Between Power and Irrelevance

BETWEEN POWER AND IRRELEVANCE

The Future of Transnational NGOs

George E. Mitchell, Hans Peter Schmitz, and Tosca Bruno-van Vijfeijken

With an afterword by Barney Tallack

OXFORD
UNIVERSITY PRESS

Oxford University Press is a department of the University of Oxford. It furthers
the University's objective of excellence in research, scholarship, and education
by publishing worldwide. Oxford is a registered trade mark of Oxford University
Press in the UK and certain other countries.

Published in the United States of America by Oxford University Press
198 Madison Avenue, New York, NY 10016, United States of America.

Library of Congress Cataloging-in-Publication Data
Names: Mitchell, George E. (Associate professor), author. |
Schmitz, Hans Peter, 1965– author. | Vijfeijken, Tosca Bruno-van, author.
Title: Between power and irrelevance : the future of transnational NGOs /
George E. Mitchell, Hans Peter Schmitz, Tosca Bruno-van Vijfeijken;
with an afterword by Barney Tallack.
Description: New York, NY : Oxford University Press, [2020] |
Includes bibliographical references and index.
Identifiers: LCCN 2019052482 (print) | LCCN 2019052483 (ebook) |
ISBN 9780190084714 (hardback) | ISBN 9780190084721 (paperback) |
ISBN 9780190084745 (epub) | ISBN 9780190084738 (updf) |
ISBN 9780190084752 (online)
Subjects: LCSH: Non-governmental organizations.
Classification: LCC JZ4841 .M58 2020 (print) |
LCC JZ4841 (ebook) | DDC 341.2—dc23
LC record available at https://lccn.loc.gov/2019052482
LC ebook record available at https://lccn.loc.gov/2019052483

9 8 7 6 5 4 3 2

Paperback printed by Marquis, Canada
Hardback printed by Bridgeport National Bindery, Inc., United States of America

CONTENTS

PREFACE

In September 2003 the idea of a research project about transnational NGOs (TNGOs) formed among a group of faculty at the Maxwell School of Citizenship and Public Affairs at Syracuse University. An interdisciplinary team of faculty, students, and staff subsequently coalesced around this concept to form the Transnational NGO Initiative within the Moynihan Institute of Global Affairs at the Maxwell School. The Initiative established an integrated approach to academic research, teaching, and consulting with an emphasis on understanding the lived experiences of practitioners. The vision was to serve the TNGO community with relevant research and instructional opportunities that addressed the sector's most pressing interests and concerns. This book represents a distillation of what we have collectively learned in our nearly two-decade-long collaboration as researchers, teachers, observers, and consultants in the areas of TNGO management, leadership, and strategy.

Under the leadership of Professor Margaret "Peg" Hermann, the Transnational NGO Initiative obtained National Science Foundation (NSF) funding in 2006 to support a large-scale, in-depth, mixed-method interview study of more than 150 TNGO leaders to develop a baseline understanding of the sector and to better understand leadership perspectives on questions of governance, effectiveness, accountability, collaboration, and related areas.[1] In addition to the authors of this book, the interdisciplinary research team included (in alphabetical order) Alejandro S. Amezcua, Derrick L. Cogburn, Peg Hermann, Jesse D. Lecy, Christiane Pagé, Paloma Raggo, Michael J. Scialdone, and Lorena Viñuela. At the time, this was among the first "large-n" (large sample size) studies of US-registered TNGOs in a field that had traditionally been dominated by "small-n" research and individual case studies.

The initial interview study not only produced research publications and educational materials, but also opened the door to years of sustained interactions with contemporary TNGO practitioners. The Transnational NGO Initiative frequently hosted senior leaders beginning in 2005 and operated a Visiting Fellows program starting in 2007 that involved collaborative research between TNGO leaders, faculty, and students. We have also been part of major organizational change processes undertaken by several large TNGOs, including Save the Children, Oxfam, CARE, and Amnesty International. Our typical role was to help these organizations document, learn from, and critically review organizational change management capabilities. Our access to internal documents, interviews, focus group discussions, surveys of staff, and our direct observation of key events and meetings resulted in case studies, internal reports, evaluations, and presentations.[2]

The Initiative also administered an annual Leadership Institute beginning in 2011, which brought together next-generation TNGO leaders from across the world to discuss organizational leadership issues and develop strategies to promote internal change. The success of the Leadership Institute led to the establishment of a tailored Senior Leadership Development Program beginning in 2013, which brought together leaders from ActionAid, Amnesty International, Greenpeace, Oxfam, and CIVICUS. A separate program for Population Council was held in 2014–2015. Additionally, from 2012 to 2016, the Transnational NGO Initiative co-facilitated an NGO Learning Group of change managers who shared and documented their experiences and observations, and also consulted with Heifer International for strategic planning exercises as they sought to change their role, strategy, and theory of change. These and other sources of data and experiential learning are summarized in the Notes on Sources.

This book seeks to address a strong demand among TNGO leaders for forward-looking sectoral analysis. After years of sustained collaboration and practitioner engagement we observed a sense of anxiety about the future relevance of TNGOs, particularly, although certainly not exclusively, among practitioners based in the United States and other Western democracies. Although typically leaders outwardly express confidence about their organizations' relevance and impact, privately we perceived many practitioners to be somewhat skeptical over the directions of many reforms; ambivalent about the sector's responses to demands for accountability, effectiveness, and evaluation; and generally concerned about the future. These feelings were particularly acute among the most analytically minded and forward-thinking leaders and observers whom we encountered.

At the broadest level, the anxiety about the future appears to be related to a dissonance between the expressed values of the sector and its actual practices. On the one hand, TNGOs occupy a moral high ground, setting themselves apart from other sectors such as government and business. On the other hand, they are similar to many other kinds of organizations in that they are likewise shaped by the need to survive as well as by internal cultures and external pressures and constraints. Although the many tensions that can arise are not new and have been described by many commentators, few have attempted a systematic explanation of the underlying context giving rise to them. In attempting this explanation, we deliberately chose to adopt the perspective of a provocative "critical friend" who cares about the success of the TNGO sector and believes that honest confrontation, not consolation or flattery, is the best means of getting to the bottom of things.

As a sector, TNGOs are surely complicit in many of their own frustrations, but we argue that their most intractable challenges derive from the institutional and normative architecture that has come to define the sector as we know it today. Time and again, specific "forms and norms" that constitute the TNGO sector inhibit its abilities to deliver on its promises, offering the seductive comfort of a particular kind of status quo in the place of the sector's own self-proclaimed vision of organizational and societal transformation. Productively confronting the sector's anxiety about its future requires an analytical understanding of the specific institutional and normative conditions under which TNGOs operate. Before it can secure its future relevance, the sector must first reexamine its history and learned behaviors.

Over the past couple of decades, many TNGOs have initiated processes of organizational transformation to prepare for the future. Some have moved headquarters to low- and middle-income countries (e.g., ActionAid and Oxfam) or increased their regional presence (e.g., Amnesty International). Some have reorganized their formal structures (e.g., World Vision) or adopted a more corporate approach (e.g., Save the Children). Regardless of whether such transformations are successful, many TNGOs can still survive because of their brand recognition and continued ability to attract resources. But whether they survive and also remain relevant is another matter. This will depend upon whether they make some very difficult choices—as individual organizations and as a sector—about their identity and purpose.

This book focuses mainly on medium- to large-sized TNGOs founded and based in North America and Western Europe. We refer to these organizations generically as "TNGOs" rather than introducing more complicated acronyms. Although there is significant variation among these organizations with regard to their missions and their size and reach, they nevertheless represent a coherent set of actors recognized by practitioners, academics, policymakers, and other observers. As the authors of this book, we are based in the United States and have been socialized by its geographical and cultural contexts. Where possible, we draw on perspectives and examples offered by the non-Western leaders whom we have encountered throughout our years of engagement with the sector. Our experiences suggest that the insights communicated in this book will be relevant to a diversity of practitioners, scholars, and students from around the world, but readers should nonetheless understand that this book is written from a particular perspective.

This book was made possible through the support of our many generous mentors, colleagues, friends, and family members. We thank Peg Hermann for her pivotal role in establishing a home for the Transnational NGO Initiative in the Moynihan Institute and for consistently supporting our initiative intellectually, financially, and as a friend and mentor. The Transnational NGO Initiative has benefited over the years from the hard work of many of its associated faculty, doctoral students, graduate assistants, undergraduate students, volunteer students, and interns, for whom we are very grateful. We also thank all the leaders and practitioners who have given us their time as interviewees, as visitors to the Maxwell School, as experts providing feedback and commentary on our work, and as friends and colleagues. There are far too many individuals to name, but a few have truly gone above and beyond in support of our project. Barney Tallack (former director of strategy, Oxfam International) has contributed immensely to several chapters of this book, particularly on the subjects of governance, change management, and mergers and acquisitions.[3] We are grateful for his feedback on draft chapters and for his commentary presented in the book's Afterword. Ramesh Singh (CEO, ActionAid International) was one of the Transnational NGO Initiative's first Visiting Fellows and during multiple visits he regularly offered his thoughtful analytical perspective. Sam Worthington (CEO, InterAction) has been a longtime supporter of our endeavors and we have greatly benefited from his experience working regularly with hundreds of TNGOs. Jeremy Hobbs (former executive director, Oxfam International) was one of the peer analysts for our work on organizational change in the sector. Sarah Ralston (CARE International), Monica Maassen (Oxfam International), and the other peer members of the INGO Learning Group on Organizational Change also heavily influenced our understanding of the topic.

We have received valuable insights and feedback on our work from many of our academic colleagues. We cannot list all the scholars who have inspired us, corrected us, and improved our understanding, but a few colleagues stand out for their extraordinary contributions. We are grateful to (in alphabetical order) Cristina Balboa, David Berlan, Elizabeth Bloodgood, Ann Marie Clark, J. Michael Dedmon, Maryam Zarnegar Deloffre, Alnoor Ebrahim, Uwe Gneiting, Mary Kay Gugerty, Nina Hall, Afsaneh Nahavandi, Christopher

Pallas, Mark Sidel, Sarah S. Stroup, Margit van Wessel, and Wendy Wong. We thank David Pervin and James Cook from Oxford University Press for their support and guidance, and we express our appreciation to four anonymous reviewers for helping us greatly improve the manuscript. We are also grateful to Conrad Hain, who provided invaluable assistance assembling the index.

Undertaking a project of this magnitude is of course impossible without the close support of family and friends. George thanks his wife, Whitney, for her limitless love and support, and for willingly and patiently bearing many hardships and sacrifices. He also thanks Robert, Cheryl, Russ, Liz, and Mary Jane for their faith, and Peg, Rosemary, and Mary Kay for their guidance and mentorship. Hans Peter thanks his spouse, Amy, for faithfully reading his drafts of academic writing, and his family for always supporting their son, brother, nephew, uncle, and in-law. Tosca is grateful to her husband Jim and her children Soren and Annika, who patiently endured all the times she was absent through frequent work-related travel or mental absences due to the many distractions that work presented. She could not have produced the body of work that she contributed to this book without their enduring support and understanding for what drove her.

The three of us also remain grateful for our ongoing mutual friendship, which has helped us to carry on our sustained collaboration despite the adversities of time and distance. We look forward to many more years of collaboration, joyful reunions, and continued intellectual and personal growth together.

Finally, we thank the many others who we have failed to mention but who have informed, inspired, and counseled us. We are indebted to you all!

George, Hans Peter, and Tosca
January 2020

REFERENCE

Lux, Steven J., and Tosca Bruno-van Vijfeijken. *From Alliance to International: The Global Transformation of Save the Children*. Syracuse: Maxwell School of Citizenship and Public Affairs, 2012

ABBREVIATIONS

ACFID	Australian Council for International Development
AED	Academy for Educational Development
ALM	agency-level measurement
ALNAP	Active Learning Network for Accountability and Performance
ARNOVA	Association for Research on Nonprofit Organizations and Voluntary Action
BACO	best available charitable option
BBB-WGA	Better Business Bureau Wise Giving Alliance
BFM	beneficiary feedback mechanisms
CAFOD	Catholic Agency For Overseas Development
CCCD	Child Centered Community Development
CCL	Center for Creative Leadership
CEDPA	Centre for Development and Population Activities
CEO	chief executive officer
CHS	Core Humanitarian Standard
COO	chief operating officer
CSIS	Center for Strategic and International Studies
CSO	civil society organization
CSR	corporate social responsibility
DAC	Development Assistance Committee
DFID	Department for International Development (UK)
E-PARCC	Program for the Advancement of Research on Conflict and Collaboration
ECHO	European Civil Protection and Humanitarian Aid Operations
EU	European Union
EUR	euro (currency)
FHI	Family Health International
FoEI	Friends of the Earth International
FPP	Forest People's Program

G7	Group of Seven
G8	Group of Eight
GIIRS	Global Impact Investing Ratings System
GIS	Geographic information systems
GNI	gross national income
GTP	Global Transition Program
HERE	Humanitarian Exchange and Research Centre
HQ	headquarters
HRBA	Human Rights-Based Approach
IARAN	Inter-Agency Research and Analysis Network
IATI	International Aid Transparency Initiative
IBASE	Brazilian Institute for Social and Economic Analysis
ICAN	International Campaign to Abolish Nuclear Weapons
ICANN	Internet Corporation for Assigned Names and Numbers
ICBL	International Campaign to Ban Landmines
ICC	International Criminal Court
ICNL	International Center for Not-for-Profit Law
ICSC	International Civil Service Commission
ICSO	international civil society organization
IGO	intergovernmental organization
IMF	International Monetary Fund
INASP	International Network for the Availability of Scientific Publications
INGO	international nongovernmental organization
INTRAC	International NGO Training and Research Centre
IRC	International Rescue Committee
ISTR	International Society for Third-Sector Research
IT	information technology
J-PAL	Abdul Latif Jameel Poverty Action Lab
L3C	low-profit limited liability company
LGBTQ	lesbian, gay, bisexual, transgender, and questioning/queer
LI	Leadership Institute
LLC	limited liability company
LMX	leader-member exchange
LTA	leadership trait analysis
M&A	mergers and acquisitions
M&E	measurement and evaluation
MEAL	monitoring, evaluation, accountability, and learning
MIC	middle-income countries
MSF	Médecins Sans Frontières (Doctors Without Borders)
NGO	nongovernmental organization

NORA	Nordic Journal of Feminist and Gender Research
NOVIB	Dutch Organization for International Aid
NSF	National Science Foundation
ODA	official bilateral development aid
OECD	Organisation for Economic Cooperation and Development
PIR	Public Internet Registry
Plan USA	Plan International USA
RBA	rights-based approaches
RELU	research, evaluation, and learning unit
SIDA	Swedish International Development Cooperation Agency
SLDP	Senior Leadership Development Program
SMS	single management structure
SOAS	School of Oriental and African Studies
TAN	transnational advocacy network
TNGO	transnational nongovernmental organization
UCODEP	Unity and Cooperation for Development of Peoples
UIA	Union of International Associations
UK	United Kingdom
UN	United Nations
UNGC	United Nations Global Compact
UNHCR	United Nations High Commissioner for Refugees
UNITA	National Union for the Total Independence of Angola
UNSC	United Nations Security Council
US	United States
USA	United States of America
USAID	United States Agency for International Development
USD	United States dollar (currency)
VP	vice president
WASH	water, sanitation, and hygiene
WSIS	World Summits on the Information Society
WWF	World Wildlife Fund
WWII	World War II
YWCA	Young Women's Christian Association

CHAPTER 1
Confrontation

Transnational non-governmental organizations (TNGOs) as a sector have grown rapidly in the past decades, both in terms of their numbers and in size. Some of these organizations have become highly professionalized and have built sustained ties to intergovernmental organizations (IGOs), governments, foundations, and the corporate sector.[1] A casual observer may conclude that the steady expansion of the sector and its growing visibility demonstrates that TNGOs have been, and will remain, impactful and relevant into the future. In addition, trends in philanthropic giving indicate a steadily increasing interest among individual and institutional donors in supporting global causes.[2]

But as the sector has expanded and large TNGOs have become global brands, these organizations have also confronted a growing gap between their historically defined identities and their new ambitions driven by organizational growth and a desire to bring about fundamental social and political change. Among other consequences, the increased visibility of the TNGO sector has made it a target for a litany of demands for more representativeness, accountability, responsiveness, efficiency, and effectiveness. As the public is increasingly used to the presence of these actors, TNGOs can no longer rely on a past consensus in which they represented a new and morally compelling answer for addressing poverty, human rights abuses, and environmental destruction. Now, they must fully embrace being accountable to those they serve and demonstrate how they contribute to solving the most pressing global issues.

TNGOs have struggled to adapt to these expectations as concerns about their credibility, legitimacy, and future relevance are increasingly dominant among the broader public and within the sector. Many TNGOs face the conflicting imperatives of, on the one hand, being large transnational organizations that can operate efficiently at scale and, on the other hand, maintaining the grassroots authenticity and consensus-oriented culture that contributed to their early successes. Some TNGOs have arguably become "too big to be small" and face seemingly irreconcilable trade-offs between competing values.[3] For example, TNGOs are expected to maintain grassroots authenticity, but while also realizing economies of scale through professionalization and standardization; they are expected to remain nimble and responsive, but while also maintaining an inclusive, consensus-oriented governance structure with broad representation on a global scale; and they are expected to meet ever-higher standards of program effectiveness, but without diverting resources from program delivery to evaluation and learning. Indeed, the sheer size of the largest TNGOs has invited criticisms about losing their rootedness in civil society and increasingly resembling the multinational corporations whose cultures and practices they seem to simultaneously embrace and disparage.[4]

Recent academic research and practitioner perspectives reflect this much more uncertain future of the sector. Typical critical assessments find these organizations to be too bureaucratic, detached, and no longer connected to organic citizen activism.[5] For example, TNGOs neither were the inspiration of major social movements in the past decade (e.g., Arab Spring, Occupy, or European anti-austerity movements), nor are they necessarily seen as the best or most relevant vehicle for social change for new generations of social entrepreneurs, impact investors, and online political activists.[6] The rise of change.org, SumOfUs, and Avaaz alongside social entrepreneurship programs across many universities[7] indicates a profound cultural shift in how younger generations envision making a difference in the world. The institutional form of the TNGO—as a registered public charity or "nonprofit" in most Western democracies—is becoming less attractive relative to other emerging mechanisms for advancing social causes. This may simply be a result of the cyclicality of activism and its patterns of exhaustion and demobilization,[8] or it may be a sign of a much broader reckoning about the relevance of a third sector standing apart from government and markets.

TNGOs therefore confront significant internal as well as external challenges—both in terms of managing organizational growth and change as well as adapting to rapidly changing operational environments. In a recent survey of TNGO leaders, for example, respondents overwhelmingly reported that their organizations were either formulating or executing significant organizational change processes (77%) and perceived the broader ecosystem within which their organizations operate to be changing either faster than before (80%) or so much faster than before that future success will require "unprecedented" measures (17%).[9] However, most leaders (60%) reported that their organizations were not yet matching the external rate of change, while only a minority (18%) described their current business models as "stable."

So why are so many TNGO leaders concerned about the future of their own organizations and the sector overall? Part of the answer is the sheer scope and complexity of social change throughout the world. Geopolitical power shifts, the emergence of newly powerful actors, closing or shifting civic spaces, generational shifts in donor expectations, difficulties demonstrating impact and efficiency, and competition for talent are among the many challenges that TNGOs must confront to secure their future relevance. Moreover, these issues must be addressed in the context of global challenges affecting TNGOs' operating environments, including demographic shifts, rising inequality, and the climate crisis.[10]

These and other change drivers have motivated major organizational change initiatives throughout the TNGO sector, as a failure to successfully adapt could further undermine the legitimacy and relevance of individual organizations or the sector more broadly. Before turning later in the book to how TNGOs have sought to confront some of these challenges and why they have faced specific difficulties, we first outline what we perceive as the three most fundamental drivers currently pressuring the sector.

CHANGE DRIVERS

During the past two decades, the legitimacy and relevance of TNGOs has been challenged. These challenges have been animated by at least three external trends shaping the sector and its future: (1) geopolitical shifts and the rise of China and other non-Western powers; (2) increasing demands for accountability and results from "above" (donors) and "below" (local communities); and (3) the emergence of other types of non-state actors and solutions competing with TNGOs—including corporate social responsibility (CSR), "triple bottom line" and "shared value"–induced corporate action, social enterprises, benefit corporations,[11] private contractors, and digital campaigning and funding platforms.

Geopolitics

The geography of power and resources has significantly shifted since many TNGOs were originally founded. China, Brazil, Mexico, South Korea, and India, for example, have for many years experienced much higher economic growth rates than the United States and most other Western democracies. China is already a major provider of foreign aid focused on infrastructure development, and it pursues different objectives than do Western donors.[12] The growing global presence of non-Western governments pushes TNGOs to develop new capacities required to navigate a different set of cultural contexts.[13] In addition, governments have become more adept at controlling transnational influences and regulating civil society,[14] while a crackdown on democratic practices across many regions of the world has shrunk the operational space for civic action.[15] Simultaneously, many Western democracies have curtailed their financial and ideational support for democratic norms, civil society, and human rights abroad.[16]

Governments in Hungary, Russia, and elsewhere have targeted foreign-funded TNGOs and have passed laws designed to crack down on transnational actors supportive of democracy, human rights, and other liberal norms.[17] Domestic politics and certain counterterrorism-inspired regulatory actions by states such as the UK, US, and Australia have added to this shrinking of the civic space. The legitimacy of civil society is broadly challenged by claims that these actors (1) do not represent local populations and are elitist and unelected, (2) advance foreign agendas, and (3) pursue illegitimate partisan and political objectives.[18] To the extent that the United States retrenches into a relatively more nationalistic and isolationist posture, while Russia, China, and other states become more assertive, such a backlash could presage a more ominous future environment for TNGOs globally. The relatively stable world order of the Cold War period has given way to a more multilayered and multipolar world with more players capable of contesting norms and institutions.[19] More important, TNGOs can no longer rely on a cultural background they have shared for decades with their own governments and relatively well-off supporters based predominantly in Judeo-Christian societies. Although the political environment for TNGOs has not uniformly deteriorated, TNGOs do face a much more complex geopolitical landscape compared to decades past, requiring greater nimbleness and adaptive capacity.[20]

Accountability

As TNGOs face an increasingly complex geopolitical environment, the core problems of global economic inequality, human rights abuses, and environmental degradation persist despite decades of lofty promises, concerted activism, and the comings and goings of different strategies and tactics. Although much progress has been made globally on many development, poverty reduction, and human rights issues,[21] TNGOs nevertheless struggle to provide credible evidence of their effectiveness and distinct value-added in contributing to positive social change. There is a growing public skepticism about the sector, reflected in declining trust of TNGOs when compared with other sectors. In 2019, an Edelman Trust Barometer survey placed trust in NGOs internationally at 56 percent—the same as for businesses[22]—while an international poll from Gallup and Wellcome found that only 52 percent of people worldwide have confidence in NGOs.[23]

For decades, TNGOs have underinvested in measuring their impact and have largely failed to meaningfully change a sectoral and philanthropic culture that often views investments in measurement, evaluation, accountability, and learning as diversions of resources. Many advocacy organizations have emphasized exposing human rights violations or environmental problems but struggle to prioritize the assessment of the outcomes of their awareness-raising and monitoring efforts. Meanwhile, many direct service-oriented organizations have documented output and "reach" numbers that fall short of providing evidence of sustainable impact. While TNGOs are increasingly pushed by their donors to measure impact, these pressures can lead to the adoption of inappropriate evaluation practices with limited value in improving programming over time.[24] The rigorous monitoring and evaluation activities that would be necessary for demonstrating results-based accountability are often viewed as too costly, complicated, infeasible, or inappropriate.

As donors and watchdog organizations have increased their demands for accountability and effectiveness, some TNGOs initially responded by expanding their claims to address the root causes of human rights violations and other deprivations. The concept of "charity," as a short-term strategy of relieving the symptoms of poverty, has largely been replaced by more ambitious goals of sustainable development and human rights protection. At the same time, many TNGOs have started to invest modestly into explaining how they plan to accomplish their missions and monitor progress through regular program evaluation. As TNGOs ramped up their promises to address root causes, they also began to implicitly predicate their legitimacy on actually achieving sustainable long-term impact. But their inability or unwillingness to produce credible evidence of this broader notion of impact[25] has created a widening credibility gap.

The gap between TNGOs' aspirational rhetoric and the available evidence of their success is large, partly due to the ambitiousness of many contemporary missions. For example, Oxfam states in its mission that it strives for a "just world without poverty," ActionAid aims for "a world without poverty and injustice," Human Rights Watch "defends the rights of people worldwide," and Plan International promises "a world in which all children realize their full potential." Even the considerable resources of the largest TNGOs seem small in comparison to the scope and complexity of these missions, and even single-issue TNGOs must wrestle with the increasing interconnectedness of global challenges.[26]

The problem is not just that TNGOs have a habit of overpromising, but that they are held accountable by increasingly vocal donors as well as local communities. While donors have been trained to view themselves as contributing to solving the world's most difficult problems, local communities have been identified primarily as in need of external support and lacking capacities or rights. Deprivations at local levels abroad remain a primary driver of fundraising, while many TNGOs struggle to let local communities represent themselves.[27] The traditional intermediary role played by TNGOs seems increasingly untenable. Local communities are more likely today to question the motives of transnational actors and express their own perspectives without the mediating role of TNGOs. Both donors and local communities are no longer as dependent on TNGOs, requiring fundamentally new identities and legitimacy practices.

Competition

As TNGOs struggle worldwide to maintain the public's trust and confidence,[28] other modes of activism are challenging the basic TNGO model with the potential to squeeze the sector from multiple sides. The expansive concept of the "social economy organization" and the rise of CSR and social impact investing invite business into areas formerly dominated by nonprofits.[29] Although for-profit contractors have long competed with TNGOs in development and humanitarian aid,[30] the expansion of base-of-the-pyramid and shared-value approaches[31] has slowly enlarged the footprint of commercial enterprises.[32] Companies such as TOMS or Warby Parker have been successful in convincing consumers that "business for good" is possible, even if their core drive is profit-making.[33] Benefit corporations, social enterprises, and other types of hybrid organizations have emerged as competition, with increasing support from venture philanthropists focused on measuring impact and seeing a return on investment.[34] Organizations such as Acumen Fund have rejected the traditional grant model of funding and view their role as investors in promising social entrepreneurs with cost-effective solutions.[35] Community foundations have grown in popularity, while traditional foundations are increasingly keen to invest directly in local organizations abroad. Meanwhile, some new philanthropic players, including the Chan-Zuckerberg Initiative, eschew the traditional nonprofit form in favor of a more flexible limited liability company (LLC).

Additionally, digital platforms are gaining traction with the potential to bypass the need for brick-and-mortar organizations. Digital platforms and technologies can often mobilize more supporters, raise money more quickly, communicate with millennials and other younger generations with more attractive narratives, and respond more quickly to social issues, arguably demonstrating a potential for "organizing without organizations."[36] For example, GiveDirectly is among the few organizations recommended by GiveWell, the online information intermediary that evaluates TNGOs based on impact and cost-effectiveness. Online digital platforms promise to directly link stakeholders together, posing a risk of disintermediation for traditional TNGOs. Meanwhile, the influx of other types of actors into spaces traditionally occupied by TNGOs erodes the underlying notion of a separate and unique third sector in which TNGOs have an inherent comparative advantage.

TNGO RESPONSES TO CHANGE DRIVERS

TNGOs have limited influence over these external changes, but they are not helpless. Many organizations have responded to these new challenges by undergoing organizational and strategic renewal. One response common across the sector is to increase promises and ambitions. Over many years, most especially larger-sized TNGOs have shifted away from presenting themselves as trustworthy charities distributing to the needy to instead adopting an explicit commitment to achieving value-adding long-term sustainable impact. Another response has been the adoption and replacement of strategic meta-frameworks (e.g., sustainable development, capacity-building, and rights-based approaches) to assure donors and the public that future approaches will be informed by previous criticisms and not repeat past mistakes. Responses at the organizational level have included significant governance reforms, investments in leadership development, enhanced collaboration within and across sectors, and mergers and acquisitions. In the process, many organizations have adopted more rigorous monitoring and evaluation practices at both the program and the organizational levels and have experimented with digital tools to empower supporters and expand supporter bases.

These mission-focused, organizational, and strategic responses by TNGOs to the challenges faced are the central focus of this book. There are hard choices to be made, and larger TNGOs are taking very different approaches to securing their futures. Some organizations, like World Vision and Save the Children, see their future as a highly professionalized, corporate, and ever-growing provider of humanitarian and development services. Save the Children narrowed its focus to child survival below the age of five, basic education, and child protection, while professionalizing to appeal primarily to large private foundations and institutional donors, for example.[37] In contrast, TNGOs like ActionAid or Oxfam are skeptical of modeling themselves as large contractors and are shifting away from service provision to a model focused on facilitating, brokering, convening, and collaborating with social movements.[38] As many TNGOs are undergoing major organizational changes at multiple levels, there is significant demand for systematically tracking and analyzing these disparate efforts at securing a future. There is no single path forward, which heightens the need for establishing a clearer sense of the challenges and opportunities associated with specific choices about the future role of individual organizations and the sector overall.

The challenges for TNGOs do not end with the need to adapt to external change drivers. Efforts at reinvention have forced many organizations to focus on themselves and to address profound internal challenges resulting from tensions about where to go next.[39] Additionally, a prevailing consultative and consensus-oriented culture and a limited willingness to invest in core organizational infrastructure and change processes have sometimes delayed necessary innovation and reforms.[40] Ironically, as the TNGO sector is pushing for urgent social and political changes elsewhere, it is often reluctant to embrace such change internally. One basic internal challenge is how to maintain global agility and cohesiveness while also fostering responsiveness to diverse local conditions and demands. For example, Amnesty International struggled with implementing an agenda of establishing regional offices, trying to change its London-centric, hierarchical structure to become more globally representative. As a result, it was able to change its organizational form, but staff morale declined and leadership failed to address significant internal problems negatively affecting the organization.[41] Amnesty is not the only TNGO struggling with regular internal tensions, and the transnational nature of these organizations has created significant challenges in sustaining credible global and local presences.[42]

While there is no one consistent overarching response across the sector, most larger TNGOs are engaged in some form of reflection and forward-thinking adaptation. This book offers perspectives on these efforts, while arguing that the sector has not yet gone far enough in understanding and redefining its own role or in narrowing the gap between rhetoric and reality. Much of the sector continues to lack the collective capacity, and perhaps the will, to effectively address many of its current and future challenges. While recognizing the significance of many of the important steps taken in the past decade, the sector has yet to fully manifest its commitments to demonstrating effectiveness, practicing accountability to local communities, and investing sufficiently in governance, leadership, organizational change, and collaborative capacities. The question is not necessarily whether TNGOs should change, but how they will be able to invest sufficiently in enhancing their capacities for the future.

OBSTACLES TO CHANGE

At surface level, many of the difficulties that TNGOs are encountering are caused by complex shifts in the external operating environment. However, in addition to these challenges, the institutional and normative architecture in which TNGOs are embedded also pose difficulties. The inherited institutional form of the TNGO and the attendant individual belief systems and cultural norms associated with the administration and operation of that institutional form have emerged as significant impediments to the realization of TNGOs' ambitions. While many critics see TNGOs at risk of being corrupted by their size and success,[43] we identify long-standing institutional and cultural factors as key explanations for many of the sector's struggles. This is of course a very broad argument, and one that will likely not apply to all TNGOs in all contexts and all subsectors at all times, but in the pages that follow we articulate an analytical framework that describes how the sector's own constitutive "forms and norms" have come to constrain its ability to effectively invest in its own future.

DEFINITION AND TERMINOLOGY

Before elaborating further, we first briefly clarify what we mean by "TNGO" and the "TNGO sector" to qualify the scope of our analysis. Transnational civil society organizations have existed for centuries, many of them with ancient religious origins.[44] However, the term "non-governmental organization" (NGO) gained currency only relatively recently, during the negotiations of the United Nations (UN) Charter in 1945, as a means to distinguish private groups from IGOs. IGOs, or "specialized agencies" created and controlled by states, were given a right to participate without vote while NGOs received a lesser consultative status.[45] For the UN, the core defining features of NGOs included (1) an independence from governments, (2) a not-for-profit status, and (3) the existence of a substantially formalized organizational structure.

We employ the term "TNGO" to identify a particular type of transnationally operating non-state actor composed of entities that are typically incorporated according to countries' national legal frameworks for nonprofits, public benefit organizations, or charities. Many definitions exist in scholarship[46] but generally include the criteria listed in Table 1.1.[47] It is useful to recognize that academic, practitioner, and policy communities not only use a wide range of terms and definitions but also adopt different views about the appropriate roles of TNGOs in society.[48]

The term "TNGO" substantially overlaps with other terms commonly used in law, everyday language, practitioner discourse, and academic scholarship. In many national legal contexts TNGOs are registered as "charities,"

Table 1.1 DEFINING FEATURES OF THE TNGO

Acting in the public interest	TNGOs work for the benefit of humankind and act in the service of a general (not particular) public interest.
Not-for-profit	TNGOs are not principally organized to generate profits. Net earnings are not distributed for private benefit.
Independent	TNGOs determine their own policies, direct their own activities, and are independent of direct government, funder, or other control.
Voluntary	Participation in the work of a TNGO is not compulsory.
Active	TNGOs are actively pursuing their missions on an ongoing basis.
Lawful	Members of the TNGO community act with integrity and within the bounds of law.
Structured	TNGOs maintain a formal organizational structure, which typically involves a governing board (or boards), defined voting rules, a mission statement, bylaws, policies, and codes of conduct.
Transnational	TNGOs are composed of entities in more than one country and regularly operate across national boundaries.

---

for example, while management scholarship usually regards TNGOs as a subtype of "nonprofit." For the purposes of this book, a TNGO represents a special case of an NGO, charity, nonprofit, public or social benefit organization, civil society organization, etc.

Larger TNGOs are rarely a single organization but instead are constellations of multiple entities operating under a coherent brand identity and coordinating their efforts in the service of a common cause. Throughout this book, we often refer to TNGO "families" that consist of multiple "members," "affiliates," "headquarters," or "offices" that may exist at local, national, regional, or global levels. In keeping with common parlance, we often refer to these families by their shorthand names by dropping the "International" (for example, "Oxfam" rather than "Oxfam International"). Overall governance structures vary considerably across TNGO families, ranging from unitary hub-and-spoke-style structures to loose confederations of relatively independent members. Table 1.2 summarizes the most common types of TNGO structures, excluding networks, alliances, and similar structures composed of multiple independent TNGO brands.[49]

This book focuses mainly, although not exclusively, on the future of so-called leading TNGOs[50] that operate in a significant number of low- and middle-income countries but were founded in the wealthier countries of the "Global North" of North America and Europe. Although the North-South dichotomy pervades discussions of TNGOs and their organizational structures, we acknowledge that this divide is increasingly problematic, as many global problems are inherently transnational and many countries in the Global South are rapidly developing into higher-income countries with increased geopolitical power, among other reasons.

To avoid the practical difficulties of complicated qualifications and a profusion of neologisms and acronyms, particularly given that TNGO families often describe their component entities using unique terms of art (e.g., member, affiliate, etc.), we generally refer to TNGO families and their member entities, regardless of subsector or location, by the generic term "TNGO."[51] We also generally follow the linguistic conventions of the sector, including referring to a Global North and Global South, with the notable exception that we favor the term primary stakeholders over "beneficiaries" in recognition of the sector's commitment to empowerment as well as increasing discomfort with the term beneficiary.[52] In addition to mainly considering the challenges of mid- to large-sized leading TNGOs, we also primarily draw on English-language research and disproportionately from examples from the United States.

Table 1.2 TNGO STRUCTURES

Structure	Description	Governance implications
Unitary	A unitary TNGO is a single organization governed and managed by a dominant central unit. National or regional branches are line managed by the center. Some groups have national or regional branches for program delivery or fundraising.	The organization is hierarchical. Unitary organizations are more straightforward to govern, can be more agile and corporate, and can engage with and make commitments to other actors more easily. The core challenge for this type of organization is the power imbalance between a central unit based in a developed country and its much less influential units abroad.
Federation	A federation consists of national members with a strong central unit with significant oversight on governance, strategy, management, finance, brand, and operating rules. Members have agreed to yield more power to the center than in the case of confederations. The federation board has ultimate authority and has the power to set global strategy for all members, to levy fees (typically with the consent of members), to control the brand (including licensing), and to intervene in high-level hiring and firing. Relations between members are relatively clearly spelled out. Some control of country-level fundraising and advocacy may be delegated, but with specific, agreed-upon rules.	Federations are integrated by common policies and standards, while programs are often managed centrally. Leaders have to be able to rely on both formal and informal authority. They are less agile in decision-making than a unitary organization but more agile than confederations. They are capable of using consultation to feed membership views into central decision-making. Consensus-building as a regular practice contributes to loyalty and shared identity, while formal power can be exercised in case of disputes and crises.
Global membership organization	A global membership organization typically has a national branch structure supporting a central federated secretariat. The federation board may be elected by and answer to a wider membership. The power at the central unit is moderate and members are independent.	A global membership organization features distributed power due the board's being downwardly accountable. The central unit usually has the power to set broad strategy, to raise funds, and to control the brand. However, in reality, this power may be restrained by (more powerful) national sections asserting influence. The central unit typically

Table 1.2 CONTINUED

Structure	Description	Governance implications
		has some limited power to intervene with national boards and CEOs, but very limited influence on high-level hiring and firing at local level.
Confederation	A confederation features a smaller and less powerful central unit (secretariat). The central unit may set standards and theoretically control the brand, but it has to regularly negotiate strategies and campaigns with national sections. It cannot intervene directly in hiring and firing of national board members and CEOs. The programs are managed either by national members (sometimes through a lead agency model) or through a central program department, but with funding for themes and countries controlled largely by national sections.	Confederations typically operate on a consensus basis to align members on common strategies, plans, and rules. Confederations may face challenges such as slow decision-making, outsized influence of veto players, conflict avoidance, and a tendency to align around a lowest common denominator.

ANATOMY OF THE TNGO SECTOR

If the sector's success could be measured by the size and number of organizations, then the modern history of the TNGO sector has generally been prosperous, although evaluating the evolution of the sector worldwide is inhibited by the absence of reliable data.[53] Several factors limit data availability, including disagreements about definitions,[54] lack of resources and political will, and the challenges associated with determining organizational dormancy and death.[55] As a result, detailed and systematic data on the nature, evolution, and geographic distribution of TNGOs worldwide (headquarters and operations) are difficult to obtain.[56]

Even without accurate annual data, there is general agreement on two trends. First, the sector has been steadily expanding[57] and growth has been particularly strong in the post–World War II period and particularly since the 1970s.[58] Second, there is significant inequality among TNGOs; they not only vary greatly in size and income, but many relatively large organizations have expanded at rates much higher than the sector overall. This is certainly contrary to the "let a thousand flowers bloom" ethos of the sector,[59] even if it is relatively easy to create new organizations in some countries. Both the UN data on "NGO consultative status" as well as tax data for international nonprofits in the United States confirm these trends.

The expansion of the TNGO sector is visible in the overall numbers of organizations, their cumulative resources, and their participation in global institutions. The Union of International Associations (UIA) records that the number of TNGOs increased from fewer than 200 in 1909 to more than 67,000 in 2014,[60] again with much of the growth occurring since the 1970s.[61] The number of NGOs with consultative status at the UN increased slowly from 41 in 1946 to 700 in 1992, or at an annualized rate of about 14 organizations per year. After the end of the Cold War, the growth rate accelerated, and by spring 2019, 5,161 NGOs had consultative status, representing an average of 172 organizations added annually since 1992.[62]

Global funding for civil society organizations (CSOs) has broadly increased over time. The World Bank reports that projects with some degree of "civil society" involvement increased from 6 percent in the late 1980s to more than 70 percent in 2006.[63] The total volume of official bilateral development aid (ODA) managed and delivered by civil society organizations increased from $18.2 billion in 2009 to $19.6 billion in 2013, or about 15 percent of total ODA for reporting countries.[64] Although a growing percentage of ODA focused on civil society is channeled to groups based outside of the countries of the relatively wealthy Development Assistance Committee (DAC), seven and a half times more ODA goes to organizations based in DAC countries rather than those based in developing countries, mainly due to the outsourcing of government-supported services.[65] In countries such as the United States, government funding continues to be an important source of income for many TNGOs.[66] Among US-based TNGOs, US Agency for International Development (USAID) funding typically accounts for roughly 8 to 12 percent of supported organizations' total revenues.[67] Moreover, growth rates often accelerate following major humanitarian crises, which "act as catalysts for longer term growth, bringing in new supporters, and providing the stimulus for strengthening global capacity."[68]

Between 2009 and 2015, the UK development NGO sector expanded from 676 to 881 organizations and the sector's spending grew by 45 percent.[69] A review of financial statements of seven major TNGOs[70] found that their combined revenues increased by 74 percent between 2004 and 2013, ahead of the 56 percent growth rate of the overall US-based TNGO sector during the same period.[71] During the period of 2008 to 2013, Save the Children grew by 12 percent, Médecins Sans Frontières by 8 percent, Plan

International by 7 percent, and Oxfam by 2 percent, while CARE's budget decreased by 2 percent.[72]

There are a variety of internal and external factors driving differential growth rates throughout the sector. Especially by the 1990s, many governments had begun to accelerate the channeling of bilateral aid through TNGOs, essentially inserting TNGOs as intermediaries in global aid chains, largely out of concern about corruption and misspending by recipient country governments.[73] Government funding has long been an important component of the income portfolios of many, although certainly not all, TNGOs. Globally, significant increases in government funding and corporate support have all played major roles in the expansion of the sector. It is likely that larger and more professionalized organizations have benefited more since they have more visible brands, greater economies of scale, and often have advantages in securing and retaining funding, particularly from official donors and large foundations with which they have established long-term relationships.

It is tempting to conflate the strong financial growth in the TNGO sector with the notion of organizational success. Continued financial support and increasing numbers may not necessarily reflect underlying successes in achieving programmatic goals, as the overall expansion of the sector does not tell us much about the relevance and impact of TNGOs' programs. However, the sector's rise to prominence has certainly attracted increased attention as stakeholders and critics raise questions about TNGOs' accountability, legitimacy, and effectiveness.

ORGANIZATION OF THE BOOK

The chapters of this book comprise a narrative driven by insights about the issues shaping the future relevance of the sector. We identify a variety of core issues and challenges confronting TNGOs and examine specific initiatives, alternatives, and lessons-learned from the experiences of leading organizations. Chapters 2–5 provide the essential context for understanding the nature, significance, and difficulties of future-oriented TNGO reforms. Chapter 2 describes the institutional and normative architecture in which TNGOs are embedded, which is increasingly at odds with the strategic shifts described in Chapter 3. Chapter 4 examines the nature of TNGO power and establishes the issue of legitimacy as a central concern for organizational change. Chapter 5 examines the problem of legitimacy in more detail. Chapters 6–11 explore the potential of digital technology, enhanced measurement and evaluation, governance reforms, leadership development, collaboration, and mergers and acquisitions, respectively, as means of addressing the challenges facing the sector. In each case, the latter chapters reveal how elements of the legacy architecture (described in Chapter 2) constrain TNGOs' efforts to successfully adapt for the future.

More specifically, Chapter 2 considers the "soul" of the TNGO and articulates an analytical framework to explain core organizational and sectoral tensions. Drawing on cultural observations and canonical theories of sectoral emergence and institutional design, the analysis interrogates the nature of the TNGO as an institutional form embedded in the specific cultural context of charity and philanthropy. The chapter draws on insights from multiple disciplines to establish an understanding of how legacy beliefs and practices limit the abilities of TNGOs to adapt to their changing external environment and realize their expanding aspirations.

TNGOs have significantly changed their strategic and tactical repertoires over the past few decades. Chapter 3 describes major shifts in the strategic orientations of TNGOs that represent a concerted movement from their historical roots as charitable conduits to social and political change agents seeking sustainable impact and long-term transformations. Three illustrative strategic shifts—from direct service delivery to championing rights and supporting entrepreneurship; from reactive advocacy to proactive global campaigning; and from capacity-building to systems thinking—underscore the growing mismatch between the inherited institutional and normative features of the TNGO and the sector's contemporary ambitions and strategies.

The power and influence of TNGOs has been the subject of great interest over the past several decades, especially as many traditionally service-oriented TNGOs have embraced advocacy in the pursuit of political or social change. Chapter 4 explains why and how TNGOs have become powerful actors in global affairs. It argues that TNGOs were at the "right place at the right time" and benefited from favorable geopolitical conditions in previous decades. The chapter examines the nature of TNGO power historically and explains how TNGOs exerted influence throughout various stages of the policy process, including issue emergence, agenda-setting, policy formation, and policy implementation. As TNGOs have largely benefited from professionalized activism and elite access, their power today is plateauing, if not waning, because of the increasing incongruity between their ambitions and the limited affordances of their legacy forms and norms. Without a collective effort to challenge its own conventional wisdoms, the sector will struggle to live up to its rhetoric of social transformation.

TNGOs require legitimacy to exercise power, yet TNGOs are often criticized for being uninvited, unelected, and unaccountable. Not all of these critiques are always valid, but TNGOs have remained too passive in matching their legitimacy practices to their expanding mandates and goals. Chapter 5 elaborates on the shift from traditional to more contemporary legitimacy expectations and practices. In the past, TNGOs were legitimate if they were principled, stayed away from politics, and demonstrated good stewardship of donor resources. More contemporary expectations include the imperative to demonstrate impact and being truly transparent and responsive to those they claim to serve. TNGOs are increasingly aware of these new demands, but often remain bound by antiquated institutional and normative conventions. New approaches to enhancing legitimacy provide a wide range of opportunities that invite organizations to proactively align their aspirations with stakeholder expectations.

Digital technologies are transforming social activism. The traditional approaches of staff-led advocacy and direct service delivery are directly challenged by digital capabilities that allow or "afford" the direct connection of stakeholders to one another. Chapter 6 examines some of the most promising strategic options provided by digital tools, including shifting away from staff-led action to more supporter-led activism. Such shifts can help TNGOs become more authentic, representative, and legitimate. Specifically, digital tools can be deployed to broaden participation as a means of generating more inclusive activism and to deepen participation to intensify supporter engagement. But despite these opportunities, features of the legacy architecture have made it difficult for TNGOs to invest in new technologies or accord them a major role in shaping programmatic strategies and organizational structures.

Most medium- to large-sized TNGOs have moved well beyond the legacy charity model to embrace a significantly more expansive commitment to creating long-term sustainable impact—at least rhetorically. Many of them have also made important strides in assessing outcomes at the program and organizational or "agency" levels. Chapter 7 describes innovations in measurement and evaluation practices and reviews the internal and external challenges that organizations have confronted. An enhanced focus on assessing impact at the program and organizational levels not only requires strategic investments that are hard to make, but also requires broader cultural changes in how TNGOs and their staff think about organizational learning and their roles in bringing about social change. Despite being an area where many organizations still struggle, TNGOs will need to improve their measurement and evaluation capabilities to demonstrate their value and relevance and satisfy changing legitimacy expectations.

Many TNGOs have undergone substantial governance reforms to better balance the need for coherence and agile decision-making in global governance bodies with growing demands for local representation and accountability through local-level governance mechanisms. Chapter 8 discusses how governance reforms have been designed to improve legitimacy and alleviate structural inequalities among TNGO (con)federation members. TNGOs governance reforms may involve centralization, decentralization, global restructuring, adding new governance bodies, and experimenting with digitally enabled global fora, although each type of governance reform carries risks and trade-offs. Specific considerations include structural inequalities; dual citizenship; board composition, roles, and culture; power centers; and resources. Governance reforms may formally address long-standing disparities within organizations, but their results remain uncertain. Additionally, organizational agility and transaction costs remain concerns, and long-established norms and patterns of learned behavior remain powerful inhibitors of successful change.

Leadership defines how an organization is perceived externally and also how it manages an increasingly complex set of internal governance mechanisms and structures. Chapter 9 identifies specific leadership blind spots that often emerge as TNGOs move to adopt more ambitious mandates and implement strategic changes to secure organizational relevance and legitimacy. Traditional leadership in the sector has often lacked a culture of inquiry while also struggling to work in an environment of growing complexity and ambiguity. While organizations in crisis may be tempted to rely on charismatic leaders and their promises, new leadership models emphasize shared, distributed forms of leadership, post-heroic leadership styles, collaborative skills, humble personalities, a capacity to self-reflect and identify personal needs, and a focus on results, credit-sharing, and the building of authentic relationships. There is growing consensus around a shift in leadership needs, but sectoral norms tend to relegate leadership development to an area of underinvestment and neglect.

Collaboration is a major strategic approach to scaling up programs or enhancing advocacy efforts. TNGOs are increasingly asked to engage with other civil society groups, the business sector, and government agencies. Chapter 10 examines different types and levels of collaboration, benefits and obstacles to collaboration, and the capacities required to collaborate strategically with a broad range of partners, including "unlike-minded" actors. Collaboration requires a greater focus on the external environment and leading without having top-down control. While contracts and memoranda of understanding matter in setting the general parameters of collaborative arrangements, their success is largely driven by the attention given to the alignment of informal expectations, understandings, and behaviors. Cultural factors thus emerge as a common obstacle to collaboration effectiveness. Additional considerations include challenges related to unequal partnerships and credit-taking for collective outcomes.

Mergers and acquisitions (M&As) can play an important role in the TNGO sector, particularly in helping TNGOs to strategically gain capabilities needed to be more effective, relevant, and competitive. Informed by a number of recent examples, Chapter 11 explains why typical M&As within the sector are rare and often reactive in nature. They usually involve the joining together of a smaller, financially stressed organization with a larger, healthier TNGO looking to expand as a means of remaining competitive. Much less common are more proactive M&A efforts where both partners come together from positions of strength. M&As appear to be underutilized as a strategic tool to increase scale and impact due to a variety of normative and institutional barriers. These include legal structures that disincentivize or prevent takeovers, cultures of uniqueness among TNGOs and their supporters, and the lack of M&A matchmakers and resources for competently exploring and executing the M&A process.

Chapter 12 summarizes the main themes of the book, with an emphasis on how the sector's future remains constrained by its normative and institutional architecture. This analysis includes discussions of organizational metamorphosis, change leadership, and sector-wide collective action to bring about fundamental transformation in the legacy architecture itself. Metamorphosis may include the emergence of a polycentric model, the development of hybrid models designed to escape the constraints of the legacy charity framework, deeper collaborations and mergers and acquisitions, and changes in organizational platforms. At the sectoral level, TNGOs can become better servants of their mission by changing the conditions in which they themselves operate.

REFERENCES

Aldashev, Gani, and Cecilia Navarra. "Development NGOs: Basic Facts." *Annals of Public and Cooperative Economics* 89, no. 1 (2018): 125–55. https://doi.org/10.1111/apce.12188.

Avula, Kavita, Lisa McKay, and Sébastien Galland. *Amnesty International. Staff Wellbeing Review*. Washington, DC: The Konterra Group, 2019.

Balboa, Cristina M. "How Successful Transnational Non-Governmental Organizations Set Themselves Up for Failure on the Ground." *World Development* 54 (February 2014): 273–87. https://doi.org/10.1016/j.worlddev.2013.09.001. http://www.sciencedirect.com/science/article/pii/S0305750X13002027.

Balboa, Cristina M. *The Paradox of Scale: How NGOs Build, Maintain, and Lose Authority in Environmental Governance*. Cambridge, MA: MIT Press, 2018.

Banks, Nicola, and Dan Brockington. *Mapping the UK's Development NGOs: Income, Geography, and Contributions to International Development*. Manchester: Global Development Institute/The University of Manchester, 2019.

Banks, Nicola, David Hulme, and Michael Edwards. "NGOs, States, and Donors Revisited: Still Too Close for Comfort?" *World Development* 66 (2015): 707–18. https://doi.org/10.1016/j.worlddev.2014.09.028.

Bloodgood, Elizabeth, and Hans Peter Schmitz. "The INGO Research Agenda: A Community Approach to Challenges in Method and Theory." In *Routledge Handbook of International Organization*, edited by Bob Reinalda, 67–79. New York: Routledge, 2013.

Bob, Clifford. *The Marketing of Rebellion: Insurgents, Media, and International Activism*. New York: Cambridge University Press, 2005.

Brass, Jennifer N., Wesley Longhofer, Rachel S. Robinson, and Allison Schnable. "NGOs and International Development: A Review of Thirty-Five Years of Scholarship." *World Development* 112 (2018): 136–49. https://doi.org/10.1016/j.worlddev.2018.07.016.

Brechenmacher, Sakia, and Thomas Carothers. *Examining Civil Society Legitimacy*. Washington, DC: Carnegie Endowment for International Peace, 2018.

Brown, L. David, Alnoor Ebrahim, and Srilatha Batliwala. "Governing International Advocacy NGOs." *World Development* 40, no. 6 (2012): 1098–108. https://doi.org/10.1016/j.worlddev.2011.11.006.

Bush, Sarah, and Jennifer Hadden. "Density and Decline in the Founding of International NGOs in the United States." *International Studies Quarterly* (August 2019). https://doi.org/10.1093/isq/sqz061.

Caldwell, Ken. *ICSO Global Financial Trends*. London: Baobab, 2015.

Carothers, Thomas. "Closing Space for International Democracy and Human Rights Support." *Journal of Human Rights Practice* 8, no. 3 (2016): 358–77. https://doi.org/10.1093/jhuman/huw012.

Chabbott, Colette. "Development INGOs." In *Constructing World Culture*, edited by John Boli and George M. Thomas, 222–49. Stanford: Stanford University Press, 1999.

Cheng, Cheng. *The Logic behind China's Foreign Aid Agency*. New York: Carnegie-Tshinghua Center for Global Policy, 2019.

Civicus. *State of Civil Society Report 2011*. Johannesburg: Civicus, 2012.

Clark, John. "Civil Society in the Age of Crisis." *Journal of Civil Society* 7, no. 3 (2011): 241–63.

Curtis, Mark. "Charity or Justice." *New Internationalist*, October 1, 2005. https://newint.org/features/2005/10/01/politics.

Davies, Thomas R. *NGOs: A New History of Transnational Civil Society*. Oxford: Oxford University Press, 2014.

Davis, Steve. "China's Emerging Role in Social Innovation for Global Good." *Stanford Social Innovation Review*, May 9, 2017. https://ssir.org/articles/entry/chinas_emerging_role_in_social_innovation_for_global_good.

Detert, James R., Roger G. Schroeder, and John J. Mauriel. "A Framework for Linking Culture and Improvement Initiatives in Organizations." *The Academy of Management Review* 25, no. 4 (2000): 850–63. https://doi.org/10.2307/259210.

DiMaggio, Paul J., and Helmut K. Anheier. "The Sociology of Nonprofit Organizations and Sectors." *Annual Review of Sociology* 16, no. 1 (1990): 137–59.

"Do You Still Use the Word 'Beneficiary'?" Feedback Labs, updated September 6, 2015, accessed August 26, 2019. https://feedbacklabs.org/blog/do-you-still-use-the-word-beneficiary/.

Dupuy, Kendra, James Ron, and Aseem Prakash. "Hands Off My Regime! Governments' Restrictions on Foreign Aid to Non-Governmental Organizations in Poor and Middle-Income Countries." *World Development* 84 (2016): 299–311.

Ebrahim, Alnoor, and V. Kasturi Rangan. "Acumen Fund: Measurement in Impact Investing." Boston: Harvard Business School Publishing, 2011.

Edelman. *2019 Edelman Trust Barometer: Global Report*. New York, NY: Daniel J. Edelman Holdings, 2019.

Edwards, Michael. *Civil Society*. 3rd ed. Cambridge: Polity Press, 2014.

Edwards, Michael. "What's to Be Done with Oxfam?, Part 2." *openDemocracy*, February 15, 2018. https://www.opendemocracy.net/en/transformation/what-s-to-be-done-with-oxfam-part-2/.

Edwards, Michael, and David Hulme. "Too Close for Comfort? The Impact of Official Aid on Nongovernmental Organizations." *World Development* 24, no. 6 (1996): 961–73.

Emmrich, Daniel. *NGOs in the 21st Century. The Opportunities Presented by Digitalization and Globalization*. Munich: Dr. Wieselhuber & Partner, 2017.

Fassin, Didier. "The Predicament of Humanitarianism." *Qui Parle* 22, no. 1 (2013): 33–48. https://doi.org/10.5250/quiparle.22.1.0033.

Fidelity Charitable. *The Future of Philanthropy. Where Individual Giving Is Going*. Boston: Fidelity Charitable, 2016.

Fisher, William F. "Doing Good? The Politics and Anti-Politics of NGO Practices." *Annual Review of Anthropology*, no. 26 (1997): 439–64.

Ganz, Marshall, Tamara Kay, and Jason Spicer. "Social Enterprise Is Not Social Change." *Stanford Social Innovation Review* 16, no. 2 (2018): 59–60.

Götz, Norbert. "Reframing NGOs: The Identity of an International Relations Non-Starter." *European Journal of International Relations* 14, no. 2 (2008): 231–58. https://doi.org/10.1177/1354066108089242. http://journals.sagepub.com/doi/abs/10.1177/1354066108089242.

Green, Duncan. *Fit for the Future? Development Trends and the Role of International Ngos*. Oxford: Oxfam GB, 2015.

Gugerty, Mary Kay, and Dean Karlan. *The Goldilocks Challenge. Right-Fit Evidence for the Social Sector*. New York: Oxford University Press, 2018.

Hannan, Michael T., and John Freeman. "The Population Ecology of Organizations." *American Journal of Sociology* 82, no. 5 (1977): 929–64.

Haynes, Emily, and Michael Theis. "Gifts to Charity Dropped 1.7% Last Year, Says 'Giving USA'." *The Chronicle of Philanthropy* 31, no. 9 (2019): 22–23.

Hopgood, Stephen. *Keepers of the Flame. Understanding Amnesty International*. Ithaca: Cornell University Press, 2006.

Hornsby, Jeffrey S., Jake Messersmith, Matthew Rutherford, and Sharon Simmons. "Entrepreneurship Everywhere: Across Campus, across Communities, and across Borders." *Journal of Small Business Management* 56, no. 1 (2018): 4–10. https://doi.org/10.1111/jsbm.12386.

IARAN. *The Future of Aid INGOs in 2030*. Inter-Agency Regional Analysts Network, 2017. http://iaran.org/futureofaid/The_Future_Of_Aid_INGOs_In_2030-33.pdf.

Ingram, George, and Kristin M. Lord. *Global Development Disrupted: Findings from a Survey of 93 Leaders*. Washington, DC: Brookings Institution, 2019.

InterAction. *Supporting Your NGO Future: US NGO Executive Thoughts on the Future*. Washington, DC: InterAction, 2019.

"In International Aid, People Should Be Seen as Consumers Not 'Beneficiaries'."
    The Guardian, updated May 13, 2015, accessed August 26, 2019. https://www.
    theguardian.com/global-development-professionals-network/2015/may/13/
    international-aid-consumers-beneficiaries.

The International Budget Partnership. *"Thats How the Light Gets In." Making Change
    in Closing Political Environments*. Washington, DC: The International Budget
    Partnership, 2016.

International Center for Not-for-Profit Law. "Closing Civic Space: Impact on
    Development and Humanitarian CSOs." *Global Trends in NGO Law* 7, no. 3
    (2016): 1–19.

Jaskyte, Kristina, and Audrone Kisieliene. "Organizational Innovation: A Comparison
    of Nonprofit Human-Service Organizations in Lithuania and the United States."
    International Social Work 49, no. 2 (2006): 165–76.

Johnson, Erica, and Aseem Prakash. "NGO Research Program: A Collective Action
    Perspective." *Policy Sciences* 40 (2007): 221–40.

Kenny, Charles. *Getting Better: Why Global Development Is Succeeding—and How We Can
    Improve the World Even More*. New York: Basic Books, 2012.

Kolk, Ans, Miguel Rivera-Santos, and Carlos Rufín. "Reviewing a Decade of Research
    on the 'Base/Bottom of the Pyramid' (BOP) Concept." *Business & Society* 53, no. 3
    (2014): 338–77.

Lecy, Jesse D., and David M. Van Slyke. "Nonprofit Sector Growth and Density: Testing
    Theories of Government Support." *Journal of Public Administration Research and Theory*
    23, no. 1 (2013): 189–214. https://doi.org/10.1093/jopart/mus010.

Liket, Kellie C., and Karen Maas. "Nonprofit Organizational Effectiveness: Analysis
    of Best Practices." *Nonprofit and Voluntary Sector Quarterly* 44, no. 2 (April 1,
    2015): 268–96. https://doi.org/10.1177/0899764013510064.

Lucchi, Elena. *Introducing "For Profit" Initiatives and Actors in Humanitarian Response*.
    Barcelona: Médecins Sans Frontières, 2018.

Lux, Steven J., and Tosca Bruno-van Vijfeijken. *From Alliance to International: The
    Global Transformation of Save the Children*. Syracuse: Maxwell School of Citizenship
    and Public Affairs, 2012.

Mangaleswaran, Ramesh, and Ramya Venkataraman. *Designing Philantropy for Impact*.
    Chennai: McKinsey & Company, 2013.

Marquis, Christopher, Andrew Klaber, and Bobbi Thomson. *B Lab: Building a New
    Sector of the Economy*. Cambridge, MA: Harvard Business School, 2011.

Marquis, Christopher, and Andrew Park. "Inside the Buy-One Give-One Model."
    Stanford Social Innovation Review, Winter 2014, 28–33.

Martens, Kerstin. "Mission Impossible. Defining Nongovernmental Organizations."
    Voluntas 13, no. 3 (2002): 271–85.

McKeever, Brice S. *The Nonprofit Sector in Brief 2015: Public Charities, Giving, and
    Volunteering*. Washington, DC: Urban Institute, 2015.

Mitchell, George E. "NGOs in the United States." In *Routledge Handbook
    of NGOs and International Relations*, edited by Thomas Davies, 415–32.
    New York: Routledge, 2019.

Organisation for Economic Co-operation and Development. *Aid for CSOs*.
    Paris: OECD, 2015.

Orlova, Alexandra V. "'Foreign Agents,' Sovereignty, and Political Pluralism: How the Russian Foreign Agents Law Is Shaping Civil Society." *Penn State Journal of Law & International Affairs* 7, no. 2 (2019): 382–417.

Porter, Michael E., and Mark R. Kramer. "The Big Idea: Creating Shared Value." *Harvard Business Review* (January–February 2011).

Prakash, Aseem, and Mary Kay Gugerty, eds. *Advocacy Organizations and Collective Action.* Cambridge: Cambridge University Press, 2010.

Rainey, Stephen, Kutoma Wakunuma, and Bernd Stahl. "Civil Society Organisations in Research: A Literature-Based Typology." *Voluntas* (December 2016): 1–23. https://doi.org/10.1007/s11266-016-9816-y.

Ransom, David. "The Big Charity Bonanza." *New Internationalist*, October 2, 2005. https://newint.org/features/2005/10/01/keynote.

Roberts, Susan M. "Development Capital: USAID and the Rise of Development Contractors." *Annals of the Association of American Geographers* 104, no. 5 (2014): 1030–51. https://doi.org/10.1080/00045608.2014.924749.

Rutzen, Douglas. "Civil Society under Assault." *Journal of Democracy* 26, no. 4 (2015): 28–39.

Salamon, Lester M. "Putting the Civil Society Sector on the Economic Map of the World." *Annals of Public and Cooperative Economics* 81, no. 2 (2010): 167–210.

Shirky, Clay. *Here Comes Everybody: The Power of Organizing without Organizations.* New York: Penguin, 2008.

Sidel, Mark. *Regulation of the Voluntary Sector: Freedom and Security in an Era of Uncertainty.* London: Routledge, 2009.

Sikkink, Kathryn. *Evidence of Hope: Making Human Rights Work in the 21st Century.* Princeton, NJ: Princeton University Press, 2017.

Sriskandarajah, Dhananjayan. "NGOs Losing the War against Poverty and Climate Change, Says Civicus Head: Charities Are No Longer Drivers of Social Change; for Many Saving the World Has Become Big Business. How Did We Lose Our Way?" *The Guardian* (London), August 11, 2014.

Stephen, Matthew D., and Michael Zürn, eds. *Contested World Orders: Rising Powers, Non-Governmental Organizations, and the Politics of Authority beyond the Nation-State.* Oxford: Oxford University Press, 2019.

Stroup, Sarah S., and Wendy Wong. *The Authority Trap: Strategic Choices of International NGOs.* Ithaca: Cornell University Press, 2017.

Tallack, Barney. *INGO Typologies and Organizational Forms.* (Unpublished manuscript) 2018.

Twersky, Fay, Phil Buchanan, and Valerie Threlfall. "Listening to Those Who Matter Most, the Beneficiaries." *Stanford Social Innovation Review* 11 (2013): 41–45.

Union of International Associations. *Yearbook of International Organizations.* 5 vols. Leiden: Brill, 2016.

Watkins, Susan Cotts, Ann Swidler, and Thomas Hannan. "Outsourcing Social Transformation: Development NGOs as Organizations." *Annual Review of Sociology* 38 (2012): 285–315.

Weiss, Thomas M., D. Conor Seyle, and Kelsey Coolidge. *The Rise of Non-State Actors in Global Governance: Opportunities and Limitations.* Broomfield, CO: One Earth Future Foundation, 2013.

Werker, Eric, and Faisal Z. Ahmed. "What Do Nongovernmental Organizations Do?" *Journal of Economic Perspectives* 22, no. 2 (2008): 73–92.

Willetts, Peter. *Non-Governmental Organizations in World Politics: The Construction of Global Governance*. New York: Routledge, 2011.

Youngs, Richard. *Civic Activism Unleashed: New Hope or False Dawn for Democracy?* Oxford: Oxford University Press, 2019.

Younis, Mohamed, and Andrew Rzepa. *One in Three Worldwide Lack Confidence in NGOs*. Gallup and Wellcome (2019). https://news.gallup.com/opinion/gallup/258230/one-three-worldwide-lack-confidence-ngos.aspx.

CHAPTER 2
Soul

If the soul of a TNGO consists of its mission and its principled vision of an improved future, then its body is its institutional form—generally some collection of charitable organizations and the rules and norms that govern them.[1] If the soul and the body are in harmony, a TNGO can concentrate its power on transforming the world that it seeks to change; when they are in disharmony, its transformative power will be frustrated. In this book, we argue that the existential angst felt by many thoughtful TNGO practitioners about the sector's future is partially the result of disharmony—a fundamental incongruity between the soul and the body of the TNGO. As TNGOs have become more ambitious and have sought to transform themselves and adapt to new organizational roles, they have discovered the limits of what is possible within their current institutional and normative architecture. To secure their futures, TNGOs may need to change more than their business models and operational strategies; they may also need to redefine the institutions and norms constituting the sector's identity.

Successfully adapting to the geopolitical shifts, new competitors, and enhanced accountability demands described in Chapter 1 will require significant organizational change efforts for many TNGOs. However, the conceptualization and execution of reforms are complicated by the embeddedness of TNGOs in an institutional and normative architecture historically defined by the charity model.[2] TNGOs founded in Northern countries such as the United States and United Kingdom, for example, are typically registered as "charities," yet relatively few TNGOs today would describe themselves as such. The term implies an arguably antiquated conception of TNGOs as stewards of self-expressive almsgiving in which value is consummated in the act of giving itself. Today, however, in the so-called impact era,[3] most especially mid-to-large-sized TNGOs would probably agree that their purpose is to achieve social transformation or sustainable impact. Over the past few decades, these TNGOs have committed themselves to moving beyond the amelioration of symptoms associated with the charity model to address the root causes of social and environmental problems with long-term solutions.

The institutional form of the charity is not particularly conducive to these lofty ambitions. The charity model emerged historically not as a vehicle for fundamental societal transformation, but as a mechanism for stewarding almsgiving. The charity framework is designed to ensure organizational trustworthiness under a set of specific assumptions about the purpose of giving, the nature of charitable activities, and the possibility of opportunistic or fraudulent behavior. What has been largely overlooked are the implications of being a charity for the abilities of contemporary TNGOs to remain relevant and competitive in today's complex and rapidly changing environment. Although the idea of impact-oriented and problem-solving philanthropy has largely overtaken conventional charity as a rhetorical and strategic frame in much discourse,[4] this shift has yet to be matched by the capacities of many TNGOs to effectively implement their new strategies and realize their new aspirations.[5]

We describe the environment of the TNGO as an *architecture*. This architecture is defined by two sets of characteristics: (1) the institutional form of the TNGO and (2) organizational cultures and sectoral norms that shape TNGO behavior. These two sets of characteristics can compound the difficulties that TNGO change managers and leaders experience when they initiate reforms to secure the future relevance of their organizations.

INSTITUTIONAL FORM

The form of a TNGO can affect its ability to serve its mission. The right form can give a TNGO's soul expression and power, but the wrong form can become a hindrance. The origin story of the charity or nonprofit provides insights into the institutional form of the TNGO. This story begins in an abstract state of the world with no charitable sector and no TNGOs. Why does the world even need these organizations? Explanations for the existence of charities can be organized into demand-side and supply-side explanations that focus on why and where charities or nonprofits form.[6]

Demand-side explanations

In the story's primordial world, the first sector to emerge in what eventually becomes the "three-sector economy" is the market. Individuals looking to maximize their own self-interests spontaneously provide for the needs of society guided by the invisible hand of the profit motive. Unfortunately, markets can fail. Needed goods may be undersupplied because potential producers cannot easily control access to consumption. Public goods typically fall into this category, such as national defense, infrastructure, and clean air. Once such goods are produced, they are available to everyone, even to those who do not pay.[7] The free market will tend to undersupply public goods because freeriding cannot be prevented and therefore profits cannot be assured.[8] Government is therefore necessary to correct market failure by using its coercive powers to levy taxes to prevent freeriding and correct supply deficiencies.

But governments can also fail. In democracies, governments are most likely to respond to majority demands with a single level of service for all their constituents, inevitably undersupplying some constituents who demand more or different goods and services.[9] For example, government has a greater incentive to provide for mainstream educational opportunities, while neglecting the needs expressed by minority communities. Seeking to satisfy such unmet demands, individuals establish special organizations—charities—to fill in the gaps left behind by the market and the state. The "third sector" thus emerges, literally as the last of three sectors.

In a society in which all three sectors already exist, government and charities are likely to be intertwined, with governments providing support to charities to produce public services. This is because philanthropic capital may be insufficient, donors may be particularistic or paternalistic, and organizations may be too amateurish to be effective, for example.[10] Government can correct so-called voluntary failure by supporting charitable organizations with grants, contracts, and tax benefits, as is common in many countries.[11]

Today, these stories of how the charitable sector emerged are reflected in conversations about its contemporary role and purpose. If we believe in the notions of market and government failures, then the nonprofit sector stands apart with a unique identity and role. If we accept the idea of voluntary failure, then the emphasis shifts to the common purpose of government and nonprofit sectors in jointly providing public goods.[12] Many TNGOs have historically ascribed to the former perspective by defining their role as addressing government failure through service provision and advocacy focused on individual relief and better treatment of those in need of help. But there is a much more fundamental problem lurking beneath the surface. Why should charities be trusted to succeed where market and government institutions have failed?

Contract failure and the charity model

In principle, anyone willing to voluntarily fund the provision of social outcomes could simply hire a business to do so, and so charities should not be necessary. The difficulty, however, is that social outcomes are often very difficult or excessively costly to measure, arguably to the extent that they may even be unmeasurable.[13] Philanthropists cannot contract with businesses to produce social outcomes because they have no way of determining whether the desired social outcomes are ever produced. This might be fine if businesses could be trusted to act in good faith, but businesses face financial incentives to cheat the buyer. They can exploit information asymmetries—essentially donor ignorance—and behave opportunistically. For example, a for-profit orphanage may stand to financially benefit by neglecting its residents to minimize costs and maximize profits. The profit motive itself potentially conflicts with promises to deliver on outcomes that donors cannot easily verify. Thus, yet another type of failure arises, one of contract failure.[14] Donors will not contract with businesses to produce social outcomes because businesses cannot be trusted.

The solution to this problem is the institutional form of the charity, the principal design feature of which is the so-called nondistribution constraint.[15] Unlike a business, the officers of a charity are prohibited from capturing net earnings for their private benefit. In other words, they do not own the resources of the organization and cannot lawfully distribute profits to themselves. The nondistribution constraint therefore imbues charities with trustworthiness. Society will trust charities to produce unobservable social outcomes because charities lack the material incentives that businesses have to defraud donors. Put differently, charities specialize in the production of unobservable outcomes because they have a comparative advantage in trustworthiness. Information asymmetry still exists but is no longer a problem because charities are trustworthy. These three features— unobservable outcomes, information asymmetry, and the nondistribution constraint—define the form of the charity. Charities are relevant because they are trustworthy; they have no reason to spend donor money on anything other than programs to help people.

Supply-side explanations

While the failure theories explain the space created for charities to exist, they do not necessarily explain the existence of philanthropists and social entrepreneurs willing to donate their own money to help other people. Generally, supply-side explanations for the existence of charities posit that there are certain kinds of people with an innate desire to contribute to the social good.[16] Such people may not necessarily create or join charitable organizations, but they often do. Through a process called entrepreneurial sorting, these people may choose to pursue social change by lobbying government, forming a socially responsible business, joining existing movements, starting a charity, or through other such means.[17]

Philanthropists, activists, and volunteers may have ideological or religious motives,[18] be driven by a sense of normative commitment, moral duty,[19] or public service motivation,[20] or they may seek affective bonding or conformity to social norms.[21] They may also be driven by a desire to exert power, control, or gains related to self-esteem and social status,[22] with research generally concluding that giving is predominantly motivated by personal benefits.[23] Interestingly, experimental research has shown that people will donate even when they are presented with a scenario in which their donation will have no impact.[24] Donors and social entrepreneurs may be motivated by the "warm glow"[25] or social accolades that they receive from giving or volunteering. For example, the phenomenon of people posting pictures of themselves participating in charitable activities on social media platforms to gain "likes" has become so widespread that it has been the subject of a vigorous transnational campaign against it.[26] The impetus for social entrepreneurship need not necessarily be pure altruism; it could also involve a mixture of self-regarding motives or what economists refer to as impure altruism.[27] The supply-side perspective reminds us that there will always be people willing to volunteer and to support the work of charities, regardless of authentic societal needs and the ability of organizations to create lasting impact.

Successful failure

If individuals derive personal benefits from giving and volunteering, then one function of the charitable sector is to provide these benefits to donors by collecting charitable contributions. In an extreme scenario in which society's problems are fundamentally unsolvable, the purpose of the sector is not to achieve sustainable impact, but instead to (1) produce an agreeable feeling that something is being done and (2) conceal the fact that nothing can be done.[28] So long as charities remain trustworthy and successfully conceal evidence of their failure, stakeholders remain satisfied. Donors receive the personal psychic benefits they desire and charities receive the funding they need to continue in perpetuity. In a sense, charities are in the business of selling licenses to feel good to donors.[29] Charities just have to remain trustworthy and manage information carefully so that donors are not disappointed.

In this scenario, social change may be so difficult and rare that "strategic ignorance" about social outcomes may be psychologically rational.[30] In this sense, charities do not just provide a "warm glow" to donors, but give them protection from unwanted information. Perhaps social outcomes are indeed observable, but society chooses not to observe them because it would rather assume the best. Or perhaps people simply choose to believe what they want to believe regardless of the evidence, as experimental research has implied.[31] In any case, an important corollary of this thought experiment is that charities do not necessarily need to achieve or demonstrate impact to be successful. The charitable sector, in other words, is prone to providing "a stable and friendly environment for low-performing, high-persistence organizations."[32]

Rationales and performance surveillance regimes

The charitable sector throughout much of the world today is extremely diverse and embodies a variety of personal and organizational rationales. The so-called instrumental rationale emphasizes results and the solving of social problems, whereas the expressive rationale emphasizes the symbolic function of the charitable sector and the need for individuals and communities to express their values, identify with causes, and conform with social expectations.[33] This may include not only donors but also TNGO staff and volunteers as well. These different rationales are not necessarily mutually exclusive, but over time, the instrumental rationale seems to have gained currency, not just among philanthropists and governments but among practitioners and thought leaders as well.[34]

The institutional form of the charity as it exists in most countries of the Global North emerged largely from religious traditions of expressive almsgiving[35] and generally lacks features that would make it more conducive to the instrumental rationale. In the United States, for example, regulation of the sector primarily focuses on tax-exempt eligibility and possible financial misconduct, especially related to fundraising.[36] In effect, charities that avoid financial scandals, maintain low overhead, and generally channel the maximum proportion of funding to current programs are considered trustworthy.[37] To survive, charities must maintain this trustworthiness, not necessarily be impactful. In principle, charities can have no impact at all and still continue to license donor warm glow, surviving indefinitely.[38]

TNGOs incorporating as charities effectually adopt an institutional form optimized not for *impact* in the context of demonstrably solving societal problems, but for *trustworthiness* in the context of encouraging benevolent donor almsgiving. While certainly both objectives are admirable (and they need not be in conflict), problems arise when organizations definitely committed to achieving sustainable impact and societal transformation are constituted instead as entities designed to steward alms. Impact-oriented organizations want to innovate, empower, facilitate, and invest in long-term change processes, whereas the architecture of the charity essentially requires organizations to immediately transfer their resources directly to "recipients" or "beneficiaries." Resources spent researching, evaluating, and investing in the future are construed as diversions of money away from the charitable mission. This is probably why so many TNGOs evidently feel obliged to display their (in)direct cost rates or program expense (or overhead) ratios on their websites and in their promotional materials, despite such metrics being widely discredited as meaningful and helpful indicators of efficiency or effectiveness.[39] The display of various pie charts and seals of approval derived from financial information demonstrate trustworthiness in the charitable architecture. Trustworthiness is required to ensure organizational survival and is maintained principally through the public performance of fiscal probity.[40]

The charity model subjects organizations to a narrow surveillance regime that cannot reliably reward or punish organizations according to their degrees of success in achieving their missions. The institutional framework rewards a focus on upward financial accountability and acceptance of the status quo, while largely disregarding organizational impact. Like an industry that becomes uncompetitive due to protectionist policies, the TNGO sector risks becoming irrelevant because organizations have not necessarily had to demonstrate their effectiveness to survive.[41]

Organizational structure

The architecture's surveillance regime also helps to explain the resilience of some problematic organizational structures in need of reform. The governance structures of many TNGOs founded in the Global North continue to reflect the historical legacies of traditional aid models based on the conveyance of material resources from the Global North to the Global South. Arguably, these structures are better optimized for serving the interests of Northern donors than maximizing relevance and responsiveness to Southern stakeholders. Even as many TNGOs are implementing significant governance reforms designed to empower their Southern members and affiliates (see Chapter 8), the architecture's emphasis on upward financial accountability still encourages deference to wealthier Northern members, whether through formal mechanisms or behind the scenes.

CULTURE AND NORMS

TNGOs are typically lauded for the norms that constitute their sector, including principled action, altruism, universalism, and a willingness to work long hours for relatively little financial reward. These are often identified as the unique qualities of the sector setting it apart from government and business. But while these espoused norms may sustain a generally positive external image for the TNGO, other norms and cultural attributes can be more problematic. Disconnects between espoused and lived values, as well as impediments to change imposed by specific cultural values and norms, have prompted an increasing number of TNGOs to question their own organizational cultures, norms, and practices. In a recent survey of TNGO leaders, for example, 96 percent were assessing, formulating, or executing significant organizational change processes and 83 percent were specifically assessing, formulating, or executing organizational cultural changes.[42] Indeed, cultural change is a major component of many broader organizational changes that TNGOs are attempting to implement. Although cultural change is widely discussed in the business literature,[43] it is a less prominent topic in the TNGO literature and remains often a not well-understood and therefore difficult task for practitioners.

Organizational culture

Organizational culture refers to the often subconscious and unspoken assumptions, values, and belief systems about the character or identity of an organization.[44] These belief systems define "how we work around here" and indicate how one should behave and how one can be successful within an organization. Culture manifests itself in widely shared everyday habits.[45]

Culture is established and reinforced through the stories and myths that an organization tells itself about what it stands for. Founders frequently play key roles in establishing an organizational culture, although subsequent leaders and dominant teams can also influence culture. The often outsized role of founders can be a major concern, especially as a significant hurdle to leadership transitions and organizational change.[46] Culture determines what the organization pays attention to (or not), which behaviors it rewards, the criteria it uses for the selection, recruitment, and termination of staff, the rituals it performs, the physical layout of offices, and its formal statements about itself. Culture is tenacious and represents a form of inertia.[47] It institutionalizes what worked in the past and is reinforced over time.

Organizational culture should be distinguished from national and regional cultures, and organizations often have multiple subcultures. These may be based on the influence of national or regional cultures or of functional specializations within an organization, such as finance, legal, or fundraising. Research on TNGOs has identified how national cultures can influence how TNGOs operate,[48] but has not often emphasized the internal workings of these organizations from a cultural perspective.

Organizational culture is both visible and invisible. It is reflected in buildings, structures, and images. It is also reflected in group behavior, decision-making, and social relations. Finally, it is driven by deeply seated beliefs about the problems the organization addresses and how it goes about doing so.[49]

Organizational cultures can vary markedly across and within organizations, and opening up the "black box" of organizations typically reveals contradictions and tensions between different and competing values.[50] But the mission focus of TNGOs alongside the emphasis on moral principles generates underlying attitudes shaping daily practices and behaviors. At the risk of overgeneralizing, three core beliefs appear to define the unique cultural character of TNGOs. These are summarized in Table 2.1 along with the other components of the architecture, and are explained below.

First, TNGO culture is characterized by consultation and deliberation that can often be excessive. In the context of leading large organizational change processes, such a consultative culture can contribute to greater diversity in inputs but can also lead to protracted discussions, delayed decision-making, and a frequent resort to the lowest common denominator. TNGO practitioners and observers have noted a tendency of extensive "navel-gazing" and often little regard for the transaction and opportunity costs of a highly consultative culture. For example, the tendency of relying on too many meetings without clearly defined action items or the emphasis

Table 2.1 ANALYTICAL CONCEPTS

Architectural component	General considerations	Specific concepts
Institutional	Demand-side	Market failure
		Government failure
		Voluntary failure
	Contract failure	Unobservable outcomes
		Information asymmetry
		Nondistribution constraint
		Trustworthiness
	Supply-side	Normative commitments
		Affective bonding
		Conformity to social norms
		Self-esteem, warm glow, social status, psychic benefits
	Successful failure	Donors prefer ignorance because impact may be unattainable
		Charities can survive financially regardless of impact
	Rationales	Expressive
		Instrumental
	Performance surveillance regime	Emphasis on organizational trustworthiness demonstrated through fiscal probity
		Focus on financial data in lieu of credible impact information
	Governance structures	Legacy models emphasize upward financial accountability over other accountabilities
		Members or sections in the Global North dominate decision-making
Normative	Attributes of organizational culture	Consultation and deliberation
		Uniqueness, in-group bias, conflict avoidance
		Process over outcomes
	Sectoral attributes	Exaggerated reliance on conformity (isomorphism) to secure legitimacy
		Perceived need to conform may impair innovation and learning

on "busyness" as a substitute for tracking performance are all indicators of an organizational culture with ineffective communication and deliberation processes. In a highly consultative culture TNGOs may also tend to reopen consultation or decision-making processes as soon as they have closed. This can also undermine organizational agility at critical junctures.

Second, TNGO practitioners tend to display a strong conviction that their organizations have a unique organizational identity, value system, and set of core competencies and approaches that are distinct from those of other organizations. This sense of uniqueness can be overstated—even bordering on "organizational narcissism"[51]—and can frustrate collaborations and impede mergers and acquisitions (see Chapters 10 and 11), among other consequences. An inflated sense of organizational uniqueness can also prevent people from accepting that the organization needs to change to remain viable and relevant for the future.

The idea of a unique organizational identity frequently leads to attitudes of "us versus them" and a strong sense of in-group (versus out-group) bias. This sense of uniqueness and superiority often cultivated in the external relations of TNGOs can also seep inside the organization and create destructive behavior including a tendency to "villainize the 'other' rather than acknowledge one's own part in any conflict or seek contact or compromise."[52] Such internal dynamics can lead to passive aggressive behaviors, including "*say* yes but *do* no."[53] Since everyone is dedicated to the mission, conflict avoidance can emerge as a response to personal or professional differences. As summarized by one TNGO leader: "We are all nice people and we are all doing our best—this is our psychological contract."[54] This set of related cultural attributes inhibits frank conversations about sensitive subjects, stymieing change.

Externally, attitudes such as "you are either with us, or you are against us" or "we are good, others are bad" negatively affect the power of TNGOs. Many TNGO practitioners have a limited awareness of, and interest in, working with unlike-minded actors and frequently lack the skills to interact with, and influence, members of out-groups. This may also lead to advocacy and campaigning attitudes focused on disparaging the values, intentions, and even the intelligence of those who are othered. This mindset does not lend itself well to influencing dissimilar actors and has become increasingly problematic as TNGOs' ambitions have expanded.

Third, many of these cultural traits ensure that TNGO cultures value loyalty, effort, and passion, more so than measurable outcomes. Many TNGO leaders and staff feel primarily accountable to the (self-defined) cause—having passion for the mission and being willing to spend long hours for a relatively low salary.[55] The psychological contract[56] between the individual and the organization usually does not emphasize a need to demonstrate sustainable impact, at least not until more recently. As one TNGO leader put it: "Asking about outcomes is like pulling teeth. It lowers your popularity as a leader when you do so."[57] This is also reflected in a lack of discipline with which individual or unit-level performance management processes tend to be executed.[58] The weak outcome orientation also reflects the historical legacy of the charity model and its emphasis on organizational inputs and processes instead of outcomes. Although TNGOs have increasingly adopted the rhetoric of outcomes and impact, accountability remains primarily tied to upward financial reporting and exhibited levels of passion and effort.

If an organization is defined primarily by its level of passion and effort, then it is also difficult to recognize the unintended consequences of its actions. Being convinced of doing good work creates a culture often incapable of recognizing harm done, including to the very people whom they claim to support. Strong organizational reflexes can exist among the staff and leadership of such organizations against the very notion that they might do harm, resulting in attempts to deny and even punish people who bring such harms to light.[59] The recent scandals that have plagued Oxfam, Amnesty International, and Save the Children, for example, indicate how damaging this can be not only to those victimized but also to an organization's reputation, financial sustainability, and staff motivation. In these cases, leadership was in some form aware of the problems, but going public raised concerns about negative effects on trustworthiness and fundraising.[60] The logic of "we can do no harm because our intentions are good" can blind organizations to critical shortcomings.

This is not to say that scandals are a necessary result of organizational cultures or that TNGOs do not often produce valuable outcomes. The point is that a lack of critical self-awareness and an underemphasis on assessing outcomes limit the ability of organizations to learn and improve over time. At the operational level, there are rarely obvious solutions to most of the problems addressed by TNGOs, so it is essential to foster an organizational culture of open dialogue, critique, and experimentation. Many TNGOs continue to struggle with establishing such a culture, primarily because their normative and institutional reward structures prioritize trustworthiness, process, and commitment above results.

Sectoral norms

In addition to organizational culture, sectoral norms play an important role in the architecture of the TNGO. Organizations need to conform to social rules and norms to appear legitimate.[61] Sectoral norms are capable of influencing organizational behavior even to the point of causing organizations to forgo activities that would technically be in their best interest.[62] Since norms are typically taken for granted, their influence on behavior is often invisible. For example, economists have pointed out that net fundraising proceeds are maximized when the cost of raising an additional dollar is one dollar, but few fundraisers would knowingly spend an additional $0.99 to raise an additional $1.00 because doing so would clearly violate sectoral norms. Organizations therefore forgo the additional $0.01, even though it could have been used to improve and expand programs.[63] Generally, TNGO behavior is constrained by what the norms of the charitable sector will allow. In this example, organizations effectually forgo increased future impact to maintain their conformity to fundraising norms.[64] Within the normative frame of the charity model, indirect expenses such as fundraising and administration are not investments in increased future impact but instead represent diversions of resources away from current programming. Funders, public agencies, information intermediaries, watchdogs, and media organizations semi-coercively enforce conformity to the charity model through mechanisms such as funding requirements and the surveillance of financial ratios.[65] Indeed, research has shown that financial ratios can have a significant impact on future donations.[66]

The importance of conforming to such norms becomes exaggerated when the external environment is uncertain. Organizations often respond to uncertainty by imitating other organizations that they perceive to be successful. This kind of mimicry—so-called mimetic isomorphism—is not based on a rational diffusion of best practices but rather on a need to maintain legitimacy when no one really knows what to do.[67] In the architecture of the charitable sector this manifests itself in phenomena such as the so-called nonprofit starvation cycle, in which organizations compete for the lowest overhead rate only to starve themselves of the capacities they need to be effective.[68] A key insight is that none of this isomorphic behavior actually improves organizational performance. For instance, there is no systematic evidence to suggest that organizations with lower overhead rates are more effective or efficient; research has instead suggested the contrary.[69]

In addition to mimetic isomorphism, professionalization and socialization are also reliable vectors of norm diffusion.[70] Especially among large TNGOs, staff, leaders, and consultants frequently circulate across organizations and diffuse shared ideas.[71] The need to maintain legitimacy under uncertainty leads individuals and organizations to perpetuate and reaffirm sectoral norms. For example, TNGOs have taken decades to move away from using ethically problematic imagery of destitute children in their fundraising appeals. Such images reliably appeal to donors, but also reinforces problematic stereotypes. On the one hand, it is professional to adopt common fundraising methods that work and are aligned with prevailing ideas of "powerful givers."[72] On the other hand, such practices undermine new mandates focused on empowerment and equity.

Uncertainty is a pervasive feature of the TNGO's operational environment, especially in fields where credible evidence about effective practices is lacking, and isomorphism is a common response to this ambiguity. Indeed, there are few clear answers about how to end poverty or advance social justice and human rights.[73] Isomorphic responses to uncertainty in the pursuit of such aims helps to explain why so many TNGOs often look so similar in terms of their rhetoric, structure, and strategy, despite most claiming to be unique. This can impair innovation and learning—two critical activities necessary for ensuring future relevance.

CONCLUSION

Despite having already largely transcended the notion of charity as a fundamental paradigm for effective social action, the TNGO nevertheless finds itself embodied in an architecture still defined by the legacy charity framework. This architecture offers little to incentivize, support, and reward strategic shifts toward new organizational roles more conducive to sustainable social transformation. This is increasingly problematic because many TNGOs have staked their legitimacy and relevance on their claims of sustainable impact, beyond merely demonstrating that they are trustworthy stewards of self-expressive almsgiving. Moreover, in conforming to the imperatives of the institutional and normative architecture, TNGOs limit their capacities to adapt. For example, the omnipresent imperative to prioritize fiscal propriety may draw resources and attention away from measuring program impact, while a weak outcome orientation may hinder learning and accountability both internally and externally. The architecture can therefore compound the already significant challenges to organizations attempting to adapt to a wide variety of developments. This is simply part of the cost of being a charity.

Arguably, the situation is a devil's bargain. TNGOs receive valuable benefits in many contexts for adopting and adhering to the charity model, but the arrangement also relieves some of the pressure to improve accountability and effectiveness in order to survive. The architecture's trustworthiness surveillance regime helps to insulate organizations from an important kind of market discipline that might otherwise force TNGOs to more urgently confront their challenges.

The problem is not one that can be solved solely at an organizational level. The larger philanthropic ecosystem in which TNGOs operate needs to provide a more conducive environment to support TNGOs that are focused on achieving and demonstrating sustainable impact.[74] Regulatory changes, new institutional forms, internal governance reforms, and large-scale collective action may be required to restore trust, confidence, and legitimacy.[75] While observers and practitioners often focus on the tactical and strategic challenges of serving communities in difficult operating environments, less attention has been paid to the architecture in which TNGOs are embedded or its core analytical features (see Table 2.1). The architecture not only can constrain the ability of TNGOs to live up to their rhetoric about impact, but it also presents significant obstacles to implementing many of the organizational reforms necessary for ensuring the sector's broader legitimacy and future relevance.

REFERENCES

Alvesson, Mats, and Stefan Sveningsson. *Changing Organizational Culture: Cultural Change Work in Progress*. New York: Routledge, 2015.

Andreoni, James. "Impure Altruism and Donations to Public Goods: A Theory of Warm-Glow Giving." *The Economic Journal* 100, no. 401 (1990): 464–77.

Andreoni, James, and A. Abigail Payne. "Charitable Giving." In *Handbook of Public Economics*, edited by Alan A. Auerbach, Raj Chetty, Martin Feldstein, and Emmanuel Saez, 1–50. Amsterdam: North Holland, 2013.

Avula, Kavita, Lisa McKay, and Sébastien Galland. *Amnesty International: Staff Wellbeing Review* Washington, DC: The Konterra Group, 2019.

Barber, Putnam, and Megan M. Farwell. "The Relationships between State and Nonstate Interventions in Charitable Solicitation Law in the United States." In *Regulatory Waves: Comparative Perspectives on State Regulation and Self-Regulation Policies in the Nonprofit Sector*, edited by Oonagh B. Breen, Alison Dunn and Mark Sidel. New York, NY: Cambridge University Press, 2017. 199-220.

Bekkers, René, and Pamala Wiepking. "A Literature Review of Empirical Studies of Philanthropy: Eight Mechanisms That Drive Charitable Giving." *Nonprofit and Voluntary Sector Quarterly* 40, no. 5 (2011): 924–73.

Beswick, Danielle, Niheer Dasandi, David Hudson, and Jennifer vanHeerde-Hudson. "International Development NGOs, Representations in Fundraising Appeals, and Public Attitudes in UK-Africa Relations." In *Britain and Africa in the Twenty-first Century*, edited by Danielle Beswick, Jonathan Fisher, and Stephen R. Hiurt, 196–213. Manchester: Manchester University Press, 2019.

Block, Stephen R., and Steven Rosenberg. "Toward an Understanding of Founder's Syndrome: An Assessment of Power and Privilege among Founders of Nonprofit Organizations." *Nonprofit Management and Leadership* 12, no. 4 (2002): 353–68. https://doi.org/10.1002/nml.12403. https://onlinelibrary.wiley.com/doi/abs/10.1002/nml.12403.

Bond and Itad. *Value for Money: What It Means for UK NGOs*. London: Bond, 2012.

Breen, Oonagh B., Alison Dunn, and Mark Sidel, eds. *Regulatory Waves: Comparative Perspectives on State Regulation and Self-Regulation Policies in the Nonprofit Sector*. New York: Cambridge University Press, 2017.

Brest, Paul. "A Decade of Outcome-Oriented Philanthropy." *Stanford Social Innovation Review* (2012). http://www.ssireview.org/articles/entry/a_decade_of_outcome_oriented_philanthropy.

Brest, Paul. "Strategic Philanthropy and Its Discontents." *Stanford Social Innovation Review* (April 27, 2015). https://ssir.org/up_for_debate/article/strategic_philanthropy_and_its_discontents.

Bright, Leonard. "Is Public Service Motivation a Better Explanation of Nonprofit Career Preferences Than Government Career Preferences?" *Public Personnel Management* 45, no. 4 (2016): 405–24. https://doi.org/10.1177/0091026016676093. http://journals.sagepub.com/doi/abs/10.1177/0091026016676093.

Bryer, David, and John Magrath. "New Dimensions of Global Advocacy." *Nonprofit and Voluntary Sector Quarterly* 28, no. 1 suppl. (1999): 168–77. https://doi.org/10.1177/089976499773746500. http://journals.sagepub.com/doi/abs/10.1177/089976499773746500.

Child, Curtis, and Eva M. Witesman. "Optimism and Bias When Evaluating a Prosocial Initiative." *Social Science Quarterly* (2019). https://doi.org/10.1111/ssqu.12585.

Coupet, Jason, and Jessica L. Haynie. "Toward a Valid Approach to Nonprofit Efficiency Measurement." *Nonprofit Management & Leadership* 29, no. 2 (2019): 299–320. https://doi.org/10.1002/nml.21336.

Crumpler, Heidi, and Philip J. Grossman. "An Experimental Test of Warm Glow Giving." *Journal of Public Economics* 92 (2008): 1011–21.

Davies, Thomas. *NGOs: A New History of Transnational Civil Society*. New York: Oxford University Press, 2014.

DiMaggio, Paul, and Walter Powell. "The Iron Cage Revisited: Institutional Isomorphism and Collective Rationality in Organizational Fields." *American Sociological Review* 48 (1983): 147–60.

Duchon, Dennis, and Michael Burns. "Organizational Narcissism." *Organizational Dynamics* 37, no. 4 (2008): 354–64.

Duchon, Dennis, and Brian Drake. "Organizational Narcissism and Virtuous Behavior." *Joural of Business Ethics* 85, no. 3 (2009): 301–8.

Edwards, Michael. "What's to Be Done with Oxfam?, Part 2." *openDemocracy* (February 15, 2018). https://www.opendemocracy.net/en/transformation/what-s-to-be-done-with-oxfam-part-2/.

Finnemore, Martha, and Kathryn Sikkink. "International Norm Dynamics and Political Change." *International Organization* 52, no. 4 (1998): 887–917.

Frumkin, Peter. *On Being Nonprofit: A Conceptual and Policy Primer.* Cambridge, MA: Harvard University Press, 2002.

Galaskiewicz, Joseph, and Wolfgang Bielefeld. *Nonprofit Organizations in an Age of Uncertainty.* New York: Aldine de Gruyter, 1998.

Gordon, C. Wayne, and Nicholas Babchuk. "A Typology of Voluntary Associations." *American Sociological Review* 24, no. 1 (1959): 22–29.

Gregory, Ann Goggins, and Don Howard. "The Nonprofit Starvation Cycle." *Stanford Social Innovation Review* (Fall 2009): 49–53.

Gross, Robert A. "Giving in America: From Charity to Philanthropy." In *Charity, Philanthropy, and Civility in American History,* edited by Lawrence J. Friedman and Mark D. McGarview, 29–48. New York: Cambridge University Press, 2003.

Hall, Peter Dobkin. "Historical Perspectives on Nonprofit Organizations in the United States." In *The Jossey-Bass Handbook of Nonprofit Leadership and Management,* edited by David O. Renz, 3–41. San Francisco: Jossey-Bass, 2010.

Hansmann, Henry B. "The Role of Nonprofit Enterprise." *The Yale Law Journal* 89, no. 5 (1980): 835–901. https://doi.org/10.2307/796089. http://www.jstor.org/stable/796089.

Heifetz, Ronald A., Marty Linsky, and Alexander Grashow. *The Practice of Adaptive Leadership: Tools and Tactics for Changing Your Organization and the World.* Boston: Harvard Business School Publishing, 2009.

Hilhorst, Dorothea, and Nadja Schmiemann. "Humanitarian Principles and Organisational Culture: Everyday Practice in Médecins Sans Frontières–Holland." *Development in Practice* 12, nos. 3–4 (2002): 490–500. https://doi.org/10.1080/0961450220149834.

Hudson, Mike. *Managing without Profit: The Art of Managing Non-Profit Organizations.* Harmondsworth: Penguin, 1999.

InterAction. Supporting *Your NGO Future: US NGO Executive Thoughts on the Future.* Washington, DC: InterAction, 2019.

Jacobs, Fred A., and Nicholas P. Marudas. "The Combined Effect of Donation Price and Administrative Inefficiency on Donations to US Nonprofit Organizations." *Financial Accountability & Management* 25, no. 1 (2009): 33–53. https://doi.org/doi:10.1111/j.1468-0408.2008.00464.x. https://onlinelibrary.wiley.com/doi/abs/10.1111/j.1468-0408.2008.00464.x.

James, Estelle. "Why Do Different Countries Choose a Different Public-Private Mix of Educational Services?" *Journal of Human Resources* 28, no. 3 (1993): 571–92.

Kitching, Karen. "Audit Value and Charitable Organizations." *Journal of Accounting and Public Policy* 28, no. 6 (2009): 510–24.

Knoke, David. *Organizing for Collective Action: The Political Economies of Associations.* New York: Routledge, 1990.

Lecy, Jesse D., and Elizabeth A. M. Searing. "Anatomy of the Nonprofit Starvation Cycle: An Analysis of Falling Overhead Ratios in the Nonprofit Sector." *Nonprofit and Voluntary Sector Quarterly* 44, no. 3 (2015): 539–63. https://doi.org/10.1177/0899764014527175.

Lecy, Jesse D., and David M. Van Slyke. "Nonprofit Sector Growth and Density: Testing Theories of Government Support." *Journal of Public Administration Research and Theory* 23, no. 1 (2013): 189–214. https://doi.org/10.1093/jopart/mus010.

Lewis, David. "NGOs, Organizational Culture, and Institutional Sustainability." *The Annals of the American Academy of Political and Social Science* 590, no. 1 (2003): 212–26.

Lohmann, Roger A. "And Lettuce Is Nonanimal: Toward a Positive Economics of Voluntary Action." *Nonprofit and Voluntary Sector Quarterly* 18, no. 4 (1989): 367–83.

MacAskill, William. "Effective Altruism: An Introduction." *Essays in Philosophy* 18, no. 1 (2017): 1–5.

Marudas, Nicholas P., TeWhan Hahn, and Fred A. Jacobs. "An Improved Model of Effects of Accounting Measures of Inefficiency on Donations." *Journal of Finance and Accountancy* 15 (2014): 1.

Meehan, William F., III, and Kim Starkey Jonker. *Engine of Impact: Essentials of Strategic Leadership in the Nonprofit Sector.* Stanford: Stanford Business Books, 2017.

Mitchell, George E. "Fiscal Leanness and Fiscal Responsiveness: Exploring the Normative Limits of Strategic Nonprofit Financial Management." *Administration & Society* 49, no. 9 (2017): 1272–96. https://doi.org/10.1177/0095399715581035.

Mitchell, George E. "Modalities of Managerialism: The 'Double Bind' of Normative and Instrumental Nonprofit Managerial Imperatives." *Administration & Society* 50, no. 7 (2018): 1037–68. https://doi.org/10.1177/0095399716664832. 2016.

Mitchell, George E. "NGOs in the United States." In *Routledge Handbook of NGOs and International Relations*, edited by Thomas Davies, 415–32. New York: Routledge, 2019.

Mitchell, George E., and Thad D. Calabrese. "Outcome-Oriented Philanthropy and the Problem of Institutional Design." Philanthropy and Social Impact: A Research Symposium, The Center on Philanthropy & Public Policy, Sol Price School of Public Policy, University of Southern California, 2019.

Mitchell, George E., and Thad D. Calabrese. "Proverbs of Nonprofit Financial Management." *American Review of Public Administration* 49, no. 6 (2019): 649–61. https://doi.org/10.1177/0275074018770458.

Mitchell, George E., and Hans Peter Schmitz. "The Nexus of Public and Nonprofit Management." *Public Performance & Management Review* 42, no. 1 (2019): 11–33. https://doi.org/10.1080/15309576.2018.1489293.

Moore, Mark H. "Managing for Value: Organizational Strategy in For-Profit, Nonprofit, and Governmental Organizations." *Nonprofit and Voluntary Sector Quarterly* 29, no. 1 (2000): 183–204.

Null, C. "Warm Glow, Information, and Inefficient Charitable Giving." *Journal of Public Economics* 95 (2011): 455–56.

O'Hara, M., and A. Omer. "Virtue and the Organizational Shadow: Exploring False Innocence and the Paradoxes of Power." In *Humanity's Dark Side: Evil, Destructive Experience, and Psychotherapy*, edited by A. C. Bohart, B. S. Held, E. Mendelowitz, and K. J. Schneider, 167–87. Washington, DC: American Psychological Association, 2013.

Olson, Mancur. *The Logic of Collective Action. Public Goods and the Theory of Groups* Cambridge, MA: Harvard University Press, 1965.

"The Overhead Myth." GuideStar, 2013. http://overheadmyth.com/wp-content/uploads/2013/06/GS_OverheadMyth_Ltr_ONLINE.pdf.

Pandey, Sanjay K., Sheela Pandey, Rachel A. Breslin, and Erica D. Broadus. "Public Service Motivation Research Program: Key Challenges and Future Prospects." In *Foundations of Public Administration*, edited by Jos Raadshelders and Richard Stillman, 314–32. Irvine, CA: Melvin and Leigh, 2017.

Pritchett, Lant. "It Pays to Be Ignorant: A Simple Political Economy of Rigorous Program Evaluation." *The Journal of Policy Reform* 5, no. 4 (2002): 251–69.

Rousseau, Denise. *Psychological Contracts in Organizations: Understanding Written and Unwritten Agreements.* Thousand Oaks, CA: Sage, 1995.

Salamon, Lester M. "Of Market Failure, Voluntary Failure, and Third-Party Government: Toward a Theory of Government-Nonprofit Relations in the Modern Welfare State." *Journal of Voluntary Action Research* 16, nos. 1–2 (1987): 29–49. https://doi.org/10.1177/089976408701600104.

Schein, Edgar H. *Organizational Culture and Leadership*. San Francisco: Jossey-Bass, 2010.

Schmidt, Arthur "Buzz." "Divining a Vision for Markets for Good." In *Selected Readings: Making Sense of Data and Information in the Social Sector*, edited by Eric J. Henderson, 61–81. N.p.: Markets for Good, 2014.

Seibel, Wolfgang. "Organizational Behavior and Organizational Function: Towards a Micro-Macro Theory of the Third Sector." In *The Third Sector: Comparative Studies of Nonprofit Organizations*, edited by Helmut K. Anheier and Wolfgang Seibel, 107–22. Berlin: de Gruyter, 1990.

Seibel, Wolfgang. "Successful Failure." *American Behavioral Scientist* 39, no. 8 (1996): 1011–24. https://doi.org/10.1177/0002764296039008006.

Steinberg, Richard. "Economic Theories of Nonprofit Organizations." In *The Nonprofit Sector. A Research Handbook*, edited by Walter W. Powell and Richard Steinberg, 117–39. Thousand Oaks, CA: Sage, 2006.

Stroup, Sarah S. *Borders among Activists: International NGOs in the United States, Britain, and France*. Ithaca, NY: Cornell University Press, 2012.

Tinkelman, Daniel, and Kamini Mankaney. "When Is Administrative Efficiency Associated with Charitable Donations?" *Nonprofit and Voluntary Sector Quarterly* 36, no. 1 (2007): 41–64.

Watkins, Susan Cotts, Ann Swidler, and Thomas Hannan. "Outsourcing Social Transformation: Development NGOs as Organizations." *Annual Review of Sociology* 38 (2012): 285–315.

Weisbrod, Burton A. *The Nonprofit Economy*. Cambridge, MA: Harvard University Press, 1989.

Weisbrod, Burton A. "Toward a Theory of the Voluntary Non-Profit Sector in a Three-Sector Economy." In *Altruism, Morality, and Economic Theory*, edited by Edmund S. Phelps, 171–95. New York: Russell Sage Foundation, 1975.

Wing, Kennard, and Mark A. Hager. *Getting What We Pay For: Low Overhead Limits Nonprofit Effectiveness*. Washington, DC: Urban Institute Center on Nonprofits and Philanthropy and Indiana University Center on Philanthropy, 2004.

Young, Dennis R. *If Not for Profit, for What?: A Behavioral Theory of the Nonprofit Sector Based on Entrepreneurship*. Heath, MA: Lexington Books, 1983.

Young, Dennis R., and Richard Steinberg. *Economics for Nonprofit Managers*. New York: The Foundation Center Press, 1995.

Zald, Mayer N., and Michael Lounsbury. "The Wizards of Oz: Towards an Institutional Approach to Elites, Expertise, and Command Posts." *Organization Studies* 31, no. 7 (2010): 963–96.

CHAPTER 3
Strategy

As many TNGOs' missions have evolved to embrace fundamental societal transformation, the constraints of the architecture described in Chapter 2 have become more problematic. Features of the charity model, individual TNGO cultures, and sectoral norms that contributed to success in the past increasingly limit the potential of TNGOs to adapt for the future. These limitations become more apparent when considering the organizational changes required for TNGOs to effectively implement new strategies.

Historically, the most prevalent TNGO strategy was to focus on immediate physical needs following disasters or in situations of persistent poverty. Appeals for funding often catered to the expressive rationale of charitable giving associated with an ethical imperative to give.[1] In the past, many TNGOs played a crucial role as intermediaries that collected donations in the Global North and conveyed those resources to the Global South. The child sponsorship programs adopted by ActionAid, Compassion International, and World Vision exemplify this approach.

Even when some organizations began to choose advocacy over service delivery as their main focus, the underlying logic generally reflected a desire for immediate relief, not long-term social transformation. For example, Amnesty International early on encouraged its dedicated membership in wealthy countries to write letters on behalf of individuals identified as "prisoners of conscience." During the Cold War, Amnesty identified such prisoners in Western, Communist, and non-aligned countries[2] while mobilizing urgent and principled action. Such an approach steered clear of overt political action and transformation and instead emphasized a desire to mobilize moral values as a means of improving the human condition.[3]

The need to adapt to changing geopolitical realities has led many TNGOs to embark on repeated strategic changes during the past decades. In the humanitarian and development sectors, this has often involved adding advocacy to the dominant practice of service delivery. In the human rights or environmental sectors, advocacy was often already a primary strategy, but specific strategies became increasingly global and complex in their ambitions. These significant strategic shifts were often driven by the emergence of new organizations challenging past approaches and promising to be more effective at delivering on the promises of the sector. For example, Médecins Sans Frontières was founded in 1971 to challenge conventional humanitarian aid practices in the aftermath of the Biafra war in Nigeria.[4] Human Rights Watch emerged in the late 1970s as a challenger to Amnesty International, promising to professionalize human rights research and advocacy.[5]

Strategic adaptation in response to geopolitical changes and sectoral competition are nothing new, but TNGOs today face more fundamental challenges mounted by external actors with very different cultural and social backgrounds. These include the rise of economies in the non-Western world, competition from organizations in the Global South, and the emergence of digital platforms and corporate actors claiming to produce global goods more efficiently and effectively than TNGOs. Meanwhile, an increased strategic emphasis on campaigning, advocacy, and public education means a greater need to secure legitimacy and demonstrate accountability. The old foundation of legitimacy based on fiscal probity and upward accountability to donors is no longer sufficient for an evolving TNGO sector that has self-adopted more expansive mandates to not just deliver direct aid but also to fundamentally transform societies.

CHARITY AND SUSTAINABLE IMPACT AS STRATEGIC FRAMES

Charity focused on perpetual aid and philanthropy focused on sustainable impact represent distinct strategic approaches to addressing society's needs and problems. Today's challenges faced by TNGOs seeking to prepare for the future are not only a matter of moving from "simpler" forms of charity to more complex interventions.[6] Both practices will always be part of what TNGOs do, and what matters is less if one prefers one over the other, but how each are practiced. For example, GiveDirectly's unconditional cash transfers could be interpreted as a regression to charity,[7] although such strategies have attracted significant attention from donors and researchers.[8] However, GiveDirectly has also employed randomly controlled trials to assess impact.[9]

Critics often label charity as short-term, superficial, and fostering of dependency. Most institutional donors and TNGOs today have adopted the rhetoric of strategic philanthropy and sustainable impact, with an emphasis on addressing the root causes of social problems. But not only does strategy matter, but also the processes used to implement strategy. For example, addressing the root causes of social problems may or may not rely on empowering local populations. Andrew Carnegie's *Gospel of Wealth* called for a shift from perpetual assistance to creating opportunities, and claimed at the same time that the "rich know better than the poor" and donors should remain in full control of their giving.[10] While the notion of sustainable impact may be more expansive and compelling than those of charity, both may still involve donor-focused practices permissive of the "successful failure" identified in Chapter 2.

Those defending charity as a viable strategy point out that it can provide natural protections against donor paternalism and the invasion of the non-profit sector by businesslike mindsets.[11] What matters then is how charity or philanthropy as normative frames are actually implemented in daily practices on the ground. TNGOs have generally moved away from charity to embrace the logic of long-term sustainable impact, but this shift has also increased their struggles to deliver on expanding promises. Without significantly investing in measurement systems and proactively reconsidering their roles as intermediaries between the rich and the poor, TNGOs risk inviting strategic ambiguities and inconsistencies that are ultimately unhelpful.

MATCHING STRATEGIES TO EXPANDING MANDATES

The pursuit of more expansive mandates has been accompanied by shifts in organizational strategy favoring advocacy over service delivery, global campaigns over local activism, and systems thinking over the shorter-term orientations of bringing immediate relief to individuals. Indeed, a recent survey found that 76 percent of TNGO leaders in the United States are assessing, formulating, or executing new or significantly increased advocacy programming and efforts to shape public sentiment.[12] Although such strategies have long existed in the TNGO sector,[13] they have become more widely accepted since the 1990s by the largest and most visible organizations.[14] Following World War II and the adoption of the Universal Declaration of Human Rights in 1948, distinct sectors of TNGO activism operated based on separate normative frameworks, from the humanitarian sector's emphasis on impartiality and neutrality to the human rights sector's principles of universality and indivisibility. Since the 1970s, environmental TNGOs advanced their own sets of ideas, and single-issue organizations became a dominant form in the sector. While advocacy played a minor role in traditional humanitarian and development activities, the widespread diffusion of the human rights framework across sectors eventually came to represent one of the key developments underlying a convergence in strategic repertoires across subsectors.[15] At the same time, advocacy across TNGOs changed over time from a primary focus on individuals to a growing emphasis on social conditions and other root causes giving rise to abuses and violations.[16]

With the rise of rights-based approaches and a growing dissatisfaction with conventional charity, most, especially large-sized, TNGOs developed some version of their own advocacy approach.[17] Some have chosen to emphasize more adversarial campaigns at global and national levels (e.g., Oxfam) while others have primarily targeted their advocacy at attitudinal and behavioral change in local communities (e.g., Plan International). Human rights TNGOs can "name and shame" their targets often at a distance. In contrast, humanitarian and development TNGOs typically maintain significant local presence with permanent staff and offices. The former then are more likely to be confrontational, while the latter have to consider how any deployment of advocacy is going to affect their operations and capacity to reach those they want to serve.[18]

TNGOs specialize in addressing social, political, or environmental problems through cross-border activity. While the sector has always addressed difficult conditions, early efforts consisted of short-term charity and relief focused on immediate symptoms. TNGOs specialized in bringing moral solutions to the world's problems, not political ones. Instead of calling for a revolution or popular uprisings, TNGOs provided assistance through services and by speaking on behalf of victims.[19] This approach worked well for many decades and organizations flourished as they were able to save lives, cause the release of prisoners, and create protected land, for example. Such achievements, while important, typically manifested themselves on a substantially smaller scale than what their missions may have suggested.

Over time, many TNGOs started to express a desire to address the root causes of societal problems and acknowledged that accomplishing their missions requires experimentation, learning, adaptation, and researching how specific interventions translate into medium-term outcomes and long-term impact. For example, humanitarian groups have supplemented their focus on delivering goods with an emphasis on strengthening community resilience. Relief is no longer viewed as a sole focus of action, and most humanitarian TNGOs today embrace a "new humanitarianism" with an emphasis on resilience, risk reduction, early-warning systems, local capacity-building, and a desire to ultimately hand over responsibility to local actors.[20] In the human rights area, TNGOs have moved away from documenting particular instances of violations, and are today more focused on identifying and addressing systemic causes of injustice.

In other words, the arc of the last several decades reveals shifts in strategy that reflect an increasing commitment to the instrumental rationale of TNGOs as agents of change. However, the architecture in which TNGOs are embedded does not easily accommodate these shifts of TNGOs into new strategic roles with more expansive mandates. Some general trends illustrate the difficulties. These include (1) efforts to augment traditional service delivery with advocacy, public education, and entrepreneurial approaches; (2) shifts among advocacy organizations to focus more on global campaigns, rather than specific local or individual conditions; and (3) efforts to introduce systems thinking as a holistic framework for analyzing and addressing root causes. Table 3.1 illustrates two dimensions along which these strategic shifts have taken place.

Table 3.1 DIMENSIONS OF STRATEGY CHANGE

		Focus	
		Individual relief	*Root causes*
Approach	*Advocacy*	Freeing prisoners of conscience and prisoners of war Blocking whaling ships	Global campaigns to change policymaker preferences and public worldviews "Naming and shaming" focused on changing worldviews, laws, and practices Rights-based approaches
	Service	Aid distribution Child sponsorship Land acquisitions for habitat protection Cash transfers	Microfinance and creating opportunities for entrepreneurship Ending harmful environmental practices in the business sector

From direct service delivery to championing rights and supporting entrepreneurship

While the immediate and short-term nature of charity continues to be an important focus for many donors, the TNGO sector as a whole has mostly embraced more complex strategies in the name of fundamental social transformation often pursued through advocacy strategies.[21] Although traditional direct service delivery will likely always remain a core strategy for many TNGOs, many organizations have expanded or shifted their strategies to embrace a greater role for advocacy. For example, in the past two decades Save the Children substantially increased its global advocacy operations,[22] CARE adopted rights-based approaches (RBA), Plan transitioned into child centered community development (CCCD),[23] and Heifer began advocating to influence the value chain for farming products. As many TNGOs have deemphasized pure service delivery, they have developed more complex theories of change and are also trying to redefine their own roles and to bolster their own legitimacy. It is in these areas of activism where TNGOs have innovated the most but also where they face the most significant pushback and questions about their accountability and effectiveness.

Among development TNGOs, the movement toward hybrid strategies that combine service delivery with human rights advocacy, and that frame material deprivations as human rights infringements, has been well documented.[24] Such RBAs attempt to address the root causes of poverty and frame "beneficiaries" as "rights-holders" rather than needy dependents.[25] The diffusion of RBA since the early 1990s was driven by the increasingly universal reach of human rights norms coupled with a growing crisis of the traditional development model based on foreign aid. RBA has played a key role in diminishing the long-standing divide between human rights advocacy and development aid, and has allowed many TNGOs to assert their legitimacy by adapting in response to growing critiques of the traditional aid system.[26] TNGOs that adopt strategies that couple traditional service delivery with advocacy are also often seen as more effective by their peers.[27]

Early adopters of RBA included ActionAid, Oxfam,[28] Plan, and CARE, most of which began by the mid-1990s to introduce the terminology into their programming.[29] Following the adoption of RBA by the UN system in 2003, UN agencies and TNGOs have often developed unique versions of RBA, differing in regards to which rights are prioritized and how those rights are advanced through advocacy, legal action, and grassroots mobilization.[30] While RBA has become widely adopted among Northern European TNGOs, many prominent US-based organizations, including World Vision, have yet to embrace the frame, presumably due to apprehensions toward RBA and international human rights more generally in the US context.[31]

Another strategy pushing beyond traditional service delivery is the growing focus on microfinance and entrepreneurship. The concept and practice destabilizes conventional distinctions between voluntarist and market-based approaches to social betterment and challenges cultural and legal demarcations between nonprofit and for-profit institutional forms. More broadly, such social innovation strategies promise to address at least four specific limitations of the traditional charity model. First, it calls for self-sustaining resource generation that avoids a perpetual reliance on often fickle donor funding, as is the case with the Grameen Bank's and BRAC's microfinancing models. Second, it replaces the project-based intervention logic with a process of iterative product or service development (prototyping) that acknowledges a need for trial and error and adaptive learning. Third, it shifts emphasis away from the TNGO as project owner and instead allows local entrepreneurs to own solutions. Fourth, by establishing peer-to-peer lending opportunities, organizations such as Kiva give donors control over who receives their financial support.[32] Lessons from the microfinance crisis[33] suggest that this approach is more likely to succeed when accompanied by complementary efforts aimed at capacity-building (e.g., incubators) and infrastructure development.

A clear strategic shift is taking place in favor of longer-term, sustainable solutions, generally involving the empowerment of local rights-holders or social entrepreneurs. The conventional notion that TNGOs should focus on addressing immediate material needs through direct service provision, rather than expending resources in support of longer-term, often more overtly political strategies, is increasingly hard to justify in the wake of sustained criticisms of traditional aid models and the availability of alternative approaches. However, although many TNGOs are augmenting, deemphasizing, or abandoning purely charitable approaches and some are experimenting with commercial approaches involving social innovation, organizations still confront a philanthropic culture heavily influenced by the legacies of the conventional charity model.

While innovation in strategies can be a significant driver of organizational change, the emphasis on novelty and likelihood of success[34] often underestimates continuity and path dependency. RBA and social innovation are very different from traditional service delivery, but they also reflect some important similarities to earlier aid efforts. Social innovation largely still avoids politicizing the conditions causing poverty and deprivation by favoring market-based solutions. Similar to the rise of the TNGO after World War II, the emphasis is on helping individuals by giving them access to opportunities to escape persistent poverty. Interestingly, RBA as the strategy most focused on politics is itself being challenged by the spread of business-driven approaches to poverty reduction.

From reactive advocacy to proactive global campaigning

Repertoires of advocacy strategies vary widely across TNGOs. They may include public interest litigation, lobbying, policy analysis, mobilization, media outreach, influencing behavioral attitudes, and the promotion and scale-up of successful interventions. Advocacy efforts may be targeted at local, national, and international levels, may rely on an outsider strategy, may be integrated into insider strategies of "tactical lobbying"[35] that involve intersectoral collaborations, or may combine both insider and outsider strategies as a means of increasing the power of under-resourced activists.[36] Underlying this diversity of advocacy efforts, there are some major trends in the trajectory of TNGO advocacy as organizations have grown their brands and resources over the past decades.

While development and humanitarian TNGOs have for some time diversified away from service delivery, human rights and environmental TNGOs have also embraced significant strategic shifts in their approaches to advocacy.[37] Early advocacy efforts were more reactive and narrowly targeted by responding to specific instances of human rights violations and environmental destruction.[38] Iconic in this regard is the practice of adopting prisoners of conscience promoted by Amnesty International[39] and Greenpeace's direct actions taken during the 1970s to end the killing of seal pups and whale hunting. These actions were focused, reactive to often visible harm, and highly effective in mobilizing moral outrage among supporters across the Global North. With increasing growth and professionalization, many TNGOs were able to expand their staff dedicated to increasingly comprehensive research and advocacy efforts. Popular support and volunteers became less relevant over time, and were even viewed as counterproductive to the future of many of these organizations.[40]

During the 1970s and 1980s, a new form of advocacy—global campaigning—emerged to match both the growth of the sector and its expanding mandates.[41] Among the development and humanitarian TNGOs, Oxfam became a major global campaigning organization, while human rights and environmental organizations began to also pay increased attention to targeting international institutions[42] to advance their agendas globally. For example, Amnesty International began in 1973 its first ever campaign to address the root causes of government-sanctioned torture around the world.[43]

It was limited to one year and only focused on awareness-raising, but was so successful in raising publicity that subsequent campaigning contributed to the creation of the UN Anti-Torture Convention in 1984. After the end of the Cold War, TNGO campaigning across many issue areas (see Chapter 4) became a dominant activity contributing to claims that TNGOs and civil society had established a powerful, alternative logic of social action competing now with markets and states in shaping global and national policies.[44] As many governments are unable or unwilling to protect the livelihoods of their populations, TNGOs have increasingly targeted non-state actors, including businesses with global supply chains and violent groups responsible for gross human rights violations.[45]

Global campaigns became attractive for advocacy TNGOs because these campaigns matched their evolving mandates and increasing ambitions. The release of a prisoner provides immediate satisfaction to those writing letters, similar to sending a monthly check to a poor child abroad. However, both action strategies have fallen out of favor over time because TNGOs wanted to accomplish more sustainable goals by addressing underlying conditions. This required adopting more proactive strategies, including advocacy at national and international levels. In theory, an international treaty against torture will force governments to no longer consider such practices in their detention facilities, while RBA was similarly designed to push governments into assuming roles as primary duty bearers providing for their own citizens. In many ways, the strategic shifts represented learning over time and a rational response to the limits of earlier efforts.

In hindsight, the rise of TNGO brands alongside global campaigns and innovative change strategies generated not just a significant backlash against this type of activism, but also left the sector less prepared for the future. Many civic spaces have shifted with various post-1990s political developments, while others have shrunk as governments and other powerful actors have sought to exploit public angst to roll back previous gains with anti-progressive politics.[46] TNGOs have been increasingly accused of being part of global governance elite with limited popular support to back up their legitimacy. They become more successful at creating laws and institutions at global levels, while having more limited capacities to support implementation at national and local levels, especially in countries with hostile governments (see Chapter 4). As the sector matured, the expertise-focused approach principally relied on staff for elite lobbying and normative mobilization, but often neglected building diverse popular support at local levels.[47] This detachment from the grassroots opened the doors for authoritarian leaders to question the legitimacy of TNGOs and reject their claims.

Staff-led expertise privileges a "naming and shaming" approach to advocacy that has been losing efficacy. In the past, advocacy organizations mainly generated reports and exposed wrongdoing, resulting in decreasing levels of mobilization and greater public fatalism about the ability of TNGOs to deliver on their promises. The reliance on negative messaging also reinforced images of victimhood and the charitable impulse of substituting virtuous almsgiving for broad social action. Often well-meaning campaigns designed to address harm unintentionally disempowered the oppressed and identified TNGOs as saviors with the necessary principled dedication and expertise.[48] In contrast to "naming and shaming," new advocacy strategies humanize rights and other issues, highlight solutions alongside problems, and move toward more distributed campaigning with less staff dominance. This growing emphasis on multiway communications in advocacy creates more space for telling stories,[49] rather than stating facts and struggling to appeal to contested norms.

From capacity-building to systems thinking

TNGOs have become more ambitious in their strategies by moving from an original focus on the individual and local issues toward addressing more abstract underlying causes on national and transnational scales. Alongside these shifts, there have also been growing questions about capacity-building and technical assistance as mainstay strategies designed to end ongoing resource transfers. Capacity-building may include the training of government officials or civil society groups, involving consultants to transfer expertise, establishing exchange programs, or providing equipment for improved organizational functionality. By the mid-2000s the OECD estimated that about 25 percent of international development aid ($15 billion) was spent on capacity-building,[50] and it has been among the most widely employed strategies among US-based TNGOs.[51]

Although the overall results have been mixed,[52] significant improvements have been achieved where the strategy has successfully run its course. However, that also means that relatively little more can be gained through continued capacity-building without complementary efforts. As donors have largely backed away from purely externally led technical interventions in favor of an "endogenous process, strongly led from within a country,"[53] TNGOs have increasingly sought to hand over control to local communities. However, relations between external actors with resources and domestic stakeholders with declared process ownership remain affected by weak partnership behaviors, misunderstandings, and power differentials.[54] There are risks of empowering local elites uninterested in comprehensive, pro-poor, equitable economic development, a problem frequently ignored when capacity-building efforts fail to include a local power analysis.[55]

One way TNGOs have sought to address the weaknesses of capacity-building programs is to move away from a short-term project-based approach to a more long-term strategy that combines capacity-building with other efforts, including advocacy and social mobilization.[56] Capacity-building is then less about a discrete effort to endow individuals or organizations with specific tools, knowledge, or skills, and more of a process of building out entire systems necessary to deliver specific services, such as healthcare and economic development.[57] Enhanced TNGO ambitions underlie these shifts, as well as a realization that many earlier strategies wrongly assumed that problems were either simple (and could be solved with rules and recipes) or complicated (and had to consider many moving parts), rather than complex (with unpredictable interactions and feedback loops). Over time, many interventions turned out to have both limited impact and often negative unintentional consequences not easily captured by simple planning and assessment tools.

A systems approach combined with an emphasis on collective impact brings several advantages, including greater awareness of limitations, more attention to understanding how systems evolve, self-organize, and consist of feedback loops, and a greater focus on relationships between different parts of the system rather than the parts in isolation.[58] For example, a systems approach focuses less on a specific training program for healthcare workers and more on how healthcare workers are situated in the overall system of healthcare. It may direct TNGOs to look beyond one-off training exercises and focus instead on enhancing the capacity of individuals to repeatedly apply and adapt new knowledge.[59] Such an approach may be difficult to implement within the contemporary aid structure focused on short-term results, but it is an important way of embedding strategies into a more holistic understanding of social problems targeted by TNGOs.[60]

CHALLENGES IN SUSTAINING STRATEGY SHIFTS

Not all TNGOs are doubling down on expanding advocacy or shifting toward RBA, social innovation, empowerment, or systems thinking; certainly many organizations will continue to maintain more traditional strategies or experiment with other approaches. But as a whole, the sector's broad embrace of more transformational missions coincides with these specific shifts in strategy. However, the organizational changes necessary to effectively sustain new strategies must be implemented in a relatively challenging architectural context.

What these shifts have in common is a focus on root causes and broad-based impact, a relatively long-term time horizon, new organizational roles that transcend the charity model, and notably, an ability to invest in organizational capacities with high short-term costs to donors and high long-term benefits to communities.

Organizational investments in more effective strategic capacities can be challenging for TNGOs due to the poor cost-benefit optics. In the near term, costs may appear excessive in relation to any immediate benefits, while in the long term the benefits are more likely to take the form of enhanced impact rather than cost savings. TNGOs implementing these strategies may simply appear to be less efficient, especially in comparison to organizations still mainly implementing traditional direct service strategies with lower indirect costs. This is partly by design. The trustworthiness surveillance regime described in Chapter 2 compels organizations to maximize current program spending and cannot easily distinguish between laudable investments in future impact and short-term inefficiency or waste. Innovative TNGOs may have difficulties justifying increased short-term costs, especially when the benefits materialize far into the future and take the form of increased impact that may never become clearly visible. Similar difficulties materialize when TNGOs initiate organizational change processes, explore mergers and acquisitions (see Chapter 11), and attempt to embark on many other future-oriented reforms.

Another commonality to these trends is the increasing difficulty of measuring impact (see Chapter 7). This is challenging due to both (1) the inherent difficulties of measurement and evaluation (M&E) in often complex and adverse operating environments and (2) the difficulties of investing in M&E systems organizationally within a broader environment of stakeholders that increasingly demands M&E but remains averse to supporting it. Although sectoral norms are slowly changing, many funders still expect M&E, accountability, learning, responsiveness, and transparency activities and capacities to be covered from unrestricted funds, while relatively few external sources of support exist to help build the requisite organizational capacities. Perhaps it is ironic that a sector so well known for capacity-building should lack such critical capacities of its own.

The obstacles to strengthening investments in areas such as M&E are particularly problematic because so much more yet needs to be learned about the effectiveness of RBA, social innovation, empowerment, facilitation, brokering, and power and systems approaches as organizational strategies. Indeed, the rate of adoption of new strategies risks outpacing the available evidence of strategy effectiveness. As described in Chapter 2, the exaggerated reliance on conformity as a strategy to secure organizational legitimacy could be crowding out innovation and learning or leading to the diffusion of inefficient or ineffective practices. At the very least, TNGOs need more leeway to invest in M&E and related approaches, capacities, and systems that are even capable of accounting for the cultural nuances, unanticipated effects, and nonlinear relationships that pervade complex change processes.[61]

Finally, a weak outcome orientation and a belief that TNGOs cannot do harm can lead to complacency and arrogance at a time when TNGOs most need to be taking measures to ensure their legitimacy and effectiveness. The assumption that a TNGO's programming is effective because its approach is sophisticated and its intentions are virtuous can allow underinvestment in organizational learning, continuous program improvement, and meaningful accountability mechanisms. The added difficulties of implementing long-term strategies in complex environments can sometimes explain why these systems may underperform or are absent. However, offering complexity as an excuse risks undermining public trust and confidence in the sector by reducing visibility into the sector's activities, ultimately harming accountability and legitimacy.

CONCLUSION

The strategic shifts taking place throughout the sector suggest a transformation in the role of TNGOs away from the traditional charity model of intermediation and direct implementation and toward an impact-oriented model focused on long-term transformation in complex contexts. TNGOs have made significant strides over the past decades to move beyond short-term interventions by adopting complex theories of change and reimagining their own roles. New tensions have emerged around the need to demonstrate results and the desire to shift away from elite-driven social change. TNGOs have greatly expanded their ambitions over time, while also declaring their desire to yield real power to those they claim to serve.

For this transition to be successful, not only TNGOs but also the philanthropic ecosystem in which TNGOs are embedded must adapt. The existing architecture has traditionally favored, and still favors, short-term direct program implementation and linear theories of change over longer-term strategies of empowerment, facilitation, innovation, and complex systems change. Traditional strategies often resonate with inherent human biases for the present and a disinclination for delayed gratification, particularly given the risk that long-term innovative strategies may not always prove effective.[62]

Bringing organizational strategies and practices into alignment with TNGOs' expanded missions requires enhanced organizational capacities, a more conducive sectoral ecosystem, and longer-term time horizons. Meanwhile, underlying shifts from direct service to enhanced advocacy and from individual relief to root causes are redefining the nature and role of the TNGO. Strategic innovations point in the direction of a fundamental transformation of organizational roles, yet broader changes are needed to enable such a transition.

REFERENCES

Albrecht, Sarah. "Shrinking, Closing, Shifting: A Changing Space for Civil Society." *Alliance Magazine*, 2017. https://www.alliancemagazine.org/blog/shrinking-closing-shifting-changing-space-civil-society/.

Bouguen, Adrien, Yue Huang, Michael Kremer, and Edward Miguel. "Using Randomized Controlled Trials to Estimate Long-Run Impacts in Development Economics." *Annual Review of Economics* 11, no. 1 (2019): 523–61. https://doi.org/10.1146/annurev-economics-080218-030333. https://www.annualreviews.org/doi/abs/10.1146/annurev-economics-080218-030333.

Brinkerhoff, Derick W., and Peter J. Morgan. "Capacity and Capacity Development: Coping with Complexity." *Public Administration and Development* 30, no. 1 (2010): 2–10. https://doi.org/10.1002/pad.559. http://dx.doi.org/10.1002/pad.559.

Bryer, David, and John Magrath. "New Dimensions of Global Advocacy." *Nonprofit and Voluntary Sector Quarterly* 28, no. 1 suppl. (1999): 168–77. https://doi.org/10.1177/089976499773746500.

Buchanan, Tom. "'The Truth Will Set You Free': The Making of Amnesty International." *Journal of Contemporary History* 37, no. 4 (2002): 575–97.

Carnegie, Andrew. *The Gospel of Wealth*. New York: Carnegie Corporation of New York, 1889/2017.

Charnovitz, Steve. "Two Centuries of Participation: NGOs and International Governance." *Michigan Journal of International Law* 18, no. 2 (1997): 183–283.

CIVICUS. *State of Civil Society Report 2018*. Johannesburg: CIVICUS, 2018. https://www.civicus.org/documents/reports-and-publications/SOCS/2018/socs-2018-overview_top-ten-trends.pdf.

Cox, Brendan. *Campaigning for International Justice*. London: Bond, 2011.

Crost, Benjamin, Joseph H. Felter, and Patrick B. Johnston. "Conditional Cash Transfers, Civil Conflict, and Insurgent Influence: Experimental Evidence from the Philippines." *Journal of Development Economics* 118 (2016): 171–82. https://doi.org/https://doi.org/10.1016/j.jdeveco.2015.08.005.

Davies, Thomas. *NGOs: A New History of Transnational Civil Society*. New York: Oxford University Press, 2014.

Denney, Lisa, "$15bn Is Spent Every Year on Training, with Disappointing Results. Why the Aid Industry Needs to Rethink 'Capacity Building'." In *From Poverty to Power* (blog), edited by Duncan Green, January 5, 2018. https://oxfamblogs.org/

fp2p/15bn-is-spent-every-year-on-aid-for-training-with-disappointing-results-why-the-aid-industry-needs-to-rethink-its-approach-to-capacity-building.

Denney, Lisa, Richard Mallett, and Matthew S. Benson. *Service Delivery and State Capacity: Findings from the Secure Livelihoods Research Consortium*. London: Secure Livelihoods Research Consortium, 2017.

Dorsey, Ellen. "Managing Change. Amnesty International and Human Rights NGOs." In *50 Years of Amnesty International: Reflections and Perspectives*, edited by Wilco de Jonge, Brianne McGonigle Leyh, Anja Mihr, and Lars van Troost, 181–219. Utrecht: Universiteit Utrecht, 2011.

Duhigg, Charles. "Why Don't You Donate for Syrian Refugees? Blame Bad Marketing." *New York Times*, June 14, 2017. https://www.nytimes.com/2017/06/14/business/media/marketing-charity-water-syria.html.

Eckel, Jan. "The International League for the Rights of Man, Amnesty International, and the Changing Fate of Human Rights Activism from the 1940s through the 1970s." *Humanity* 4, no. 2 (2013): 183–214.

Fassin, Didier. *Humanitarian Reason: A Moral History of the Present*. Berkeley: University of California Press, 2011.

Fernández-Aballí, Ana. "Advocacy for Whom? Influence for What? Abuse of Discursive Power in International NGO Online Campaigns: The Case of Amnesty International." *American Behavioral Scientist* 60, no. 3 (2016): 360–77. https://doi.org/10.1177/0002764215613407.

Fox, Renée C. *Doctors without Borders: Humanitarian Quests, Impossible Dreams of Médecins Sans Frontières*. Baltimore: Johns Hopkins University Press, 2014.

Gready, Paul. "Rights-Based Approaches to Development: What Is the Value-Added?" *Development in Practice* 18, no. 6 (2008): 735–47. http://www.informaworld.com/10.1080/09614520802386454.

Green, Duncan. *How Change Happens*. New York: Oxford University Press, 2017.

Green, Duncan. "If Top Down Control Is Unavoidable, Can We Still Make Aid More Compatible with Systems Thinking?" In *From Poverty to Power* (blog), July 17, 2019. https://oxfamblogs.org/fp2p/if-top-down-control-is-unavoidable-can-we-still-make-aid-more-compatible-with-systems-thinking/.

Gross, Robert A. "Giving in America: From Charity to Philanthropy." In *Charity, Philanthropy, and Civility in American History*, edited by Lawrence J. Friedman and Mark D. McGarview, 29–48. New York: Cambridge University Press, 2003.

Gruskin, Sofia, Dina Bogecho, and Laura Ferguson. "'Rights-Based Approaches' to Health Policies and Programs: Articulations, Ambiguities, and Assessment." *Journal of Public Health Policy* 31, no. 2 (2010): 129–45.

Haushofer, Johannes, and Jeremy Shapiro. "The Short-Term Impact of Unconditional Cash Transfers to the Poor: Experimental Evidence from Kenya." *The Quarterly Journal of Economics* 131, no. 4 (2016): 1973–2042. https://doi.org/10.1093/qje/qjw025.

Holcombe, Susan H. "Structuring a Global NGO for a Rights-Based Change Agenda." In *Change Not Charity: Essays on Oxfam's First 40 Years*, edited by Laura Roper, 362–75. Boston: Oxfam America, 2010.

Holmén, Hans. *Snakes in Paradise: NGOs and the Aid Industry in Africa*. Bloomfield, CT: Kumarian Press, 2010.

ICNL. "Survey of Trends Affecting Civic Space: 2015–2016." *Global Trends in NGO Law* 7, no. 4 (2016): 1–21.

INASP. *Approaches for Developing Capacity for the Use of Evidence in Policy Making*. Oxford: INASP, 2016.

InterAction. *Supporting Your NGO Future: US NGO Executive Thoughts on the Future.* Washington, DC: InterAction, 2019.

Kabeer, Naila, Simeen Mahmud, and Jairo Guillermo Isaza Castro. *NGOs' Strategies and the Challenge of Development and Democracy in Bangladesh.* Ids Working Paper 343. Brighton: IDS, 2010.

Keck, Margaret E., and Kathryn Sikkink. *Activists beyond Borders. Advocacy Networks in International Politics.* Ithaca, NY: Cornell University Press, 1998.

Kennedy, David. *The Dark Sides of Virtue: Reassessing International Humanitarianism.* Princeton, NJ: Princeton University Press, 2004.

Kumar, Raj. *The Business of Changing the World: How Billionaires, Tech Disrupters, and Social Entrepreneurs Are Transforming the Global Aid Industry.* Boston: Beacon Press, 2019.

Lindenberg, Marc, and Coralie Bryant. *Going Global: Transforming Relief and Development NGOs.* Bloomfield, CT: Kumarian Press, 2001.

Lux, Steven J., and Tosca Bruno-van Vijfeijken. *From Alliance to International: The Global Transformation of Save the Children.* Syracuse: Maxwell School of Citizenship and Public Affairs, 2012.

Ly, Pierre, and Geri Mason. "Individual Preferences over Development Projects: Evidence from Microlending on Kiva." *Voluntas* 23, no. 4 (2012): 1036–55. https://doi.org/10.1007/s11266-011-9255-8.

Lyon, Thomas P. *Good Cop/Bad Cop: Environmental NGOs and Their Strategies toward Business.* Washington, DC: Resources for the Future, 2010.

Mader, Philip. "Rise and Fall of Microfinance in India: The Andhra Pradesh Crisis in Perspective." *Strategic Change* 22, nos. 1–2 (2013): 47–66. https://doi.org/10.1002/jsc.1921. http://dx.doi.org/10.1002/jsc.1921.

Marin, Andrei Florin, and Lars Otto Naess. "Climate Change Adaptation through Humanitarian Aid? Promises, Perils, and Potentials of the New Humanitarianism?" *IDS Bulletin* 48, no. 4 (2017): 15–30.

Matta, Adriana, Fábio da Gonçalves, and Lisiane Leyser Bizarro. "Delay Discounting: Concepts and Measures." *Psychology & Neuroscience* 5, no. 2 (2012): 135–46.

Mitchell, George E. "The Attributes of Effective NGOs and the Leadership Values Associated with a Reputation for Organizational Effectiveness." *Nonprofit Management & Leadership* 28, no. 1 (2015): 39–57.

Mitchell, George E. "The Strategic Orientations of US-Based NGOs." *Voluntas* 25, no. 5 (2014): 1874–93. https://doi.org/10.1007/s11266-014-9507-5.

Mitchell, George E., and Thad D. Calabrese. "Instrumental Philanthropy and the Problem of Institutional Design." Philanthropy and Social Impact: A Research Symposium, The Center on Philanthropy & Public Policy, Sol Price School of Public Policy, University of Southern California, 2019.

Mitchell, George E., and Sarah S. Stroup. "The Reputations of NGOs: Peer Evaluations of Effectiveness." *The Review of International Organizations* 12, no. 3 (2016): 397–419. https://doi.org/10.1007/s11558-016-9259-7.

Moyo, Dambisa. *Dead Aid: Why Aid Is Not Working and How There Is a Better Way for Africa.* New York: Farrar, Straus and Giroux, 2009.

Mutua, Makau. "Savages, Victims, and Saviors: The Metaphor of Human Rights." *Harvard International Law Journal* 42, no. 1 (2001): 201–46.

Nelson, Paul J., and Ellen Dorsey. "At the Nexus of Human Rights and Development: New Methods and Strategies of Global NGOs." *World Development* 31, no. 12 (2003): 2013–26.

Nelson, Paul J., and Ellen Dorsey. "Who Practices Rights-Based Development? A Progress Report on Work at the Nexus of Human Rights and Development." *World Development* 104 (2018): 97–107.

O'Brien, Paul. "Politicized Humanitarianism: A Response to Nicolas de Torrente." *Harvard Human Rights Journal* 17 (2004): 31–40.

O'Brien, Robert, Anne Marie Goetz, Jan Aart Scholte, and Marc Williams. *Contesting Global Governance: Multilateral Economic Institutions and Global Social Movements.* Cambridge: Cambridge University Press, 2000.

OECD. *The Challenge of Capacity Development. Working towards Good Practice.* Paris: OECD, 2006.

Piron, Laure-Hélène. *Learning from the UK Department for International Development's Rights-Based Approach to Development Assistance.* London: Overseas Development Institute, 2003.

Plan International. *Promoting Child Rights to End Child Poverty.* Working, UK: Plan Limited, 2010. https://plan-international.org/publications/ promoting-child-rights-end-child-poverty#download-options.

Plipat, Srirak. *Developmentizing Human Rights. How Development NGOs Interpret and Implement and Human Rights–Based Approach to Development Policy.* PhD thesis, University of Pittsburgh, 2005.

Rabben, Linda. *Fierce Legion of Friends: A History of Human Rights Campaigns and Campaigners.* Hyattsville: Quixote Center, 2002.

Rodley, Nigel S. "Amnesty International's Work on Personal Integrity—A Personal Reflection." In *50 Years of Amnesty International: Reflections and Perspectives*, edited by Wilco de Jonge, Brianne McGonigle Leyh, Anja Mihr, and Lars van Troost, 51–74. Utrecht: Universiteit Utrecht, 2011.

Saunders-Hastings, Emma. "Charity, Philanthropy, and Trusteeship." *HistPhil* (November 18, 2015). https://histphil.org/2015/11/18/charity-philanthropy-and-trusteeship/.

Schmitz, Hans Peter. "A Human Rights–Based Approach (HRBA) in Practice: Evaluating NGO Development Efforts." *Polity* 44, no. 4 (2012): 523–41. https://doi.org/10.1057/pol.2012.18. <Go to ISI>://WOS:000309694200005.

Schmitz, Hans Peter. "Menschenrechtswächter: Partielle Midlife-Crisis. INGOs, Vereinte Nationen, und Weltöffentlichkeit." *Vereinte Nationen* 49, no. 1 (2001): 7–12.

Schmitz, Hans Peter. "Non-State Actors in Human Rights Promotion." In *The Sage Handbook of Human Rights*, edited by Anja Mihr and Mark Gibney, 352–72. London: Sage, 2014.

Schmitz, Hans Peter, and George E. Mitchell. "The Other Side of the Coin: NGOs, Rights-Based Approaches, and Public Administration." *Public Administration Review* 76, no. 2 (2016): 252–62. https://doi.org/10.1111/puar.12479. http://dx.doi.org/ 10.1111/puar.12479.

Singer, Peter. *The Life You Can Save: How to Do Your Part to End World Poverty.* New York: Random House, 2010.

Soskis, Benjamin. "The Indeterminate Politics of the Charity vs. Philanthropy Divide." *HistPhil* (November 30, 2015). https://histphil.org/2015/11/30/ the-indeterminate-politics-of-the-charity-vs-philanthropy-divide.

Starr, Kevin, and Laura Hattendorf. "GiveDirectly? Not So Fast." *Stanford Social Innovation Review* (March 11, 2014). https://ssir.org/articles/entry/givedirectly_ not_so_fast.

Swedlund, Haley. *The Development Dance: How Donors and Recipients Negotiate the Delivery of Foreign Aid.* Ithaca, NY: Cornell University Press, 2017.

Uvin, Peter. "From the Right to Development to the Rights-Based Approach: How 'Human Rights' Entered Development." *Development in Practice* 17, nos. 4/5 (2007): 597–606.

Uvin, Peter. *Human Rights and Development.* Bloomfield, CT: Kumarian Press, 2004.

Woodward, Aniek, Andre Griekspoor, Shannon Doocy, Paul Spiegel, and Kevin Savage. "Research Agenda-Setting on Cash Programming for Health and Nutrition in Humanitarian Settings." *Journal of International Humanitarian Action* 3, no. 1 (2018): 7. https://doi.org/10.1186/s41018-018-0035-6.

Yanacopulos, Helen. "The Strategies That Bind: NGO Coalitions and Their Influence." *Global Networks* 5, no. 1 (2005): 93–110. https://doi.org/10.1111/j.1471-0374.2005.00109.x.

CHAPTER 4

Power

TNGOs exercise power, especially in relations with local partners and communities but also with global actors like states and multinational corporations. Many TNGOs use advocacy based on universal principles on behalf of others as one of their strategies to exert influence. Advocacy strategies have evolved over time, mainly by becoming increasingly global and by putting increased emphasis on root causes, especially by addressing the need for policy change. As a result, the sector has enjoyed a number of signature victories at the global level, from improved business behaviors to the adoption of human rights treaties. These actions propelled individual TNGO brands to greater prominence and led to responses ranging from acclaim[1] to backlash. Many of the major global advocacy accomplishments of TNGOs took place in the 1980s and 1990s, while successes were less frequent after the turn of the millennium as geopolitical shifts began to limit TNGO influence in some areas. TNGOs benefited for decades from the close elite ties created with politicians and bureaucrats in Western capitals,[2] and have been able to exercise influence well above their collective material and coercive resources.

Meanwhile, civic spaces that opened up after the end of the Cold War have changed or become increasingly restricted (again), particularly in the shadow of the global "War on Terror," creeping ethnonationalism and anti-globalism, and adverse reactions to past successes.[3] Many TNGOs are looking to expand their advocacy capabilities and scale up campaigns at a time when their operating environments have become less hospitable. This underscores just some of the adversities confronting TNGOs as they attempt to realize ever more ambitious visions of the future through sophisticated campaigns to address underlying conditions. To be legitimate and effective change agents in the dynamic geopolitical environment, TNGO campaigners need to understand the nature and operation of "ideational power" and how this power can be successfully applied to influence policy at multiple levels.

During the 1980s and 1990s, TNGOs benefited from a geopolitical window of opportunity to push their agendas onto states and global institutions. The problems they are facing now and in the future are partly driven by geopolitical changes over which the sector has little control. But TNGOs still have choices to make, and they can do more to build more solid foundations to sustain their influence. As TNGOs have largely benefited from professionalized activism and elite access, their power base has become less secure because of the increasing disharmony between their ambitions and the architecture of the sector. TNGOs are today widely recognized actors in global institutions and negotiations, but they lack a corresponding international legal status to enhance their legitimacy[4] and their domestic status in national institutional and normative contexts often imposes significant constraints. The rhetoric of transformation has translated into a proliferation of advocacy success stories, but has yet to lead to fundamental changes in how the sector operates, is legitimized, and understands its own power and role.

IDEATIONAL POWER

Lacking the coercive capabilities of states, TNGOs primarily mobilize power in ideational form through tactics such as knowledge dissemination, framing, venue-shopping (the seeking out of favorable fora in which to debate issues), and naming and shaming. Central to this kind of power is acquiring authority[5] through a combination of a mission focus, professional competency, and the espousing of universal norms rhetorically shared by the global community. TNGOs contribute to processes of collective social learning when global issues arise and solutions are needed.[6]

To generate authority, TNGOs rely on the currency of legitimacy or "a generalized perception or assumption that the actions of an entity are desirable, proper, or appropriate within some socially constructed system of norms, values, beliefs and definitions."[7] TNGOs actively seek legitimacy by acting as discursive entrepreneurs,[8] shaping norms and belief systems, and mobilizing universal principles and symbols of global (in)justice.[9] They produce knowledge in four distinct areas: (1) the extent of a social problem and its harm, (2) the provision of policy solutions for addressing a problem, (3) the process focused on adopting specific policies, and (4) the capacities to implement and monitor policy solutions and new practices. TNGOs may try to shape population worldviews and social norms, or use direct action[10] and more expressive strategies to change public attitudes and behavior.[11]

A fundamental tension emerges when TNGOs engage overtly in the policy process itself. Traditionally, TNGOs' legitimacy and trustworthiness has been linked to their explicit avoidance of politics, including in processes of policy formulation and adoption.[12] However, networks of experts have always produced knowledge about both policy problems and solutions, and many advocacy organizations have shifted over time to pay more attention to questions of policy formation and implementation. For example, tobacco research in the 1950s and 1960s focused mainly on the causal link between smoking and lung cancer, but later on it increasingly emphasized the relative effectiveness of specific policy solutions including cessation programs, taxation, and bans on indoor smoking.[13] In the humanitarian space, a number of TNGOs have taken more overtly political positions following perceived failures of global responses to mass atrocities in a number of high-profile cases, including Rwanda in 1994 and Darfur after 2003.[14] Specifically, the strengthening of international law became a key focal point for many TNGOs attempting to increase their impact by addressing root causes.

To get policies adopted, TNGOs have to acquire expertise about the decision-making processes and arenas. Knowledge about the policy process may shape coalition-building, venue-shopping, access to policymakers, and strategies for dealing with opponents. Finally, policy implementation creates new knowledge challenges related to translating and adapting programs to local conditions[15] and monitoring their effectiveness. In these last two stages of adoption and implementation, TNGOs may be part of co-governance arrangements exerting direct power through binding decisions implemented locally.[16]

The expanding ambitions of TNGOs entail a growing need for different types of capacities related to issue and process expertise. Applying these different types of expertise may generate tensions, potentially negatively affecting the legitimacy of TNGOs. A focus on producing issue knowledge emphasizes a non-partisan image whereby organizations have to be perceived as neutral in order to not "lose authority with their target audience."[17] TNGOs expressing particularistic interests or participating in overt political bargaining processes may face a backlash based on violating the expectations of their supporters. But to ignore the political arena and decision-making processes risks becoming irrelevant or leaving it up to policymakers to ignore or selectively refer to provided expertise.

The role of TNGOs has evolved over time from primarily engaging in agenda-setting and gatekeeping to increasingly participating in the governance of important global issues. Decades ago, the roles of TNGOs in the creation of the UN anti-torture convention (1984) or the anti-landmines treaty (1997) were groundbreaking. More recently TNGOs have played expansive roles, especially in supporting new global institutions such as the International Criminal Court[18] or in areas with weak or absent state institutions.[19]

TNGOs may lack the power to coerce outcomes by force, but they frequently compensate by relying on less overt forms of influencing, including shaping shared understandings of issues.[20] TNGOs have to be adept at framing issues in ways that are more likely to resonate with audiences. TNGOs often navigate power relations across multiple levels while also seeking to address hidden forms of power and discrimination.[21] Exerting less visible forms of power is often reflected in the reliance on discursive strategies and socialization processes meant to change people's notions and behaviors through strategic communications. Human rights campaigns redefine undesirable practices as inappropriate and impermissible, eliminating them from what policymakers consider as feasible. For example, anti-apartheid activists effectively constructed a particular understanding of the international community that excluded policies based on racialized social control.[22] Even when TNGOs fail to change behavior through ideational pressure, they still force other actors into defending their actions by relying on elaborate counter-narratives as justifications.[23]

ADVOCACY EFFECTIVENESS

Four categories of factors affect TNGO advocacy and its success: (1) issue characteristics, (2) the policy environment, (3) the internal capacities and characteristics of TNGOs and their coalitions, and (4) target characteristics.[24] The relative importance of these factors (and sub-factors) can vary over time[25] and TNGOs can deploy strategies such as venue-shopping,[26] coalition building,[27] and fundraising to acquire new capabilities. Adaptation over time is a key capacity for remaining relevant throughout the policy process as well as for working across different national and cultural contexts. Agenda-setting and policy formation at the global level may require adding expertise in elite lobbying and navigating international institutions,[28] for example, while implementing global policies domestically may require additional capacities to understand and adapt to local conditions.[29] Table 4.1 summarizes these factors affecting policy advocacy effectiveness.

Table 4.1 ADVOCACY EFFECTIVENESS FACTORS

Category	Factors
Issue characteristics	Severity and type
	Tractability
	Perceptions of affected groups
Policy environment	Political windows of opportunity
	Salience of issues
	Allies and opponents
	Domestic political structures
Internal capacities	Network density and composition
	Leadership
	Governance structure
	Knowledge, skills, and norm entrepreneurship
	Adaptive capacities
	Organizational culture
Target characteristics	Identifiability
	Degree of interdependence
	Vulnerability to sanctions and incentives

Issue characteristics

Specific issues have inherent and ascribed characteristics that affect the success of campaigns. In the global health area, for example, three important issue characteristics have emerged: (1) severity, (2) tractability, and (3) perceptions of affected groups.[30] Using different labels, these factors can also be found in the analysis of TNGO power in other policy areas. Each of these characteristics can be subject to framing efforts to influence public perceptions and encourage action.

Severity can be framed both quantitatively and qualitatively based on the type of harm and its relation to universally held beliefs or effects on dominant interests. Issues involving bodily harm are particularly susceptible to campaigns.[31] Scientists may be more likely to present information about deaths, injuries, economic damages, and other measurable disruptions.[32] Other groups may look beyond the numbers and develop frames resonant with existing ideas, ideologies, and transcultural beliefs. For example, health issues can be linked to national security concerns or the justice frame can be used to explain how the climate crisis creates greater loss and damage for vulnerable populations.[33] Severity is a compelling issue characteristic, but its effects are often ambiguous because responses can range from denial to repression, and frames can be easily appropriated by other actors.

Tractability matters because problems that are viewed as solvable are more likely to get addressed.[34] Issues may be characterized by high levels of severity, but mobilization may only foster fatalism in the absence of realistic solutions and changes in public perceptions about the likelihood of success. Prior to Amartya Sen's work on famines, for example, Western audiences largely believed that such conditions in the Global South were natural. Sen's work not only identified specific political causes and responsible parties, but forcefully argued that democratic governance and public accountability could prevent famine.[35]

Proposed solutions are often key to initial advocacy success, but they are also frequently contested as they are implemented. During the past decades, humanitarian intervention has become a highly contested practice where human rights TNGOs have often clashed with humanitarian groups about the use of military force or the power of international courts to deter future heinous crimes.[36] In the environmental area, Greenpeace won a major victory in 1995 by forcing the oil company Shell to recycle, rather than dispose of the storage buoy Brent Spar. However, soon after this advocacy win Greenpeace admitted that it had gotten many of the facts about the pollution hazards wrong.[37] While the presence of tractable solutions to a problem is a key condition for campaign success, advocating for them often politicizes the efforts of TNGOs and carries risks for legitimacy. Greenpeace forced Shell into submission by making a case for recycling, but it ultimately lost credibility because its focus on short-term publicity led to shortcuts in evaluating a complex environmental problem.

Tractability is closely linked to perceptions about affected groups. Differences in the relative power of, and perceptions about, specific population segments shape the responses of decision-makers.[38] TNGOs typically work with already vulnerable populations, and stigma[39] can play a powerful role in undermining action. Stigma can deter TNGOs and others from taking up a cause in the first place[40] and also make it more difficult for activists to persuade the public about taking action.

Framing focused on issue characteristics is often about telling a causal story with a "villain" and victims suffering as an innocent group.[41] Government agents seen arresting dissidents provides a much simpler causal story than harms caused by abstract global markets or climate change. TNGOs face trade-offs between presenting an issue in simplified ways and the often more complex realities on the ground. Although it may be tempting to simplify and exaggerate for greater short-term resonance, this may create unintended risks of long-term damage to a cause if the reality turns out to be more complex.

Policy environment

The policy environment consists of structural factors shaping access or timing as well as the universe of supporters, opponents, and bystanders relevant to a specific issue. Political opportunity structures, including high-profile events, can offer activists rare openings to get attention for a specific cause.[42] Relevant stakeholders in the broader policy environment are often seen as either potential partners in a coalition-building process or as representing countervailing interests. The political skills needed to build such coalitions and respond to counter-mobilization pushes practitioners to leave their comfort zones and engage in more strategic action, including approaching "unlike-minded" actors and looking at issues from the perspectives of other stakeholders. This may be particularly challenging for TNGOs with organizational cultures driven by a strong in-group cultural bias.

An environment dense with existing organizations benefits transnational activists by offering a larger arena for coalition-building and for legitimating mobilization efforts.[43] Even if activists are critical of policies proposed by international institutions, the existence of such institutions provides opportunities to develop and advance campaigns.[44] At domestic levels TNGOs may find open and democratic societies easier to access from the outside, but domestic pluralism may also make it more difficult to build winning coalitions. In contrast, authoritarian societies may be harder to get access to, but if one can gain the trust of elites the policy impact can be significant.[45]

Internal capacities of TNGOs and their coalitions

The capacities of a TNGO or an activist network are shaped by internal factors, such as the types of leadership and governance structures, underlying organizational cultures, and the ability to adapt over time. Internal governance helps organizations and networks distribute tasks and generate consensus about a coherent agenda for mobilization.[46] A governance structure has to define conditions of membership, balance nimbleness with the needs for deliberation and representation, and facilitate organizational learning and adaptation. Structures can have shared decision-making, have a strong lead, or involve a special authority delegated with governance tasks.[47]

Norm entrepreneurship is a major internal capacity attributed to TNGOs.[48] So-called policy entrepreneurs have defined interests and knowledge of the policy process and are "waiting for problems to float by to which they can attach their solutions."[49] For example, civil society groups play an important role in everyday human rights lawmaking because they show up, share the basic goals of officials, and exchange their knowledge for influence.[50] Similar to international bureaucrats, policy entrepreneurs can trade valuable information and operate often unsupervised by states in shaping complex policies.[51] Within the TNGO sector, more research-focused organizations can participate alongside others whose emphasis is primarily on awareness-raising or on representing local communities.[52] This division of labor creates benefits associated with networked activism, including combining different sources of legitimacy with expertise in mobilization and campaigning.

Global coalitions are a particularly powerful form of TNGO campaigning because they operate in a more focused and time-limited manner.[53] The International Campaign to Ban Landmines (ICBL) coalition not only grew very rapidly shortly after its creation, but brought together likeminded organizations with diverse expertise, including humanitarian and human rights organizations versed in international law, victims groups representing those injured, and disarmament groups with specific knowledge in weapons.[54] Apart from substantive expertise, such coalitions also need to be able to reach outside their comfort zone. The ICBL recruited former generals to add credible military voices. Publish What You Pay worked with oil companies in pushing the Extractive Industries Transparency Initiative.[55]

Many TNGOs are coalitions of more or less independent units collaborating under a common brand identity. This raises questions of centralization and decentralization, including how to create coherence across a network of affiliates.[56] Managing these governance issues successfully contributes to effectiveness by establishing decision-making rules based on the required outcomes. For example, Amnesty International was able to establish a governance structure that centralized proposal and enforcement powers, but decentralized implementation powers.[57] Centralization at the top contributes to coherence and agility, while decentralization at the bottom facilitates adapting messages to different contexts and ensuring the flexibility needed to respond to local conditions.

The organizational culture underlying the daily operations of an organization remains frequently overlooked as a key factor in shaping the internal capacities of a TNGO. The sector is populated by organizations with different identities, missions, and deliberative practices. Organizational culture can contribute to overall success by drawing in dedicated staff willing to invest extraordinary time and resources, but it can also generate major tensions between different groups convinced of their own positions.[58] The belief in a unique identity often leads to enhanced in-group/out-group thinking and can undermine the collaboration needed to scale up outcomes. Finally, mission focus can become a litmus test for loyalty and dedication, which does not necessarily foster a culture of measuring results and organizational learning.

Target characteristics

Policy advocacy is more likely to be effective when targets are easily identifiable and vulnerable to economic or reputational pressures.[59] Specific targeting is generally more effective than targeting abstract structures and systems because only real individuals or organizations have vulnerabilities that activists can exploit to gain leverage. For example, transnational boycotts against entire industries are difficult to organize and sustain, and ultimately less likely to be effective than targeting specific companies, bureaucrats, and politicians. The Nestlé boycott of the 1970s represented a key learning opportunity for modern transnational activists[60] and became a major inspiration for subsequent campaigns. Similarly, development and humanitarian TNGOs are well aware that relying on abstract statistics and complex analyses of social conditions does not always attract donor attention and money. Oxfam's Behind the brands[61] campaign targeted specific food companies, not abstract supply chains or the capitalist system overall.

Interdependence plays a key role in defining target vulnerability. States and corporations are more vulnerable to pressures if they are well integrated into their social environment and regularly exposed in interactions with their peers. Corporations may be more vulnerable if they are more directly exposed to consumers through retail outlets or if their corporate social responsibility units report to top-level executives.[62] Anti-sweatshop activism has been shown to be selectively targeted at companies with perceived vulnerabilities, including having already good reputations for social responsibility and visibility in the marketplace.[63]

Assessing the impact of TNGOs and their campaigns is challenging for a number of reasons. First, TNGOs often raise issues that are poorly tracked and lack credible data. For example, statistics on domestic violence or female genital cutting were for many years unreliable because the issues were not viewed as serious problems by those in positions to collect the data. One of the first tasks of activism then is to develop an initial understanding of the extent of the problem. Second, TNGOs have increasingly adopted complex theories of change involving collective impact and systems thinking to address the underlying causes of social problems (see Chapter 3). As TNGOs have adopted more ambitious goals and strategies, establishing cause and effect has become more challenging. Third, TNGO participation in specific issue areas is frequently informal and difficult to observe with traditional social science methods. In addition, many TNGOs have experimented with taking less visible roles focused on facilitating, brokering, or supporting the activities of others. The methodological challenges create significant risks of either over- or underestimating impact, particularly when the individual contributions of multiple actors are hard to disentangle.

Many of the classic examples of TNGO activism reflect direct leadership and mobilization by broad coalitions.[64] These advocacy efforts typically span the four stages of (1) issue creation, (2) agenda-setting, (3) policy formation, and (4) policy implementation. All four stages frequently overlap and feedback effects are likely. Table 4.2 summarizes TNGO activities, factors affecting TNGO power, and relevant risks across the four stages of the policy process.

Issue creation

Issue creation is the process of identifying a previously taken-for-granted condition and transforming it into a problem and campaign cause. Typically, TNGO efforts focus on strategically framing issue characteristics to elicit a response from policymakers and the public. Basic information combined with a specific frame constitutes the core of many awareness-raising campaigns. Human interest stories are often central to communicating abstract global issues, although this may be an incidental byproduct of campaigning. For example, Friends of the Earth International (FoEI) received an unexpectedly high number of public responses when it started to highlight crop spraying in a pesticides campaign. People started to tell their

Table 4.2 TNGO ACTIVITIES AT DIFFERENT STAGES OF THE POLICY PROCESS

Stage of the policy process	Illustrative activities	Factors affecting TNGO power	Risks
Issue creation	Gatekeeping Developing issue expertise Dissemination of research Awareness-raising Developing human interest stories	Issue and communications expertise	Ignoring deserving causes
Agenda-setting	Framing and goal setting Conflict expansion Venue-shopping Norm grafting Recruitment of high-profile champions	Framing resonance Coalition diversity Venue favorability	Unintended negative consequences of messaging
Policy formation	Power analysis Propose solutions Mobilization Coalition-building Insider/outsider strategies Monitoring of negotiations and opponents	Process expertise Having a clear "ask" Internal cohesion and conflict resolution mechanisms Access to venues	Preemptive compromising
Policy implementation	Resource transfer Education Developing culturally sensitive practices Knowledge brokerage	Adaptive capacities at local levels Legitimacy among target audiences	Inappropriate or untested policy responses

stories about being affected by the practice, which offered a more human side of an abstract focus on scientific research about harm caused.[65]

Issue creation in a world of finite resources means that TNGOs are major gatekeepers in determining what issues are deserving of global attention.[66] Amnesty International's 1977 decision to focus on capital punishment represents such a gatekeeping activity since it meant that a major human rights organization would now expend significant resources on one particular issue. While activists had been debating the issue for some time,[67] only Amnesty's involvement ensured that the topic became a global issue and enabled mobilization leading to a growing number of states to abolish capital punishment.[68]

Issue creation is frequently enabled by linking a problem to existing belief systems. After years of quiet efforts by the International Committee of the Red Cross to highlight the deadly effects of landmines, a number of TNGOs entered the issue area in the 1990s arguing that landmines were no ordinary weapons, but killed indiscriminately in violation of international humanitarian law. By "grafting" existing norms against indiscriminate weapons of mass destruction onto the landmines case,[69] the campaign redefined the issue to paint the picture of a global humanitarian crisis involving bodily harm to innocent civilians.[70]

Many global campaigns have been effective at raising awareness, but forget to develop a clear plan for what happens next. A limited focus on awareness-raising can increase risks for unintentional harm, wasted resources, or resistance and backlash.[71] For example, the organization Invisible Children had worked for many years in US high schools to raise awareness about the violence of the Lord's Resistance Army operating in Eastern and Central Africa. When the organization decided to use social media to promote a 30-minute video called *Kony 2012*, it had no clear strategies on how to capitalize on its viral success or what to exactly accomplish with its campaign. Critics quickly pointed out that the campaign provided little room for local African voices and relied on the "patronizing sympathy"[72] of often uninformed Western audiences.

In contrast, the Jubilee 2000 campaign was more effective in framing the issue of debt relief in the poorest countries with simple messaging, a deadline, and a straightforward "ask" of debt cancellation.[73] Similarly, issue creation around neonatal mortality originated by developing and spreading knowledge about new solutions for preventing newborn deaths. Research done at the local level in low-income countries led to the emergence of cheap and effective interventions. Transnational mobilization then contributed to generating global awareness about an issue previously viewed as impossible or too expensive to address.[74]

Agenda-setting

Agenda-setting involves capturing the attention and shaping the priorities of decision-makers and the general public. It not only turns an abstract social condition into an issue and problem, but causes the media and policymakers to consider the topic in a serious and sustained way.[75] In addition to issue framing, successful agenda-setting typically involves conflict expansion and dealing with institutional constraints. Conflict expansion reflects efforts to appeal to a greater number of stakeholders and increase their interest in a topic. To circumvent institutional constraints, activists engage in venue-shopping to select favorable fora and engage in related strategies.

In the "blood diamond" case, for example, agenda-setting commenced with the 1998 publication of *A Rough Trade* by Global Witness. The report charged diamond trader De Beers with complicity in the violation of UN sanctions (UNSC resolution 1173) against the rebel group UNITA in Angola. Shortly thereafter, a coalition of TNGOs started the campaign Fatal Transactions to raise awareness among consumers and the general public. The campaign benefited from having to target only one major industry player and could credibly threaten economic damages. De Beers was vulnerable to the mobilization because "gem diamonds have no intrinsic value apart from the sentimental, and high market prices were manipulated for years."[76] Conflict expansion was successful when states such as South Africa and Belgium became involved because they stood to benefit from regulations or hosted important trading centers.

In the anti-personnel landmines case, the campaign had success in agenda-setting by creating a diverse global coalition, recruiting likeminded states as early champions, and relying on an aggressive public advocacy strategy. Conflict expansion relied on recruiting more allies and shifting the burden of proof to opponents who were put on the defensive. But those efforts may not have been enough without proactively lobbing for a more favorable venue. The decision of Canada and other states to shift the negotiations out of the UN Conference of Disarmament into a separate platform—the Ottawa process—was crucial for the emergence of the anti-landmines treaty.

In the case of the International Criminal Court (ICC), TNGOs had called for the establishment of a global judicial body already envisioned in the 1948 Genocide Convention.[77] As the UN Security Council remained resistant to such ideas during the Cold War, the issue of criminal responsibility for government officials could only take hold regionally in Southern Europe during the 1960s and in Latin America in the 1970s and 1980s.[78] After the end of the Cold War, the UN General Assembly in 1989 called on the International Law Commission to study the establishment of such a court. As global venues became more favorable to the issues, TNGOs formed the Coalition for an International Criminal Court in 1995. Although the ICC certainly has its critics, the fact that it emerged at all represents considerable progress for the norm of international criminal responsibility.

While it is relatively easy to establish a campaign goal, it is more difficult to identify specific "asks" designed to recruit allies or gain access to favorable venues. Agenda-setting success requires ongoing power analysis to understand who has decision-making power, why issues may struggle to get traction, and what shapes the interests and identities of key stakeholders.[79] TNGOs must weigh different venue and framing options and assess what power resources new stakeholders may add during conflict expansion. Issue creation often relies primarily on substantive expertise about the extent of a problem and its possible solutions. In contrast, agenda-setting requires procedural expertise and knowledge about the political process.

Policy formation

The right framing and venue are essential to ensuring that mobilization can shift from general awareness-raising to getting specific policies adopted or changed. Policy formation as a distinct stage directs attention to the interests of decision-makers and the structure of the policy environment. Activists may dominate processes of issue creation and agenda-setting, but their roles in negotiations during policy formation often diminish. Once other actors pay attention and become involved, the field becomes more crowded, actors with more resources appear, and TNGOs may not necessarily have a seat at the table.

Greater participation rights may be a sign of increased civil society prominence, but it does not automatically translate into policy impact. Factors that contribute to success include substantive and process expertise, an ability to define a clear and realistic "ask" separate from the broader campaign goals, coalition leadership that balances nimbleness and deliberation, and the ability to manage the power of dominant actors. These factors often work together, with outcomes more easily observed in formalized negotiations where policy formation is reflected in the establishment of treaties or other types of agreements.[80]

Substantive and process-related expertise helps TNGOs get access and enhance their stature during negotiations. Civil society actors frequently provide blueprints for language they seek and can marshal frames that resonate with others. Intergovernmental bodies often grant access to their venues in exchange for the information offered by TNGOs.[81] Similarly, TNGOs often work with representatives of smaller countries with more limited capacities than major powers. TNGOs also typically monitor negotiations closely and seek to expose secret deals to increase transparency and enhance their own ability to influence results. In the case of the ICC negotiations, civil society groups regularly surveyed state delegations about their specific positions on controversial articles, including the creation of an independent prosecutor. When these surveys established an overwhelming majority of states supporting a prosecutor independent of state influence, this substantially undercut the counterarguments of powerful countries including China, Russia, and the United States.[82]

Two risks faced by TNGOs involved in policy formation are incrementalism and co-optation. Critics have pointed out that many TNGO campaigns, such as those around the Copenhagen Summit, end up with very limited results. Additional examples include Jubilee 2000's debt cancellation for only a limited number of countries, and the ICBL's acceptance of a narrowed focus on anti-personnel landmines only. In both cases, the initial goals of the campaigns were more ambitious and narrowed substantially during the policy formation process.[83] Kumi Naidoo, attending the World Economic Forum in Davos in 2012, charged that such venues were about "incremental thinking—baby steps. They talk more about system recovery than about system design."[84]

Cases of co-optation are also common, especially when TNGOs and other civil society actors cannot agree on key demands in the policy formation process. The two UN World Summits on the Information Society (WSIS) held during the 2000s in Geneva and Tunis are examples for such outcomes.[85] The WSIS process provided ample opportunities and extensive participation rights for TNGOs. Despite the multi-stakeholder format, TNGOs from the Global North benefited from their already extensive experience working within UN structures,[86] and the coalition of civil society groups failed to effectively advance the interests of citizens in low- and middle-income countries.[87] In the WSIS process, extensive participation did not translate into influence because TNGOs from the Global North and South, having failed to level the playing field among themselves in terms of negotiating capacity, access, and voice, struggled to agree on demands and were easily co-opted into negotiations about technical aspects, rather than transformational outcomes. More radical demands became marginalized over time, and the future participation of TNGOs in the process became a major end in itself.[88]

More participation and mobilization alone do not automatically translate into impact. Expertise about substantive and procedural issues matter and can often be exchanged for access. Once access is secured, influence is enhanced by an ability to organize and mobilize internally and externally and by the analytic capacity to identify specific demands that are both likely to gain overall support and are also likely to set the stage for future gains toward the more long-term goals of a campaign. TNGOs from the Global North have dominated many of the agenda-setting and policy formation processes of the past decades. Coalitions are dominated by TNGOs with more resources, and these organizations also often prevail when negotiations move fast and opportunities for internal deliberation are limited.[89] Agendas tend to be set by Western elites with very particular understandings of both problems and solutions and with only limited input coming from those most affected.

Policy implementation

Policy implementation is not automatic and a government or other targeted actors may be either unable or unwilling to implement adopted policies.[90] When policymakers offer resistance, TNGO power depends on the ability to secure access, frame issue characteristics for local audiences, and build "winning coalitions."[91] In the case of failed states or other targets with limited capacities,[92] TNGOs may work collaboratively with government or other domestic actors to implement policies. For example, since the end of the Cold War, TNGOs have worked more frequently with business other non-state actors that often have more direct control over the livelihoods of individuals.[93]

Multipronged policy engagement at global, national, and local levels creates major challenges for the capacity of TNGOs. Issues of cultural appropriateness and power inequities regularly emerge as TNGOs shift from talking about how things should be in aspirational rhetoric to actually favoring specific policies and programs. Agenda-setting and policy formation at the international level typically focus on one or very few venues, while the implementation of global agreements requires "boots on the ground" in multiple venues with vastly different social, cultural, and political circumstances.[94] As a result, transnational activists are often more successful at pressuring relatively weak countries, but fail to change the behavior of more powerful states.[95] States can develop counter-frames emphasizing alternative norms,[96] for example by emphasizing national security concerns over human rights protections, or they can use their power to remove topics from public contention, such as by stifling free speech and thus limiting activists' ability to even deploy discursive tools in challenging behavior. TNGOs dependent on access and funding may choose to not offend governments and agree to abandon their focus on fundamental political or social transformation.[97]

Nevertheless, norm socialization pressures can be very powerful independently of material leverage.[98] Initial denials by governments can lead to tactical concessions, lending emerging norms a form of recognition as a step toward prescriptive status. States are particularly vulnerable to such pressures if they have a track record of prior commitment to a given norm and are aspiring members of a community that already respects the norm. International norms are rarely implemented without contestation or modification. This may occur in three separate steps leading from (1) domestic debates about the norms to (2) the adoption of specific laws and (3) the actual implementation in daily practice.[99]

For successful policy implementation, local salience and the relative coherence of external policies and norms are key factors.[100] High norm resonance at the global level can increase material and normative pressures, and also improve the quality of networking and messaging.[101] However, significant global pressure can also generate local pushback. Issue salience and local resistance influenced the campaigns against female genital mutilation and early marriage, for example.[102] While the campaign against female genital mutilation developed much greater global salience and impact over time, it also generated significant local resistance.[103] In comparison, efforts to end early marriage gained less attention both globally and locally, which translated into less funding and attention, but also lower local resistance against external activists. Much of this complex alignment in global resonance and local resistance can be traced to how activists framed female genital mutilation in ways that frequently highlighted Western perceptions focusing on bodily harm, rather than community views about a traditional cultural practice.[104]

TNGOs may attempt to increase the salience and precision of a norm to limit opportunities to evade implementation pressures. The capacities of activists to develop appropriate strategies of localization matter,[105] as does who transmits and translates norms and how.[106] For example, many TNGOs now aspire to empower local communities to be co-owners of development and other programs, a process that profoundly shapes the very meaning of effectiveness in the process. An emphasis on local ownership is not only about enhancing objectively assessed outcomes, but it highlights that "the formation, operation and linkages of a network can be seen as both the means and the result of advocacy work."[107]

Local conditions have also mattered greatly in the case of advocacy for LGBTQ rights in Europe. Campaigns targeting Eastern European countries looked distinctly different from those emerging in established European democracies. In the new democracies, a "brokered transnational channel," that is, the embeddedness of local activist groups in regional and global networks, played a more significant role,[108] while in Western European democracies such channels were less relevant.

The role of external activists in pushing for domestic policy change frequently faces backlash and local pushback.[109] Examples of well-meaning programs advancing inappropriate frames and solutions are widespread and have given rise to an entire literature on the "White Savior complex."[110] TNGOs and other external actors typically have more resources than local communities, but their efforts may fail because of poorly adapted interventions.[111] The majority of mid-sized and larger TNGOs has addressed these issues for some time by hiring and promoting many more local staff across their organizations, including in leadership positions, by equalizing salary and benefits policies across local and international staff, and by establishing explicit policies focused on empowering the voices of local communities.[112] Led by organizations such as ActionAid, such practices have spread more widely in the sector over the past decade. At the same time, many TNGOs have also embraced less prominent roles traditionally associated with project-based or advocacy work and instead chose to remain in the background by investing in capacity-building and the provision of core funding for civil society ecosystems, as well as in strategies of brokering, facilitating, and convening.[113]

CONCLUSION

How and why have TNGOs risen to prominence since the 1970s and 1980s? Some of it certainly has to do with the innovative strategies that the sector has developed over time, as described in Chapter 3. However, the sector has also often simply been in the "right place at the right time," as TNGOs benefited from geopolitical changes including post–Cold War liberalization in many countries. Demand for TNGO services increased, trust in government decreased, and TNGOs and other private actors came to be viewed as the preferred conduits for aid and providers of public services. The détente between the United States and the Soviet Union in the 1970s and then the end of the Cold War opened up important opportunities for advocacy TNGOs to advance their agendas. At domestic and regional levels, the mobilization against authoritarian regimes in Southern Europe and Latin America during the 1970s and 1980s also played a key role in building the capacities of TNGOs to advance global campaigns once political conditions were more favorable in the 1990s.

TNGOs exploited these opportunities by playing to their comparative advantage in trustworthiness and emphasizing their (untested) solutions to market and government failures. The idea of channeling development aid through TNGOs also emboldened the sector to define ever more ambitious goals beyond short-term service delivery. While not all mid- to large-sized TNGOs have embraced advocacy or have become involved in global campaigning, the sector as a whole has shifted markedly in this direction in the service of new and expanded missions.

As long as TNGOs found favorable global conditions for their actions, policy advocacy provided a path to addressing root causes, contributing to

TNGOs' international prominence. But since the 2000s, the sector has faced an increasingly hostile operating environment as the gap between their increased ambitions and their abilities to follow through has become more apparent. Challenges from authoritarian governments, local populations, and even decreasing support in their home countries are mounting. In the near future, the sector is unlikely to be able to enjoy the same levels of influence as it did during the 1980s and 1990s.

As TNGOs became increasingly powerful actors in global policy change, they have faced criticism not just because of their growing influence, but also because their organizational forms are often out of step with their rhetoric and aspirations. For example, the internal structures of many TNGOs still often reflect and reproduce problematic power disparities between the Global North and South. Without significant reforms in the service of enhanced legitimacy, ambitious TNGOs risk becoming ill-adapted to the purposes of authentic social and cultural change through transformative advocacy.

REFERENCES

Ackerman, John. "Co-Governance for Accountability: Beyond 'Exit' and 'Voice'." *World Development* 32, no. 3 (2004): 447–63. http://www.sciencedirect.com/science/article/pii/S0305750X03002341.

Ahmed, Meena. *The Principles and Practice of Crisis Management: The Case of Brent Spar.* Basingstoke: Palgrave, 2006.

Allan, Jen Iris, and Jennifer Hadden. "Exploring the Framing Power of NGOs in Global Climate Politics." *Environmental Politics* 26, no. 4 (2017): 600–20. https://doi.org/10.1080/09644016.2017.1319017.

Aluttis, Christoph, Thomas Krafft, and Helmut Brand. "Global Health in the European Union—A Review from an Agenda-Setting Perspective." *Global Health Action* 7, no. 1 (2014). https://doi.org/10.3402/gha.v7.23610.

Arensman, Bodille, Margit van Wessel, and Dorothea Hilhorst. "Does Local Ownership Bring About Effectiveness? The Case of a Transnational Advocacy Network." *Third World Quarterly* 38, no. 6 (2017): 1310–26. https://doi.org/10.1080/01436597.2016.1257908.

Ayoub, Phillip M. "Contested Norms in New-Adopter States: International Determinants of LGBT Rights Legislation." *European Journal of International Relations* 21, no. 2 (2015): 293–322.

Bang, Abhay T., Rani A. Bang, Sanjay B. Baitule, M. Hanimi Reddy, and Mahesh D. Deshmukh. "Effect of Home-Based Neonatal Care and Management of Sepsis on Neonatal Mortality: Field Trial in Rural India." *The Lancet* 354, no. 9194 (1999): 1955–61.

Bartley, Tim, and Curtis Child. "Shaming the Corporation: The Social Production of Targets and the Anti-Sweatshop Movement." *American Sociological Review* 79, no. 4 (2014): 653–79. https://doi.org/10.1177/0003122414540653.

Betsill, Michele M., and Elisabeth Corell. *NGO Diplomacy: The Influence of Nongovernmental Organizations in International Environmental Organizations.* Cambridge, MA: MIT Press, 2008.

Bex, Sean, and Stef Craps. "Humanitarianism, Testimony, and the White Savior Industrial Complex: *What Is the What* Versus *Kony 2012.*" *Cultural Critique* 92, no. 1 (2016): 32–56.

Bloomfield, Michael John. *Dirty Gold: How Activism Transformed the Jewelry Industry.* Boston: MIT Press, 2017.

Breen, Oonagh B., Alison Dunn, and Mark Sidel, eds. *Regulatory Waves: Comparative Perspectives on State Regulation and Self-Regulation Policies in the Nonprofit Sector.* New York: Cambridge University Press, 2017.

Brown, L. David, and Vanessa Timmer. "Civil Society Actors as Catalysts for Transnational Social Learning." *Voluntas* 17, no. 1 (2006): 1–16. https://doi.org/10.1007/s11266-005-9002-0.

Burroughs, John, and Jacqueline Cabasso. "Confronting the Nuclear-Armed States in International Negotiating Forums: Lessons for NGOs." *International Negotiation* 4, no. 3 (1999): 459–82.

Busby, Joshua W. "Bono Made Jesse Helms Cry: Jubilee 2000, Debt Relief, and Moral Action in International Politics." *International Studies Quarterly* 51, no. 2 (2007): 247–75.

Bush, Sarah Sunn. *The Taming of Democracy Assistance: Why Democracy Promotion Does Not Confront Dictators.* Cambridge: Cambridge University Press, 2015.

Carpenter, R. Charli. *Forgetting Children Born of War. Setting the Human Rights Agenda in Bosnia and Beyond.* New York: Columbia University Press, 2010.

Carpenter, R. Charli. *"Lost" Causes: Agenda-Setting and Agenda-Vetting in Global Issue Networks.* Ithaca, NY: Cornell University Press, 2014.

Carpenter, R. Charli. "Studying Issue (Non)-Adoption in Transnational Advocacy Networks." *International Organization* 61 (2007): 643–67.

Chandler, David G. "The Road to Military Humanitarianism: How the Human Rights NGOs Shaped a New Humanitarian Agenda." *Human Rights Quarterly* 23, no. 3 (2001): 678–700.

Charnovitz, Steve. "Nongovernmental Organizations and International Law." *The American Journal of International Law* 100, no. 2 (2006): 348–72. http://www.jstor.org/stable/3651151.

Choi-Fitzpatrick, Austin. *What Slaveholders Think. How Contemporary Perpetrators Rationalize What They Do.* New York: Columbia University Press, 2017.

Christiano, Ann, and Annie Neimand. "Stop Raising Awareness Already." *Stanford Social Innovation Review* (Spring 2017).

CIVICUS. *State of Civil Society Report 2018.* Johannesburg: CIVICUS, 2018. https://www.civicus.org/documents/reports-and-publications/SOCS/2018/socs-2018-overview_top-ten-trends.pdf.

Cloward, Karisa. *When Norms Collide: Local Responses to Activism against Female Genital Mutilation and Early Marriage.* New York: Oxford University Press, 2016.

Cobb, Roger W., and Charles D. Elder. *Participation in American Politics: The Dynamics of Agenda-Building.* Baltimore: Johns Hopkins University Press, 1972.

Cole, Teju. "The White-Savior Industrial Complex." *The Atlantic* (March 21, 2012).

Cox, Brendan. *Campaigning for International Justice*. London: Bond, 2011.

Cross, Mai'a K. Davis. "The Limits of Epistemic Communities: EU Security Agencies." *Politics and Governance* 3, no. 1 (2015): 90–100. https://doi.org/doi:10.1017/S0260210512000034.

Dany, Charlotte. "Ambivalenzen der Partizipation: Grenzen des NGO-Einflusses auf dem Weltgipfel zur Informationsgesellschaft." *Zeitschrift für Internationale Beziehungen* 19, no. 2 (2012): 71–99.

Dany, Charlotte. *Global Governance and NGO Participation: Shaping the Information Society in the United Nations*. London: Routledge, 2013.

Dixon, Jennifer M. "Rhetorical Adaptation and Resistance to International Norms." *Perspectives on Politics* 15, no. 1 (2017): 83–99.

Editors. "Losing the Johnson Amendment Would Destroy the Unique Political Role of Nonprofits." *Nonprofit Quarterly*, February 6, 2017. https://nonprofitquarterly.org/2017/02/06/losing-johnson-amendment-destroy-unique-political-role-nonprofits/.

Edwards, Michael. *Civil Society*. 3rd ed. Cambridge: Polity Press, 2014.

Eilstrup-Sangiovanni, Mette, and Teale N. Phelps Bondaroff. "From Advocacy to Confrontation: Direct Enforcement by Environmental NGOs." *International Studies Quarterly* 58, no. 2 (2014): 348–61.

Farquharson, Karen. "Influencing Policy Transnationally: Pro- and Anti-Tobacco Global Advocacy Networks." *Australian Journal of Public Administration* 62, no. 4 (2003): 80–92.

Finnemore, Martha, and Kathryn Sikkink. "International Norm Dynamics and Political Change." *International Organization* 52, no. 4 (1998): 887–917.

Gaventa, John. *Power after Lukes: A Review of the Literature*. Brighton: Institute of Development Studies, 2003.

Glasius, Marlies. *The International Criminal Court: A Global Civil Society Achievement*. London and New York: Routledge, 2006.

Gneiting, Uwe. "From Global Agenda-Setting to Domestic Implementation: Successes and Challenges of the Global Health Network on Tobacco Control." *Health Policy and Planning* 31, no. suppl. 1 (2016): i74–i86. https://doi.org/10.1093/heapol/czv001.

Green, Duncan. *Fit for the Future? Development Trends and the Role of International NGOs*. Oxford: Oxfam GB, 2015.

Green, Duncan. *How Change Happens*. New York: Oxford University Press, 2017.

Haddad, Heidi Nichols. *The Hidden Hands of Justice: NGOs, Human Rights, and International Courts*. New York: Cambridge University Press, 2018.

Hall, Nina. "What Is Adaptation to Climate Change? Epistemic Ambiguity in the Climate Finance System." *International Environmental Agreements: Politics, Law, and Economics* 17, no. 1 (2017): 37–53. https://doi.org/10.1007/s10784-016-9345-6.

Hertel, Shareen. *Unexpected Power: Conflict and Change among Transnational Activists*. Ithaca, NY: Cornell University Press, 2006.

Holzscheiter, Anna. "Discourse as Capability: Non-State Actors' Capital in Global Governance." *Millennium* 33, no. 3 (2005): 723–46. https://doi.org/doi:10.1177/03058298050330030301.

Hopgood, Stephen. *Keepers of the Flame: Understanding Amnesty International*. Ithaca, NY: Cornell University Press, 2006.

Jetschke, Anja. *Human Rights and State Security: Indonesia and the Philippines*. Philadelphia: University of Pennsylvania Press, 2011.

Johnson, Tana. *Organizational Progeny: Why Governments Are Losing Control over the Proliferating Structures of Global Governance.* New York: Oxford University Press, 2014.

Keck, Margaret E., and Kathryn Sikkink. *Activists beyond Borders: Advocacy Networks in International Politics.* Ithaca, NY: Cornell University Press, 1998.

Kingdon, John W. *Agendas, Alternatives, and Public Policies.* New York: Longman, 1995.

Klotz, Audie. *Norms in International Relations: The Struggle against Apartheid.* Ithaca, NY: Cornell University Press, 1995.

Klugman, Barbara, Daniel Ravindra, Denise Dora, Maïmouna Jallow, and Marcelo Azambuja. *Towards a New Ecology of the Human Rights Movement.* Johannesburg: Barbara Klugman Concepts, 2017.

Koenig, Rebecca. "Some International Groups Saying Hiring More Locals Boosts Results." *Chronicle of Philanthropy,* May 21, 2018. https://www.philanthropy.com/article/International-Groups-Shift/243469.

Lake, Milli. "Strong NGOs and Weak States: Pursuing Gender Justice in the Democratic Republic of Congo and South Africa." Cambridge: Cambridge University Press, 2018.

Leebaw, Bronwyn. "The Politics of Impartial Activism. Humanitarianism, and Human Rights." *Perspectives on Politics* 5, no. 2 (2007): 223–39.

Lukes, Steven. *Power. A Radical View.* 2nd ed. Basingstoke: Palgrave Macmillan, 2005.

Mamudu, Hadii M., MariaElena Gonzalez, and Stanton Glantz. "The Nature, Scope, and Development of the Global Tobacco Control Epistemic Community." *American Journal of Public Health* 101, no. 11 (2011): 2044–54. https://doi.org/10.2105/ajph.2011.300303.

Margolin, Drew B., Cuihua Shen, Seungyoon Lee, Matthew S. Weber, Janet Fulk, and Peter Monge. "Normative Influences on Network Structure in the Evolution of the Children's Rights NGO Network, 1977–2004." *Communication Research* 42, no. 1 (2015): 30–59. https://doi.org/10.1177/0093650212463731.

McAteer, Emily, and Simone Pulver. "The Corporate Boomerang: Shareholder Transnational Advocacy Networks Targeting Oil Companies in the Ecuadorian Amazon." *Global Environmental Politics* 9, no. 1 (2009): 1–30. https://doi.org/10.1162/glep.2009.9.1.1.

McCambridge, Ruth. "National Council of Nonprofits Launches Coalition Campaign to Oppose Repeal of Johnson Amendment." *Nonprofit Quarterly,* March 2, 2017. https://nonprofitquarterly.org/2017/03/02/national-coalition-nonprofits-launches-campaign-oppose-repeal-johnson-amendment/.

Merry, Sally Engle. *Human Rights and Gender Violence: Translating International Law into Local Justice.* Chicago: University of Chicago Press, 2006.

Meyer, David S., and Debra C. Minkoff. "Conceptualizing Political Opportunity." *Social Forces* 82, no. 4 (2004): 1457–92. https://doi.org/10.1353/sof.2004.0082.

Mitchell, George E., and Sarah S. Stroup. "The Reputations of NGOs: Peer Evaluations of Effectiveness." *The Review of International Organizations* 12, no. 3 (2016): 1–23.

Murdie, Amanda M., and David R. Davis. "Shaming and Blaming: Using Events Data to Assess the Impact of Human Rights INGOs." *International Studies Quarterly* 56 (2012): 1–16.

Nash, Thomas, and Richard Moyers. *Global Coalitions: An Introduction to Working in Civil Society Partnerships.* London: Action on Armed Violence, 2011.

Nasiritousi, Naghmeh, Mattias Hjerpe, and Björn-Ola Linnér. "The Roles of Non-State Actors in Climate Change Governance: Understanding Agency through Governance Profiles." *International Environmental Agreements: Politics, Law, and Economics* 16, no. 1 (2016): 109–26. https://doi.org/10.1007/s10784-014-9243-8.

O'Brien, Robert, Anne Marie Goetz, Jan Aart Scholte, and Marc Williams. *Contesting Global Governance: Multilateral Economic Institutions and Global Social Movements.* Cambridge: Cambridge University Press, 2000.

Olesen, Thomas. *Global Injustice Symbols and Social Movements.* Basingstoke: Palgrave Macmillan, 2015.

Olesen, Thomas. "Power and Transnationalist Activist Framing." In *Power and Transnational Activism,* edited by Thomas Olesen, 1–19. Abingdon: Routledge, 2011.

Paumgarten, Nick. "Magic Mountain. What Happens at Davos?" *New Yorker* (February 28, 2012), 44–53.

Pollard, Amy, and Julius Court. *How Civil Society Organisations Use Evidence to Influence Policy Processes: A Literature Review.* London: ODI, 2005.

Pralle, Sarah B. *Branching Out, Digging In: Environmental Advocacy and Agenda Setting.* Washington, DC: Georgetown University Press, 2006.

Price, Richard. "Reversing the Gun Sights: Transnational Civil Society Targets Land Mines." *International Organization* 52, no. 3 (1998): 613–44.

Price, Richard. "Transnational Civil Society and Advocacy in World Politics." *World Politics* 55, no. 4 (2003): 579–606.

Princen, Sebastiaan. "Agenda-Setting in the European Union: A Theoretical Exploration and Agenda for Research." *Journal of European Public Policy* 14, no. 1 (2007): 21–38. https://doi.org/10.1080/13501760601071539.

Provan, Keith G., and Patrick Kenis. "Modes of Network Governance: Structure, Management, and Effectiveness." *Journal of Public Administration Research and Theory* 18, no. 2 (2008): 229–52. https://doi.org/10.1093/jopart/mum015.

Quissell, Kathryn. "The Impact of Stigma and Policy Target Group Characteristics on Policy Aggressiveness for HIV/AIDS and Tuberculosis." PhD diss., American University, 2017.

Reiners, Nina. "Transnational Lawmaking Coalitions for Human Rights." PhD diss., Universität Potsdam, 2017.

Risse, Thomas, ed. *Governance without a State: Policies and Politics in Areas of Limited Statehood.* New York: Columbia University Press, 2013.

Risse-Kappen, Thomas. "Introduction." In *Bringing Transnational Relations Back In: Non-State Actors, Domestic Structures, and International Institutions,* edited by Thomas Risse-Kappen, 3–33. Cambridge: Cambridge University Press, 1995.

Risse-Kappen, Thomas, ed. *Bringing Transnational Relations Back In: Non-State Actors, Domestic Structures and International Institutions.* Cambridge: Cambridge University Press, 1995.

Rose, Chris. *How to Win Campaigns: Communications for Change.* London: Earthscan, 2010.

Sabatier, Paul A. "An Advocacy Coalition Framework of Policy Change and the Role of Policy-Oriented Learning Therein." *Policy Sciences* 21 (1988): 129–68.

Schabas, William A. *The Abolition of the Death Penalty in International Law.* New York: Cambridge University Press, 2002.

Schmitz, Hans Peter. "International Criminal Accountability and Transnational Advocacy Networks (TANs)." In *Oxford Handbook of International Security,* edited by

Alexandra Gheciu and William C. Wohlforth, 697–710. New York: Oxford University Press, 2018.

Schneider, Anne, and Helen Ingram. "Social Construction of Target Populations: Implications for Politics and Policy." *American Political Science Review* 87, no. 2 (1993): 334–47.

Sen, Amartya. *Development as Freedom*. Oxford: Oxford University Press, 1999.

Shetty, Salil. "The Value of International Standards in the Campaign for Abolition of the Death Penalty." *Brown Journal of World Affairs* 21, no. 1 (2014): 41–60.

Shiffman, Jeremy. "Network Advocacy and the Emergence of Global Attention to Newborn Survival." *Health Policy and Planning* 31, no. suppl. 1 (2016): i60–i73. https://doi.org/10.1093/heapol/czv092.

Shiffman, Jeremy, Kathryn Quissell, Hans Peter Schmitz, David L. Pelletier, Stephanie L. Smith, David Berlan, Uwe Gneiting, et al. "A Framework on the Emergence and Effectiveness of Global Health Networks." *Health Policy and Planning* 31, no. suppl. 1 (2016): i3–i16. https://doi.org/10.1093/heapol/czu046.

Sikkink, Kathryn. *The Justice Cascade. How Human Rights Prosecutions Are Changing World Politics*. New York: W. W. Norton, 2011.

Smilie, Ian. *The Kimberley Process Certification Scheme for Rough Diamonds: Comparative Case Study 1*. London: Verifor/ODI, 2005.

Stone, Deborah A. "Causal Stories and the Formation of Policy Agendas." *Political Science Quarterly* 104, no. 2 (1989): 281–300.

Stroup, Sarah S., and Wendy Wong. *The Authority Trap: Strategic Choices of International NGOs*. Ithaca, NY: Cornell University Press, 2017.

Suchman, Mark C. "Managing Legitimacy: Strategic and Institutional Approaches." *The Academy of Management Review* 20, no. 3 (1995): 571–610.

Symons, Jonathan, and Dennis Altman. "International Norm Polarization: Sexuality as a Subject of Human Rights Protection." *International Theory* 7, no. 1 (2015): 61–95. https://doi.org/10.1017/S1752971914000384.

Tallberg, Jonas, Lisa M. Dellmuth, Hans Agné, and Andreas Duit. "NGO Influence in International Organizations: Information, Access, and Exchange." *British Journal of Political Science* 48, no. 1 (2015): 1–26. https://doi.org/10.1017/S000712341500037X.

Tarrow, Sidney. *The New Transnational Activism*. Cambridge: Cambridge University Press, 2005.

Tosun, Jale, Sebastian Koos, and Jennifer Shore. "Co-Governing Common Goods: Interaction Patterns of Private and Public Actors." *Policy and Society* 35, no. 1 (2016): 1–12. https://doi.org/10.1016/j.polsoc.2016.01.002.

Wang, Haidong, Mohsen Naghavi, Christine Allen, Ryan M. Barber, Zulfiqar A. Bhutta, Austin Carter, Daniel C. Casey, et al. "Global, Regional, and National Life Expectancy, All-Cause Mortality, and Cause-Specific Mortality for 249 Causes of Death, 1980–2015: A Systematic Analysis for the Global Burden of Disease Study 2015." *The Lancet* 388, no. 10053 (2016): 1459–544. https://doi.org/10.1016/S0140-6736(16)31012-1.

Wapner, Paul. "Horizontal Politics: Transnational Environmental Activism and Global Cultural Change." *Global Environmental Politics* 2, no. 2 (2002): 37–62.

Williams, Jody, Stephen D. Goose, and Mary Wareham. *Banning Landmines: Disarmament, Citizen Diplomacy, and Human Security*. Lanham: Rowman & Littlefield, 2008.

Wong, Wendy H. *Internal Affairs: How the Structure of NGOs Transforms Human Rights.* Ithaca, NY: Cornell University Press, 2012.

World Health Organization. *Eliminating Female Genital Mutilation: An Interagency Statement.* Geneva: World Health Organization, 2008.

Zimmermann, Lisbeth. "Same Same or Different? Norm Diffusion between Resistance, Compliance, and Localization in Post-Conflict States." *International Studies Perspectives* 17, no. 1 (2016): 98–115. https://doi.org/10.1111/insp.12080.

CHAPTER 5
Legitimacy

Legitimacy is an important construct both enabling and restricting TNGO actions. Negative reports about TNGOs often include references to legitimacy issues and reflect a broad range of frequently conflicting understandings of where legitimacy comes from and what legitimate behavior looks like. Typical occasions of such debates are major humanitarian crises, including the aftermaths of the Rwandan genocide in 1994, the Indian Ocean tsunami in 2004, and the Haiti earthquake in 2010. In the case of Rwanda, TNGOs debated the legitimacy of helping suspected Hutu perpetrators of genocide in refugee camps,[1] and in the aftermath of the Haiti earthquake local politicians and activists challenged the legitimacy of the TNGO presence and dominance in relief efforts. When Oxfam International failed to adequately investigate mistreatment and abuses committed by its Haiti staff, the scandal not only affected one organization,[2] but also created broader negative publicity for the entire sector.

Legitimacy is an essential currency for the TNGO sector. It is an essential part of generating authority and income. Diminished legitimacy due to eroding public trust creates vulnerabilities, including to funding, recruitment, collaboration, and access to decision-makers. A challenge faced by many TNGOs today is a loss of legitimacy based on a growing gap between what they promise and their lack of capacities to deliver. TNGOs have successively expanded their missions to emphasize root causes and have adopted more sophisticated strategies, including expanded advocacy and campaign efforts. As a result of the increasing involvement of TNGOs in governance and their evolution beyond missions of charity and amelioration, the sector today faces new legitimacy challenges and also greater scrutiny from more diverse sets of stakeholders.

Critics of TNGOs have called them unelected, unaccountable, and self-appointed organizations that have assumed many traditional governance responsibilities (e.g., enforcing rights or providing social services) without being meaningfully accountable to those they claim to serve.[3] TNGOs remain vulnerable to these challenges not necessarily because they are always valid, but because much of the sector has failed to develop a new understanding of its legitimacy consistent with its expanded mandates and ambitions. Organizational reforms designed to enhance the listening capacities of TNGOs and a greater focus on diversity and inclusion in hiring practices move TNGO legitimacy practices closer toward TNGOs' current and future aspirations. However, many of current efforts remain limited because TNGOs remain often too passive and unwilling to challenge the traditional architecture and its increasingly antiquated legitimacy model.

Traditionally, TNGO legitimacy has in large measure derived from the so-called nondistribution constraint (see Chapter 2) that imbues organizations with a certain kind of financial trustworthiness. Additionally, many TNGOs have become adept at mimicking the strategies and practices of more well-known and financially successful organizations, adhering to financial benchmarks, and adapting to donor preferences as means of gaining legitimacy through conformity or "isomorphism." In the past the TNGO sector also derived some degree of legitimacy from its independence from the business and government sectors. Over time, however, intersectoral collaborations increased not only for pragmatic reasons, but also for—ironically—the legitimizing effects that such collaborations can often provide for TNGOs, given that TNGOs may lack other readily apparent bases for claiming legitimacy.[4] Indeed, it is hard to imagine successful large-scale social change without the cooperation, if not collaboration, of market and state actors of some kind and to some degree. As TNGOs have become more collaborative and have made increasingly expansive claims about their goals and missions, the grounds for their legitimacy has destabilized and has become increasingly linked to their effectiveness (outcome legitimacy) and their relationships with an expanding set of stakeholders (process legitimacy). Moreover, the adoption of new organizational roles that embrace brokering, convening, facilitation, and research demand new bases of legitimacy that differ from those that were relevant for legitimating past roles more focused on direct service delivery.

THE CONTEXT OF TNGO LEGITIMACY

The concept of legitimacy evolves and its definition remains fluid, varying across subsectors. During the past decades, two important factors have contributed to an increasingly challenging landscape for TNGO legitimacy. First, TNGOs operate across borders and work with a wide array of stakeholders with diverse interests, including governments granting legal access, donors providing resources, and local communities with specific expectations. Second, TNGOs have adopted more expansive goals and strategies, requiring new sources of legitimacy. As the sector has shifted away from the architecture's traditional emphasis on perpetual intermediation and direct service, which was legitimated by fiscal propriety and scandal avoidance, it has embraced more indirect and transformative roles, which require more complex means of legitimation.

TNGO legitimacy is embedded in social relationships and is based on the "perception or assumption that their actions are desirable, proper, or appropriate within a socially constructed system of norms, values, beliefs, and definitions. . . . Legitimacy is bestowed by a collective audience."[5] Accountability practices may contribute to perceptions of legitimacy, but they are not the only factor shaping how stakeholders evaluate TNGO behavior. Legitimacy reflects a "stamp of approval"[6] used by organizations as an "instrumental and strategic resource that is constructed in relation to an audience."[7] As a result, TNGOs must have clarity about how they relate to different stakeholders, what matters to those stakeholders, and how to negotiate competing claims.[8]

Legitimacy emerges from at least three distinct sources: (1) legal recognition, (2) a set of shared norms, and (3) "actions expressing consent."[9] For TNGOs, all three issues raise complex challenges requiring proactive management. First, TNGOs have no formal international legal status analogous to national registration to legitimate their institutional "personalities" with respect to international law. Instead, TNGOs have to secure such status in multiple domestic contexts, where they usually incorporate as charitable organizations or their equivalent. Second, TNGOs work across culturally diverse contexts where shared norms are often not present. TNGOs also regularly address culturally sensitive issues (e.g., relating to women's empowerment, LGBTQ communities, or indigenous peoples) and face challenges based on working in diverse normative contexts. Third, TNGOs often lack a coherent, dominant constituency[10] that can generate regular expressions of consent, and the lack of broad and deep ownership in home and program locations can be a significant problem overall. Comparatively, businesses have owners or shareholders, while democratic governments face regular elections by defined electorates. TNGOs typically face conflicting stake-holder demands and cannot rely on elections or profits as a mechanism of legitimation.[11] If they fail to recognize and actively manage the legitimacy issues associated with their presence and purpose, then TNGOs face the prospect of diminished trust, confidence, authority, and ultimately, power.

Recognizing the multiple criteria or dimensions of legitimacy facilitates practical responses to the challenges faced by the sector. For example, legitimacy frameworks have included components related to representativeness, distinctive values, effectiveness and goal achievement, and empowerment and participation;[12] democratic, moral, and technical claims;[13] and purpose, performance, processes, and people.[14] While principled and representational claims are important, effectiveness has become an increasingly important dimension for how TNGOs are expected to demonstrate their legitimacy.[15] This has many practical implications for areas such as organizational culture, measurement and evaluation (M&E) processes, and information technology (IT) systems, for example.

TRADITIONAL DIMENSIONS OF TNGO LEGITIMACY

Traditional notions of TNGO legitimacy emphasize charity, financial probity, conspicuous altruism (including working long hours for little or no pay), and abstaining from direct involvement in political activities. These legitimacy dimensions are well-established across different TNGO subsectors and have come under greater scrutiny over time. In the humanitarian sector, for example, the core principles of neutrality, independence, and impartiality have long defined organizational legitimacy.[16] These principles legitimated access to populations during violent conflict, while not tipping the balance between the parties to conflicts. Over time, TNGOs emerged with different understandings of legitimate humanitarian action, emphasizing increased advocacy and greater responsiveness to victims of violence.

TNGOs performing service delivery in the development sector have long been viewed as legitimate simply because they visibly conveyed needed resources from the Global North to the Global South. Almost any actions would lead to improvements on the ground, even if they were inefficient or temporary. Being primarily responsible to donors for fiscal propriety and resource conveyance provided a clear path for accountability and legitimacy. Most TNGOs have abandoned a sole emphasis on perpetual charity and have embraced instead much more complex interventions requiring a broader set of legitimating practices.

Finally, advocacy TNGOs emerging during the 1960s and 1970s derived their primary legitimacy from the norms of human rights and environmental protection as defined by states in international treaties and their own constitutions. Similar to humanitarian and development TNGOs, it was important for these organizations to be politically neutral and emphasize research expertise and principled action. This is prominently reflected in Amnesty International's practice of deliberately defending prisoners of conscience from all major ideological camps during the Cold War, including Western democracies, the Communist bloc, and non-aligned countries. The practice of "bearing witness" based on universalist claims reflected a desire to occupy a moral high ground that often ignored the significant political consequences of TNGO actions.[17] As advocacy TNGOs have moved toward more ambitious advocacy strategies focused on underlying causes (see Chapter 3), the grounds for legitimating such practices have also shifted. For example, when advocacy TNGOs such as Amnesty began to mobilize in defense of social, economic, and cultural rights, their advocacy became more politicized and focused on public policies governing national economies.[18]

Parallel to the significant changes in TNGO strategies and ambitions during the 1980s and 1990s, donors started to look for more reliable information about the organizations they supported. In the United States, Charity Navigator was founded in 2001 with a mission to provide better intelligence about where to invest charitable contributions. Charity registers and information intermediaries improved access to registration and financial data. At the same time, benchmarks and governance standards emerged for evaluating and even rating and ranking organizations. However, in the absence of data on how organizations actually secure consent or deliver on their promises, these efforts reinforced the architecture's traditional legitimacy standards focused on donor interests and the surveillance of officer salaries and overhead spending ratios. Over time, many organizations found ways to conform to these standards to receive favorable ratings in a system that provided few or no incentives to prioritize outcomes for primary stakeholders.[19]

As TNGOs' rhetoric increasingly committed them to predicating their legitimacy on their impact, they have undertaken significant efforts to enhance legitimacy through procedural and self-expressive means, such as by relying on improved representation, participation, and value articulation. However, the sector has faced greater difficulties in measuring and demonstrating impact as another source of legitimation. Nevertheless, TNGOs have made rhetorical claims about their impact as a primary source of their legitimacy,[20] and they have increasingly emphasized impact in their communications with outside audiences.[21] Obstacles to delivering on these promises not only include the challenges of measuring impact, but often point to deeper constitutive issues. TNGOs' identities often remain defined by claims of being virtuous organizations whose existence by definition implies impact and whose actions can do no harm.[22]

FROM OVERHEAD TO OUTCOMES

Compared to legacy strategies of short-term assistance to the needy, many, if not most TNGOs today are committed to addressing underlying conditions with sustainable solutions. Still emerging behind this shift is a new legitimacy model focused less on financial probity and overhead rates and more on accountability for outcomes and impact.[23] Cultural, institutional, and demographic forces increasingly favor organizations that can demonstrate their effectiveness, especially as new competitors such as social enterprises and digital platforms continue to promote data-driven approaches.[24] Advances in data collection and processing enable the analysis of complex transnational interventions and challenge the claims that measuring outcomes or impact is either too expensive to be worthwhile or is impractical or impossible. Whether through reporting initiatives such as the International Aid Transparency Initiative (IATI) or data transparency platforms such as GuideStar Platinum (which allows organizations in the US to self-report about their outcomes), TNGOs' public-facing personas will be increasingly mediated by data-focused digital platforms.[25] As online data transparency platforms mature, it will ratchet up expectations for TNGOs to define clearly what they want to accomplish and to report on their effectiveness. These platforms will also make it much harder for organizations to gain legitimacy without offering supporting evidence.

While the philanthropic sector begins to shift its attention from overhead rates to outcomes, the old "lean and mean" mentality still remains an integral part of the architecture.[26] Many funders still cap indirect cost rates and few provide dedicated resources to support rigorous program evaluation. Moreover, funders often require TNGOs to focus on costs more so than meaningful outcomes, causing TNGOs to adopt parallel accounting and reporting systems that can distract from measuring what matters most. Evaluation and reporting requirements from funders can increase the use of outcome measurement in principle,[27] but mandated evaluation—particularly if unaccompanied by sufficient resources and genuine staff buy-in—can lead to evasive behaviors,[28] similar to the misrepresentation of financial information. This underscores the importance of establishing stronger outcome orientations and learning cultures within organizations[29] that are grounded in an internal consensus about the importance of evaluation for organizational learning and, also, legitimacy.

The movement toward outcomes mirrors not only the change in the social contract for establishing TNGO legitimacy, but also reflects a deeper transformation in the sector. When TNGOs operated primarily in the style of charities, they established legitimacy for their performance not necessarily by demonstrating results but by demonstrating trustworthiness. Trustworthiness was achieved by minimizing the perceived risk of fraud and misappropriation, which traditionally meant exhibiting low overhead, suppressing salaries, and avoiding debt, reserve accumulation, financial risk, and so on.[30] More recently, thoughtful observers have pointed out that a fixation on cost ratios inhibits investments in core capacities necessary for effectiveness,[31] such as those related to leadership development, more representative governance structures, program innovations, and improvements in measurement, evaluation, accountability, learning, transparency, and stakeholder responsiveness. These new dimensions of TNGO legitimacy are transformative not only because they require TNGOs to be accountable to their own promises, but also because they represent a fundamental departure from the conventional architecture in which TNGOs are embedded across the globe.

SECTORAL EFFORTS TO ENHANCE LEGITIMACY

The TNGO sector is increasingly recognizing the need to embrace new dimensions of organizational legitimacy,[32] but many organizations struggle to translate their new rhetoric into sustained action. As described in Chapter 3, many TNGOs have shifted their strategies toward more comprehensive and impact-oriented approaches emphasizing systems thinking, facilitation, and empowerment more so than direct service provision or elite-led advocacy. Insofar as performance is understood in terms of impact, TNGOs can foster their legitimacy by articulating impact as (1) an expressive value and (2) an instrumental claim. The expressive approach emphasizes rhetorical commitments that present impact as an organizational and sectoral value, while the instrumental approach relies on data transparency to demonstrate evidence of impact. Although the two may be used in tandem, rhetorical commitments do not necessarily substantiate instrumental claims.

Expressive approaches

As an expressive value, numerous sets of voluntary global standards, codes of conduct, and "accountability clubs" have emerged that allow TNGOs to express their commitments to community norms and performance standards.[33] For example, the Global Standard for CSO (Civil Society Organization) Accountability expresses commitments for organizations to continuously monitor, evaluate, learn, and adapt with a focus on lasting results; to evaluate long-term results in consultation with stakeholders; to identify the unintended effects of programs; and to invite and act on stakeholder feedback.[34] Similarly, the Sphere Project and Core Humanitarian Standard (CHS) express commitments to use evidence for learning and improving, to share learning internally and externally, to incorporate feedback and complaints from stakeholders, to use participatory methods, and to consider failures as well as successes.[35] TNGOs that voluntarily subscribe to such standards affirm commitments to achieving sustainable impact, among many other normative commitments. However, due to the voluntary nature of compliance, these initiatives have limited credibility. In some cases, self-certification is a requirement for formal membership in an alliance,[36] but enforcement remains voluntary. Moreover, many stakeholders may not recognize brands such as the Global Standard or CHS, especially as the number of standard-setting initiatives and accountability clubs has multiplied into the hundreds globally. This risks a "race to the bottom" that benefits the standard-setting initiatives with the lowest expectations with regard to disclosures of credible evidence of compliance. In terms of establishing performance-based legitimacy, the potential of rhetorical commitments to voluntary standards is limited.[37]

In some cases, voluntary initiatives have emerged to preempt or substitute for absent or inadequate state regulation. This appears to be most likely in countries where public trust in the sector is low and either stakeholders are unable to agree on the details of a formal regulatory framework or the responsible parties are unable to exercise meaningful oversight.[38]

Accountable Now (formerly the INGO Accountability Charter) is one initiative that has taken a more proactive approach by providing systematic feedback to TNGO accountability reports, as well as engaging members over time with a goal of improving practices. It also facilitates peer learning networks and has supported the emergence of shared accountability standards across nine established civil society accountability networks. These kinds of practices have begun to move individual organizations decidedly toward new legitimacy practices, but they remain relatively obscure and may have very limited effects on how these organizations and the sector are perceived by the broader public.

Instrumental approaches

An elaborate information intermediation ecosystem has been emerging to provide external stakeholders with more and better-quality information about TNGOs and their impact. It provides TNGOs with platforms and other mechanisms to facilitate data transparency about their missions, goals, and outcomes.[39] Information intermediaries and data platforms and services can provide stakeholders access to more detailed performance information and subject TNGOs to greater accountability for outcomes-based performance. Additionally, a variety of market-based initiatives have been introduced that emphasize data about outcomes and cost-effectiveness.

Individual donors increasingly perceive TNGOs through data transparency platforms or seek out third-party reviews because such ratings and rankings have greater credibility than organizations' own claims and self-certification schemes. Information intermediaries provide ratings, rankings, and other types of information about organizations to the public.[40] Examples of such intermediaries include Charity Navigator, the Better Business Bureau Wise Giving Alliance (BBB-WGA), GiveWell, and Philanthropedia in the United States, Charity Intelligence in Canada, Mido in Israel, and Filantrofilia in Mexico. Their ratings variously use financial disclosures, informational requests, websites, annual reports, and even crowdsourcing to evaluate or convey information about TNGOs.

GiveWell in the United States is rare within the universe of information intermediaries because of its long-standing focus on impact and cost-effectiveness, particularly with its emphasis on the marginal benefit of donations. However, out of the hundreds of promising organizations reviewed up to 2019, GiveWell was only able to recommend eight TNGOs that met its standards for achieving demonstrable results cost-effectively.[41] Tellingly, much of the data upon which GiveWell bases its recommendations is not produced by the TNGOs themselves but is drawn from academia and others outside of the TNGO community.[42] Such an approach is labor-intensive and is unlikely to be scalable to the thousands of TNGOs registered in the United States alone.

In acknowledgment of the limitations of financially oriented accountability systems and the difficulties of scaling impact auditing approaches, intermediaries have been experimenting with directly (e.g., Charity Navigator 2.0 and 3.0) and indirectly (e.g., GuideStar/Candid's medal designations) evaluating organizations based on transparency. The more information an organization discloses to the public, the more favorable designations it receives. In the United States, both Charity Navigator 3.0 and GuideStar Platinum allow TNGOs to display self-reported information about outcomes in a standardized format.[43] Such external transparency practices are only as good as the data on which they are based. And better data can only emerge if TNGOs have robust internal systems for monitoring and evaluation. Although information intermediation runs the risk of misreporting and other counterproductive behaviors,[44] these mechanisms can call attention to deficiencies in organizations' internal systems and provide an impetus for strengthening them.[45] Similar to Accountable Now, such mechanisms ultimately require commitment from organizational leadership to be used meaningfully and productively.

Some donors may be willing to shift away from rewarding financial probity toward valuing transparency and impact. There is some evidence that general social trust, awareness of accreditation systems,[46] and increased internet disclosure[47] positively affect donations, revealing that donors are effectively willing to "pay" for enhanced disclosure.[48] While evidence about how donors respond to financial versus performance disclosures yields mixed conclusions, younger donors appear particularly receptive to information about programmatic performance.[49]

The TNGO community has an historic opportunity to get out in front of these developments by strengthening their internal systems for results reporting. Given the proliferation and increasing sophistication of online platforms, technical barriers no longer inhibit greater strides in communicating results as a legitimating feature of what the sector does. The emergence of more mature online platforms also means that stakeholders will increasingly expect TNGOs to be more engaged in such disclosures and be more specific about their goals and accomplishments. Due to these developments and the self-professed impact-oriented commitments of many TNGOs, legitimacy based on performance now means demonstrably achieving outcomes, not just espousing righteous principles, avoiding scandals, and minimizing overhead.

In addition to initiatives from within the civil society sector and externally driven initiatives from information intermediaries and digital platforms, a variety of market-based innovations have emerged with a strong emphasis on results and cost-effectiveness. The increasing availability and appeal of alternatives to the charity model that are based on outcomes and cost-effectiveness, rather than just effort and probity, directly challenge the comparative advantage that TNGOs have enjoyed for decades. Social impact investment is catalyzing significant innovations in outcome accounting as investors seek out tools for determining how best to allocate their scarce resources. Organizations such as the Acumen Fund have attracted attention to their innovative method of capital allocation in which they calculate the cost per unit of impact for a project in relation to the best available charitable option (BACO).[50] Organizations such as First Light, Hub Ventures, Toniic, Unitus Seed Fund, the Unreasonable Institute, Village Capital; market exchanges such as Mission Markets, Impact Investment Exchange, and MaxImpact; and other resources for facilitating impact investing such as ImpactSpace, Investor's Circle, Global Impact Investing Networking, Aspen Network of Development Entrepreneurs, and the Impact Investing Policy Collaborative are all supporting this new approach to achieving social impact. Despite the market orientation of most impact investing, to the extent that organizations other than TNGOs are better capacitated to innovate and demonstrate their impact, they will enjoy a competitive advantage over TNGOs in performance-based legitimacy. Over time this can erode the appeal and relevance of TNGOs in relation to other actors better adapted to the expectations of impact-oriented funders.

Alongside impact-oriented philanthropy and impact investing, social impact bonds, pay-for-performance schemes, benefit corporations, and low-profit limited liability companies (L3Cs)[51] are all emerging and providing opportunities for channeling scarce resources to their most socially impactful uses.[52] The introduction of the Global Impact Investing Ratings System (GIIRS) implemented by B-Lab provides comprehensive and comparable social and environmental impact ratings for thousands of companies and funds from around the world.[53] The existence of these data can improve investor confidence, attract increased capital, and promote learning and continuous program improvement. These developments will impact the TNGO sector directly or indirectly by shaping expectations about what a legitimate approach to addressing global problems looks like.

The emergence of social impact investing in particular may be fundamentally changing the contours of philanthropy. Much of its growth has probably been driven by the capacity of new players to mobilize new sources of funding, potentially leading to major changes in the larger financial-philanthropic ecosystem.[54] Indeed, impact investing has grown into a $502 billion market globally.[55] The percentage of that sum that was diverted away from the TNGO sector is unknown, but even a small fraction could represent a considerable threat to the sustainability of TNGO models that are still playing to the traditional architecture.

How will the TNGOs of the future fare in a social sector increasingly composed of alternative social change vehicles? One step TNGOs can take to improve their competitiveness and relevance now is to strengthen their internal data systems to produce more systematic and rigorous evidence of their impact. However, this is much easier said than done, especially as the traditional architecture makes it exceedingly difficult to invest in such systems. Nevertheless, TNGO leaders and practitioners might consider that their ability to derive organizational legitimacy and relevance based on performance will depend upon how their organizations compare to increasingly sophisticated competition from adjacent sectors.

LEGITIMACY AND RESPONSIVENESS

Apart from outcome-based legitimacy, TNGOs have made strides in the area of process legitimacy by focusing attention on primary stakeholder participation and feedback as well as general stakeholder responsiveness. Feedback can be used in various ways, including to prevent and stop harm and to adapt and improve programs over time. TNGO safeguarding policies represent a relatively recent example of the former and focus on ensuring that "staff, operations and programmes do no harm to children and vulnerable adults, or expose them to abuse or exploitation."[56] In this case, "first movers" may not always be rewarded by the public for being more transparent. While Oxfam has self-reported on safeguarding incidents since 2011, the wider public only learned in early 2018 about the 2010 sexual misconduct of staff in Haiti.[57] As Oxfam was criticized for being too lenient in its response, its own trail of information was interpreted as evidence of systemic failure, rather than early but insufficient attempts to be more transparent.

In recent years a veritable movement focused on "beneficiary feedback" and "constituency voice" has gained traction throughout much of the TNGO community. Often labeled as "downward accountability,"[58] the intention behind such practices is to improve programs by involving local communities throughout the entire process of planning, implementation, and evaluation. Rather than asserting legitimacy by claiming to "speak for" or "speak about" local communities at international events or when asking donors for money,[59] TNGOs establish meaningful feedback mechanisms and other channels of two-way communications.

Research on "beneficiary feedback mechanisms" (BFM) reveals that their design and implementation plays a major role in their effectiveness.[60] For example, a pilot program led by Word Vision UK tested three mechanisms: (1) unsolicited feedback through technology-based channels, (2) solicited feedback through analog channels, and (3) feedback channels designed with the participation of primary stakeholders, which involved focus groups, community meetings, and suggestion boxes. The evaluation determined that the third mechanism was the most effective, likely because it was the only one explicitly designed with user input. The evaluation also determined that such feedback mechanisms require proactive outreach by TNGO staff to enhance inclusion, consideration of literacy levels, and a financial capacity to actually respond appropriately to requests made.

In addition to BFMs at the program level, TNGOs can also implement more effective systems for responsiveness at the organizational level as a means of enhancing organizational legitimacy. For example, in the aftermath of the 2010 Haiti earthquake, the Disaster Accountability Project[61] systematically contacted TNGOs that had received significant support for the Haiti earthquake response to determine how the money was being spent and what results were being achieved. By their account, TNGOs not only lacked sufficient online transparency about their operations in Haiti but also were systematically unresponsive to their requests for information. Similar issues have also arisen for environmental TNGOs pursuing their missions without sufficient regard for local community views. In 2016, Survival International became the first TNGO to charge another TNGO, the Worldwide Fund for Nature (WWF), of violating OECD Guidelines for Multinational Enterprises by denying the rights of indigenous peoples in their conservation work.[62]

As much as enhanced responsiveness can improve an organization's legitimacy, a lack of responsiveness can undermine it. Although TNGO practitioners may be well aware of the difficulties and tensions associated with reporting and responsiveness (including security concerns related to transparency), external stakeholders may have a different set of assumptions and expectations. Whether at the program or organizational level, information transparency and responsiveness are becoming increasingly important components of TNGO legitimacy.

THE CHANGING DIMENSIONS OF TNGO LEGITIMACY

Legitimacy is a social construction, and as such its components or dimensions change with the changing assumptions and expectations of stakeholder groups. Whereas the legacy basis for organizational legitimacy was built upon principled commitments, representational claiming, elite expertise, financial propriety, charity, and conformity, the new or emerging basis focuses on effectiveness, strategy, leadership, governance, transparency, and responsiveness, as summarized in Table 5.1.

Table 5.1 EVOLVING LEGITIMACY FRAMEWORKS

	Legitimating criteria	Behavioral expressions
Traditional legitimacy basis	Principles	Espousing universal values and taking a moral high-ground
	Representation	"Speaking for or speaking about" disadvantaged communities
	Elite expertise	Capacities to carry out independent research and design and implement programs
	Financial propriety	Prioritizing upward financial accountability to donors Minimizing overhead and accumulated financial reserves Avoiding financial misconduct and exhibiting trustworthiness
	Charity	Intermediation between donors and recipients Perpetually delivering direct and immediate aid Projecting a distinct identity from business and government
	Conformity (isomorphism)	Financial benchmarking Adapting to donor preferences Mimicking practices of well-known and financially successful organizations
Emerging legitimacy basis	Effectiveness	Demonstrable, cost-effective goal attainment
	Strategy	Emphasizing long-term sustainable transformation, complexity, innovation, learning, and adaptation
	Leadership	Community and supporter-driven (rather than staff or elite-driven)
	Governance	Multi-directional accountability Internal structures and processes provide appropriate multi-stakeholder representation
	Transparency	Proactive sharing of information with stakeholders Participation in data transparency platforms
	Responsiveness	Listening and "speaking with" communities and supporters Satisfying inquiries and requests in a timely manner Reacting appropriately to feedback

Because the TNGO sector itself helped to bring about this evolution of the legitimacy model, it is ironic that TNGOs should be lagging so far behind on some of its most important dimensions. Although it may be tempting to place blame on individual TNGOs for failing to live up to their own standards, the gap points also to the structure of the underlying charity architecture that still prioritizes the older dimensions of legitimacy. For example, while many regulatory frameworks and information intermediaries routinely scrutinize TNGO financial information, no such commensurate infrastructure exists for obtaining and assessing information about organizational responsiveness or effectiveness. Moreover, the legacy architecture socially constructs and reconstructs TNGOs in ways that limit their abilities to adapt and reform. To the extent that TNGOs are incentivized to prioritize perpetual service delivery and upward financial accountability to donors, they are deterred from investing in long-term organizational change processes that could enhance their effectiveness and improve their strategies, leadership, governance, transparency, and responsiveness.

CONCLUSION

Legitimacy is essential for generating the authority required for TNGOs to be powerful advocates for the populations they claim to serve. In the past, TNGOs embraced traditional notions of legitimacy by espousing specific principles and representational claims, providing elite expertise, exhibiting financial probity and trustworthiness, filling gaps left by the market and governments through charitable service provision, and conforming to other traditional sectoral norms. Today, legitimacy is increasingly based on criteria such as effectiveness, strategy, leadership, governance, transparency, and responsiveness to multiple stakeholders. TNGO performance and legitimacy require the capacities to rigorously listen to those that TNGOs claim to help and to iteratively develop new solutions. If the sector does not become more proactive in such regards, competitors outside of the sector will continue to challenge the roles TNGOs—likely with increasing success.

There is no one-size-fits-all approach to the legitimacy challenges faced by the sector. Even as new dimensions increase in importance, TNGOs will still need to consistently express and live their core values, ensure that resources are used appropriately, and address issues that the business and government sectors fail to address. Some organizations may choose to attenuate their claims to narrow the gap between their promises and their actual practices and accomplishments. Those that remain committed to expansive claims to bring about transformational change will need to invest and improve.

Resource investments in these areas force real trade-offs that organizations must make between meeting the demands of the legacy architecture and breaking free of those limitations to fulfill new commitments and roles. As TNGOs predicate their organizational legitimacy and authority on instrumental claims of achieving impact, investments in organizational capacities to listen and assess results become more important. Although organizational changes and investments will impose significant costs, TNGOs at least have a variety of opportunities to improve their legitimacy. As discussed in Chapters 6, 7, 8, 9, and 10, digital technologies, measurement systems, governance reforms, leadership development, and collaboration all offer paths to enhanced organizational legitimacy. A greater awareness of the significance of organizational legitimacy to organizational power and authority (see Chapter 4) should motivate TNGOs to more deliberately consider the grounds upon which their organizations can claim a mandate to pursue their missions.

REFERENCES

Atack, Iain. "Four Criteria for Development NGO Legitimacy." *World Development* 27, no. 5 (1999): 855–64.

Balboa, Cristina M. *The Paradox of Scale: How NGOs Build, Maintain, and Lose Authority in Environmental Governance.* Cambridge, MA: MIT Press, 2018.

Beetham, David. *The Legitimation of Power.* Basingstoke: Palgrave Macmillan, 2013.

Bekkers, René. "Trust, Accreditation, and Philanthropy in the Netherlands." *Nonprofit and Voluntary Sector Quarterly* 32, no. 4 (2003): 596–615.

Berger, Ken, Robert Penna, and Jeremy Kohomban. "Mergers and Collaborations for Charity Navigator?" *Stanford Social Innovation Review*, August 10, 2012.

BFM. *Using Beneficiary Feedback to Improve Development Programmes: Findings from a Multi-Country Pilot.* N.p.: World Vision, INTRAC, Social Impact Lab, and CDA, 2016. http://feedbackmechanisms.org/public/files/BFM-key-findings-summary.pdf.

Bhattacharya, Rinku, and Daniel Tinkelman. "How Tough Are Better Business Bureau/ Wise Giving Alliance Financial Standards?" *Nonprofit and Voluntary Sector Quarterly* 38, no. 3 (2009): 467–89.

Bond. "Safeguarding Guidance and Resources." 2018. https://www.bond.org.uk/ngo-support/safeguarding.

Breen, Oonagh B., Alison Dunn, and Mark Sidel, eds. *Regulatory Waves: Comparative Perspectives on State Regulation and Self-Regulation Policies in the Nonprofit Sector.* New York: Cambridge University Press, 2017.

Brest, Paul. "A Decade of Outcome-Oriented Philanthropy." *Stanford Social Innovation Review* (2012). http://www.ssireview.org/articles/entry/a_decade_of_outcome_oriented_philanthropy.

Carman, Joanne G. "The Accountability Movement: What's Wrong with This Theory of Change?" *Nonprofit and Voluntary Sector Quarterly* 39, no. 2 (2010): 256–74.

Carman, Joanne G. "Nonprofits, Funders, and Evaluation: Accountability in Action." *The American Review of Public Administration* 39, no. 4 (2009): 374–90.

Carman, Joanne G. "Understanding Evaluation in Nonprofit Organizations." *Public Performance and Management Review* 34, no. 3 (2011): 350–77.

Deloffre, Maryam Zarnegar. "NGO Accountability Clubs in the Humanitarian Sector: Social Dimensions of Club Emergence and Design." In *Voluntary*

Regulation of NGOs and Nonprofits: An Accountability Club Framework, edited by Mary Kay Gugerty and Aseem Prakash, 169–200. Cambridge: Cambridge University Press, 2010.

Deloffre, Maryam Zarnegar, and Hans Peter Schmitz. "INGO Legitimacy: Challenges and Responses." In *Routledge Handbook of NGOs and International Relations*, edited by Thomas Davies, 606–20 (New York: Routledge, 2019).

Disaster Accountability Project. "The Transparency of Relief Organizations in Haiti." In *Tectonic Shifts: Haiti since the Earthquake*, edited by Mark Schuller and Pablo Morales, 65–68. Sterling, VA: Kumarian Press, 2012.

Ebrahim, Alnoor, and V. Kasturi Rangan. *Acumen Fund: Measurement in Venture Philanthropy*. Cambridge: Harvard Business School, 2009.

Edwards, Michael. "What's to Be Done with Oxfam?" *openDemocracy* (August 1, 2016). https://www.opendemocracy.net/transformation/michael-edwards/what-s-to-be-done-with-oxfam.

Edwards, Michael. "What's to Be Done with Oxfam?, Part 2." *openDemocracy* (February 15, 2018). https://www.opendemocracy.net/en/transformation/what-s-to-be-done-with-oxfam-part-2.

Ellis, Peter. "The Ethics of Taking Sides." In *Ethical Questions and International NGOs*, edited by Keith Horton and Chris Roche, 65–86. New York: Springer, 2010.

Feldmann, Derrick, Joanna Nixon, Justin Brady, Lara Brainer-Banker, and Lindsay Wheeler. *The 2013 Millennial Impact Report*. The Millennial Impact Research (2013). http://www.themillennialimpact.com/past-research.

Gandia, Juan L. "Internet Disclosure by Nonprofit Organizations: Empirical Evidence of Nongovernmental Organizations for Development in Spain." *Nonprofit and Voluntary Sector Quarterly* 40, no. 1 (2011): 57–78.

Gugerty, Mary Kay. "The Effectiveness of NGO Self-Regulation: Theory and Evidence from Africa." *Public Administration and Development* 28, no. 2 (2008): 105–18.

Gugerty, Mary Kay. "Signaling Virtue: Voluntary Accountability Programs among Nonprofit Organizations." *Policy Sciences* 42, no. 3 (2009): 243–73.

Gugerty, Mary Kay, and Aseem Prakash, eds. *Voluntary Regulation of NGOs and Nonprofits: An Accountability Club Framework*. New York: Cambridge University Press, 2010.

Gugerty, Mary Kay, Mark Sidel, and Angela L. Bies. "Introduction to the Minisymposium: Nonprofit Self-Regulation in Comparative Perspective—Themes and Debates." *Nonprofit and Voluntary Sector Quarterly* 39, no. 6 (2010): 1027–38.

Gutterman, Ellen. "The Legitimacy of Transnational NGOs: Lessons from the Experience of Transparency International in Germany and France." *Review of International Studies* 40 (2014): 391–418.

Heifetz, Ronald A., Marty Linsky, and Alexander Grashow. *The Practice of Adaptive Leadership: Tools and Tactics for Changing Your Organization and the World*. Boston: Harvard Business School Publishing, 2009.

HERE Geneva. *Humanitarian Priorities for People in Crises—The Foundations for a More Effective Response*. Geneva: Humanitarian Exchange and Research Centre, 2016.

Hope Consulting. *Money for Good: The US Market for Impact Investments and Charitable Gifts from Individual Donors and Investors*. (May 2010). https://thegiin.org/assets/binary-data/RESOURCE/download_file/000/000/96-1.pdf.

Houchin, Susan, and Heather Johnston Nicholson. "Holding Ourselves Accountable: Managing by Outcomes in Girls Incorporated." *Nonprofit and Voluntary Sector Quarterly* 31, no. 2 (2002): 271–77.

INTRAC. *Dfid Beneficiary Feedback Mechanisms (BFM) Pilot: End-Point Review: Synthesis Report*. N.p.: Social Impact Lab, INTRAC, and World Vision,

2016. http://feedbackmechanisms.org/public/files/BFM End-point Synthesis—full report.pdf.

Koppell, Jonathan G. S. "Pathologies of Accountability: ICANN and the Challenge of 'Multiple Accountabilities Disorder'." *Public Administration Review* 65, no. 1 (2005): 94–108. https://doi.org/10.1111/j.1540-6210.2005.00434.x.

Krishnan, Ranjani, Michelle H. Yetman, and Robert J. Yetman. "Expense Misreporting in Nonprofit Organizations." *The Accounting Review* 81, no. 2 (2006): 399–420.

Lischer, Sarah Kenyon. *Dangerous Sanctuaries: Refugee Camps, Civil War, and the Dilemmas of Humanitarian Aid.* Ithaca, NY: Cornell University Press, 2015.

Lynch, K., and Kate Cooney. "Moving from Outputs to Outcomes: A Review of the Evolution of Performance Measurement in the Human Service Nonprofit Sector." *Administration in Social Work* 35, no. 4 (2011): 364–88.

Marquis, Christopher, Andrew Klaber, and Bobbi Thomson. *B Lab: Building a New Sector of the Economy.* Cambridge, MA: Harvard Business School, 2011.

McCollim, Elena. "A Tale of Two Influences: An Exploration of Downward Accountability in World Vision International." PhD diss., University of San Diego, 2019.

Meyer, Michael, Renate Buber, and Anahid Aghamanoukjan. "In Search of Legitimacy: Managerialism and Legitimation in Civil Society Organizations." *Voluntas* 24 (2013): 167–93.

Mitchell, George E. "Collaborative Propensities among Transnational NGOs Registered in the United States." *American Review of Public Administration* 44, no. 5 (2014): 575–99. https://doi.org/10.1177/0275074012474337.

Mitchell, George E. "The Construct of Organizational Effectiveness: Perspectives from Leaders of International Nonprofits in the United States." *Nonprofit and Voluntary Sector Quarterly* 42, no. 2 (2013): 322–43. https://doi.org/10.1177/0899764011434589.

Mitchell, George E. "Creating a Philanthropic Marketplace through Accounting, Disclosure, and Intermediation." *Public Performance and Management Review* 38, no. 1 (2014): 23–47.

Mitchell, George E. "Fiscal Leanness and Fiscal Responsiveness: Exploring the Normative Limits of Strategic Nonprofit Financial Management." *Administration & Society* 49, no. 9 (2017): 1272–96. https://doi.org/10.1177/0095399715581035.

Mitchell, George E. "Modalities of Managerialism: The 'Double Bind' of Normative and Instrumental Nonprofit Managerial Imperatives." *Administration & Society* 50, no. 7 (2018): 1037–68. https://doi.org/10.1177/0095399716664832.

Mitchell, George E. "Fiscal Leanness and Fiscal Responsiveness: Exploring the Normative Limits of Strategic Nonprofit Financial Management." *Administration & Society* 49, no. 9 (2017): 1272–96. https://doi.org/10.1177/0095399715581035.

Mitchell, George E., and Thad D. Calabrese. "Proverbs of Nonprofit Financial Management." *American Review of Public Administration* 49, no. 6 (2019): 649–61. https://doi.org/10.1177/0275074018770458.

Mudaliar, Abhilash, and Hannah Dithrich. *Sizing the Impact Investing Market.* New York: Global Impact Investing Network, 2019. https://thegiin.org/assets/Sizing the Impact Investing Market_webfile.pdf.

National Contact Point of Switzerland. *Final Statement: Specific Instance Regarding the World Wide Fund for Nature International (WWF) Submitted by the Survival International Charitable Trust.* Berne: Swiss NCP, 2017.

National Council of Nonprofits. *Investing for Impact. Indirect Costs Are Essential for Success.* Washington, DC: National Council of Nonprofits, 2013.

Nelson, Paul J. "Social Movements and the Expansion of Economic and Social Human Rights Advocacy among International NGOs." In *Closing the Rights Gap: From Human Rights to Social Transformation*, edited by LaDawn Haglund and Robin Stryker, 149–70. Berkeley: University of California Press, 2015.

O'Hara, Maureen, and Aftab Omer. "Virtue and the Organizational Shadow: Exploring False Innocence and the Paradoxes of Power." In *Humanity's Dark Side: Evil, Destructive Experience, and Psychotherapy*, 167–87. Washington, DC: American Psychological Association, 2013.

"The Overhead Myth." *GuideStar*, 2013, accessed June 24, 2013. http://overheadmyth.com/wp-content/uploads/2013/06/GS_OverheadMyth_Ltr_ONLINE.pdf.

Pallas, Christopher L., David Gethings, and Max Harris. "Do the Right Thing: The Impact of INGO Legitimacy Standards on Stakeholder Input." *Voluntas* 26, no. 4 (2015): 1261–87. https://doi.org/10.1007/s11266-014-9475-9.

Parsons, Linda M. "The Impact of Financial Information and Voluntary Disclosures on Contributions to Not-for-Profit Organizations." *Behavioral Research in Accounting* 19 (2007): 179–96.

Prakash, Aseem, and Mary Kay Gugerty. "Trust but Verify?: Voluntary Regulation Programs in the Nonprofit Sector." *Regulation & Governance* 4, no. 1 (2010): 22–47.

Richardson, Beth. "Sparking Impact Investing through GIIRS." *Stanford Social Innovation Review*, 2012. http://ssir.org/articles/entry/sparking_impact_investing_through_giirs.

Ronalds, Paul. *The Change Imperative: Creating the Next Generation NGO*. Sterling, VA: Kumarian Press, 2010.

Rubenstein, Jennifer C. "The Misuse of Power, Not Bad Representation: Why It Is beside the Point That No One Elected Oxfam." *Journal of Political Philosophy* 22, no. 2 (2014): 204–30. https://doi.org/10.1111/jopp.12020.

Saxton, Gregory D., Daniel G. Neely, and Chao Guo. "Web Disclosure and the Market for Charitable Contributions." *Journal of Accounting and Public Policy* 33, no. 2 (2014). 127–144.

Slim, Hugo. "By What Authority? The Legitimacy and Accountability of Non-Governmental Organisations," International Meeting on *Global Trends and Human Rights—Before and after September 11*, Geneva, January 10–12, (2002). http://www.gdrc.org/ngo/accountability/by-what-authority.html.

Thrandardottir, Erla. *NGO Audiences: A Beethamite Analysis*. London: City University of London, 2017.

Tremblay-Boire, Joannie, Aseem Prakash, and Mary Kay Gugerty. "Regulation by Reputation: Monitoring and Sanctioning in Nonprofit Accountability Clubs." *Public Administration Review* 76, no. 5 (2016): 1–11. https://doi.org/10.1111/puar.12539.

Wellens, Lore, and Marc Jegers. "Beneficiary Participation as an Instrument of Downward Accountability: A Multiple Case Study." *European Management Journal* 32, no. 6 (2014): 938–49.

Yanacopulos, Helen. *International NGO Engagement, Advocacy, Activism: The Faces and Spaces of Change*. Basingstoke: Palgrave Macmillan, 2015.

CHAPTER 6
Digital

The twin developments of digitization and disintermediation fundamentally challenge traditional models of TNGO activism. Digital organizations such as 38 Degrees, 350.org, GetUp!, Avaaz, Jhatkaa, and GiveDirectly have changed how individuals—especially younger generations—participate in civic and political life both domestically and transnationally. Such organizations and digital platforms represent a different mode of collective action by encouraging supporter-led activism, replacing research-based advocacy with an issue-agnostic approach, and emphasizing the short-term mobilization of individuals through sharing, petitioning, and donating.[1] Rather than committing to a long-term relationship with a specific TNGO, individuals today can choose from a broad menu of online opportunities that provide a sense of being directly involved in causes that they care about. A growing number of transnational and national digital organizations now coexist with traditional modes of top-down transnational campaigning.

Digital organizations disrupt the traditional TNGO model by having supporters, donors, and primary stakeholders engage with each other without the need for costly intermediation through a conventional "brick-and-mortar" organization. For example, digital organizations such as Kiva, GiveDirectly, and Watsi channel donations directly to recipients. This is especially appealing to new generations of donors, including "web kids"[2] who grew up online and prefer greater autonomy and less long-term commitment in social activism.[3] These organizations typically appeal to donors' traditional demands for low or no overhead spending while also giving them significant control over where their donations go. In the advocacy arena, 350.org and #FridaysforFuture are building the kind of agenda-setting power that traditional TNGOs previously enjoyed in the 1980s and 1990s.

Central to their success is not networking with elites, but the use of digital capabilities or "affordances"[4] in creating self-sustained networks among supporters.

As the costs of legacy intermediation and staff-directed campaign models keep increasing,[5] digital platforms become comparatively more attractive. Many TNGOs have responded to this disruptive change by adding their own digital strategies with goals including breaking into new supporter markets in low- and middle-income countries where they have struggled to attract donors. However, the digital challenge goes well beyond attracting new supporters within the traditional system of transnational advocacy and resource transfers. Digital tools push TNGOs to reconsider their basic role and purpose by enabling faster responses and more direct, timely, and authentic input and feedback from stakeholders. They provide new means of collecting data about program and organizational effectiveness and thus can lead to more data-driven decision-making with accelerated testing and adaptation.[6] Digital tools also facilitate the adoption of new advocacy strategies no longer built around elite actions and mass media strategies, but focused on empowering supporters to lead advocacy efforts themselves.

The digital age challenges TNGOs to (re-)define their value propositions and comparative advantages, and to be more responsive and communicative with stakeholders. The digital turn is not simply about how to fit digital tools into an existing organizational model, but how to adapt the organization to a digital world. The emergence of online competition increases pressures among traditional TNGOs to better facilitate direct consultation and participation by supporters and other stakeholders. It also creates pressures for TNGOs to increase their awareness of "where the eyeballs are" at any moment in time, with respect to salient issues, media platforms, and the imperative to communicate persuasively with younger digitally native audiences. TNGOs now face a choice about whether to deploy digital technology primarily to broadcast charitable appeals within the existing architecture or to transform themselves by proactively incorporating digital affordances into their goals and strategies.

GOING DIGITAL

In a recent survey, TNGO leaders reported that "digital transformation" was the top trend impacting their organizations.[7] Indeed, digital innovations are relevant across the entire spectrum of TNGO activities, including income generation, program and campaign design, internal and external communications, and even governance. Specific applications include money transfers via cellular phones and the use of global informational systems to map areas of natural or man-made disasters.[8]

Digital technologies can be mobilized to enhance both advocacy inputs and outputs. On the input side, TNGOs have used open-source maps and satellite images to provide data to local governments about where to locate facilities and provide services, to address humanitarian crises, and to identify human rights abuses. For example, in 2016, Amnesty International's Decode Darfur campaign mobilized more than 26,000 volunteers to scan satellite images for evidence of government attacks on villages in Darfur. Digital tools can also facilitate access in areas of limited statehood and speed up data collection after natural disasters.[9] This use of technology primarily improves efficiency by reducing costs or expediting data collection, and it can work well in support of traditional professionalized and staff-led advocacy work.[10] Geographic information systems (GIS) and other technologies are not just letting TNGOs provide better programming; they are also changing understandings of social problems and informing strategies.[11]

Digital tools can also be used to enhance advocacy outputs by giving supporters more control of campaign topics and strategies or by widening and broadening participation in a given campaign.[12] Usually digital adoption patterns are driven by a TNGO's existing organizational preferences and the underlying theory of change. For example, organizations with a focus on elite lobbying may view their online presence primarily as a means to broaden support, while organizations with a history of grassroots engagement may be more interested in member participation as an end in itself.[13] The core activities enhanced by digital tools include (1) identifying campaign topics and strategies, (2) organizing supporters to lead on their own, and (3) responding more rapidly to external opportunities.

Giving supporters more control over campaign topics represents a departure from the traditional model of TNGO campaigning. However, organizations such as SumOfUs and Avaaz have long encouraged participation by empowering supporters to choose advocacy topics and strategies.[14] Although these groups are also dedicated to social and political change, they rely much less on staff to run campaigns. Instead, they have embraced more of a start-up and measurement-focused culture that regularly listens to and assesses what supporters want. Tools such as A/B testing[15] play a greater role in efforts to "test multiple storylines with different social media audiences to determine what works best to shift mindsets and the narratives prevalent in mainstream media."[16] Rather than just disseminating abstract facts and research, digital tools can encourage the empowerment of supporters to increase impact overall.

Digital tools transform not only how organizations relate to their supporters, but also how they make decisions internally. Many digital organizations purposively keep their organizations lean and flat to allow for maximum agility and responsiveness to supporter preferences and innovations. Some seek to transform into online organizing communities.[17] Digital organizations offer a broad range of opportunities for engagement, and members can feel included in broader movements by undertaking even relatively small actions. Digital technologies can lower entry barriers for new members[18] and facilitate the pooling of smaller actions to generate larger impact. TNGO staff shift their attention to creating meaningful and "personalized experiences" for their supporters.[19] Digital organizations marry an emphasis on facilitating the growth of "leaderful" movements and supporter-centric approaches with giving staff authority to make decisions on campaigns or other actions without lengthy consensus-building processes. This makes TNGOs not only less hierarchical and more agile, but projects a grassroots orientation where power is exercised by members and supporters rather than elite organizational leadership.

Digitally facilitated communication is a tool for rapid responsiveness to events that supporters care about. Instead of a narrow mission statement, what an organization stands for emerges from its members and its members emerge from the organization's actions. The emphasis is on nimbleness and the minimization of bureaucracy so that organizations can exploit unexpected moments of convergence between "high information" and "high actionability" with swift action. Within a deliberately small organization, staff are empowered to make decisions within their realms of expertise and focus primarily on facilitating members' actions.

The digital age represents a major generational shift that challenges older TNGOs to rethink their models and theories of change. Social media and other digital affordances have fundamentally changed how individuals think about their own roles and political behaviors. Younger generations are more interested in causes than organizations, and they view digital media as a means to anchor their lifestyles in social networks.[20] They exhibit greater independence and a preference to act on their own terms in ways that support their social visibility and standing with their peers and networks.[21] As a result, digital forms of engagement now compete with traditional group and institutional affiliations in the context of established movement organizations, the mainstream media, parties, and churches.[22] The idea of "connective action"[23] may complement or compete with conventional social movements and with TNGOs that historically have been built around formal organizing, strong leadership, brokered coalitions, and action frames that draw on ideology or group identity.[24]

Digital technologies fundamentally challenge traditional service delivery and advocacy strategies that rely on expertise and elite-driven activity. Digital tools provide new affordances that offer TNGOs new opportunities for engagement, mobilization, and empowerment, but the actual adoption patterns are shaped by organizational cultures and the specific personal experiences of leaders and staff. The vast majority of TNGOs have yet to take bold steps in the digital realm, as many in the sector are skeptical about how these technologies affect (1) their control over messaging, and (2) their brand and credibility. As a result, surveys on digital adoption patterns continue to find that "nonprofits are struggling mightily with how to structure their digital programs" and "one-way broadcast campaigns continue to dominate the way nonprofits campaign."[25]

Digital media as an access point to informal spaces challenges the fundamental norms and behaviors of organizations as bureaucratic structures often driven by staff expertise and cultural values that prize consensus-oriented decision-making. While new generations of supporters are digital natives, many TNGO leaders and board members today did not grow up with Instagram or WhatsApp. As a result, digital tools may be favored by younger generations, but broader organizational and strategic decisions will continue to be dominated by an older generation of activists. Practitioners in the sector generally score higher on intrinsic motivation,[26] and their passion is often driven by strong convictions and normative views about how the world should be.[27] Their self-identity may be strongly associated with working in or working with a TNGO and engaging in courageous and self-righteous actions.[28] This culture can stand in the way of embracing a new paradigm in which TNGOs play the role of enablers of (online) citizen activism.[29]

Cultural resistance may be reinforced by a sense of uniqueness or of being irreplaceable, as well as the sunk costs associated with the difficulties of steering a large organization historically focused on research, mass media, and staff-driven action onto a new course. TNGOs have often developed a comfortable niche of specialized subject matter expertise and social networks with peers and elite decision-makers. This can generate skepticism about relying on short-term actions or small donations for reaching goals of longer-term, structural change. As TNGOs claim to focus on root causes and increasingly embrace systems thinking (see Chapter 3), digital tools often invite skepticism and perceptions of fostering "slacktivism."[30] More fundamentally, most TNGOs are driven by an overriding interest in fostering mainly transactional relationships with their supporters and donors. With a few exceptions, the sector still tends to underemphasize community-building among supporters, and has found limited use for digital engagement as a tactic for promoting transformation. Granted, digital tools can certainly be used in a purely transactional fashion to solicit donations and "clicks" while remaining firmly in control of campaigns and messaging. However, this reinforces both an acquiescence to the traditional donor-centric architecture as well as a failure of imagination to see digital affordances as an opportunity for entertaining new organizational values, practices, roles, and forms (see Chapter 2). Such a mindset also suggests that such TNGOs are failing to "get it" in terms of adapting to the digital age and are risking their future relevance especially in the eyes of younger (and increasingly, older) stakeholders.

Major barriers to embracing digital technologies include ethical questions arising from going online. TNGOs will face backlash if they use supporter data without consent and will be held to high standards by the general public. They may also struggle to establish a reliable digital infrastructure[31] capable of protecting user data and will be subject to board oversight cognizant on the many trade-offs introduced by adopting digital tools. Digital resources will vary with regard to accessibility and long-term costs, and may generate different perceptions of alignment with an organization's mission and values among stakeholders. For example, when Kiva and Mercy Corps announced their intention to partner with Facebook's Libra Association, they argued that transactions in cryptocurrency would advance their missions to serve the poor and expand financial inclusion.[32] Critics quickly pointed out that such a partnership is likely to benefit Facebook by improving its reputation while generating significant risks to participating TNGOs.[33]

An aversion to risk and a desire to retain control of priorities, branding, and messaging can present obstacles to going digital, as can apprehensions about "trolling," disinformation, and other online pathologies. However, a lack of online engagement is unlikely to be an effective reaction to such fears. Instead, TNGOs can focus on learning how to protect and promote civility, to communicate productively (or at least not counterproductively) with unlike-minded actors, and to advance and defend their legitimacy to participate in online spaces.

DIGITAL STRATEGIES AND ORGANIZATIONAL FORMS

TNGOs can integrate a variety of different digital tools into their strategic repertoires.[34] Different platforms, such as Instagram, WhatsApp, and Twitter, offer a variety of opportunities to engage supporters. Individual

Table 6.1 DIGITAL STRATEGIES

Who leads?

		Staff-driven	Supporter-driven
Participation goals	*Broader*	Digital broadcasting	Digital analytics
	Deepen	Digital conversing	Distributed organizing

organizations also differ greatly with regard to their levels of resource invest-ment, integration of digital into the overall organization,[35] and perceptions of leadership and staff about the risk and potential of digital organizing. Patterns of adopted digital strategies can be understood as flowing from a TNGO's overall understanding of what role it plays in social change and how it sees its relationship to stakeholders. Table 6.1 identifies four types of digital engagement providing analytical categories for understanding specific practices.[36] TNGOs may adopt several different strategies over time and they may embrace each of them in a more or less dedicated manner. Larger organizations can have significant advantages with regard to their relative ability to invest in digital capabilities, although their more corpo-rate cultures can sometimes entail a control orientation that can inhibit dig-ital risk-taking.

Digital broadcasting

Digital broadcasting uses digital technologies exclusively to amplify campaigns and market the message to potential donors and supporters. The effects on the organization and its strategies are minimal, and social media serves mainly the purpose of one-way communication. There is variation within digital broadcasting in terms of the platforms used (e.g., Instagram, Snapchat, Facebook, Twitter, etc.), the frequency of communica-tion (hourly, daily, weekly, etc.), the type and content of messages sent (e.g., photos, videos, etc.), and the target audiences. A core benefit for TNGOs is the potential to reach more people online at lower costs. In addition, they can make claims about having a broader support base by counting an-yone interacting with the organization online.[37] For example, in 2015 the World Widelife Fund (WWF) segmented its email list to identify the most influential Twitter users and targeted them with specific messaging to increase the reach of their campaigns. It also sent targeted text messages to those identified as already effective social influencers.[38]

Digital broadcasting represents a strategy compatible with the existing architecture and traditional organizational models since it only changes the channels used for communicating messages. TNGOs remain intermediaries in resource exchanges and employ staff-led strategies mainly designed to garner media attention and support fundraising. Internally, TNGOs are likely to integrate digital teams into their fundraising and communications departments. Internal digital teams are primarily the recipients of messaging developed in other parts of the organization.

Digital conversing

Digital conversing involves sustained multi-way conversations between TNGO staff and supporters. Staff remain in charge of these conversations, but there is greater emphasis on feeding supporter views into an organization's decision-making processes. The primary purpose is to make organizational boundaries more permeable and to draw supporters closer to the cause. Conversing focuses on regularly soliciting member feedback about campaign topics, strategies, and other issues. There is no explicit focus on expanding membership, but a main emphasis on working more closely with those dedicated to the mission. The purpose is primarily to derive greater value from the existing membership, rather than to transform the organization and its supporters. This strategy requires organizational changes that ensure members' input is adequately captured and transmitted to relevant decision-makers. Digital teams have increased standing and capacity to transmit member views to other parts of the organization. As a result, the action and tactical repertoires of the organization may adapt based on feedback, although the overall mission remains untouched.

Digital analytics

Digital analytics is defined by a culture of listening and regular testing of members' responses to emails, social media, and other digital communications, which subsequently guides organizational strategy. Campaigners prioritize listening to their members' preferences and behavior through digital channels, including emerging topics and interests. For example, digital-based advocacy organizations, such as Avaaz, MoveOn, and SumOfUs, collect data on members' responses to their digital communications, including email open and action rates, Facebook likes, and Twitter retweets. They also test their tactics and messaging to determine campaign strategy and framing. This digital approach is rarely single-issue focused, but more agnostic and seeks to "chase the energy."[39] Supporters drive the campaigns chosen[40] and this type of "analytic activism"[41] requires a large membership base to conduct meaningful tests and to aggregate member preferences. Digital teams and their outputs are central to the organization's decision-making and its core purpose of facilitating successful collective actions such as through donating or signing an online petition. Organizational cultures supporting digital analytics differ significantly from those of the traditional architecture by privileging experimentation and supporter empowerment, and by promoting topics based on supporter interest more so than elite expertise.

Distributed organizing

Distributed organizing is defined by an organization's decision to hand over entire campaigns to supporters by both broadening and deepening participation. The primary purpose of social media and other technologies is not to understand preferences or converse, but to empower and facilitate independent actions.[42] Action repertoires are controlled by supporters whose entrepreneurialism provides direction, even if this generates more disagreements.[43] The theory of change emphasizes the transformation of supporters into leaders in the process of achieving campaign goals. Relying on social media, distributed campaigning facilitates independent and self-promoting actions at a scale that conventional staff-led efforts cannot reach.

Distinct digital practices provide a menu for strategic action. TNGOs may choose to limit digital tools to efforts aimed at expanding immediate fundraising, asking for short-term, staff-defined, and directed action, or collecting information from supporters. Alternatively, digital tools can be used to entirely transform how TNGOs relate to their stakeholders and think about their own role and purpose. TNGOs seeking to transform to a digital facilitation and empowerment role will need to consider whether their organizations are prepared for such a major cultural adjustment, not only in handing over greater control to supporters but also in growing a stronger outcome orientation with a data-driven culture of continuous testing and learning.[44]

Transformative applications of digital technology, especially for supporter-led campaigning, may force significant changes in institutional form relative to the charities of the traditional architecture. Unlike most traditional TNGOs, some leading organizations in digital campaigning are not registered as charitable organizations. For example, Change.org is a for-profit public benefit corporation in the United States[45] and 38 Degrees is a for-profit registered company in the UK. And although special tax benefits are among the most important advantages of the charity model in many countries, a few digital organizations have forgone these benefits in exchange for greater freedom to undertake political activity. For example, Australia's GetUp! sacrificed donation tax-deductibility for greater independence from government[46] and Avaaz in the United States traded it for the freedom to engage in political activism.[47] Meanwhile, in Germany, two prominent campaigning organizations, Attac and Campact, lost their charitable status because their work allegedly violated tax laws prohibiting political activities.[48] The institutional form of the charity described in Chapter 2 is designed to maximize broad-based trustworthiness, necessitating a degree of political neutrality. However, this constitutive feature is often incompatible with the contentious strategies that supporters may demand to achieve social change. In the US context, for example, recent legislative efforts to revise the tax code to allow charities to engage in politics were widely condemned by charities for fear that such a change would critically erode public trust in the sector.[49] While digital strategies like distributed supporter-led campaigning seem to offer significant potential, it is unclear whether TNGOs are culturally and institutionally prepared to adapt. On the one hand, charitable status imbues TNGOs with a degree of automatic legitimacy and trustworthiness, but on the other hand, it also often limits their ability to pursue the more transformative political changes that may be necessary to remain relevant to activists and advance expanding mandates.

BREADTH AND DEPTH OF DIGITAL ENGAGEMENT

Understanding differences in digital practices is a key step toward applying them effectively in advancing organizational goals. Many different objectives may be pursued online, including fundraising, bolstering membership and legitimacy for causes, reducing costs, soliciting fast feedback, and enhancing program effectiveness. Technology has long served as a major boon for activists, either by lowering the costs of connecting with likeminded individuals or by facilitating access to closed and politically unstable regions.[50] In this largely elite-based transnational perspective, individual supporters mostly based in the Global North played a relatively minor role in advocacy campaigns. What is different about digital technologies is their capacity to transform the TNGO itself and how it relates to its key

Table 6.2 DIGITAL PARTICIPATING PATTERNS

		Depth	
		Shallow	*Deep*
Breadth	*Broad*	Inclusive	Transformative
	Narrow	Transactional	Intensive

stakeholders. Rather than serving as an intermediary in transnational networks, the new role of such organizations will be to primarily broaden or deepen civic participation to drive legitimate democratic processes.[51]

The focus on breadth emphasizes who is involved and why some groups are more engaged than others. Issues of diversity and inclusion move to the foreground as organizations consider how their supporter base enables or limits specific social actions. The focus on depth encompasses the level of engagement and commitment, ranging from being a follower or observer to becoming a supporter or advocate and leader. Digital organizations such as Change.org, 38 Degrees, and SumOfUs have demonstrated that they can recruit millions of supporters, far outpacing the memberships of most traditional TNGOs, while many organizations continue to struggle with moving their supporters from low-threshold participation toward greater engagement. Table 6.2 elaborates how moving toward broadening or deepening participation allows organizations to reach specific goals related to inclusivity, intensity, transactionalism, or transformation.

Breadth of participation

A focus on the breadth of participation emphasizes the role of digital communications in reaching disadvantaged audiences. Research focused on this issue points to the success of a number of social and political movements in recent years, including the Arab Spring protests, Occupy Wall Street, and anti-austerity movements in Europe.[52] Similarly, research on electoral campaigns claims that increased democratic engagement has been augmented by the advent of digital tools.[53] Online interactions create a "major reservoir of civic energy"[54] because they can create "a sense of belonging" and collective identity.[55] With the increased professionalization of progressive activism, populist and nativist movements have seen significantly more success in mobilizing aggrieved sections of society to protest and vote in elections.[56] In contrast, many TNGOs have relied for decades on relatively privileged and wealthy supporters and a traditional normative emphasis on shared cultural understandings, stewardship of resources, and trustworthiness.

Digital tools have the potential to lower entry barriers and encourage faster collective responses to events, but socioeconomic status remains a powerful predictor of civic participation, offline and online. There is some evidence that digital tools draw younger and more female audiences, but socioeconomic differences persist in shaping who becomes engaged in the first place.[57] Wealthier sections of society are more likely to develop political interests and pass on educational backgrounds supporting civic participation.[58] In addition to socioeconomic status, age, and gender, TNGOs also have to consider if more supporters actually means greater diversity and inclusion with regard to race, ethnicity, (dis)ability, sexual and gender identity, geographical location, rural versus urban dwelling, and so forth.[59] Except for organizations that focus on issues related to specific identity groups, relatively few mainstream brick-and-mortar TNGOs have invested significantly in strategies and data collection efforts designed to actively track and diversify membership.

Most TNGOs have focused on broadening participation, either because they want to reach new and younger donors or because they want to shed the stigma of being viewed as a Northern-based organization with little support in the Global South. One prominent example of an effort to broaden participation is Greenpeace's incubation of Mobilisation Lab[60] and its Greenwire Digital Initiative. Greenwire was created in 2011 to serve as a platform for supporters to collectively organize without staff leadership.[61] Greenwire supports the creation of online communities around skills, local issues, and campaign topics, and it explicitly encourages members to define their own topics around which to mobilize. Instead of staff-led activism focused on awareness-raising, this initiative emphasizes organizing individuals for independent social action and distributed campaigning.

Some of the broadening of participation is simply an artifact of new technologies generating new forms of social activism embedded in everyday activities. These consumer-related actions lower the entry barrier for some audiences, especially urban and younger audiences.[62] This can help accomplish goals of making TNGOs less professionalized and elite-focused, but it also requires active outreach and capacity-building targeting disadvantaged audiences. A limited investment in this area is likely to draw only the same people the sector has always attracted and to fail to motivate supporters to escalate their commitments. TNGOs face important trade-offs here. If they seriously pursue new audiences and supporters with very different socioeconomic and cultural backgrounds, they may experience greater intra-organizational tensions, lose ground with their existing donor base, and de-stabilize the forms and norms behind their past successes. Commitments to diversity and inclusion represent a major area of expanding TNGO aspirations that remain often unmatched by current practices.

Depth of participation

Adding more and different kinds of supporters using digital tools may be necessary for expanding and rejuvenating the supporter base, for claiming greater popular legitimacy, and for diversifying inputs for the organization. But such membership expansion may or may not translate into deeper engagement, greater civic agency by supporters, and ultimately greater impact. In some cases, focusing only on broadening participation may lead to lower levels of engagement, fostering "slacktivism."[63] Beyond widening participation, TNGOs have to consider how digital media can be used to sustain and increase individual civic engagement.

In the context of digital communications, the deepening of social activism connotes either the conversion from online to offline engagement (e.g., sign the online petition and then participate in street demonstrations) or the escalation of individual commitments and actions in either domain. Such escalation can take the form of shaping messaging (rather than just consuming, liking, or sharing content), donating time, talent, and money, and also spurring others to do the same by taking initiative or exercising leadership to organize others.[64]

There are two main reasons TNGOs would pursue enhanced civic agency as a goal. First, the organization wants to move some of its supporter base toward becoming a core of "champions" invested not only in certain causes, but also in the well-being of the organization. These supporters may donate more regularly, take consistent action and initiative, and recruit new members. Second, enhanced agency also means that dedicated supporters will strengthen the legitimacy of a cause by adding not only numbers, but skill sets. Such crowd campaigning reflects a belief that sustainable social change must rely on the broad empowerment of individuals and enhance their ability to collectively run a campaign without relying on traditional organizational resources.

Social media use can enhance overall participation in civic and political life,[65] but it remains unclear if there is a reliable way of motivating those starting out at low levels of online activity toward sustained and escalating engagement over time. For example, a Chilean study found that heavy social media users were much more likely to participate in street protests or marches.[66] In the case of the 2014 Umbrella Movement protests in Hong Kong, survey research found that social media usage was correlated with deeper commitment and movement leadership.[67] The strongest evidence for a positive correlation emerges from studies focused on youth, likely because they are both intense social media users and less politically active initially.[68] Social media allowed young Indian feminists to organize much more quickly online in response to mass sexual assaults, but it also facilitated increased offline activities such as marches and demonstrations.[69]

While there are many promising examples of how social media increases the quantity and quality of activism, what remains uncertain is who ultimately gets drawn into greater civic participation. Some research suggests that those most active online and offline are already predisposed and would have acted no matter what tools were available to them.[70] Compared to the relatively easy task of lowering thresholds of engagement by creating an online presence, deepening participation requires more extensive strategic investments. For example, the digital organization Change.org began in 2015 to develop tools for petitioners to acquire additional skills, such as how to approach the media and negotiate with decision-makers.[71] Greenpeace's Greenwire also offers specific tools to activists, including an "Online Leader Lab" with training sessions, an "Activist Toolbox," and also technical assistance from national offices. Such efforts are deliberate attempts to move individuals toward different forms of engagement,[72] and assessing their effectiveness requires the challenging task of tracking supporter journeys online and offline.

In sum, there is evidence that digital tools can contribute to a broadening and deepening of civic participation, but it requires significant organizational investments to avoid reinforcing existing participatory inequalities. If TNGOs want to move beyond quantity as a measure of online success, they have to make explicit efforts to empower those with less access and capacity. These insights stand in contrast to the lag in investments with regard to a digital infrastructure. Larger TNGOs may enjoy an advantage here because of the greater availability of resources, but they may still be held back by the omnipresent demands and expectations of legacy forms and norms, including organizational cultures unwilling to cede top-down control. Effective organizations for the future invest in digital expertise at more senior levels, incorporate digital leaders in designing and executing campaigns, and distribute digital responsibilities throughout the organization.[73] To effectively promote deeper engagement, digital teams need to be thoroughly integrated into organizational strategy and decision-making or even "dissolved" into the overall organization to fully embed digital into virtually all organizational functions.

Even when organizations are successful at broadening and deepening supporter engagement, they face choices about how much control over campaign development they ultimately want to yield to supporters and how they think about linking online activism to traditional policy arenas dominated by elite decision-makers. If an organization sees itself primarily as a facilitator and no longer as the "hero of the story,"[74] then organizational strategies will emphasize not only reaching an ever-increasing number of supporters, but also enhancing the agency of those individuals. Offering digital opportunities is a good start, but building civic agency is a goal that many TNGOs have historically tended to neglect in favor of staff-led and elite-focused campaigning.

Although digitization raises the possibility of disintermediation and the fading out of the brick-and-mortar organization, early experiences with digital organizing reaffirm the importance of organizational capacities and strategies.[75] Fully realizing the potential of digital activism requires formal organizations with specialized skills, resources, and connections to empower disadvantaged sections of society and convert online petitions into policy wins. Organizing requires leadership development among supporters who have shown a commitment to increasing their engagement so that they can mobilize wider circles. Cross-fertilization between online and offline activism remains critical, and expert-driven, elite forms of "inside activism" will continue to be necessary supplements to secure victories with legislators and policymakers.

MEASURING DIGITAL IMPACT

Evaluating the success of digital strategies is a central task for their successful adoption and diffusion. Many digital organizations pride themselves on what they perceive as having a stronger evidence-based, data-driven decision-making culture than traditional TNGOs, especially a culture of testing.[76] In this regard, they mirror the Silicon Valley start-up culture of innovative tech companies that make similar claims about their data-driven cultures as compared to traditional companies. Digital campaigning makes some measurement easier, but also poses risks that organizations chase superficial "vanity metrics," such as numbers of clicks or likes, rather than pursuing deeper engagement goals. Like traditional measures of "reach" or "outputs" in traditional TNGO evaluation reports, vanity metrics are often short-term and myopic and can lead to problematic impressions and decisions. Focusing on output or supporter numbers can create the wrong incentives for staff.

More advanced online engagement efforts emphasize matching content to different platforms, getting supporters to tell their stories (distributed campaigning), and using the digital realm to constantly solicit meaningful feedback (digital conversing).[77] While the traditional advocacy model privileges methods of broadcasting and one-way communications, new generations of digital natives are skeptical of self-serving promotional activities, seek authenticity, and want to engage at various levels of action. Engaging with supporters online is an important way of moving beyond mere transactional relationships.

Ultimately, however, the use of any metrics is only as good as what gets considered in actual decision-making. Changing an organizational culture so that metrics are regularly discussed is among the most important shifts an organization can undertake in this new environment.[78] This "culture of testing" emphasizes experimentation, data analytics, and frequent and rapid change and adaptation.[79] Among traditional TNGOs, especially mid- to large-sized organizations, the aspiration toward evidence-based decision-making is becoming more popular, and some organizations are consciously working toward such a practice—strategically, procedurally, and culturally—but this is still a nascent movement. Cultural belief systems that prize virtuous intentions and efforts often at the expense of rigorous, data-driven decision-making, still pervade the normative component of the architecture in which TNGOs operate. Efforts to change culturally can take TNGOs a long way toward bringing their practices in line with their expanding mandates and promises, but it will be difficult for individual organizations to challenge traditional ways of thinking and working that may be deeply ingrained.

CONCLUSION

While digital tools are widely adopted among TNGOs, the willingness of staff and leaders to embrace the digital age varies widely across the sector. Generational change will help, but current digital expertise among senior leadership remains limited, which creates major gaps between how TNGOs think about digital opportunities and the expectations of millennial and younger stakeholders. This may remain a source of internal conflict within TNGOs whose traditional ways of operating highlight research, mobilization, and actions driven by elite staff. Those working inside of TNGOs today may worry whether their professional expertise, willingness to sacrifice salary, and engage in risk-taking will still be valued in digitally native organizations. Moreover, in TNGO campaigns individual staff may strongly identify with, and be strongly motivated by, the cause, and individual leaders may remain skeptical of handing control over to outsiders. In a supporter-driven approach, such motivations and drives may be counterproductive as staff need to be a lot more sensitive to cues from membership and the public to focus on enablement and empowerment.

To remain relevant advocates in the future, TNGOs will need to move beyond the conventional broadcasting and staff-led models of online engagement. Listening to and empowering supporters can help to build the democratic legitimacy that TNGOs need by enhancing listening and responsiveness. At the same time, any effort to develop a digital presence is not necessarily transformative on its own and requires an awareness of potential risks. The significance of technological change is shaped by adoption patterns and the way that organizations elect to become digital actors. As with traditional interventions and campaigns, measures of breadth—whether in terms of reach or output numbers or click or like numbers—do not automatically translate into sustainable social or political change. Moreover, sustained local level credibility, relationships, and social capital will remain essential for achieving long-term impact for many organizations, which digital platforms cannot easily provide. In addition, activists will continue to face disinformation and other negative online developments,[80] highlighting the need for developing capabilities for dealing with such threats.

To accomplish the task of organizationally enabled activism across multiple platforms and venues, TNGOs have to develop not only greater capacities to collect data, but also abilities to analyze and learn from such data in a timely fashion. They also have to invest in data security, whether it concerns data about primary stakeholders or communications between other supporters. TNGO websites are also becoming more regularly the target of distributed denial-of-service attacks by hackers.[81] In addition, TNGOs are increasingly a target for malware, phishing, botnets, and other forms of attacks. As TNGOs increasingly commit to receiving feedback and listening to stakeholders, the data cannot simply remain unused either because there is no processing capacity or because strategic planning and theories of change have not been updated to reflect a digital shift.

Improving digital capabilities in the pursuit of sustainable impact will require significant investments in skill sets, infrastructure, and processes. However, these investments will not resemble conventional expenditures on traditional charitable activities and outputs related to immediate aid provision. Although norms may be changing across many parts of the sector, the legacy architecture still prefers organizations that look and behave more like charities. Adapting to a digital future may mean pushing the boundaries of what donors, regulators, and other key stakeholders are ready to accept. For example, TNGOs will have to find funding for costly "tech stacks" (software subscriptions) that may look more like overhead than program expenditures, while also avoiding crossing regulatory lines, such as political restrictions that circumscribe appropriate behavior for charitable organizations.

For some TNGOs, digitization may ultimately be about how they think about and respond to the existential threat of disintermediation. The significance of this threat depends on the value proposition that TNGOs embrace for the future. If they conform to the architecture and operate essentially as pass-through conduits for donations from the Global North to the Global South, then they will face greater difficulty competing with digital organizations that can reach "recipients" around the world much more efficiently. But if TNGOs can leverage digital affordances to make the transformation into conveners and facilitators of authentic supporter-led activism, and if they can demonstrate credible evidence of their impact, then they will still have a viable future role to play. However, to realize this digital future the sector's forms and norms will need to adapt.

REFERENCES

Achieve. *The 2016 Millennial Impact Report: Cause Engagement Following an Election Year.* Washington, DC: Case Foundation, 2016.

Bakardjieva, Maria. "Subactivism: Lifeworld and Politics in the Age of the Internet." *The Information Society* 25, no. 2 (2009): 91–104.

Ballart, Xavier, and Guillem Rico. "Public or Nonprofit?: Career Preferences and Dimensions of Public Service Motivation." *Public Administration* 96, no. 2 (2018): 404–20. https://doi.org/doi:10.1111/padm.12403.

Bennett, W. Lance, and Alexandra Segerberg. *The Logic of Connective Action: Digital Media and the Personalization of Contentious Politics.* New York: Cambridge University Press, 2013.

Bernholz, Lucy, and Lyndon Ormond-Parker. "The Ethics of Designing Digital Infrastructure." *Stanford Social Innovation Review* 16, no. 3 (2018): 34–39.

Bond, Becky, and Zach Exely. *Rules for Revolutionaries: How Big Organizing Can Change Everything.* White River Junction, VT: Chelsea Green Publishing, 2016.

Boulianne, Shelley. "Social Media Use and Participation: A Meta-Analysis of Current Research." *Information, Communication, & Society* 18, no. 5 (2015): 524–38.

Brandzel, Ben. *The 8-Fold Path of New Organizing: DNA-Level Operating Principles for Building a Progressive People's Movement in the 21st Century.* Unpub. manuscript on hand with authors: n.d.

Chadwick, Andrew. *The Hybrid Media System: Politics and Power.* New York: Oxford University Press, 2013.

Chadwick, Andrew, and James Dennis. "Social Media, Professional Media, and Mobilisation in Contemporary Britain: Explaining the Strengths and Weaknesses of the Citizens' Movement 38 Degrees." *Political Studies* 65, no. 1 (2017): 42–60. https://doi.org/10.1177/0032321716631350.

Chadwick, Andrew, and Jennifer Stromer-Galley. "Digital Media, Power, and Democracy in Parties and Election Campaigns: Party Decline or Party Renewal?" *The International Journal of Press/Politics* 21, no. 3 (2016): 283–93. https://doi.org/10.1177/1940161216646731.

"Charitable Status of Not-for-Profits under Threat in Germany." Nexus News Agency. Updated April 5, 2019. http://www.nna-news.org/news/article/?tx_ttnews%5Btt_news%5D=2747&cHash=99b6f54447971ea00def1acb6303ad5a.

Cole, Teju. "The White-Savior Industrial Complex." *The Atlantic* (March 21, 2012).

Czerski, Piotr. "We, the Web Kids (Trans. M. Szreder)." *The Atlantic* (February 21, 2012).

Dichter, Sasha, Tom Adams, and Alnoor Ebrahim. "The Power of Lean Data." *Stanford Social Innovation Review* (Winter 2016): 36–41.

Editors. "Losing the Johnson Amendment Would Destroy the Unique Political Role of Nonprofits." *Nonprofit Quarterly* (February 6, 2017). https://nonprofitquarterly.org/2017/02/06/losing-johnson-amendment-destroy-unique-political-role-nonprofits/.

"Facebook's Digital Currency Libra: Why Nonprofits Are Joining." DevEx, Updated June 24, 2019. https://www.devex.com/news/facebook-s-digital-currency-libra-why-nonprofits-are-joining-95142.

Feldmann, Derrick. *A Generation for Causes. A Four-Year Summary of the Millennial Impact Report*. Indianapolis: Achieve/Case Foundation, 2014.

Fraussen, Bert, and Darren Halpin. "How Do Interest Groups Legitimate Their Policy Advocacy? Reconsidering Linkage and Internal Democracy in Times of Digital Disruption." *Public Administration* 96, no. 1 (2018): 23–35. https://onlinelibrary.wiley.com/doi/abs/10.1111/padm.12364.

"GIS for SDGs: 'See Things That Were Impossible to See,' Esri Founder Says." DevEx, Updated July 12, 2019. https://www.devex.com/news/gis-for-sdgs-see-things-that-were-impossible-to-see-esri-founder-says-95255.

Hale, Sadie, and Erin Niimi Longhurst. *Make It Social: Tips & Tricks for #Socialmedia Success*. London: Social Misfits Media, 2019.

Hall, Nina, and Phil Ireland. "Transforming Activism: Digital Era Advocacy Organizations." *Stanford Social Innovation Review* (July 6, 2016). https://ssir.org/articles/entry/transforming_activism_digital_era_advocacy_organizations.

Hall, Nina, Hans Peter Schmitz, and J. Michael Dedmon. "Transnational Advocacy and NGOs in the Digital Era: New Forms of Networked Power." *International Studies Quarterly* (2019). https://doi.org/10.1093/isq/sqz052.

Heaven, Sally. "How World Wildlife Fund Used Segmentation to Activate Social Influencers for Their Cause." *npEngage* (March 10, 2017). https://npengage.com/advocacy/how-world-wildlife-fund-used-segmentation-to-activate-social-influencers-for-their-cause/.

Heimans, Jeremy, and Henry Timms. *New Power: How Power Works in Our Hyperconnected World*. New York: Doubleday, 2018.

Hernandez, Kevin, and Tony Roberts. *Leaving No One Behind in a Digital World*. K4d Emerging Issues Report. Brighton: Institute of Development Studies, 2018.

Hestres, Luis E. "Climate Change Advocacy Online: Theories of Change, Target Audiences, and Online Strategy." *Environmental Politics* 24, no. 2 (2015): 193–211.

InterAction. *Supporting Your NGO Future: US NGO Executive Thoughts on the Future*. Washington, DC: InterAction, 2019.

Jacob, Frank. "The Role of M-Pesa in Kenya's Economic and Political Development." In *Kenya after 50: Reconfiguring Education, Gender, and Policy*, edited by Mickie Mwanzia

Koster, Michael Mwenda Kithinji, and Jerono P. Rotich, 89–100. New York: Palgrave Macmillan, 2016.

Karpf, David. *Analytic Activism: Digital Listening and the New Political Strategy.* New York: Oxford University Press, 2016.

Kaurin, Dragana. "Why Libra Needs a Humanitarian Fig Leaf." *Medium* (July 8, 2019). https://medium.com/berkman-klein-center/why-libra-needs-a-humanitarian-fig-leaf-79ae6a463c8.

Keck, Margaret E., and Kathryn Sikkink. *Activists beyond Borders: Advocacy Networks in International Politics.* Ithaca, NY: Cornell University Press, 1998.

Kohavi, Ron, and Stefan Thomke. "The Surprising Power of Online Experiments." *Harvard Business Review* 95, no. 5 (2017): 74–82.

Lee, Francis, and Joseph Man Chan. "Digital Media Activities and Mode of Participation in a Protest Campaign: A Study of the Umbrella Movement." *Information, Communication, & Society* 19, no. 1 (2016): 4–22.

Light, Jennifer S. "Putting Our Conversation in Context: Youth, Old Media, and Political Participation 1800–1971." In *From Voice to Influence: Understanding Citizenship in a Digital Age*, edited by Jennifer S. Light and Danielle Allen, 19–34. Chicago: University of Chicago Press, 2015.

Livingston, Steven, and Gregor Walter-Drop, eds. *Bits and Atoms: Information and Communication Technology in Areas of Limited Statehood.* New York: Oxford University Press, 2014.

Loader, Brian D., and Dan Mercea. "Networking Democracy?: Social Media Innovations and Participatory Politics." *Information, Communication, & Society* 14, no. 6 (2011): 757–69.

Marin, Milena. "Amnesty International on Small Tasks, Big Data, and Massive Engagement." *Exposing the Invisible* (January 23, 2017). Accessed January 23. https://exposingtheinvisible.org/resources/micro-tasking-amnesty-international.

Mascheroni, Giovanna. "Performing Citizenship Online: Identity, Subactivism, and Participation." *Observatorio* 7, no. 3 (2013): 93–119.

McAdam, Doug. *Political Process and the Development of Black Insurgency, 1930–1970.* 2nd ed. Chicago: University of Chicago Press, 1999.

McCambridge, Ruth. "National Council of Nonprofits Launches Coalition Campaign to Oppose Repeal of Johnson Amendment." *Nonprofit Quarterly* (March 2, 2017). https://nonprofitquarterly.org/2017/03/02/national-coalition-nonprofits-launches-campaign-oppose-repeal-johnson-amendment/.

Meier, Patrick. *Digital Humanitarians: How Big Data Is Changing the Face of Humanitarian Response.* London: Routledge, 2015.

Micó, Josep-Lluis, and Andreu Casero-Ripollés. "Political Activism Online: Organization and Media Relations in the Case of 15m in Spain." *Information, Communication, & Society* 17, no. 7 (2014): 858–71.

MobLab. The Anatomy of People-Powered Campaigns. Mobilisaiton Lab (n.d.). https://mobilisationlab.org/resources/the-anatomy-of-people-powered-campaigns/.

Mogus, Jason, and Austen Levihn-Coon. "What Makes Nonprofit Digital Teams Successful Today?" *Stanford Social Innovation Review* (February 6, 2018). https://ssir.org/articles/entry/what_makes_nonprofit_digital_teams_successful_today.

Morozov, Evgeny. "Why Social Movements Should Ignore Social Media." *New Republic* (February 5, 2013).

Oh, Sarah, and Travis L. Adkins. *Disinformation Toolkit.* Washington, DC: InterAction, 2018.

Oser, Jennifer, Marc Hooghe, and Sofie Marien. "Is Online Participation Distinct from Offline Participation? A Latent Class Analysis of Participation Types and Their Stratification." *Political Research Quarterly* 66, no. 1 (2013): 91–101. https://doi.org/10.1177/1065912912436695.

Penney, Joel. "Social Media and Symbolic Action: Exploring Participation in the Facebook Red Equal Sign Profile Picture Campaign." *Journal of Computer-Mediated Communication* 20, no. 1 (2015): 52–66.

Ruesga, G. Albert, and Barry Knight. "The View from the Heights of Arnstein's Ladder: Resident Engagement by Community Foundations." *National Civic Review* 102, no. 3 (2013): 13–16.

Saratovsky, Kari Dunn, and Derrick Feldmann. *Cause for Change: The Why and How of Nonprofit Millennial Engagement.* San Francisco: Jossey-Bass, 2013.

Schlozman, Kay Lehman, Sidney Verba, and Henry E. Brady. "Weapon of the Strong?: Participatory Inequality and the Internet." *Perspectives on Politics* 8, no. 2 (2010): 487–509.

Schroeder, Ralph. *Social Theory after the Internet. Media, Technology, and Globalization.* London: UCL Press, 2018.

Selander, Lisen, and Sirkka Jarvenpaa. "Digital Action Repertories and Transforming a Social Movement Organization." *Management Information Systems Quarterly* 40, no. 2 (2016): 331–52.

Silberman, Michael. "What Advocacy Organizations Need to Win Today." *MobLab* (March 28, 2019). https://mobilisationlab.org/stories/what-advocacy-organisations-need-to-win-today/.

Silberman, Michael, and Jackie Mahendra. "Moving beyond Vanity Metrics." *Stanford Social Innovation Review* (2015).

Sloam, James. "'The Outraged Young': Young Europeans, Civic Engagement, and the New Media in a Time of Crisis." *Information, Communication, & Society* 17, no. 2 (2014): 217–31.

Titus, Divya. "Social Media as a Gateway for Young Feminists: Lessons from the #Iwillgoout Campaign in India." *Gender & Development* 26, no. 2 (2018): 231–48. https://doi.org/10.1080/13552074.2018.1473224.

Valenzuela, Sebastián. "Unpacking the Use of Social Media for Protest Behavior: The Roles of Information, Opinion Expression, and Activism." *American Behavioral Scientist* 57, no. 7 (2013): 920–42.

Vissers, Sara, and Dietlind Stolle. "The Internet and New Modes of Political Participation: Online Versus Offline Participation." *Information, Communication, & Society* 17, no. 8 (2014): 937–55.

"Want to Fund the Resistance? Test Everything. How Greenpeace UK Went on a Mission to Test Everything and What They Learned about Process, Culture (and Engagement) along the Way." MobLab. Updated May 22, 2017. https://mobilisationlab.org/stories/want-to-fund-the-resistance-test-everything-fast/.

Wicks, Robert H., Jan LeBlanc Wicks, Shauna A. Morimoto, Angie Maxwell, and Stephanie Ricker Schulte. "Correlates of Political and Civic Engagement among Youth during the 2012 Presidential Campaign." *American Behavioral Scientist* 58, no. 5 (2014): 622–44. https://doi.org/10.1177/0002764213515226.

Word, Jessica, and Heather Carpenter. "The New Public Service?: Applying the Public Service Motivation Model to Nonprofit Employees." *Public Personnel Management* 42, no. 3 (2013): 315–36. https://doi.org/10.1177/0091026013495773.

Yanacopulos, Helen. *International NGO Engagement, Advocacy, Activism: The Faces and Spaces of Change.* Basingstoke: Palgrave Macmillan, 2015.

CHAPTER 7
Measurement

In 2006, the Center for Global Development released a report lamenting the absence of credible evidence about the impact of fifty years of international development interventions by TNGOs and other actors.[1] Following the study, the International Initiative for Impact Evaluation (3ie) was established to support rigorous impact evaluations by TNGOs and to disseminate knowledge about evaluation methodology and intervention effectiveness.[2] Despite mounting evidence that quality measurement and evaluation is associated with better programs, continued underinvestment in such capacities still pervades the development sector.[3]

Many TNGOs have attempted to address their own evaluation gaps internally by improving their monitoring, evaluation, accountability, and learning (MEAL) systems and even by introducing "agency-level" measurement systems to collect and aggregate data at the organizational level. Although most of these initiatives are distinct from scientific research that attempts to determine the effectiveness of specific intervention strategies (i.e., through the use of experimental and quasi-experimental methods), they nevertheless represent a major development for organizations that have historically underinvested in measurement and evaluation systems. Through systematic MEAL processes, TNGOs can better hold themselves accountable for serving their missions and achieving their goals. If successful, these organizations will not only become more effective through enhanced learning and accountability but will also be able to more credibly demonstrate their effectiveness, bolstering their legitimacy and relevance.

Enhanced MEAL is also a central capacity for moving beyond the traditional legitimacy model prioritizing upward financial accountability and financial stewardship. However, absent new mechanisms for legitimating TNGO actions through MEAL,[4] legacy accountability systems will remain in place. The architecture's problematic surveillance regime (see Chapter 2) cannot be reoriented from overhead to outcomes until TNGOs start producing better outcome data. However, many TNGOs struggle to do so, perhaps fittingly, because of the obstacles posed by the sector's own norms. Investing in MEAL is difficult within an architecture that tends to construe MEAL activities as diversions from the mission and MEAL costs as wasteful overhead. Nevertheless, TNGOs will have to break the cycle if they are to transform from a sector forced to minimize overhead to one empowered to maximize sustainable impact.

MEASUREMENT FRAMES

Over the past decade, measurement and evaluation activities in the TNGO sector have become increasingly sophisticated, but progress remains limited and has yet to amount to a sector-wide transformation. The change is also primarily concentrated in mid- to large-sized TNGOs, not surprisingly, although some smaller TNGOs have also made significant progress.

Measurement and evaluation assumes many forms across the TNGO sector, including qualitative observations, participatory assessments, counting, and formal impact evaluations. Some TNGOs adopt an "effectiveness frame" that focuses on evaluating whether programs achieved their intended goals, usually in terms of whether programs were implemented as planned or produced their intended outputs. Relatively few TNGOs systematically employ an "impact frame" that attempts to establish causal attribution, although this approach is sometimes adopted as a form of applied research.[5] In practice, terms such as effectiveness, impact, outcomes, reach, and so forth tend to be used very informally and interchangeably, complicating greater sectoral alignment about measurement and evaluation. Within many TNGOs, leaders and board members may be more likely to embrace the impact frame, usually at the level of the whole organization. They typically want to know "what works" across broad categories of programs so that they can make high-level strategic decisions about resource allocations.

Leaders and board members are typically not experts in the details of impact evaluation, however, and may be frustrated when they are told that impact is hard to measure, that establishing causal attribution is prohibitively complicated, or that highly technical methodological issues need to be considered before reports can be produced or reviewed. Staff, usually more consumed with details at the program and project levels, are often highly averse to the impact frame. For staff, use of the impact frame may imply the application of certain technical standards that they may not have the resources, capabilities, or inclination to meet. Staff may also consider such standards as creating accountability expectations for results that they may feel are beyond their control. Staff instead may prefer the effectiveness frame that focuses on determining whether program activities were carried out as planned, as well as on relatively more tractable data-gathering efforts that do not purport to scientifically measure causal effects (e.g., compiling output and reach numbers, monitoring outcomes not causally attributable to programs).[6]

The result is that within many TNGOs there is a gap between the impact-oriented, public-facing discourse promoted by leadership and through fundraising channels, on the one hand, and organizations' technical abilities to substantiate that rhetoric with credible evidence, on the other hand. Exacerbating this disconnect is a tendency for many stakeholders to exhibit confirmation bias, interpreting even ambiguous or contradictory performance information as evidence of success.[7] Moreover, a belief that TNGOs can do no harm because their intentions are good, combined with often weak outcome orientations, can blind stakeholders to the truth that impact is frequently more complex and elusive than they want to believe. Even if credible measurement and evaluation does take place, "publication bias" often leads to profusions of success stories while negative results rarely see the light of day.

Overall, research reveals that the state of the art of measurement and evaluation practice across the TNGO sector lags substantially behind the expanding mandates and claims of bringing about sustainable impact. For example, research on US nonprofits (including TNGOs) shows that outcomes and impacts are the least often measured logic model components, and the strongest evaluation designs are the least often used.[8] Overwhelmingly, the most commonly employed evaluation design is one that collects data only on program participants and only after the conclusion of the program.[9] This type of "single group, post only" design is incapable of credibly measuring program impact because it lacks a counterfactual condition.[10] The credibility of the counterfactual scenario is largely what determines the validity of an evaluation's conclusions, although there is significant skepticism toward counterfactual analysis among measurement and evaluation specialists throughout the TNGO sector—particularly in areas such as long-term public education and advocacy, conscientization, mobilization, and policy research.

The challenges and controversies around impact measurement have only grown as TNGOs have adopted increasingly complex theories of change, particularly those aimed at fundamental societal transformations. Formal impact evaluation methods for statistically estimating average treatment effects are less relevant and applicable to evaluating the kinds of transformational advocacy campaigns that many TNGOs have embraced. The adoption of more transformational agendas, especially in the context of highly unstable and unpredictable operating environments, only exacerbates existing measurement and evaluation challenges. Recognition of the growing difficulties and complexities involved has spawned a variety of alternative evaluative frameworks involving process tracing, contribution analysis, case studies, the general elimination method, episode study, qualitative comparative anaylsis,[11] outcome mapping[12] and harvesting,[13] and "fitness for purpose"[14] assessments, among others. Many of these alternative approaches reject the possibility of simple answers (or sometimes even of measurement itself[15]), often citing the complexity of social change. However, at the same time TNGOs may run the risk of using, or being seen to use, "complexity" as a "fuzzword" to deflect criticism or justify absent or ambiguous evidence. Skeptical external stakeholders may easily mistake claims that impact is too hard to assess as more evidence of a failing model of social change. Undertaking and evaluating transformational change is indeed extremely complex, and the sector has to continue to develop—and use—methodological and evidentiary practices and standards that are appropriate to their expanded ambitions.[16]

Taking on the measurement challenge is complicated by the many obstacles that TNGOs confront both internally and externally. TNGOs operate in an environment full of adversities and disincentives against systematic measurement and evaluation, even while they simultaneously face mounting expectations to provide more and better evidence of results.

OBSTACLES TO MEASUREMENT AND EVALUATION

Decades of research and experiential learning point to reasons why organizations might underperform and underinvest in the area of measurement and evaluation.[17] Generally, obstacles to evaluation include insufficient time and money,[18] low prioritization,[19] lack of funder interest,[20] inconsistent funder requirements, differences in the informational needs of funders and organizations, evaluation being seen as an indirect cost,[21] fear, avoidance,[22] inadequate interest,[23] inadequate knowledge or expertise,[24] technical challenges (including difficulties operationalizing variables and acquiring and using computer software),[25] and general complexity.[26] Funders acknowledge lack of resources and inadequate technical capacity as the main obstacles to evaluation,[27] although some research suggests that challenges related to data collection, data quality, expertise, technology, prioritization, and time may be more significant than resource availability.[28]

Nevertheless, funding obviously matters a great deal. For example, in a survey of 41,000 grantees and 284 foundations, the Center for Effective Philanthropy found that less than 10 percent of grantees reported receiving any dedicated assistance for performance measurement:

> It's not just that funders don't generally step up to support nonprofits with needed financial and non-financial support to build performance management systems. It's that many continue to focus on administrative cost ratios and impose arbitrary limits on "overhead," which is often ill-defined, in ways that actually create a disincentive for nonprofits to do this kind of work.[29]

On the other hand, evaluations mandated by funders may produce a "need to respond to funder-defined measures" that "may divert resources from reporting performance data that are relevant to decision making within the organization."[30] Moreover, funder-defined measures may also make it difficult for TNGOs to prioritize measures that primary stakeholders consider to be more relevant, inhibiting constituency voice. Indeed, many TNGOs consider monitoring and evaluation to be an "extractive industry" that serves external needs without contributing to program success.[31] TNGOs may see funder reporting requirements as a means of ensuring compliance and asserting control, which can lead to ceremonial and symbolic practices instead of producing meaningful and useful evidence for learning and improvement.[32] TNGO practitioners may understandably come to regard evaluation as a useless bureaucratic burden imposed by outsiders rather than an essential tool necessary for mission success.

Measurement and evaluation may also risk unintended consequences, especially in diverting organizations from a long-term focus on sustainable impact to a short-term focus on easily measurable outputs.[33] Moreover, measurement and evaluation is often criticized for promoting technocracy and managerialism and ignoring context and politics[34] despite the inherently political and subjective nature of measurement and evaluation.[35]

Empirically, high-quality evaluations are more likely to be done when those in charge are confident that they will reveal success, when they are required internally, or when they are valued by the organizational culture. Organizations that are larger, that have larger staff payrolls, and that internally require evaluation are more likely to have organizational cultures that are supportive of evaluation. Through this mechanism of organizational culture, these organizations are able to conduct more frequent and better-quality evaluations.[36]

Probably the most interesting finding in this body of research is that the most significant contributor to quality monitoring and evaluation is actually not time or money, but an organizational culture supportive of open-ended inquiry. This includes (1) a culture that values evaluation, (2) a genuine desire to understand or improve program effectiveness, and (3) internal evaluation requirements.[37] What these factors suggest is that rigorous evaluation is most likely to be meaningful and useful when it is internalized, rather than being an externally imposed requirement.

A wealth of advice and lessons-learned is available for TNGOs that wish to improve their measurement and evaluation practices[38] and systems for "outcome accounting."[39] Among the most ambitious initiatives TNGOs have tried are attempts to measure results at the organizational or agency level. TNGOs experiences in agency-level measurement offer lessons-learned about the factors that promote or inhibit the development of stronger evaluation practices.

AGENCY-LEVEL MEASUREMENT

A number of mid- to large-sized TNGOs in the past decade have committed to undertaking measurement and evaluation at the organizational level, through so-called agency-level measurement.[40] This is both technically and methodologically very demanding and typically requires significant organizational change to initiate. TNGOs have had varying levels of success in designing and implementing agency-level measurement systems, and a number of US-registered TNGOs have documented and shared their experiences. These experiences can inform future efforts to close the evaluation gap and help TNGOs meet greater demands for results-based accountability and legitimacy. Although the lessons-learned are primarily based on the experiences of TNGOs in the development subsector, campaigning organizations can also apply many of the same insights to address some of their complex evaluation challenges. Table 7.1 summarizes the key issues to consider when planning the adoption of agency-level measurement systems.

Investing in agency-level measurement systems

TNGOs increasingly experience both internal and external pressures to ratchet up their measurement systems to the agency level, even as this represents a significant challenge for many organizations that still struggle with measurement at the project and program levels. Internal pressures to demonstrate

Table 7.1 LESSONS-LEARNED ABOUT AGENCY-LEVEL MEASUREMENT

Consideration	Lesson-learned
Organizational structure	Organizational level measurement systems are even more complex and resource-intensive to set up in decentralized TNGOs where decision-making depends on reaching consensus among many different parts of the organization.
Organizational change	If there is a clear vision for the direction and process of change, setting up an agency-level measurement system can reinforce that vision. However, the overall set of changes may also tax the agency too heavily to be absorbed.
Sequencing	Because a new agency-level strategy may take several years to implement, a gradual approach to building a system, starting with the collection of basic project data, then sectoral data, and later strategy-level indicators, may be preferable to a more rapid rollout.
Expectations	Developing an agency-level measurement system often takes more time, funding, and skills than anticipated. The necessary capacity-building investment that first may be required to raise the standards of data collection may cause a significant time lag before results materialize.
Staffing	Organizations need to dedicate sufficient numbers of skilled measurement and evaluation staff to build and maintain a useful system. Organizations must have the capacity to collect, analyze, synthesize, and present data in meaningful ways.
Usability	User-friendly data platforms enable staff across the organization to store, access, and analyze data easily and allow them to use data for their own purposes. The human interaction around the platform may be more important than the platform itself.
Buy-in	Agency-level measurement systems may not respond well to country program needs, harming field staff buy-in. However, measures can be selected to benefit field staff, and field staff can use the opportunity to build new skill sets that directly support their own work in addition to the system.

agency-level results typically come from boards, leadership, and staff. Boards and senior leadership teams often request data to enable them to form an overall picture of organizational results, as through dashboards, for example. For some board members, the ability to produce dashboards provides symbolic evidence of an organization's sophistication. Demonstrating and marketing organizational reach numbers and results is also considered to be good practice for public relations, communications, and fundraising. Given signs of lessening public trust and confidence in TNGOs (see Chapter 1), there is ample reason for organizations to invest in measurement and evaluation.

Internally, too, leaders and staff desire to know what their organizations are accomplishing, at a very minimum in terms of how many people are reached, and through what types of activities. Moreover, leaders and staff increasingly want to be able to gauge progress against organizational goals to assess their theories of action or change. A few are as ambitious as wanting to measure progress toward overarching mission achievement. Finally, from an internal organizational perspective, agency-level measurement can help break down organizational silos, and especially in the case of larger (con)federated TNGOs, support efforts to unify national sections.

Of course, external pressures often first prompt TNGOs to attempt to develop agency-level measurement systems. Symbolically, some TNGOs also believe that sharing agency-wide results data related to presence, reach, and activities signals transparency. Some also assume that by providing agency-level results data and by showing the reach of TNGO programs, organizations can enhance their legitimacy, especially in the eyes of government stakeholders. Demonstrations of agency-level results are often key to successful advocacy to influence government policy and practice, especially if the goal is to scale up or hand over programs.[41]

The perceived purposes of agency-level measurement vary according to stakeholders' profiles. High-level decision-makers want aggregated data that help them make executive decisions for strategic adaptation and resource allocation (although whether they get what they expect is less evident). Program- and technical-level staff want more specific data that can inform program decision-making (and they are more sensitive to data system reporting burdens). Marketing and communications staff want data that help position the organization favorably within a crowded marketplace.

Expectations about what it takes to build and maintain agency-level measurement systems are often greatly underestimated. This includes the time, funding, expertise, and ongoing technical assistance, project, and change management capacities, and the capacities for data collection, analysis, and synthesis. Change management capacities are often especially overlooked. The success of agency-level measurement also appears to critically depend on not just having an organizational culture that values data and evidence, but also staff focused on the interest of the broader organization, not just the interest of a specific project, sector, or country.

One common experience for TNGOs is that once agency-level measurement data are generated, there will be strong internal organizational pressures to use the data for marketing, communications, and fundraising purposes. This may have the effect of influencing the kinds of data that are collected in the first place by introducing biases that favor positive evidence. Data generated for internal organizational learning may or may not be desirable for external marketing and may carry reputational risks. Also, such a pressure to produce data suitable for marketing purposes may be in tension with what senior leadership desires for internal decision-making. Very few agency-level measurement systems manage to produce data that are both specific enough for program managers and technical staff while also being useful for executive leadership and for marketing and fundraising staff.

Approaches to agency-level measurement systems

Agency-level measurement systems can be implemented top-down or bottom-up. With top-down approaches, TNGOs start by identifying organizational-level measures that are generally aligned with their strategic plans or with themes present in their organizational missions. Next, they ask different parts of the organization to track indicators associated as closely as possible with those measures. Alternatively, they can make use of existing internal indicators that relate to their overarching measurement constructs. Some TNGOs choose to conduct meta-evaluations, thematic evaluations, or focused impact evaluations on themes of interest at the organizational level.

A bottom-up approach starts with existing systems and aggregates country program-level data to the organizational level. It may rely on existing project indicators that have already been standardized or that can be standardized, and that are already measured across country programs. The approach could also sample from project, program, thematic, or sector evaluations to develop evidence of the reach or impact of the organization.

In both top-down and bottom-up systems, the aggregated data provide a sense of breadth, while the individual evaluations that the system comprises provide context and depth. Both have their benefits and challenges. Top-down systems reflect organizational priorities (reflected in missions and high-level strategies) and tend to put significant additional burdens on country program-level staff. Unless the organization-level and country program-level strategies are closely aligned, the latter may not be able to relate to the information collection demands inherent in agency-level measurement and thus may lack motivation to collect high-quality data. Bottom-up systems put less demand on country program-level staff, but aggregating data in a way that takes context into consideration and uses meaningful measures can be challenging. Different country offices do not necessarily report on the same indicators, and the quality of program evaluations can vary significantly across countries. Bottom-up systems also tend to generate a large number of indicators (in some cases many hundreds), which can place extraordinary demands on analysis and synthesis.

In the early days of agency-level measurement, most systems ended up focusing on outputs rather than outcomes or impacts. Outputs, after all, are easier to measure and standardize and impose fewer additional demands on country offices. But output measures may not be sufficiently linked to outcomes and impact. Unless evidence has established that the outputs are clearly linked to specific outcomes or impacts, aggregated output level data can be vague and not especially meaningful. Many agency-level measurement initiatives have included a hybrid of standardized indicators combined with qualitative data to provide context. After all, indicators provide only part of the story and must be augmented by additional evaluation data that provide depth, rigor, and context. This can be provided through meta-evaluations, systematic reviews, and impact evaluations.

Some TNGOs have explicitly chosen not to aggregate data at the agency level because they have determined that it exceeds their current evaluation capacity or because they are not persuaded by its value. Instead, they have opted to collect country or sector-level data that they compare with other countries and sectors over time.

Data management platforms

While the choice and capacity of data management platforms is important, TNGOs have found that the human component is also critically important. The data management platform needs to respond to the realities and constraints of country program-level staff. This implies the need for good collaboration between evaluation and information technology staff in the choice and management of such platforms. Equally, the platform managers require good communication with those in charge of data collection, especially within country programs. Having an information technology manager with deep country experience is extremely helpful. If all staff have access to the data (uploading and downloading) this can positively influence staff buy-in as well as broad uptake of the data for decision-making. In the experience of many TNGOs there appears to be no consistent, direct relationship between dollars spent on a data management platform and its success.

User satisfaction is generally unrelated to budgets spent on systems. Users care about a system functioning online and offline, easy access, and an intuitive interface. It needs to communicate with other data management platforms within the organization so that there is no need for double reporting. Users need easy access to ongoing technical support, while some staff will need access to evaluation specialists to help them make sense of the data for analysis

Table 7.2 IMPLEMENTING AGENCY-LEVEL MEASUREMENT SYSTEMS

Consideration	Implications for practice
Purpose	Ensure a clearly defined purpose and use for the system and remember that no one system can satisfy the data demands of all stakeholders.
Alignment	Align the agency-level measurement system with agency values, mission, and strategy to ensure usage.
Culture	Establishing an organizational culture of evidence-based decision-making will dramatically improve uptake. People are hired and rewarded both formally and informally for the effective use of data. Staff who act accordingly are lauded. Executive leaders align their decision-making to such data. The symbols and language that the agency uses internally and externally reflect the importance of data.
Champion	Invest in cultivating ownership and championing of the agency level measurement system at the top.
Resourcing	Allocate adequate resources, including staff, funding, and time, to build and implement the system. This includes measurement and evaluation, information technology, and project management capacity.
Buy-in	Take explicit steps to ensure broad staff buy-in into the system. This can happen by building on to existing country or program-level data collection systems, through constantly communicating the purpose of the system, through choosing indicators relevant to countries and data providers, by making data collection, management, and analysis as simple and user-friendly as possible, and by providing all staff with access to the data.
Standardization	Indicators must be standardized if they are going to be used for aggregation. Aggregating non-standardized measures is too complex and takes too much time.
Context	Recognize and communicate that indicators do not tell a full story. They speak to the organization's breadth of results, but not necessarily to their depth and significance. Understanding context remains essential.
Usability	Ensure that the information management system is user-friendly.

and interpretation. Table 7.2 summarizes the key issues that often emerge when implementing and using agency-level measurement systems.

Beyond technical design

The successful design and rollout of an agency-level measurement system depends on several "organizational readiness factors." These include (1) an organizational learning culture that values data-driven decision-making, (2) a champion within executive leadership who invests time in it, (3) a clear organizational strategy, theory of change, and set of priorities, (4) an identified audience and purpose, and (5) adequate skills and resources for data collection, management, analysis, and use.

A TNGO with an organizational learning culture conducive to evaluation has staff who value data and are rewarded for using data. They are thus more likely to provide quality and timely data input and to use this information to inform decision-making. Creating such a culture, while critical for evaluation quality, is still very much a work in progress in many TNGOs.

Having a consistent champion within the TNGO's executive leadership team can bolster the system's success. Critically, this champion must be from outside the measurement and evaluation leadership function, must devote time to this effort, and must understand the options and attendant needs, constraints, costs, and benefits. They need to take time to analyze and genuinely understand and use the data, and importantly, they need to be seen to do so.

A clear organizational strategy, theory of change, and priorities tell a TNGO what is important to measure at the agency level. In cases where the linkage between strategy and system is less clear, staff are less convinced of the system's relevance and value. Within the broader organizational strategy, TNGO leaders must define the specific purpose and ultimate use of the system. A system should not be designed to do too many things for too many people.

If staff capacity to manage projects and collect, manage, and monitor data is not broadly available, at least at a basic level, it is better to invest in that basic capacity first before venturing down the agency-level measurement path. TNGOs that have examined the feasibility and desirability of measurement at the agency level have found a "gap analysis" to be extremely helpful. This process seeks to identify existing basic evaluation capacities and integrate capacity-building into the core of its measurement and evaluation functions.

Agency-level data usage

Most agency-level measurement systems are designed for and used by a TNGO's leadership. In addition, boards of directors, marketing and communications, and program staff are also prominent users. Regional and country staff use the data less. Boards and executive leaders express the most satisfaction, while country-level and other frontline staff report lower satisfaction levels. These constituency groups are particularly dissatisfied if they feel that the aggregation of data make it less meaningful. Staff involved in developing and managing the system sometimes report being happier with the process outcomes than with the actual data. For example, the process of identifying meaningful organization-level indicators can help staff develop a shared understanding of the organization's goals and the interrelatedness of their work. Similarly, the way in which the development of an agency-level measurement system can reveal weaknesses and gaps in general measurement and evaluation capacity and can usefully draw attention to the importance of investing in those needs. If the primary users among these various groups have not been clearly identified upfront, the system may fall between the cracks, not satisfying anybody.

Centralized decision-making facilitates timely agreement on system design and staff buy-in. This means that (con)federated TNGOs have to invest more time and staff hours in the rollout process. Producing a measurement system that generates data meaningful to country staff, program managers, and executive leadership is very challenging, and is more likely to succeed if prior to adopting agency-level measures there is already considerable consensus across national offices with regard to what is being measured and valued.

Data generated by agency-level measurement systems are most often used for accountability to leadership and the board. Usage for communications and to ensure project management and technical quality are also prominent. In contrast, data are somewhat less likely to be used for strategic decision-making or learning. Overall, the general pattern suggests that data are used most to raise important questions that require further exploration, rather than to provide answers regarding what works or why.

Misuse or failure to use information

When data from agency-level measurement systems are not effectively used, the most frequently named reasons include that (1) the information does not respond to strategic decision-making needs, (2) the aggregated data are not considered meaningful, (3) the data quality is in question, and (4) the data are difficult to access. Underlying these explanations are often an absence of a culture that promotes the use of data to inform decision-making as well as insufficient prioritization. Organizations may be tempted to use project-level data for comparison across countries when such comparisons are inappropriate due to differences in country context. There are also concerns that performance related information collected for learning may reach external audiences without proper context.

TNGOs regularly report that their capacities to analyze and make sense of data cannot keep up with their ability to collect information. Indicators are often designed on what is easiest to measure, rather than what is useful for analysis, and unintended consequences or unplanned outcomes are difficult to integrate into existing measurement systems.[42] Similar to the case of adopting new digital tools, if measurement and evaluation systems are treated as an added burden, a broader culture of learning is unlikely to emerge.[43] Tensions between a desire for rigor and the need to be adaptive in response to complex and dynamic challenges are common across a range of TNGO subsectors.[44]

Costs and benefits

The largest costs are those involved in setting up and implementing the data management platform. Staff costs are also significant for project management, the shoring up of measurement and evaluation capacity, and enhanced information technology capacity. Country program-level staff tend to carry most of the burden of data collection, while data usage tends to benefit those at other levels of the organization.

The most important benefits of agency-level measurement systems mentioned by staff include the ability to assess progress and results and the corresponding assessment of project management and measurement and evaluation capacities. Staff also report how efforts to pursue agency-level measurement can promote a more positive, data-driven, globally aligned evaluation culture. Such efforts can help break down internal silos and unify an organization by helping staff see how their programs fit together and contribute to the broader mission. The vast majority of practitioners indicate that the benefits outweigh the costs.[45]

THREE ILLUSTRATIVE APPROACHES TO MEASUREMENT

Adopting agency-level measurement systems, building out internal MEAL units, and investing in data collection, management, and analysis capabilities are inevitable steps for preparing many TNGOs for the future. Individual TNGOs have approached the measurement challenge from different angles and have had mixed experiences. In a sector with no generally agreed-upon accounting standards for measuring and reporting impact, the path forward will require organizations to keep experimenting, learning, and sharing. The cases of Pact, Mercy Corps, and the International Rescue

Committee summarize these organizations' experiences with measurement in particular settings. All three organizations stand out from the average TNGO with regard to their consistent commitment to measurement and evaluation.

Measuring Pact's mission

Pact CEO Mark Viso and COO Will Warshauer advanced a vision for an innovative organization-wide system for evaluation and reporting. Pact's leadership wanted to manage by results and imagined a data system that would allow them to ascertain which projects were performing best and worst. Such information could then be used to inform internal strategic decision-making for future programming. One of their ultimate goals was to use such a system to develop a single measure of organizational reach that could quantify Pact's global impact. After several years of internal negotiations, Pact launched its global indicators initiative in 2011.[46]

Pact's global indicators were chosen to reflect its strategic foci across three impact areas (health, livelihoods, and natural resource management) and three core approaches (capacity development, livelihood and governance, and business and markets), yielding a total of six unique indicators. Pact identified interested and engaged stakeholders throughout the organization at both the headquarters and field-levels and held a series of working group meetings to discuss its global indicators. Four to six separate groups formed to identify a single indicator for each area. Some indicators, such as in health, were relatively easy to arrive at and consensus was reached rapidly, but others, such as in livelihood and governance, proved to be more complex and multidimensional. Eventually, reaching agreement on the livelihood and governance indicators required compromises. Pact subsequently explored ways of adjusting its indicators and adding new indicators ahead of its following reporting cycle. There is always a temptation to change and improve indicators, but it is also important to keep indicators consistent over time to allow year-to-year comparisons.

At such a high level of aggregation, any summary indicators would have to be very general, and Pact's six indicators were primarily measures of reach counting the numbers of people affected. For example, health impact was measured by the number of people with improved access to health and social services, and natural resource management impact was measured by the number of hectares of ecosystems under improved community management. Although such reach numbers are problematic as proxies for impact,[47] they can still provide general information about how the global reach of an organization's programs changes over time. Annual changes in these indicators can call attention to important operational and economic changes in the environment and can help leadership identify possible new challenges.

To generate indicators for capacity-building—a relatively abstract area of programming—Pact created a special index called the organizational performance index. The index was used to rate Pact's partners in each of four domains using four-point scales. The four domains were effectiveness, efficiency, relevance, and sustainability, with each domain being further composed of two subcategories. In 2018, for example, Pact's system indicated improved performance for 1,192 partners.[48]

In its first year its proponents feared that project managers might fail to report on their indicators. To address this Pact used customer relations management software to create a simple user interface with a small number of fields to allow managers to easily input information. Reporting on the global indicators occurred only once a year, minimizing the time commitment. By reducing the reporting burden on managers, Pact was able to obtain the necessary information from all their projects, whereas a more onerous system might have resulted in incomplete reporting. Additionally, Pact's relatively data-driven culture helped to facilitate the system's implementation.

Mission Metrics at Mercy Corps

In 2011, Mercy Corps introduced its Mission Metrics initiative to measure agency-level results. Following several years of rollout and implementation, the initiative was eventually discontinued amid sustained concerns, divisions, and frustrations, but the process also brought about lasting positive change within the organization, aligning expectations, boosting internal measurement and evaluation capabilities, fostering a conducive culture of evaluation, and ultimately strengthening Mercy Corps' commitment to its mission and to measuring impact.[49]

The Mission Metrics initiative was a top-down process. Mercy Corps' leadership envisioned a data system in which individual program results would be aggregated into broad categories at the agency level. Mercy Corps' 2013 Mission Metrics report organized twenty-seven agency-level metrics into three primary categories defined by its organizational mission of building more (1) secure, (2) productive, and (3) just communities. Under the rubric of building security, for example, the report noted that 3.2 million individuals improved their access to critical water and health services, while under the rubric of building just communities 7,168 communities increased the participation of marginalized groups in community services and local governance.[50] The system allowed stakeholders to drill down underneath the highly aggregated measures to examine program accomplishments at a more detailed level to understand specifically how people were affected. To facilitate the initiative, Mercy Corps implemented a sophisticated data management system throughout the organization.

Although the culture of Mercy Corps was highly supportive of high-quality measurement and evaluation, internal resistance emerged to the centralized nature of the process and the absence of field-level input early on. In addition, the adopted system suffered from ambiguities over data usage and ownership. During implementation, the Mission Metrics data management system was used in parallel with other program-level data management systems. This introduced additional reporting requirements for staff without adding significant value in a way that was useful for program management. The system did not produce actionable data for decision-making, so even though the process was long and inclusive, the purpose of the system remained unclear.[51] Ultimately, the initiative's value proposition was unsustainable given its limitations and the time and resources required to maintain it relative to the usability of the data.

Although the Mission Metrics initiative was discontinued, the process itself was valuable to the organization. The process of indicator selection initiated useful conversations that helped to clarify goals and theories of change. It also helped to focus attention on measurement and evaluation throughout Mercy Corps and made evaluation a priority. Widespread participation in the process brought attention to gaps at the program-level and identified programs that were under-capacitated. After the discontinued initiative, accountability for data became a key principle of measurement and evaluation. Data ownership also devolved more to the program level, and the organization experimented with information technology platforms that implemented measurement and evaluation systems as a program management tool.

Mercy Corps' experience with Mission Metrics suggests that having a high-quality data management platform for storing and preserving data and lessons-learned may have been more useful than the actual aggregation of agency-level results. Another important lesson is the importance of organizational culture for motivating and sustaining innovations in measurement and evaluation systems. Key stakeholders can facilitate cultural change, even in large organizations, to achieve strategic goals.

International Rescue Committee: Monitoring and research for accountability and learning

Monitoring and evaluation activity within the International Rescue Committee (IRC) is centralized within its Research, Evaluation, and Learning Unit (RELU) in coordination with its local program offices. The RELU is located at IRC's headquarters, with additional staff distributed within and across projects around the world. The RELU provides technical support and quality control for measurement and evaluation activity and sets the strategic vision for research, evaluation, and learning throughout the organization.[52]

One of the most important areas of the IRC's commitment to measurement rests with the research function of the RELU. The IRC collaborates with academic partners to conduct rigorous impact evaluations.[53] These evaluations are motivated by key research questions and knowledge gaps in the humanitarian field. The impact evaluations are mainly intended to promote sectoral learning. In fields such as health and education, practitioners can draw upon a relatively large body of evidence to inform their interventions, but in other areas of programming around issues such as domestic violence, empowerment, and children's development, fewer credible studies are available. The effectiveness of these intervention strategies is obviously important to understand, and so too is their cost-effectiveness.

Being among the first organizations to generate credible evidence about the impact and cost-effectiveness of humanitarian interventions introduces a variety of challenges. Part of the challenge of being an innovator is the lack of context for new evidence. For example, without an established evidence base for comparison, it is hard to determine whether a particular program is any more or less cost-effective than alternatives. Another challenge is understanding what role cost-effectiveness data ought to have in decision-making in relation to normative judgments about strategic priorities. Data can reveal difficult trade-offs without necessarily providing clear answers. Moreover, tensions can exist between the short-term focus of humanitarian work as an implementing agency and the long-term time horizon of research activity.

The IRC's commitment to rigorous evaluation and transparency was tested when an evaluation of a major multimillion-dollar community-driven reconstruction program revealed that the intervention failed to accomplish many of its goals. Many thought that the program should be a success, but the results proved to be disappointing. The study became a focal point for organizational and sectoral learning. It was well received internally in part because of the "strong culture of learning and questioning" within IRC.[54]

Commitment at the top also helped. The new president at the time was "extremely committed to the learning agenda for the organization, including value for money and cost-effectiveness,"[55] which helped to prioritize measurement and evaluation, including research, as important components to support the organization's mission.

INVESTING IN MEASUREMENT

The lessons-learned and case studies illustrate the importance of a conducive organizational culture for creating and sustaining momentum for meeting the measurement challenge. For TNGOs with weaker outcome orientations, this may necessitate significant organizational change. Additionally, attributes of an organization's internal culture and external environment can interact in ways that make this prioritization and investment difficult. Culturally, although most TNGO practitioners seem to be rhetorically supportive of impact measurement, they often believe that *their* work is simply too unique, special, and complex to be measured. Moreover, measurement and evaluation may not seem necessary because the organization's intentions and efforts are virtuous, while stakeholders who demand evidence may be seen as simply having lost faith. Such attitudes, combined with frequent staff resistance and relatively weak systems for performance-based accountability across the sector,[56] can reinforce an unhealthy status quo that ultimately excuses complacency in the face of an urgent need for change.

As TNGOs have increasingly based their legitimacy on their claims of generating impact, delaying further on developing adequate measurement and evaluation systems can only increase negative perceptions among external stakeholders. Many TNGOs can still rely on donors with a preference for low overhead and fiscal trustworthiness, but TNGOs also face new and emboldened competitors, including for-profit companies and digital organizations focused on data-driven and results-oriented approaches (see Chapter 6). TNGOs, by contrast, may compare themselves to other TNGOs, but rarely position themselves as leaders in evidence generation and data-driven decision-making across all the relevant sectors operating in their space. More broadly, as philanthropists and other funders increasingly embrace effective altruism,[57] strategic[58] or outcome-oriented[59] philanthropy, intelligent philanthropy,[60] smart giving,[61] investing in results,[62] value for money,[63] and similar evidence-driven philosophies, TNGOs will need to adapt quickly to position themselves for future relevance in the emerging data-hungry ecosystem.

Part of the problem for TNGOs is that they remain caught in an accountability architecture that is unfit for their future. The historical legacy of the charity model requires TNGOs to secure accountability and legitimacy principally by demonstrating trustworthiness (typically through upward financial reporting) rather than by providing evidence of organizational effectiveness or mission impact. But despite many TNGOs already having moved beyond the traditional model of the charitable intermediary, many TNGO stakeholders remain invested in traditional approaches. For example, both Mercy Corps and IRC prominently display pie charts depicting their program, administrative, and fundraising cost ratios on their main website landing pages.[64] By contrast, Pact prominently features results data on its website.[65] Symbolically, the Mercy Corps and IRC websites are catering to the existing architecture, whereas Pact is communicating a commitment to a future-oriented impact orientation. Even for organizations actively seeking to improve and adapt their measurement capabilities for the future, the pull of the legacy architecture remains strong.

TNGOs face significant challenges if they move forward with investing more resources to improve their measurement and evaluation capacities. In the existing architecture, agency-level measurement systems, modern information technology platforms, and even measurement and evaluation activity itself all represent diversions of resources away from the mission. The language of this architecture is echoed by media organizations, charity watchdogs, information intermediaries, and even funders and regulators throughout the world that hold TNGOs accountable based not on their impact but on their spending practices.[66] This puts TNGOs in a double bind: to maintain their perceived "efficiency" as charities, they must forgo overhead-increasing investments to improve their capacities for effectiveness and impact.[67] Yet these are precisely the kinds of investments that TNGOs need to make to ensure their future relevance.

CONCLUSION

The TNGOs that have experienced the greatest success with measurement, and those poised for the greatest success in the future, are those with the strongest commitment toward organizational learning in their cultures and leadership. Organizational cultural change takes time, and agency-level measurement is an especially complex and ambitious undertaking for nearly any organization. In the meantime, TNGOs not yet prepared to conduct rigorous impact evaluations or to introduce agency-level measurement systems can still work on improving their core capacities and systems for data collection and usage.[68] The gap between the rhetoric and evidence of impact has become unsustainable. TNGOs will need to either walk back their ambitions and claims or devise more transparent and sustained ways of demonstrating their accomplishments.

Most especially, mid- to large-sized TNGOs have evolved well beyond the legacy model of the ameliorative charity to embrace a significantly more expansive commitment to creating long-term sustainable impact. However, this commitment is not yet fully reflected in organizational practices, and TNGOs need to continue to adapt and evolve if they are to realize their impact-oriented aspirations. TNGOs cannot afford ambivalence: a genuine commitment to impact means a genuine commitment to measurement.

Granted, impact measurement, especially at the organizational level, is a high bar, and one that many organizations may not realistically be able to reach in the near term. Luckily, measuring outcomes and outputs can often provide reasonable proxy evidence of impact, particularly where causal links are already well-established.[69] Additionally, organizations not yet prepared or able to measure impact can work on building up their basic evaluation capabilities, developing their measurement strategies (for instance, by identifying valid indicator or proxy variables), validating their theories of change, and tracking program implementation, for example.[70] The key point is that TNGO measurement systems need to catch up with the expanded goals and claims of TNGOs.

REFERENCES

Andrei, Kyle, Elizabeth Pope, Amandie Hart, and Laura S. Quinn. *The State of Nonprofit Data*. Idealware. Portland, OR: NTEN, 2012.

Arvidson, Malin, and Fergus Lyon. "Social Impact Measurement and Non-Profit Organisations: Compliance, Resistance, and Promotion." *Voluntas* 25, no. 4 (2013). https://doi.org/10.1007/s11266-013-9373-6.

Bartlett, Valerie, Antony Bugg-Levine, David Erickson, Ian Galloway, Janet Genser, and Jennifer Talansky, eds. *What Matters: Investing in Results to Build Strong, Vibrant Communities*. New York: Federal Reserve Bank of San Francisco and Nonprofit Finance Fund, 2017.

Behn, Robert D. "The Psychological Barriers to Performance Management: Or Why Isn't Everyone Jumping on the Performance-Management Bandwagon?" *Public Performance & Management Review* 26, no. 1 (2002): 5–25.

Bond and Itad. *Value for Money: What It Means for UK NGOs*. London: Bond, 2012.

Brest, Paul. "A Decade of Outcome-Oriented Philanthropy." *Stanford Social Innovation Review* (2012). http://www.ssireview.org/articles/entry/a_decade_of_outcome_oriented_philanthropy.

Brest, Paul. "Strategic Philanthropy and Its Discontents." *Stanford Social Innovation Review* (April 27, 2015). https://ssir.org/up_for_debate/article/strategic_philanthropy_and_its_discontents.

Bruno-van Vijfeijken, Tosca, Uwe Gneiting, Hans Peter Schmitz, Ricardo Gomez, and Otto Valle. *Rights-Based Approach to Development: Learning from Guatemala.* Syracuse, NY: Moynihan Institute of Global Affairs, 2010.

Buchanan, Phil. "Which Data? And Who Will Pay for It?" In *Markets for Good: Selected Readings: Making Sense of Data and Information in the Social Sector*, 25–26. 2014. https://digitalimpact.io/wordpress/wp-content/uploads/2014/01/Markets-for-Good-Selected-Readings-eBook.pdf.

Carman, Joanne G. "Nonprofits, Funders, and Evaluation: Accountability in Action." *The American Review of Public Administration* 39, no. 4 (2009): 374–90.

Carman, Joanne G., and Kimberly A. Fredericks. "Evaluation Capacity and Nonprofit Organizations: Is the Glass Half-Empty or Half-Full?" *American Journal of Evaluation* 31, no. 1 (2010): 84–104.

Carnochan, Sarah, Mark Samples, Michael Myers, and Michael J. Austin. "Performance Measurement Challenges in Nonprofit Human Service Organizations." *Nonprofit and Voluntary Sector Quarterly* 43, no. 6 (2013). https://doi.org/10.1177/0899764013508009.

Cavalluzzo, Ken S., and Christopher D. Ittner. "Implementing Performance Measurement Innovations: Evidence from Government." *Accounting, Organizations, and Society* 29, no. 3/4 (2004): 243–67.

Center for Global Development. *When Will We Ever Learn? Improving Lives through Impact Evaluation.* Washington, DC: Center for Global Development 2006.

Child, Curtis, and Eva M. Witesman. "Optimism and Bias When Evaluating a Prosocial Initiative." *Social Science Quarterly* (2019). https://doi.org/10.1111/ssqu.12585.

Coe, Jim, and Rhonda Schlangen. *No Royal Road: Finding and Following the Natural Pathways in Advocacy Evaluation.* Center for Evaluation Innovation (2019). https://www.evaluationinnovation.org/wp-content/uploads/2019/03/No-Royal-Road.pdf.

Crowley, James, and Morgana Ryan. *Building a Better International NGO: Greater Than the Sum of the Parts.* Boulder, CO: Kumarian Press, 2013.

Crowley, James, and Morgana Ryan. *Navigating Change for International NGOs: A Practical Handbook.* Boulder, CO: Kumarian, 2017.

Dillon, Neil, and Amelie Sundberg. *Back to the Drawing Board. How to Improve Monitoring of Outcomes.* London: ODI/ALNAP, 2019.

Earl, Sarah, Fred Carden, and Terry Smutylo. *Outcome Mapping: Building Learning and Reflection into Development Programs.* Ottawa: International Development Research Centre, 2001.

Easterling, Doug. "Using Outcome Evaluation to Guide Grantmaking: Theory, Reality, and Possibilities." *Nonprofit and Voluntary Sector Quarterly* 29, no. 3 (2000): 482–86.

Ebrahim, Alnoor. *NGOs and Organizational Change: Discourse, Reporting, and Learning.* New York: Cambridge University Press, 2005.

Ebrahim, Alnoor, and V. Kasturi Rangan. "What Impact?: A Framework for Measuring the Scale and Scope of Social Performance." *California Management Review* 56, no. 3 (2014): 118–41.

Eyben, Rosalind. *Uncovering the Politics of "Evidence" and "Results". A Framing Paper for Development Practitioners.* The Big Push Forward (2013). http://bigpushforward.net/wp-content/uploads/2011/01/The-politics-of-evidence-11-April-20133.pdf.

Gandia, Juan L. "Internet Disclosure by Nonprofit Organizations: Empirical Evidence of Nongovernmental Organizations for Development in Spain." *Nonprofit and Voluntary Sector Quarterly* 40, no. 1 (2011): 57–78.

Gardner, Annette L., and Claire D. Brindis. *Advocacy and Policy Change Evaluation: Theory and Practice.* Stanford, CA: Stanford Business Books, 2017.

Gordillo, Gustavo, and Krister Andersson. "From Policy Lessons to Policy Actions: Motivation to Take Evaluation Seriously." *Public Administration and Development* 24 (2004): 305–20.

Grantmakers for Effective Organizations. *Four Essentials for Evaluation*. Washington, DC: GEO, 2012.

Gugerty, Mary Kay, and Dean Karlan. *The Goldilocks Challenge: Right-Fit Evidence for the Social Sector*. New York: Oxford University Press, 2018.

Gugerty, Mary Kay, and Dean Karlan. "Ten Reasons Not to Measure Impact—And What to Do Instead." *Stanford Social Innovation Review* (Summer 2018): 41–47.

Hatry, Harry P. *Performance Measurement: Getting Results*. 2nd ed. Washington, DC: Urban Institute Press, 2007.

Hoefer, Richard. "Accountability in Action?: Program Evaluation in Nonprofit Human Service Agencies." *Nonprofit Management and Leadership* 11, no. 2 (2000): 167–77.

International Rescue Committee. *Research at the International Rescue Committee: Top Insights from 2018, What to Watch for in 2019*. New York: IRC, 2019. https://www.rescue.org/report/ircs-top-research-findings-2018-and-2019.

"International Rescue Committee." 2019, accessed July 10, 2019, https://www.rescue.org/.

IRC. *Research at the International Rescue Committee: List of Projects by Outcome*. New York: International Rescue Committee, 2018. https://www.rescue.org/sites/default/files/document/2655/researchprojectlist5172018.pdf.

Jaeger, Hans-Martin. "'Global Civil Society' and the Political Depoliticization of Global Governance." *International Political Sociology* 1 (2007): 257–77.

Levine, Carlisle J., Tosca Bruno van-Vijfeijken, and Sherine Jayawickrama. *Measuring International NGO Agency-Level Results*. InterAction (May 2016). https://www.interaction.org/sites/default/files/ALR_WhitePaper_FINAL_0.pdf.

MacAskill, William. *Doing Good Better: How Effective Altruism Can Help You Help Others, Do Work That Matters, and Make Smarter Choices about Giving Back*. New York: Avery, 2016.

MacAskill, William. "Effective Altruism: An Introduction." *Essays in Philosophy* 18, no. 1 (2017): 1–5.

MacDonald, Neil, and Nigel Simister. *Outcome Mapping*. Oxford: INTRAC, 2015.

"Mercy Corps." 2019, accessed July 10, 2019, https://www.mercycorps.org/.

Mercy Corps. *Mission Metrics 2013 Report*. Portland, OR: Mercy Corps, 2013. http://www.mercycorps.org/sites/default/files/Mission%20Metrics%202013%20Report.pdf.

Mitchell, George E. "Accounting for Outcomes: Monitoring and Evaluation in the Transnational NGO Sector." In *Leading and Managing in the Social Sector: Strategies for Advancing Human Dignity and Social Justice*, edited by Aqeel Tirmizi and John Vogelsang, 263–82. New York: Springer, 2017.

Mitchell, George E. "Creating a Philanthropic Marketplace through Accounting, Disclosure, and Intermediation." *Public Performance and Management Review* 38, no. 1 (2014): 23–47.

Mitchell, George E. "Fiscal Leanness and Fiscal Responsiveness: Exploring the Normative Limits of Strategic Nonprofit Financial Management." *Administration & Society* 49, no. 9 (2017): 1272–96. https://doi.org/10.1177/0095399715581035.

Mitchell, George E. "Modalities of Managerialism: The 'Double Bind' of Normative and Instrumental Nonprofit Managerial Imperatives." *Administration & Society* 50, no. 7 (2018): 1037–68. https://doi.org/10.1177/0095399716664832.

Mitchell, George E. "*Why* Will We Ever Learn? Measurement and Evaluation in International Development NGOs." *Public Performance and Management Review* 37, no. 4 (2014): 605–31.

Mitchell, George E., and David Berlan. "Evaluation and Evaluative Rigor in the Nonprofit Sector." *Nonprofit Management & Leadership* 27, no. 2 (2016): 237–50. https://doi.org/10.1002/nml.21236.

Mitchell, George E., and David Berlan. "Evaluation in Nonprofit Organizations: An Empirical Analysis." *Public Performance and Management Review* 41, no. 2 (2018): 415–37. https://doi.org/10.1080/15309576.2017.1400985.

Mitchell, George E., and Thad D. Calabrese. "Proverbs of Nonprofit Financial Management." *American Review of Public Administration* 49, no. 6 (2019): 649–61. https://doi.org/10.1177/0275074018770458.

Morariu, Johanna, Katherine Athanasiades, and Ann Emery. *State of Evaluation 2012: Evaluation Practice and Capacity in the Nonprofit Sector.* Washington, DC: Innovation Network, 2012.

Morino, Mario. *Leap of Reason: Managing to Outcomes in an Era of Scarcity.* Washington, DC: Venture Philanthropy Partners, 2011.

Murray, Vic, and Bill Tassie. "Evaluating the Effectiveness of Nonprofit Organizations." In *The Jossey-Bass Handbook of Nonprofit Leadership and Management*, edited by Robert D. Herman and Associates, 303–24. San Francisco: Jossey-Bass, 1994.

Organisation for Economic Co-operation and Development. *Measuring and Managing Results in Development Cooperation: A Review of Challenges and Practices among Dac Members and Observers.* Paris: OECD, 2014. https://www.pactworld.org.

Pact. *Measuring Pact's Mission 2018.* Pact (2018). https://www.pactworld.org/sites/default/files/Pact%20MPM%202018_WEB.pdf.

Penna, Robert M. *The Nonprofit Outcomes Toolbox.* Hoboken, NJ: John Wiley & Sons, 2011.

Perrin, Burt. *Linking Monitoring and Evaluation to Impact Evaluation.* Washington, DC: InterAction/Rockefeller Foundation, 2012.

Quinn, Laura. "In Search of Better Data about Nonprofits' Programs." In *Markets for Good*, 11–14: Bill & Melinda Gates Foundation, 2013. https://digitalimpact.io/wordpress/wp-content/uploads/2014/01/Markets-for-Good-Selected-Readings-eBook.pdf.

Ramalingam, Ben, Leni Wild, and Anne L. Buffardi. *Making Adaptive Rigour Work: Principles and Practices for Strengthening Monitoring, Evaluation, and Learning for Adaptive Management* London: ALNAP, 2019.

Roberts, Susan M., John Paul Jones III, and Oliver Frohling. "NGOs and the Globalization of Managerialism: A Research Framework." *World Development* 33, no. 11 (2005): 1845–64.

Roche, Chris, and Linda Kelly. *The Evaluation of Politics and the Politics of Evaluation.* Birmingham, UK: Developmental Leadership Program, 2012.

Rogers, Patricia J. and BetterEvaluation. *Introduction to Impact Evaluation.* Washington, DC: InterAction/Rockefeller Foundation, 2012.

Schmidt, Arthur "Buzz." "Divining a Vision for Markets for Good." In *Selected Readings: Making Sense of Data and Information in the Social Sector*, edited by Eric J. Henderson, 61–81. Stanford, CA: Markets for Good, 2014.

Shutt, Cathy, and Rosie McGee. *Improving the Evaluability of INGO Empowerment and Accountability Programmes.* Brighton, UK: Centre for Development Impact, 2013.

Simister, Nigel, and Allison Napier. *Outcome Harvesting.* Oxford: INTRAC, 2017.

Singer, Peter. *The Most Good You Can Do: How Effective Altruism Is Changing Ideas about Living Ethically.* New Haven, CT: Yale University Press, 2017.

Sjöstedt, Martin. "Aid Effectiveness and the Paris Declaration: A Mismatch between Ownership and Results-Based Management?" *Public Administration and Development* 33 (2013): 143–55.

Stern, Elliot, Nicoletta Stame, John Mayne, Kim Forss, Rick Davies, and Barbara Befani. *Broadening the Range of Designs and Methods for Impact Evaluation.* London: Department for International Development, 2012.

Twersky, Fay, and Lori Grange. *A Practical Guide to Outcome-Focused Philanthropy.* Menlo Park, CA: Hewlett Foundation, 2016. https://hewlett.org/wp-content/uploads/2017/05/OFP-Guidebook-updated.pdf.

Weinstein, Michael M., and Ralph M. Bradburd. *The Robin Hood Rules for Smart Giving.* New York: Columbia University Press, 2013.

White, Howard. "Theory-Based Impact Evaluation: Principles and Practice." New Delhi: International Initiative for Impact Evaluation, 2009.

Wilson-Grau, Ricardo, and Heather Britt. *Outcome Harvesting.* Cairo: Ford Foundation, 2012.

World Bank. *World Development Report.* Washington, DC: World Bank, 2016.

York, Peter J. *Learning as We Go: Making Evaluation Work for Everyone.* New York: TCC Group, 2003.

CHAPTER 8

Governance

The modern TNGO sector emerged over the past century to address urgent needs around the world. Major organizations, such as Oxfam and CARE, were founded in the 1940s to deliver aid to civilians suffering during and after World War II. Throughout the 1950s and 1960s, the focus of these organizations shifted toward long-term transfers of resources from the Global North to the Global South,[1] with TNGOs often serving as conduits for official development assistance provided by Northern governments.[2] With the rapid expansion of the sector since the 1970s, many more organizations entered the field to establish an increasingly professionalized aid industry. During the same time, human rights and environmental advocacy organizations began to constitute distinct TNGO subsectors with unique missions and strategies. As the sector and many individual TNGOs have substantially grown over the past decades, most mid- to large-sized organizations have undergone substantial and sometimes repeated organizational restructuring to improve their operations and effectiveness. Their missions have evolved alongside increasing ambitions and more sophisticated strategies.

Geopolitical and economic shifts are core drivers of many governance reforms in the TNGO sector, with poverty now recognized as an issue in high- and middle-income countries. At least 73 percent of poor people today live in middle-income countries,[3] while traditional aid structures often still focus on the remaining 27 percent of the poor in places like sub-Saharan Africa. To impact the majority of the world's poor, TNGOs need to have more presence and influence in middle-income countries (e.g., Brazil, China, and India),[4] whose governments also wield increasing geopolitical power.

The issue is not just that TNGOs need to consider geographic shifts in their efforts, but also that their expanding mandates no longer match their often very specific subsector missions (e.g., conflict resolution, humanitarian aid, development, human rights, and environmental protection). To truly address root causes, TNGOs are developing multi-sectoral perspectives that require more knowledge and capacities outside of their original areas of operation.[5] For example, the climate crisis has broad implications for nearly all TNGO sectors by increasing demand for disaster relief and altering how development efforts are designed to include programmatic components related to adaptation and resilience.[6]

At the same time, funding models for the sector are rapidly changing and traditional sources in the Global North have plateaued or are declining.[7] Oxfam India, for example, needs to be locally governed and to offer locally devised solutions to be legitimate, and these programs have to be funded to a growing extent from Indian sources.[8] This has repercussions for country program fundraising capacity, of course, but also for who is represented on Oxfam India's board. In many TNGOs, organizational structures are still shaped by a history of dominance of Global North sections, while increasing multipolarity has shifted centers of power and decision-making elsewhere.

If TNGOs are to remain relevant, effective, and legitimate actors in global governance, they must confront major organizational challenges related not only to their roles and strategies, but also to their governance structures and leadership capacities (see Chapter 9). Governance and leadership often evolve together as organizations introduce reforms to enhance organizational legitimacy while seeking to remaining agile. However, there are many factors that can affect the effectiveness of such changes, and ultimately the ability of organizations to successfully adapt for the future. A critical awareness of the many issues at stake, including the opportunities and risks of key governance reform initiatives and specific governance reform considerations, can help prepare organizations for their present and future challenges.

THE NATURE OF TRANSNATIONAL GOVERNANCE: THE CASE OF OXFAM INTERNATIONAL

The essential background to governance reform is defined by how TNGOs emerge and change in the composition of their members and affiliates. While each TNGO has taken a different path, the case of Oxfam offers some general lessons about how the addition of new members affects the internal balance of power and requires changes to governance arrangements over time.[9] Notably, Oxfam's path to growing as a confederation has included several mergers (see also Chapter 11). Of the twenty affiliates in 2018, five emerged from mergers between autonomous organizations joining together, seven were national organizations with similarities but entirely different names and histories, and eight were created by individual affiliates or evolved from country programs in the Global South. The organizations with different names are the affiliates from Australia (formerly called Community Aid Abroad), Denmark (IBIS), France (Agir Ici), Italy (UCODEP), Mexico (VAMOS), Netherlands (NOVIB), and Spain (Intermon).

A prominent strategic driver for affiliates joining has been the increased effectiveness of advocacy work when conducted with global reach and voice. Since its founding in 1996, the Oxfam confederation has coalesced around advocacy and campaigning, or "influencing," followed by humanitarian and long-term development work. Most of the mergers were preceded by long-term collaboration, and eventually moved toward more formal alliances and then merger. For example, UCODEP had worked with Oxfam for many years, hosted Oxfam for the 2009 G8 summit in Italy, and then joined shortly afterward.

In the case of IBIS (Denmark), the organization had discussed the idea of joining a TNGO family in the early 2000s, but only much later was encouraged by the Danish government to do so to increase global program impact. When the general-secretary of IBIS attended an event organized by INTRAC in 2012,[10] he witnessed a presentation by the Oxfam's international director and director of strategy explaining its new strategic plan. Realizing the similarities in goals across the two organizations, a series of informal conversations then took place in Copenhagen. Following more high-level meetings of the chairs and CEOs, IBIS joined Oxfam in 2015 benefiting now from a combined and increased programmatic and thematic expertise as well as much-needed resources to invest in fundraising and other necessary improvements.

Oxfam affiliates display a relatively strong alignment around vision, mission, and values that is expressed in a jointly created "Purpose and Beliefs" document outlining their theory of change and strategy.[11] As each new member joins, there is also a need to manage and align different identities, approaches, funding models, and country portfolios. Even twenty years after the creation of the confederation, there are still passionately held differences in perspective among staff that require regular reconciliation. This includes differences about program approaches, policy positions, emphasis on staff versus volunteers, preferences for public campaigning versus insider lobbying, and which governments, foundations, and business to work with. These differences are driven less by national origin than by the specific preferences of leaders and long-serving staff from the top all the way to middle management.

Within the Oxfam confederation each of its affiliates brings its own history, culture, discourse, and identity to bear in confederation-wide debates and decision-making. In the absence of a hierarchical structure, new topics, such as gender justice, for example, can struggle to gain traction in a culture of "thorough consultation through meetings" that is only slowly shifting to become more agile and responsive.[12] As described in Table 8.1, a TNGO such as Oxfam and its transnational governance is composed of multiple— sometimes complementary, and sometimes conflicting—visions of an organization.

GOVERNANCE REFORMS

Governance defines how decisions are made through explicit rules, who participates in decision-making, and how decision-makers are held accountable. It is about who has authority, how an organization arrives at its collective actions, and how responsiveness within the organization is exercised. In the operation of TNGOs, its leadership must balance specific values associated with good governance, including fairness, transparency, responsiveness, mission dedication, participation, consensus, and performance. Governance reforms typically respond to perceived imbalances among values and seek to manage emerging tensions, including the need for agility in decision-making and the desire to be responsive to all constituents.

Governance structures usually embody trade-offs between competing values, such as inclusiveness versus agility, that carry specific risks. For example, some TNGOs may find that certain more democratic governance models—such as those that expand membership in the Global South, add governance layers at the regional or country levels, or add direct representation of primary stakeholders—are too cumbersome and slow, or they discover that the "power of the purse" still predominates. Additionally, some TNGOs have boards consisting entirely of executive directors or national member board chairs and lack a critical mass of even as many as three or four independent board members. This can make such boards more at risk of delving into management and operations rather than governing or of introducing self-interest into governance deliberations, and it can make the top executive leader more bound to member demands and less able to do "whole-of-the-organization" thinking and decision-making. It also makes the development of dual or twin citizenship capacities (in which board members are able to simultaneously represent both their national member

Table 8.1 ONE OXFAM, MULTIPLE ROLES

	What energizes staff	Discourse	Defining moments
Humanitarian aid	Life-saving work, rapid response	Humanitarian operations (e.g., engineering, logistics, project management, expertise, agile response, chain of command)	Major humanitarian crises
Sustainable development	Participatory approaches, consensus decision-making, partnerships	Long-term planning and partnerships; relationships with communities through multiple progressive periods; leveraging and scale-up	Changes achieved with partners at local and national levels at moments of disjuncture (e.g., Tunisia partners during Arab Spring, Aristide's organization in Haiti, IBASE in Brazil)
Emancipation and liberation	Raising political awareness, policy wins, confronting power, supporting movements to confront oppressive regimes	Political liberation, advocacy, campaigns, solidarity with partners, activists, networks	Liberation struggles, including the anti-apartheid movement and others in Latin America and elsewhere
Think tank	Insider advocacy, thought leadership monitoring, evaluation, learning	Evidence-based policymaking, academic research, convening, brokering, and influencing	Specific changes in law, policy (e.g., G8, DAVOS, IMF/World Bank meetings, Dodd Frank Act, Arms Trade Treaty), and public worldviews
Global actor	Overcoming North-South divides; addressing issues of race, gender, and ethnicity	Internal reorganization for greater diversity, equity, and inclusion	Influx of Global South membership; moving headquarters to Nairobi, Kenya

entity and the whole of the transnational organization) less likely. Indeed, a recent International Civil Society Centre survey found that over two-thirds of respondents reported that their organizations' governance structures were "at least sometimes too slow, too cumbersome, and much too focused

Table 8.2 TNGO GOVERNANCE REFORMS

	Goals	Risks
Centralization	More agile decision-making	Limits democratic participation and legitimacy
Decentralization	Enhanced legitimacy Sense of public ownership	National interests and accountabilities prevail over global action and decision-making Less globally coherent strategy implementation
Global structure	Better geopolitical alignment Greater influence for Southern members	Limited capacity to tailor to local needs Unrealistic expectations regarding pace, fundraising, and need for external support
New bodies	Enhanced legitimacy and more diverse inputs	Fragmentation, reduced decision-making agility Multiple accountabilities disorder
Digitally enabled global fora	Improved stakeholder voice and downward accountability Enhanced diversity through broader participation Reduced decision-making costs	Excessive deliberation and consultation, or eventual fatigue and cynicism, unless expectations are managed carefully Unequal access to digital tools reproduces existing inequalities

on balancing national interests."[13] Table 8.2 summarizes some of the goals and risks of specific TNGO governance reforms that have been adopted or explored over the past decades.

Most TNGOs have considered governance reforms within a broader context of rethinking their own roles, such as shifting away from service delivery and embracing advocacy, campaigning, and social movement building. For example, Save the Children narrowed its primary focus to humanitarian work and long-term development interventions to scale up operations, embrace efficiency, and attract large institutional donors.[14] It also pursued mergers and acquisitions opportunities to primarily strengthen its operations and remain competitive with other service providers.[15] Such a choice resulted in an emphasis on the centralization of program implementation and the standardization and integration of business systems and processes. However, this may not lead to opening up governance as quickly to voices in the Global South. In contrast, Oxfam has instead focused on a future role of influencing policies across local, national, and global levels.[16] This requires governance reforms focused on empowering and mobilizing all national members and affiliates to do an equal share of activism. Finally, Amnesty International has resolved to become more responsive to regional and local inputs, and has been willing to decentralize some of the traditional concentrated proposal power to gain more legitimacy with middle-income country governments and populations. Variation in governance reforms will be largely driven by how TNGOs define their identity and role within a larger ecosystem of social change activism. What is true across all of them is that their mandates and ambitions continue to grow, no matter if they want to be identified as a community, a platform, an influencer, an organizer, or an implementer.

Centralization and decentralization

For the larger TNGO "families," strategic governance reforms usually aspire to include a better balance between global centralization and local customization and accountability, following the subsidiarity principle.[17] Global secretariats, centers, headquarters, and boards want to be able to make agile decisions in response to rapid changes in the external environment, but simultaneously avoid too much centralization resulting in the erosion of local participation. Degrees of centralization or decentralization can vary with regard to specific governance functions within the organization. Three core powers within each TNGO consist of the abilities (1) to propose issues, (2) to enforce decisions, and (3) to implement agreed-upon actions.[18] In a transnational context, successful organizations have to find ways of centralizing some decision-making to secure coherence and agility, while giving sufficient room to field staff and local entities to adapt implementation practices to the specifics of a given context. In the future, this devolution of decision-making power has to also extend to proposal power insofar as organizations are inclined to shift from a staff-based to a supporter-based model of activism (see Chapter 6).

The complications of adapting well-established forms of governance such as boards and assemblies to the imperatives of twin citizenship and locally relevant forms of oversight[19] show how difficult it is to aim for a fundamental overhaul of governance structures while also trying to preserve what has worked in the past. Community-based forms of governance for national members, sections, and affiliates might offer a better alternative, but larger, older organizations may be understandably reluctant to undergo such significant organizational change.[20] Although most TNGOs outwardly espouse bottom-up, democratic principles, internally many still practice more traditional approaches,[21] including allowing higher-income-generating members to carry more weight behind the scenes.

Global structure

The goal of governance reforms can often be understood as a desire to create a truly global organization, rather than remain stuck in a framework that only manages the different views and demands expressed by a range of national members.[22] Whereas traditional governance structures are typically dominated by members from the Global North with control over more resources, global governance structures can also mitigate differences in relative power within the organization and allow for its leadership to establish more coherent and focused objectives.[23]

Moving toward more global structures is a key complement to many TNGOs focused on modernizing and streamlining their operations. In the past, it was common for wealthy Northern affiliates of development TNGOs to establish separate offices and programs abroad. For example, until 2008 as many as five to seven Oxfam affiliates would often operate independently in the same local context. This created significant inefficiencies and resource investment in parallel program structures without necessarily increasing overall effectiveness. After adopting the idea of a single management structure (SMS), Oxfam moved toward establishing a single lead affiliate responsible for all programming in one country.[24] Such fundamental changes in operations have significant repercussions for overall governance and typically absorb considerable leadership and staff resources to negotiate, agree upon, and implement.

A desire to empower Southern relative to Northern members has implications for income generation and budget allocation globally, especially as members from formerly low-income countries are increasingly expected to be more self-reliant. Such changes can enhance the legitimacy of global TNGO brands, but also introduce new challenges, particularly for members in "recipient" countries. For example, India's transformation toward middle-income status threatened outside income for Oxfam India, forcing it to rely more upon a relatively less developed culture of philanthropy inside India.[25] For many mid- to large-sized TNGOs seeking to expand and empower Southern membership, it may take much longer, fundraising may grow much more slowly, and it may require more sustained external financial and institutional support from centers and high-income country members than expected.

New bodies

As large TNGOs have grown in membership and affiliates, many have developed increasingly complex governance structures that include international assemblies and national boards or advisory councils in addition to international or global boards.[26] Amnesty International, ActionAid, Oxfam International, and Greenpeace International provide examples of such (growing) complexity. Some have added regional or constituency-based advisory bodies to this (e.g., Amnesty International) or national member or constituent assemblies (e.g., ActionAid), further increasing the complexity of leading and managing these governance structures.

Some TNGOs—such as ActionAid, Amnesty International, and WWF—that are membership-based have adopted additional governance layers in the form of global assemblies or advisory councils. Often, these assemblies directly represent member or affiliate perspectives that in turn elect an international board. Such bodies typically complicate the balancing act between democratic legitimacy and decision-making agility. In addition, some membership-based organizations such as Amnesty International note a trend in which younger-generation individual members are less interested to participate in governance and more interested in engaging in self-directed action (see Chapter 6). Amnesty, in response to this trend, has recently decided to decrease its emphasis on the generation of new dues-paying members in favor of an increased emphasis on generating broad supportership across regions, ages, and income levels.[27] The focus on individual supporters remains central to many TNGOs trying to secure new funding sources and legitimacy across the globe.

Additionally, such complexities can create tensions and contradictions between multiple organizational accountabilities to different and overlapping constituencies.[28] Changes of governance structures have significant impact on specific accountability practices (e.g., who sits at the table?) as well as external perceptions about output and process legitimacy (see Chapter 5).[29]

Digitally enabled global and local fora

Possible governance reforms extend beyond the increased role for Global South membership that has already generated significant challenges for fostering greater participation rights while also retaining agility in decision-making. Democratic legitimacy can also be improved by developing deeper roots in local civil societies and by expanding domestic constituencies beyond often narrow urban-educated and (largely male) middle class elites. As explained in Chapter 6, digital tools can provide new opportunities to reach and organize new audiences, especially socioeconomically disadvantaged constituents. This may be complemented by more sustained collaborations with national social movements, trade unions, churches, and other parts of domestic civil society.

Many TNGOs seek to become more attached to local civil societies, whether in the North or South, and to secure and strengthen public ownership in their own societies.[30] This entails facilitating meaningful representation of supporter and beneficiary interests and perspectives, not just in programs but also in constituent assemblies, advisory councils, and governing organs. Integrating digital technologies into governance constitutes a step toward enhancing both agility of decision-making and responsiveness to constituents. Making digital technologies part of organizational cultures and processes[31] provides new ways of soliciting input without necessarily compromising other values, such as performance or timely actions. This is already a practice in some intergovernmental organizations such as the World Bank for global consultations on changes in policies or other strategic shifts.[32]

While many of the governance reforms in the past have taken the form of extensively deliberative processes designed to create new bodies and structures, digital tools offer opportunities to facilitate governance functions in a nimbler fashion. Decisions that lend themselves to voting or polling after deliberation could be moved online, even across an entire global organization. Just as many web conferencing platforms now allow for deliberation, polling, or voting within team contexts, it is conceivable that this technology could be adapted for governance. This can reduce the problem of sunk costs, reduce the risk of creating resistance against change, and help to shift an overall culture to one of regularly testing and evaluating new practices.

Digitally enabled global fora may support agile, democratic governance, but they can only do so if the organization overall is committed to a culture of inquiry and openness. Concerns about the "digital divide" and the reproduction of inequities in moving online have to be addressed and organizations have to do more than adopt specific tools. For example, if polling of members or staff becomes a regular feature of governance, then such results and information need to be made available in a timely fashion to those voting, even if expressed views challenge leadership or question existing practices. Additionally, insofar as TNGOs move toward digital forms of constituent input for strategy or governance purposes, they need to very clearly communicate whether they are consulting constituents for listening purposes or for participation in decision-making. Otherwise, it may lead to consultation fatigue or cynicism.

Each of these possible governance reforms carries both opportunities and risks. Although most of the reforms summarized here reflect a desire to secure greater legitimacy, organizations must strike a balance between responsiveness and agility. Considering the highly deliberative and consensus-oriented cultures of many organizations, TNGOs will need to be careful that the benefits of enhanced legitimacy are not outweighed or nullified by excessive transaction and decision-making costs. A digital culture with a clear understanding of its opportunities and limits can aid TNGOs in lessening the tensions between different objectives pursued within their governance frameworks.

TENSIONS AND TRADE-OFFS IN GOVERNANCE REFORMS

TNGOs' governance structures often mirror competing values that can be introduced by the expanding ambitions of the sector. For example, TNGOs increasingly value professionalization, but also want to maintain grassroots authenticity and staff and supporter passion and involvement. They want to be globally capable and integrated under one brand, but also recognized as uniquely local. From a managerial perspective, a complex array of governance mechanisms generates significant transaction costs and can distract from other important objectives, including the overall mission. Key considerations generated by governance reforms are summarized in Table 8.3.

More-participatory governance structures have long been a goal for many TNGOs. Many practitioners assume that the democratic legitimacy of TNGOs needs to be strengthened, and view governance reform as a principal vehicle for achieving this change. Many leaders see such reforms as contributing not just to enhancing equity, but also to overall civic engagement and learning. An example of such emphasis on input legitimacy is ActionAid's participatory model of governance, in which all member countries—regardless of whether they are net income generating or consuming—are regarded as equal. In addition, ActionAid also formally enhanced inclusion by establishing a quota for "rights-holders" in their national assemblies and boards.[33]

In contrast, other TNGOs put much greater emphasis on output legitimacy, which de-emphasizes democratic decision-making processes and seeks instead timely decisions and actions producing results. In this view, global CEOs and boards often have too little authority, and although participatory decision-making is important in TNGO program contexts, it should

Table 8.3 GOVERNANCE REFORM CONSIDERATIONS AND TENSIONS

Consideration	Tensions
Structural inequalities	Tensions between members that are net contributors and net receivers, smaller and larger members, older and newer members
Dual citizenship	Tensions between the interests of national member organizations and those of the global organization
Board composition	Tensions between espoused values of the sector and lack of diversity and inclusion (ethnicity, class, etc.) reflected in governing bodies
Board roles	Tensions between fiduciary, strategic, and "generative" board roles
Board culture	Tensions between national cultures, including adversarial and consensus-oriented contexts; variation in national presence shaping board member perspectives
Power centers	Tensions between power centers, such as between strong national affiliates that bring in significant income and between CEOs and senior teams, international assemblies, and community-based mechanisms
Resources	Tensions between attention to governance reform and pursuing current programming and other concerns; pressure on unrestricted resources and indirect cost rates versus benefits of enhanced governance

not be the goal for global board decision-making.[34] For example, Human Rights Watch's governance structure has not changed much over the decades and reflects a global corporate board structure focused on fostering agility, responsiveness to institutional donors, and overall mission coherence.

Generally, the question of governance reform will require addressing three structural inequalities that have emerged over time within many organizations. These structural inequalities typically exist between (1) those who spend money in the organization and those who generate it (and the attendant power differentials), (2) smaller and larger sized members and affiliates, and (3) those who have historically dominated decision-making at the governance level (typically members from the Global North) and those who have joined later (i.e., members from the Global South). ActionAid, Oxfam, CARE, and Plan International are examples of TNGOs that have attempted to level the playing field at the governance level between those that primarily generate and spend resources through collective resource allocation and management frameworks. However, rewriting rules and procedures does not necessarily change the ways in which resource inequities still informally sustain power differences. Some TNGOs have also found that entrenched power differentials have resulted in enduring and problematic leadership behaviors. For example, Global North members can exhibit a "donor mentality" with attendant patron-client attitudes and tendencies to push their weight around behind the scenes. This and other less-than-helpful leadership behaviors can erode trust at important moments in organizational change processes and are misaligned with the professed leadership models of many organizations.

Structural inequalities can be handled in a variety of ways. Some TNGOs have introduced weighted voting, where the weight of each vote is determined by the contributions that members bring to the whole, such as in the case of CBM. Others have been more explicitly pragmatic and less concerned with imposing equity in governance. For example, the Save the Children global board has more individuals from the United States and the UK, plus one each for Swedish and Norwegian members, which reflects its financial reality. A number of TNGOs now operate a model in which each member sends a delegate to the assembly, which then appoints the board (for example, ActionAid and Islamic Relief). Again, political reality means that the board needs to include members from the biggest affiliates because they need those affiliates to buy in to decisions for the money to flow. Larger members in these scenarios can decide to give up power during the governance design phase, as in the case of ActionAid,[35] or they can insist on an elevated role on the assumption that in addition to providing the most money they are also in possession of more capacities and knowledge needed to operate successfully.

No matter how TNGOs handle internal power dynamics, there are increasing demands for external and downward accountabilities to the general public, primary stakeholders, peers, and partners. TNGOs are being asked to be more radically transparent than ever before, and they can no longer simply rely on being viewed as unquestioned moral leaders. Instead, they are expected to respond to anyone who either seeks information or wishes to challenge the organization's legitimacy.[36] Such expectations are enhanced by the pervasive role of technology, including proliferating online data transparency standards and platforms. Organizational transparency and responsiveness are increasingly essential for the legitimacy and credibility of TNGOs. As TNGOs develop more participatory governance structures, they simultaneously address questions about internal power balancing and sharing more power and information with external audiences. These pressures frequently clash with existing staff-led cultures focused on information as a source of distinctive power and influence.

Boards and senior management teams often struggle to reflect the people they claim to serve in their compositions. For example, a recent study of US nonprofit boards found severe overrepresentation of white men across the largest 100 organizations and observed "barely perceptible" progress over time for the representation of women.[37] A 2013 analysis of 100 TNGOs and their boards found that 66 percent of board members were of European descent and 75 percent of their university degrees were acquired at Western institutions.[38] Additionally, while 72 percent of the organizations were headquartered in the Global North, 79 percent of their activities took place elsewhere. Such gaps are increasingly morally indefensible.[39]

In general, the relative power of the international boards of larger TNGOs is limited by the existence of strong national affiliates, strong CEOs, strong senior teams that may be able to skillfully manage and maneuver the board, and the existence of international assemblies with which international boards must share power.

Current reform efforts often seek to enhance some form of twin or dual citizenship with respect to simultaneously representing multiple interests and constituencies.[40] This implies a need for governing mechanism members to consider the collective well-being of the whole organization, not just their specific member interests. One possible means of addressing such representational challenges in governing bodies is to share or swap staff or board members. For example, independent representatives from centers, international secretariats, and global boards can also sit on national boards to imbue national governance bodies with "whole-of-the-organization" perspectives. Additionally, national board chairs and members can sit on the boards of other national members.

Reforms in federated, confederated, and network-structured TNGOs struggle with not just bringing about formal institutional change, but also fostering behaviors and decisions based on a more balanced understanding of needs and mutual accountability across national member organizations.[41] One way in which TNGOs attempt to move from the formal to the informal side of changing governance is by increasing the interdependencies between different parts of the organization, with a view toward inculcating organizational culture with a doctrine of mutual accountability.[42]

If board members and others are asked to consider the overall interests of an organization, they have to shift away from a singular focus on traditional roles of fiduciary oversight and strategic guidance. To foster dual citizenship, individuals have to embrace a more "generative" role by regularly asking questions about purpose and the future role of an organization.[43] While board members can serve important roles as watchdogs, fundraisers, or strategists, the role of generating the right questions about how to fulfill the mission remains often neglected in how leaders define their governance roles. Only few TNGOs have explicitly focused on the generative role of boards. ActionAid, for example, has specifically taken up the aspiration to establish a distinct form of generative board leadership.[44]

Generative work means that there is a role for the board in framing the issues and problems that are on the horizon for TNGOs, such as identifying what to pay attention to in the external environment, what those issues mean, and what to do about them. In generative work, the board acts as a "sense maker" and discerns what future challenges and opportunities the TNGO should pay attention to. Because some boards struggle with fulfilling their fiduciary (inclusive of rapidly increasing compliance issues) and strategic roles, setting expectations that go beyond these duties may require significant investments in leadership recruitment and development. Expert assessments of TNGO boards regularly find major gaps in their capacities, and especially a lagging ability to scan the horizon and anticipate the future.[45]

Apart from well-defined roles of the board, differences in national culture affect board norms and behavior. Even within the Anglo-Saxon governance model there is great difference between US boards, which typically have far more major donors as members, and UK boards, which might have none in favor of recruiting more practitioners and other experts. Whereas US board discourse can be adversarial in weighing up alternatives in the pursuit of a decision, in the UK, New Zealand, and on Islamic TNGO boards this is less culturally acceptable and a more consensus-based form of decision-making is preferred.

Some national boards also include a percentage of former staff members or volunteers (e.g., MSF), which introduces yet another dynamic compared to those populated by corporate board members. Boards populated with professionals and their expertise may be more likely to focus on oversight issues, including efficiency and outcomes. Boards with a more diverse composition, including staff or volunteers, may be likely to engage in more generative debates about the purpose and future of the organization. Overly consultative, consensus-driven, and historically rooted boards can produce decisions that try to be consistently inclusive, but are not necessarily best for the organization overall. The desire to include everyone's views can lead to discussions and decisions that are at too high a level of abstraction, that reflect the lowest common denominator, and that include "motherhood and apple pie" statements. This latter issue impacts negatively on the ability of TNGO boards to make the tough choices needed to transform themselves.

Furthermore, in the case of (con)federated organizations, board members typically have intermittent contact with higher levels of their TNGO and consequently their picture is informed largely by the way they see it in their local context. Not all TNGOs are present on the same scale across countries. For example, Save the Children has a large footprint in the United States, while Oxfam does not; World Vision has a considerable presence in the United States, Canada, and Australia, but not the UK, and; SOS Children's Villages has its main presence in Austria and Germany, where it originated. This means that each board member is thinking about a different set of peers and competitors and is informed by different thinking in their own countries.[46]

Variation in power, norms, and individual lived experiences can contribute to diversity and creativity in governance structures, but it can also lead to more fragmentation. Those TNGOs that still have unitary boards— usually dominated by the founding members—may be missing out on the necessary perspectives to be truly global, but they are also less susceptible to the higher transaction costs, conflicts, and "lowest-common-denominator" type of decisions that can beset more decentralized TNGOs. This may explain why leaders of more centralized TNGOs tend to self-report higher levels of organizational effectiveness, whereas more decentralized TNGOs are seen as more effective by their peers—the latter possibly due to greater perceived legitimacy.[47]

While complex governance arrangements clearly have important political and symbolic significance,[48] it is less clear whether many organizations have sufficient managerial and leadership capacity in place to fully realize the potential value of highly distributed governance structures. Also unclear is whether the benefits received in advice, strategic direction, and accountability are worth the significant transaction costs involved in complex, multi-level deliberations. Moreover, the higher financial costs associated with more elaborate and legitimate governance structures may be viewed by external audiences as "wasteful" overhead spending that typically must be paid out of unrestricted resources. This means that as large TNGOs expand their Global South membership and enhance the voices of Southern members in governance, more hard-to-find unrestricted resources have to be raised.[49] In the desire to gain greater democratic legitimacy and a greater leveling of South-North power discrepancies, there are clearly trade-offs. Enhanced legitimacy may come at the expense of agility, and it may also invite reputational and funding risks if TNGOs are perceived as diverting time and resources away from program delivery to support internal processes.

Realizing the benefits of governance reform requires facilitating complex changes related to informal politics and power, as well as new and ongoing investments in maintaining more substantial organizational "backbones," particularly in the form of higher costs related to administration and deliberative processes. Governance reform thus represents another crucial area in which TNGOs and their supporters must decide how much they value more democratic forms of participation and accountability relative to other competing priorities. TNGOs must also consider what practical role specific governance reforms might play within the context of a broader need to enhance organizational legitimacy. For example, as described in Chapter 5, many, if not most TNGOs have already at least partially predicated their legitimacy on instrumental claims about their outcomes and impact, either in addition to, or instead of, procedural claims about being democratic and representative (yet responsive and agile). In the case of governance reform, as in other areas, changing imposes costs that can test TNGO capabilities and force difficult trade-offs.

Governance reforms occasionally lead to individual members and affiliates leaving the larger body. There are few such examples, but prominent ones include ActionAid Spain, IBIS Denmark (leaving Alliance 2015), Islamic Relief (France, 2006), CBM (Austria), Concern Worldwide (United Kingdom), and Fairtrade (US, 2011). Discontent within federated TNGOs is not uncommon and often results from irreconcilable differences between members about strategy and goals. National members may also resent the power of the global organization. In spite of this, such separations remain relatively rare when considering the amount of tensions on display in some TNGO families. Members of a (con)federation have to consider trade-offs associated with being part of a larger global entity. The latter provides increased presence and global voice, more capacity and ability to leverage knowledge, and access to more funding sources. But for some national members and their leadership, being part of a global body generates too many constraints on overall autonomy and spending. The power to shape program approaches, policy positions, and core beliefs has to be shared across all members, and a national affiliate may feel that such decision-making is too cumbersome. Most important, members are typically subject to a set percentage of charges for overhead and investment in the global body.[50] Since many of these factors are not easily quantifiable, calculating such trade-offs is complex and decisions about staying or leaving are often driven by how top leadership perceives the particular current situation of a national member.[51]

CONCLUSION

TNGOs confront important governance challenges as they attempt to adapt for the future. They want to be viewed as legitimate based on their practices, they want to accomplish ambitious missions, and they want to secure their own survival and growth. The imperative to secure new bases of accountability and legitimacy has instigated significant attempts at governance reform to bring TNGOs into better alignment with their rhetoric and aspirations. By matching their form to their desired roles and functions, TNGOs have taken different paths based on how they see their future role and relationships to other stakeholders. While some have chosen more centralization, a greater number have attempted to balance decision-making efficiency with the goals of empowering affiliates in the Global South and inviting input from primary stakeholders. Although TNGO forms are evolving, many organizations still confront significant challenges inherited from their pasts, including entrenched structural inequalities and attendant practices held over from previous operational and governance models. Such legacies, if not addressed, can slow the pace of change or impede adaptation.

Governance reforms can impose tensions and trade-offs, most notably in the form of reduced decision-making agility that can be exacerbated by organizational cultures characterized by excessive deliberation. The form of the TNGO itself makes improving accountability and legitimacy through the mechanism of governance difficult. TNGOs operate within complex webs of multiple accountabilities externally, and layers of mutual accountabilities internally. Board members, for example, are often asked to simultaneously represent domestic and global interests, while in some cases only having relatively infrequent contact with many parts of the organization, let alone distant offices. Whereas businesses typically have clearer lines of ownership and accountability, TNGOs have no owners and accountabilities are continuously negotiated and often in tension.

Although many TNGO governance reforms have aimed at broadening representation and enhancing downward accountability, the legacy of traditional organizational structures and board practices tends to orient accountability upward to donors and other traditionally privileged stakeholders often in the Global North.[52] Governance reforms can attempt to counteract these tendencies, but such efforts may face internal political resistance, may be seen as consuming attention and resources better expended elsewhere, and may be unlikely to contribute to greater efficiency and effectiveness in the short term. Finally, although much of the sector seems to be embracing more complex governance mechanisms, it may also need to (re)consider other alternatives. For example, TNGOs could shift to a different basis for board or assembly membership altogether or adopt unitary corporate global boards with independent members only (despite many having (con)federated membership structures).

TNGOs with missions that emphasize sustainable impact and social transformation can bolster their legitimacy by adapting their organizational forms through governance changes. They will likely face difficulties, however, especially if such changes do not pay off relatively quickly in ways that stakeholders can easily recognize. Nevertheless, if TNGOs are to have both enhanced missions and the legitimacy to carry out those enhanced missions effectively, then governance reforms will often be necessary.

REFERENCES

ActionAid International. *ActionAid International Annual Report to INGO Accountability Charter 2015*. Johannesburg: ActionAid International, 2017.

ActionAid International. *Good Practices for ActionAid International Governance* Johannesburg: ActionAid International, 2014.

Balboa, Cristina M. *The Paradox of Scale: How NGOs Build, Maintain, and Lose Authority in Environmental Governance*. Cambridge, MA: MIT Press, 2018.

Banks, Nicola, David Hulme, and Michael Edwards. "NGOs, States, and Donors Revisited: Still Too Close for Comfort?" *World Development* 66 (2014): 707–18.

Bolman, Lee G., and Terrence E. Deal. *Reframing Organizations: Artistry, Choice, and Leadership*. 6th ed. San Francisco: Jossey-Bass, 2017.

Brown, L. David, Alnoor Ebrahim, and Srilatha Batliwala. "Governing International Advocacy NGOs." *World Development* 40, no. 6 (2012): 1098–108.

Interview with Marcy Vigoda, deputy secretary general, CARE International, by Tosca Bruno-van Vijfeijken. April 25, 2013.

Chabbott, Colette. "Development INGOs." In *Constructing World Culture*, edited by John Boli and George M. Thomas, 222–49. Stanford: Stanford University Press, 1999.

Chait, Richard P., William P. Ryan, and Barbar E. Taylor. *Governance as Leadership: Reframing the Work of Nonprofit Boards*. Hoboken, NJ: Wiley, 2005.

Cook, Stephen. "Analysis: Merlin and Save the Children." *Third Sector* (July 30, 2013). https://www.thirdsector.co.uk/analysis-merlin-save-children/governance/article/1193125.

Costa, Daniela, Alan Fowler, Burkhard Gnärig, Sherine Jayawickrama, Charles MacCormack, Wayne Parchman, and Peter Strüven. *Taking a Strategic Approach to Governance Reform in International Civil Society Organisations*. Berlin: International Civil Society Center, 2012.

Crewe, Emma. "Flagships and Tumbleweed: A History of the Politics of Gender Justice Work in Oxfam GB 1986–2015." *Progress in Development Studies* 18, no. 2 (2018): 110–25. https://doi.org/10.1177/1464993417750286.

Crowley, James, and Morgana Ryan. *Building a Better International NGO: Greater Than the Sum of the Parts*. Boulder, CO: Kumarian Press, 2013.

Ebrahim, Alnoor. "The Many Faces of Nonprofit Accountability." In *The Jossey-Bass Handbook of Nonprofit Leadership and Management*, edited by David O. Renz, 101–24. San Francisco: Jossey-Bass, 2010.

Edwards, Michael, and David Hulme. "Too Close for Comfort?: The Impact of Official Aid on Nongovernmental Organizations." *World Development* 24, no. 6 (1996): 961–73.

El Tom, Fairouz. "Diversity and Inclusion on NGO Boards: What the Stats Say." *The Guardian* (May 7, 2013). https://www.theguardian.com/global-development-professionals-network/2013/apr/29/diversity-inclusion-ngo-board.

Eriksen, Siri, Lars Otto Naess, Ruth Haug, Aditi Bhonagiri, and Lutgart Lenaerts. "Courting Catastrophe?: Humanitarian Policy and Practice in a Changing Climate." *IDS Bulletin* 48, no. 4 (2017): 1–14.

Freiwirth, Judy. "Community-Engagement Governance: Systems-Wide Governance in Action." *Nonprofit Quarterly* (May 9, 2011). https://nonprofitquarterly.org/community-engagement-governance-systems-wide-governance-in-action/.

Gnärig, Burkhard, and Charles F. Maccormack. "The Challenges of Globalization: Save the Children." *Nonprofit and Voluntary Sector Quarterly* 28, no. 1 suppl. (1999): 140–46. https://doi.org/10.1177/089976499773746483.

Green, Duncan. *Fit for the Future?: Development Trends and the Role of International Ngos.* Oxford: Oxfam GB, 2015.

Hunt, Vivian, Sara Prince, Sundiatu Dixon-Fyle, and Lareina Yee. *Delivering through Diversity.* New York: McKinsey & Company, 2018.

ICSC. "Power Shift and Governance Reform: Towards More Legitimate and Effective Global Governance." News release, 2018. https://icscentre.org/wp-content/uploads/2018/05/CONCEPT-Power-Shift-and-Governance-Reform_footer-updated.pdf.

Jamann, Wolfgang, "Digital Leadership in the International Civil Society Sector." *Disrupt & Innovate* (April 24, 2018). https://icscentre.org/2018/04/24/digital-leadership-in-the-international-civil-society-sector/.

Jayawickrama, Sherine S. *Oxfam International: Moving toward "One Oxfam."* Cambridge, MA: Center for Public Leadership/Harvard Kennedy School, 2012.

Koppell, Jonathan G. S. "Pathologies of Accountability: ICANN and the Challenge of 'Multiple Accountabilities Disorder'." *Public Administration Review* 65, no. 1 (2005): 94–108. https://doi.org/10.1111/j.1540-6210.2005.00434.x.

Lux, Steven J., and Tosca Bruno-van Vijfeijken. *From Alliance to International: The Global Transformation of Save the Children.* Syracuse, NY: Maxwell School of Citizenship and Public Affairs, 2012.

Nelson, Paul J., and Ellen Dorsey. "At the Nexus of Human Rights and Development: New Methods and Strategies of Global NGOs." *World Development* 31, no. 12 (2003): 2013–26.

Oxfam. *Oxfam Purpose and Beliefs.* Oxfam International (March 24, 2011). https://www.oxfam.org/sites/www.oxfam.org/files/oxfam-purpose-and-beliefs-mar-2011.pdf.

Queenan, Jeri Eckhart, Jacob Allen, and Jari Tuomala. *Stop Starving Scale: Unlocking the Potential of Global NGOs.* The Bridgespan Group (April 2013). https://www.bridgespan.org/bridgespan/Images/articles/stop-starving-scale-unlocking-the-potential/stopstarvingscale-unlockingthepotentialofglobalngos.pdf.

Robinson, M. "Privatising the Voluntary Sector: NGOs as Public Service Contractors." In *NGOs, States, and Donors: Too Close for Comfort?*, edited by D. Hulme and M. Edwards, 59–78. London: Macmillan, 1997.

Schmitz, Hans Peter, Paloma Raggo, and Tosca Bruno-van Vijfeijken. "Accountability of Transnational NGOs: Aspirations vs. Practice." *Nonprofit and Voluntary Sector Quarterly* 41, no. 6 (2012): 1175–94. https://doi.org/10.1177/0899764011431165.

Sumner, Andy. *The New Bottom Billion: What If Most of the World's Poor Live in Middle-Income Countries?* London: Center for Global Development, 2011.

Tallack, Barney. "How We Developed the Last Oxfam Strategic Plan." Paper Presented at the Maxwell School of Citizenship and Public Affairs, Syracuse, NY, 2017.

Tallack, Barney. *INGO Typologies and Organizational Forms.* Unpublished manuscript. 2018.

Theis, Michael, and Jimena Faz Garza. "White Men Still Dominate CEO Offices at Big Charities." *The Chronicle of Philanthropy* (September 4, 2019). https://www.

philanthropy.com/article/White-Men-Still-Dominate-CEO/247039?cid=pt&source=
ams&sourceId=4723264.

Tran, Long. "International NGO Centralization and Leader-Perceived Effectiveness."
Nonprofit and Voluntary Sector Quarterly 49, no. 1 (2020): 134–59. https://doi.org/
10.1177/0899764019861741.

Wong, Wendy H. *Internal Affairs: How the Structure of NGOs Transforms Human Rights.*
Ithaca, NY: Cornell University Press, 2012.

Worthington, Sam, and Alexander Grashow. *NGO Board Reckoning.* Washington,
DC: InterAction and Good Wolf Group, 2018.

CHAPTER 9
Leadership

Leaders play a key role in facilitating the profound organizational changes that many TNGOs are undergoing. Those serving at the very top of organizations have not just overall responsibility for their organizations, but also sit at the intersection of complex internal and external challenges. With increasing demands from a broader range of stakeholders, leaders have to be capable of regularly scanning the external environment, identifying the issues that matter the most, and translating them into actionable items for others in the organization. In many (con)federated TNGOs, leaders are increasingly asked to manage more collaborative and equal relations among members and affiliates. They have to be able to properly respond to external demands and crises and also have to be proactive in envisioning future organizational roles and facilitating participatory, yet timely processes designed to get TNGOs closer to fulfilling their promises.

Considering how the demands on TNGO leadership are rapidly changing, much of the sector has underinvested in leadership development for decades and has viewed such expenditures as incompatible with donor expectations for low overhead spending. Moreover, many organizations, especially those focused on campaigning, often exhibit skepticism toward leadership, with some observers characterizing the sector overall as "leadership averse."[1] Leadership and its development remain an area of limited attention where expanding mandates and ambitions have often outrun existing internal capacities. The structural leadership challenges faced by many TNGOs result in a dearth of sufficient talent for important leadership positions,[2] a tendency to look at the business sector for solutions, and some emerging efforts to instate more systematic leadership development programs with a specific focus on the future challenges faced by the sector.

Compared to government and business, the TNGO sector has relatively few sources of guidance and information on leadership offered in academic and applied literatures. What insights are available are often derived from the business context, and lessons-learned are rarely adapted to the TNGO sector's distinctive values and context. The notion of becoming more "businesslike" is a common point of discussion and contention, although it is not always clear what imitating another sector actually means.[3] What is clear is that TNGOs are often ambivalent about businesslike values and approaches. On the one hand, the business sector is often viewed as causing many of the problems that TNGOs address, such as inequality, poor working conditions, and environmental destruction. On the other hand, TNGOs reaching a certain size sometimes cannot avoid looking to businesses for inspiration about talent management, defining value propositions, marketing, generating earned revenue, and other issues.

Professionalization as a result of organizational growth challenges the maintenance of more informal management and leadership cultures.[4] The typical trade-offs emerging include (1) corporatization versus informal management styles, (2) standardization of practices versus localization and decentralization, and (3) efficiency and agility versus procedural legitimacy and democratic representation. Although the field of leadership development is dominated by private-sector perspectives and experiences, such advice requires contextualization and adaptation not only to the TNGO sector overall,[5] but also to the specifics of different subsectors. For example, humanitarian organizations delivering aid are more likely to be concerned about logistical efficiencies than advocacy organizations focused on digitally enabled activism. The former may benefit from improved supply chain management strategies, while the latter may benefit more from implementing deliberative processes that build popular support for a cause. Since many TNGOs explicitly focus on the generation of public goods, they are typically more similar to government agencies than businesses and more appropriate guidance may often be found in the "public and nonprofit management" literature.[6]

Since TNGOs usually want to do more than just fill gaps left behind by markets and government (see Chapter 2), the sector and its leaders have to embrace certain norms of risk-taking and innovation traditionally associated with business. Major technological advances have often come from the corporate sector (sometimes with explicit government support), while the nonprofit sector cannot point to a commensurate track record largely because of the absence of investment capital and the architecture's restrictive normative expectations. With the sector taking up more ambitious mandates and goals, organizations have begun also to embrace new roles as social innovators, idea incubators, and thought leaders. These new roles require a greater capacity to learn and innovate, which means strengthening monitoring, evaluation, and accountability systems (see Chapter 7) as well as investing more in leadership development and organizational cultural change.

Rather than remaining risk avoidant, tolerance of risk and failure are important for innovation and the rapid design of new solutions with increasingly better results. This risk-taking orientation and willingness to fail transparently is still largely incompatible with many organizational cultures and donor expectations. However, some large TNGOs such as World Vision and CARE, and also mid-size organizations like PATH and Pact, are incorporating innovation units and funds, chiefs of innovation, and even futurologists to integrate nontraditional mindsets into their organizations. Many TNGOs understand the need to move on from their traditional roles, and leadership plays a key role in developing a proactive path informed by relevant lessons from other TNGOs and other sectors.

TNGO LEADERSHIP BLIND SPOTS

Common leadership "blind spots" in the TNGO sector are often caused by the cultural norms and values of the architecture. More traditional leadership in the sector prizes dedication to the mission, consensus seeking, charisma, motivational ability, and valiant heroism. It is designed to gather followers inside and outside of the organization as well as signal moral superiority to everyone else. Armed with principles and supporters, charismatic leadership can neglect bad news, avoid complexities and learning,[7] and view the outside world as largely hostile. Although certainly not all TNGO leaders in the past can be categorized as traditional in this sense, there are specific blind spots to be addressed if TNGOs are to be led successfully into the future. Table 9.1 summarizes key leadership blind spots and the problems they can cause.[8]

Externally, TNGO leaders often lack sufficient political acumen to influence other actors. Leaders do not necessarily understand politicians' motivations or frames of thinking, and often fail to take the individual leadership styles and incentive systems of decision-makers into account in their efforts to influence policymakers. Often driven by a focus on their mission and its urgency, TNGO leaders may not pay sufficient attention to the incentives and time horizons of policymakers. Leaders often underappreciate

Table 9.1 LEADERSHIP BLIND SPOTS

Blind spot areas	Problems caused
External politics	Insufficient understanding of motives, frames, and needs of (political and government senior civil servant) decision-makers and other stakeholders Assuming immutable positions, rather than framing issues in terms of interests and possible win-win scenarios, or alternatively, compromises Dominance of advocacy over inquiry forecloses possibilities
In-group versus out-group bias	"Othering" and limited diversity fosters skepticism toward out-groups
Internal politics	Neglect of political frame to understand interests and issues
Diversity and inclusion	Resistance (strong "antibodies") against internal changemakers and rebels because any dissent is framed as undermining consensus or the mission
Leadership development	General aversion against leadership and insufficient resources devoted to leadership development due to architectural imperatives Focus on "doing" rather than learning and investing
Outcomes focus	Emphasis on process and personal commitment rather than results Underinvestment in measurement, evaluation, accountability, and learning systems

the importance of chiefs of staff and advisers to politicians, making access to aides and gatekeepers crucial. Such access, as well as the right framing of information, is important in getting on the agenda now, rather than later (or never). The ideational and informational power of TNGOs to offer salient information and knowledge is well established (see Chapter 4), but knowing when to act requires more of a lobbyist's experience and approach to the political process. TNGO leaders are often very focused on promoting their cause, but less experienced in knowing how to recognize sudden political opportunities, engage with diverse audiences, and frame issues to resonate with skeptical officials and policymakers. Being able to influence a broad range of stakeholders on a given topic requires pitching specific types of evidence based on the preferences and needs of an audience. Politicians will be more inclined to listen when confronted with positive visions and "quick wins," while civil servants need credible data and technical details.[9]

TNGO leaders often struggle in their external communications when advocacy (making statements about what you want or need) dominates inquiry (seeking information about what others want or need). They then are more likely to conflate positions and interests and initiate any interaction with their own advocacy, rather than with listening and inquiring. Positional discussions tend to box leaders in, while interest-based conversations create flexibility for movement. In negotiations and collaborations, a key step involves moving from an initial transparent exchange of positions to exploring underlying interests. Such inquiry into what actually matters to other actors is particularly important when working with unlike-minded governments or businesses and when confrontational tactics will end communications. By not exploiting the benefits of interest-based inquiry, TNGO leaders are more likely to end up with lowest-common-denominator compromises, rather than gaining more trust and understanding as a pre-condition to higher-level collaboration.[10]

The lack of empathy with other stakeholders is often grounded in strong in-group versus out-group bias separating virtuous insiders and "bad" outsiders. Advocacy organizations often explicitly foster such a per-spective in their mobilization because having a clearly identifiable villain is more effective in generating media and public attention. Some TNGO leaders seem to lack a genuine interest in how to interact with and influence members of an out-group. This is all too often translated into an attitude to campaigning that essentially presumes and communicates to the other actor that they are ignorant or have the wrong values. Much less common are leadership attitudes that "assume the people we are criticizing are as smart as we are, and that some of them at least will already have thought about our criticisms," which is why leaders can "seek those people out and try and involve them in your work as early as possible, and . . . avoid lazy generalizations."[11] Greater openness to the critical perspectives of out-groups can contribute to improving one's own arguments over time, while also generating opportunities to engage more directly with opponents and attempt to influence their positions by understanding their interests.

Internally, TNGOs and their leaders also struggle with in-group versus out-group issues,[12] a lack of diversity and inclusion (e.g., social class, education, disability, sexual and gender identity, etc.), and a neglect of leadership devel-opment designed to mitigate the leadership blind spots common across the sector. New perspectives and cultural changes are often necessary to correct such shortcomings. However, some have observed that "NGOs have strong antibodies against changemakers or rebels who are brought in. They are fought all the time, and there is a high chance the system will spit them out."[13] Organizational cultures vary in the extent to which they are amenable to being changed in their ways of working, values, and work styles as a result of the inflow of younger generations and those with more diverse backgrounds.

Diversity of leadership has certainly been a preoccupation of many larger TNGOs, resulting in an increased emphasis on recruiting, developing, and retaining talent from the Global South. While significant progress has been made at the national and regional levels, at the leadership level in head-quarters, international secretariats, and more recently in global centers, these organizations still struggle to diversify leadership. Some (such as ActionAid, for example) play the role of early adopters with a seemingly bigger initial political commitment than others. Organizations such as Amnesty International admit that recruitment and retention of such leaders has been a challenge while undergoing a process of decentralization and establishing regional offices across the globe.[14] Such diversification is all the more necessary where cross-sectoral diversity is a precondition for advancing expanding mandates. In the past, TNGO leaders often advanced through the ranks, limiting the infusion of government and for-profit sector perspectives and experiences, especially below the CEO level. Moreover, in sectors such as human rights and the environment, staff generally develop their careers within their own sector, which further limits the infusion of new ideas. While most TNGOs have accepted that diversity is important for upholding principles of fairness and nondiscrimination and providing for constituency representation, far fewer have committed to moving beyond simply assimilating those who are different to instead encourage the existing culture to substantively change as a result of enhanced diversity.[15]

A number of larger, US-based TNGOs have been more open to for-profit sector hires than, for instance, European-based TNGOs that are typically more critical of the business sector. TNGOs with an already more "corporate" culture such as World Vision and Save the Children have more consistently recruited across different levels from the for-profit sector. In TNGOs that do hire people from the business sector, this leads to a faster adoption of business processes and systems, as is to be expected, while at the same time producing tensions between various parts of the organizational culture, or the strengthening of contrasting subcultures. Such tensions offer opportunities to engage in self-reflection around competing institutional logics and what is the "soul" of the TNGO (see Chapter 2).

TNGO leaders often display distinct gaps in capacities required to effectively handle the external and internal politics of making their organization more effective and responsive. This includes not just recognizing the growing external emphasis on outcomes-based accountability, impact-oriented philanthropy, and competition for resources and attention, but also the ability to translate these demands into a conducive organizational culture with internal systems for monitoring and evaluating organizational effectiveness and clarifying operational and programmatic goals, performance expectations, information ownership, and lines of accountability. Effective leadership in this regard is more than about process and doing things appropriately in accordance with conventional norms. For TNGOs to remain competitive, leadership must also be about achieving demonstrable results and incentivizing an organizational culture that genuinely values measurement, evaluation, accountability, and learning. This requires prioritizing investments in appropriate staff and systems, especially systems and processes that are standardized, scalable, and integrated across the organization (and that ideally can deliver long-term cost savings).[16] It also requires communicating the importance of outcomes to stakeholders, and in many cases leading organizational cultural changes to create an environment more conducive to an outcome orientation. TNGO leaders play a key role in translating external pressures into internal policies and processes that foster enthusiasm for adaptive change.

Such fundamental change in the focus of an organization from exhibiting dedication to a cause to being an effective learning organization highlights the importance of leading internal "change coalitions" and adopting a political frame to drive change.[17] Many leaders see their organization partially as a "jungle" in which people and caucuses jockey for power and position, seek access to influencers through gatekeepers, rally resources to their cause, and use coercive strategies, bargaining, persuasion, and negotiation to advance the goals of the organization. If top leaders cannot manage this "jungle" by taking decisive actions and recruiting allies, they are likely to lose control and their blind spots can undermine the goals of the change process. For example, CARE 2020's change process partially struggled to get on track because the change coalition lacked "positive politics" skills to increase its membership and power. It did not fully deploy process-related tools, including stakeholder and power analysis, power brokering, player strategies, bargaining, persuasion, or coercion strategies sufficiently. This opening of the political space left by the top leadership could then be exploited by other CARE members to implement their own coercion strategies, backroom deals, and stalling techniques.[18]

As the cases of CARE and other TNGOs indicate, change leadership is a critical competence for TNGO leaders.[19] Organizational change processes, especially in larger organizations, tend to be very complex, and the leadership and management abilities that are required are therefore extensive.[20] In the business sector, large organizational change processes have high failure rates, with many change processes fizzling out or imploding due to mismanaged conflict, stasis, and deliberation.[21] Organizational change leadership especially in larger TNGOs often requires integrating decentralized, horizontally connected, networked forms of management. Organizational size will typically create major structural barriers against change because it leads to bureaucratization, a greater focus on organizational survival, and the emergence of potentially powerful veto players.[22] Addressing specific leadership blind spots with regard to change management in a relatively large organization may increase the odds of success, but major organizational risks remain beyond the role of leadership.

The various leadership blind spots point to an underlying lack of leadership development. The TNGO sector, on the whole, underinvests in leadership development, as is also true throughout the nonprofit sector more broadly.[23] In the United States, for example, the Foundation Center calculated nonprofit sector spending on leadership development in 2011 at $400 million—a mere 0.03 percent of the sector's $1.5 trillion in total annual spending. This equates to per-capita spending of just $29 in the nonprofit sector as compared to $120 in the for-profit sector. Foundations are partially responsible for this underinvestment, allocating no more than 1 percent per year toward leadership development initiatives in their grantee organizations over several decades.[24] There are many reasons for such underinvestment, including pressure to minimize overhead, insufficient resources, a cultural preference for doing rather than improving, and general leadership aversion.[25] All these architectural factors are interrelated and can produce a highly adverse context for investment in leadership development.

LEADERSHIP TRAIT ANALYSIS

Leadership development as a precondition for addressing leadership blind spots begins with an assessment of a leader's current capabilities. TNGO leaders bring their individual personality traits and leadership styles to work, including when they drive large-scale change in their organizations. Leadership trait analysis (LTA) is one specific tool that can be applied in leadership development. LTA involves analyzing the content of statements made by leaders to detect underlying psychological dispositions that condition leadership behavior. Individual leaders are compared to the norms of their peer group along a variety of dimensions, and these comparisons determine a leader's overall "leadership style."[26] An assessment of TNGO leadership styles provides context for understanding leadership blind spots and development needs, while also suggesting insights about organizational cultures.

Leadership trait analysis as applied to TNGO leadership styles is grounded in a contingency model of leadership.[27] This approach emphasizes the match between what the leader is like, what stakeholders want, what the setting calls for, and the nature of the relationship between the leader and the led. It emphasizes the importance of context to leadership, and recognizes that people tend to choose leadership positions that match their leadership style so that they feel most comfortable. Analysis of TNGO leadership styles differentiates "how important it is to leaders to exert control and influence over the environment they find themselves in, and the constraints that environment poses—as opposed to being adaptable to the situation and remaining open to responding to the demands of stakeholders."[28] This categorization is based on two underlying psychological variables relating to the belief in one's ability to control events (working within or challenging constraints) and the need for power. Leaders willing to challenge constraints often come to their positions with an agenda and "seek 'true believers' to work with them in implementing that agenda."[29] They are interested in controlling the flow of information and see constraints as obstacles to be overcome. In contrast, leaders who respect constraints tend to focus on their surroundings and seek out others' perspectives. They are open to bargaining, trade-offs, and compromise. Leaders exhibiting these traits view constraints as parameters for action.[30] These leaders respond to problems on a case-by-case basis, whereas leaders who challenge constraints do so based on what they want or need.[31]

Leadership trait analysis applied to a large sample of US-based TNGO leaders has found that the majority of leaders are not constraint challengers.[32] Fifty-seven percent favored collaboration, compromise, and consensus as opposed to attempting to pursue change directly by challenging constraints. These leaders were highly sensitive to context, preferred incremental to rapid change, and maintained openness to stakeholder demands. Of the remaining 43 percent of leaders more apt to challenge constraints, 13 percent adopted a "head-on," "take-charge" approach, 11 percent worked "behind the scenes," and 19 percent varied their approach based on the situation. Leaders from smaller sized TNGOs were more likely to respect constraints, leaders from medium-sized TNGOs were more likely to challenge constraints directly, and leaders of large organizations preferred to work behind the scenes. Moreover, 64 percent of leaders from the sustainable development sector respected constraints, seeking compromise and consensus. This is likely an expression of a need to secure access for their programming and a focus on working within a larger aid industry. When TNGO leaders have been presented with these findings, they often express surprise, and sometimes some displeasure, since they do not align with the mental models that many leaders tend to have of themselves and of their sector.[33]

One of the conclusions from this and additional research and observations from leadership training programs (see the Note on Sources) is that knowing what leaders bring to leadership—their "leading self"—is crucial.[34] This is true both when it comes to the human resources dimension of leading and managing change—how people in organizations respond to large-scale organizational change—as well as to the dimensions of power and politics in organizational change processes. TNGO leaders need to know first what motivates them in the workplace, such as a sense of accomplishment, need for power, or affiliation,[35] and what their preferences are in conflict management. Some primarily focus on the "organizational-structural" or human resources dimensions of organizational change, while others pay more attention to the need to use the political or symbolic frames.[36] Not surprisingly, leading change requires all of these frames. An awareness of a leader's natural tendencies and preferences, his or her willingness to strengthen frames that are weak, and the presence of peers who complement a leader's natural tendencies are crucial. TNGO leaders are finding that it is possible to train oneself over time to use additional lenses and to increase self-awareness as a precondition to adopting a culture and mode of inquiry.[37]

FUTURE-ORIENTED LEADERSHIP AND LEADERSHIP DEVELOPMENT NEEDS

The external environmental shifts and organizational change imperatives confronting the sector generate substantially new leadership and leadership development needs for TNGOs and their coalitions. Of course, this does not mean that all existing leadership capacities are no longer important. Indeed, "certain leadership skills are always in demand; leaders still need to be flexible and adaptive, they need to be able to mobilize people, ideas, and resources, and they need to have a personally compelling style of leading others."[38] At the same time, leaders are often the first ones to be confronted with demands for change and greater evidence of organizational impact. Their ability to instill entrepreneurship, to innovate, to effectively lead change in their organizations, to communicate and collaborate with multiple types of stakeholders, and to instill such interest, willingness, and capacity to do so in their organizations have become much more urgent.

TNGO leaders today must be able to listen to even more voices and be able to synthesize that "noise" into a few overarching themes that staff, boards, and constituents can understand and act upon. Coupled with other rapid changes in the external environment, these demands on leaders translate into a need for a high degree of tolerance for ambiguity and uncertainty, while also retaining agility. The needs for strategic foresight and direction, on the one hand, and rapid adaptability and agility, on the other, create a paradox for TNGO leaders. Instead of three-to-five-year strategic planning cycles,[39] TNGOs today and in the future must be able to more rapidly evaluate what works, manage more inputs more quickly (including by using digital tools), and regularly rethink their overall role in social and political change. Leadership in such changing contexts has to be particularly adept at facilitating more supporter-led activism, being able to work within broader alliances and coalitions, and conceiving of hybrid forms of approaches and solutions. Table 9.2 provides an overview of key leadership foci and issues.

Greenpeace represents one example of an organization proactively adapting to rapidly changing external conditions. Greenpeace has shifted away from a staff-led and media-driven campaigning model to a more supporter-led form of activism.[40] This has required shifts in organizational culture away from hands-on, sometimes "heroic," and "macho" forms of leadership by Greenpeace staff and toward a strategy of enabling and serving citizens to engage in their own campaigning modalities, often through digital means (also see Chapter 6). Given the limitations of what staff-led activism can do in accomplishing expanding ambitions, a transition to supporter-led campaigning is a timely experiment that puts the organization on the forefront of generating scalable models for broad-based social and environmental change consistent with contemporary realities.

Table 9.2 LEADERSHIP FOCI AND ISSUES

Focus	Issues
Collaborative leadership	Organizational hybridity
	Polyglot perspective
	Working with unlike-minded actors
	Personal traits and skills
	Conflict management
Post-heroic leadership	Supporter-led activism
	Emotional intelligence
	Connective leadership
	Skills and talents of co-leaders
Generational leadership	Faster career cycles
	Need for feedback
	Desire for immediate impact
Change leadership	Environmental scanning
	Delegation
	Mode of inquiry
	Maintained outcome focus
	Leadership development

Leadership increasingly requires effective habits of collaborating with likeminded, as well as unlike-minded parties to achieve impact (also see Chapter 10). Focused on collective impact, TNGOs increasingly participate in multi-stakeholder partnerships, collaborative participatory governance, inter-organizational networks, coalitions, and alliances to achieve greater synergy.[41] Leading and managing these collaborative arrangements requires addressing leadership blind spots by acquiring different skills, experience profiles, and repertoires of expertise. Effective leadership in this context demands that leaders be aware of their individual attributes and be able to see themselves as others do and be able to change their leadership lens.[42]

The personal traits and skills of leaders engaged in collaborations play an important, although often underappreciated, role in successful collaborations. Such specific individual traits include open-mindedness and patience, interpersonal skills (e.g., communicating and listening), and group process skills (e.g., facilitation, negotiation, and interest-based, collaborative problem-solving). While leadership in the past may have been less focused on understanding group and intercultural dynamics, the growing emphasis on collaborative approaches requires an ability to work with different personalities. It also includes strategic leadership skills, such as the ability to see the big picture and a willingness to share power, resources, and credit. In contrast, substantive and technical skills are becoming relatively less important in collaborative settings.[43]

Leaders can approach external collaborations more strategically than opportunistically, but this demands an attentiveness to, and critical awareness of, potential collaborators as informed by thoughtful analysis. To address the leadership blind spot preventing a full understanding of others' interests (see Table 9.1), a careful stakeholder analysis prior to partner selection can determine the degree of overlap in values and ideas about how change happens. As the process moves forward, leaders can influence group process norms, pursue clarity over goals, ascertain responsibilities, and reach agreement about the nature of ties to other stakeholders. Taking a more interest-based perspective also facilitates conflict management and resolution, because a divergence in perspectives is not viewed as resulting from uncompromising positions and principles. While conflict is often stigmatized among TNGOs, it can foster innovation and generate new ideas, provided that leaders and staff can avoid tying disagreements back to personal failures.[44] Given the emphasis on inter-organizational collaboration and the growing need to work across a wide range of contexts, future leaders may aspire to be "polyglot" leaders.[45] This involves an ability to speak many institutional "languages" and work with different types of institutional forms.

Some TNGOs have recently embraced new forms of leadership models, including "post-heroic leadership."[46] These models depart from what historically were business sector–inspired "hero leader" models to instead emphasize the importance of leading horizontally through facilitative processes. Post-heroic leadership models promote notions of shared leadership with a primary role for leaders to facilitate staff development and empowerment in alignment with a shared leadership model that distributes leadership roles throughout an organization.[47] Leadership traits such as collaborative leadership skills, emotional intelligence, understanding leadership as a social process,[48] leading up,[49] and connective leadership[50] are all important in this post-heroic leadership model. Less important are hierarchical or positional forms of leadership. These transformational models of leadership align well with TNGOs' democratic, participatory values, and are increasingly seen to be the most viable style of leading in networked, (con)federated organizations, and in TNGO coalitions, networks, and alliances.

Post-heroic leadership models may generate their own blind spots, but they have become a key to both managing major internal organizational change processes and to becoming a successful collaborator with other organizations in alliances and coalitions. The "hero" type leader may be able to envision needed organizational changes and to rally support, but may not necessarily have the political skills to address skepticism and build broad-based "change coalitions."

In addition to the growing significance of multi-stakeholder collaborations (either within or between organizations), many TNGOs are also experimenting with new institutional forms of organizational hybridity through the introduction of social enterprises and impact-investing vehicles inside of or parallel to their organizations.[51] New institutional forms introduce additional new challenges. Given the rise of multi-stakeholder collaborations, hybridity,[52] and the introduction of social enterprise and impact investing models into the TNGO space, forward-thinking TNGO leaders increasingly need to cultivate an ability to collaborate productively with actors from other organizational and sectoral cultures, including businesses and social-impact investors. These cultures are often quite dissimilar to those of traditional TNGOs.

Apart from new organizational forms requiring new leadership skills, results-oriented philanthropy and impact investing as well as digital technologies generate new sets of expectations among new generations of stakeholders relatively unhampered by the norms of pre-millennial organizational models and development paradigms. In addition to presenting external challenges, these cultural changes mean that leaders need to lead younger generations of staff members differently to attract, motivate, and retain their talent. Their documented need for faster career cycles, on-the-job growth opportunities, regular feedback, and their desire to have immediate impact require different managerial styles and systems than those that may have worked for previous generations.[53] Leaders' capacities to empower others and to grow multi-layered and decentralized leadership, and their abilities to inspire employees, must adapt accordingly.[54] TNGO leaders who can be both inspirational as well as managerial will likely resonate better with younger generations of professionals who often have matured outside of the TNGO sector.

The internal orientation of many traditional brick-and-mortar TNGOs is striking when compared with, for instance, the culture and practices of explicitly public-facing digital organizations, such as change.org, 38 Degrees, or Avaaz (see Chapter 6). These are very member- and supporter-centric in their orientation, and claim to see themselves primarily as facilitators of member activism.[55] Many contemporary TNGO leaders will have to become more externally oriented and attuned to the opportunities and threats in the external environment, instead of being primarily internally oriented. This external orientation is also important for their staff, especially at the mid to senior levels, where the ability to scan the external environment to detect changes can result in the most rapid adaptations. The dynamism of the external environment for TNGOs also means that TNGOs with leadership models focused primarily at being reactive and defensive will quickly fall behind.[56] Leaders must deliberately initiate organizational changes to anticipate, as well as respond strategically to, external developments.

Change leadership requires an ability to maintain an external focus through the strong delegation and empowerment of managers and staff, which in turn frees up time for leaders to scan the environment for strategic opportunities and threats.[57] This also implies a consultative yet efficient internal decision-making process that does not overly distract leaders from developments in the external environment so that they have the opportunity to look beyond the horizon. Distributing this responsibility to employees deployed throughout the organization provides more receptive capacity toward the external environment. In addition, leaders themselves can proactively develop tools and relationships to enhance their own abilities to scan their external environments.[58]

The shift toward a greater outward orientation for leadership is broadly aligned with some of the envisioned changes in the overall role and purpose of TNGOs. Post-heroic leadership at the organizational level suggests a new and different global presence expressed in aspirations, such as becoming a community, a network, a platform, or a broker. Such major structural shifts are designed to move away from the notion of TNGOs as traditional

Table 9.3 TRADITIONAL AND FUTURE-FIT LEADERSHIP PROFILES

Traditional leadership	Future-fit leadership
Dedication to the organization	Community orientation
Position-driven advocacy	Interest-driven inquiry
Focus on in-groups versus out-groups	Collaborative within and across sectors
Linear strategic planning	Embrace complexity and ambiguity
Transactional relationships	Authentic relationships
Claim credit	Share credit
Project success	Embrace failure as a learning opportunity
Donor orientation emphasizing organizational trustworthiness and financial propriety	Results orientation emphasizing measurement, evaluation, accountability, learning, transparency, and stakeholder responsiveness
Hero and savior personality	Humble personality
Virtuous self-sacrifice	Self-reflection, continuous learning and self-development, work-life balance

charitable organizations toward more "rhizomatic" forms of dynamic networks where initiative can originate at any level or location and spread from there.[59] This idea stands in contrast to the more predictable behavior of the "arborescent" model constrained to vertical, tree-like growth.[60] Many TNGOs currently aspire to be both and insist that their organization can manage different operating and institutional logics. Their leaders are asked to oversee major organizational transformations, while also showing greater capacities to forecast and respond to external changes affecting the organization. What is clear is that core leadership skills and perspectives will need to adapt alongside the significant changes that TNGOs are undergoing with respect to organizational forms and roles. Table 9.3 suggests several ways in which leadership profiles can adapt for future fitness.[61]

CONCLUSION

Although leadership in the TNGO sector shares many similarities with leadership in other sectors, the TNGO sector's commitment to sustainable impact and social transformation, and its embeddedness within a distinct architecture of traditional forms and norms, present unique challenges for TNGO leaders. As a sector, TNGOs typically underinvest in leadership development, which contributes to potential blind spots that can limit TNGOs' abilities to adapt and change. To better serve their organizations and sector, TNGO leaders can pursue greater self-awareness and self-knowledge and try to do more to enhance their capacities for collaborative leadership, post-heroic leadership, generational leadership, and change leadership. However, investment in these capacities and related skill sets is complicated by the overarching context in which TNGO leaders operate. Culturally, many organizations still value, and respond to, traditional rather than future-fit leadership values and behaviors, while many organizational cultures exhibit leadership aversion. Moreover, the broader philanthropic ecosystem is itself relatively unconducive to supporting leadership development. This is increasingly problematic for a sector facing an urgent need to invest in its own future to adapt to a rapidly changing environment. Overall, many such traditional norms and expectations constrain TNGOs' abilities to build new capacities, experiment with less conventional roles, and successfully advance more transformative missions.

TNGOs and their leaders face rapidly evolving leadership demands while simultaneously operating under constraints that make fulfilling those demands especially challenging. To some extent, even transformative leaders must respect many of the constraints of the traditional architecture, even as they may continue to push the architecture's boundaries and advocate for change. Individual leaders must be cautious when challenging traditional ways of operating that could potentially expose organizations to risks.

During times of crisis, TNGOs may be tempted to look again for charismatic leaders promising to quickly solve their problems.[62] Unfortunately, this is rarely the most effective approach, as more humble and community-oriented leaders will likely be more successful in mobilizing entire organizations and their supporters to address current challenges and prepare for new opportunities.[63] Such leadership qualities are required to not just secure organizational survival, but also to enhance organizational impact. TNGOs and their leaders may be able to survive by remaining close to the paths that they have taken in the past, but they are then less likely to be part of the change that will be necessary for ensuring the sector's future relevance.

REFERENCES

Achieve. *The 2016 Millennial Impact Report. Cause Engagement Following an Election Year.* Washington, DC: The Case Foundation, 2016.
Bohn, Roger. "Stop Fighting Fires." *Harvard Business Review* 78, no. 4 (2000). 82-91.

Bolman, Lee G., and Terrence E. Deal. *Reframing Organizations: Artistry, Choice, and Leadership*. 6th ed. San Francisco: Jossey-Bass, 2017.

Cable, Daniel M. "How Humble Leadership Really Works." *Harvard Business Review* (April 23, 2018). https://hbr.org/2018/04/how-humble-leadership-really-works.

Cabrey, Tricia S., Amy Haughey, and Terry Cooke-Davies. *Enabling Organizational Change through Strategic Initiatives*. Newtown Square, PA: Project Management Institute, 2014.

Chadwick, Andrew, and James Dennis. "Social Media, Professional Media, and Mobilisation in Contemporary Britain: Explaining the Strengths and Weaknesses of the Citizens' Movement 38 Degrees." *Political Studies* 65, no. 1 (2017): 42–60. https://doi.org/10.1177/0032321716631350.

Cormier, Dave. "Rhizomatic Education: Community as Curriculum." *Innovate: Journal of Online Education* 4, no. 5 (2008). https://www.learntechlib.org/p/104239/.

Crowley, James, and Morgana Ryan. *Building a Better International NGO: Greater Than the Sum of the Parts*. Boulder, CO: Kumarian Press, 2013.

Crowley, James, and Morgana Ryan. *Navigating Change for International NGOs: A Practical Handbook*. Boulder, CO: Kumarian Press, 2017.

Emerson, Kirk, Tina Nabatchi, and Stephen Balogh. "An Integrative Framework for Collaborative Governance." *Journal of Public Administration Research and Theory* 22, no. 1 (2012): 1–29.

Eslen-Ziya, Hande, and Itır Erhart. "Toward Postheroic Leadership: A Case Study of Gezi's Collaborating Multiple Leaders." *Leadership* 11, no. 4 (2015): 471–88. https://doi.org/10.1177/1742715015591068.

Feldmann, Derrick, Joanna Nixon, Justin Brady, Lara Brainer-Banker, and Lindsay Wheeler. *The 2013 Millennial Impact Report*. The Millennial Impact Research (2013). http://www.themillennialimpact.com/past-research.

Fiedler, Fred E. "The Contingency Model and the Dynamics of the Leadership Process." In *Advances in Experimental Social Psychology*, edited by Leonard Berkowitz, 59–112. London: Academic Press, 1978.

Fletcher, Joyce K. "The Paradox of Post Heroic Leadership: An Essay on Gender, Power, and Transformational Change." *The Leadership Quarterly* 15 (2004): 647–61.

Fowler, Alan, Elizabeth Field, and Joseph McMahon. "The Upside of Conflict." *Stanford Social Innovation Review* (Winter 2019). https://ssir.org/articles/entry/the_upside_of_conflict.

Goleman, Daniel. *Emotional Intelligence*. New York: Bantam Books, 2005.

Graen, George B., and Mary Uhl-Bien. "Relationship-Based Approach to Leadership: Development of Leader-Member Exchange (LMX) Theory of Leadership over 25 Years: Applying a Multi-Level Multi-Domain Perspective." *The Leadership Quarterly* 6, no. 2 (1995): 219–47.

Heifetz, Ronald A., Marty Linsky, and Alexander Grashow. *The Practice of Adaptive Leadership: Tools and Tactics for Changing Your Organization and the World*. Boston: Harvard Business School Publishing, 2009.

Hermalin, Benjamin E. "At the Helm, Kirk or Spock? The Pros and Cons of Charismatic Leadership." Berkeley: University of California Press, 2014.

Hermann, Margaret G. "Assessing Leadership Style: Trait Analysis." In *The Psychological Assessment of Political Leaders*, edited by Jerrold Post, 178–212. Ann Arbor: University of Michigan Press, 2003.

Hermann, Margaret, Jesse D. Lecy, George E. Mitchell, Christiane Pagé, Paloma Raggo, Hans Peter Schmitz, and Lorena Venula. "Transnational NGOs: A Cross-Sectoral Analysis of Leadership Perspectives." (December 18, 2012). Available at SSRN: https://ssrn.com/abstract=2191082 or http://dx.doi.org/10.2139/ssrn.2191082.

Hermann, Margaret G., Jesse D. Lecy, George E. Mitchell, Christiane Pagé, Paloma
    Raggo, Hans Peter Schmitz, and Lorena Viñuela. "The Transnational NGO
    Study: Rationale, Sampling and Research Process." (January 18, 2010). Available
    at SSRN: https://ssrn.com/abstract=2191090 or http://dx.doi.org/10.2139/
    ssrn.2191090.

Hirshfield, Ira. "Investing in Leadership to Accelerate Philanthropic Impact." *Stanford
    Social Innovation Review* (2014). https://ssir.org/articles/entry/investing_in_
    leadership_to_accelerate_philanthropic_impact.

Kajenthira, Arani, and Philippe Sion. "Collective Impact without Borders: Successful,
    Multi-National, Collective Impact Efforts Require That Organizations Carefully
    Consider Two Dimensions of Their Approach." *Stanford Social Innovation Review*
    (2017).

Kania, John, and Mark Kramer. "Collective Impact." *Stanford Social Innovation Review*
    (Winter 2011): 36–41.

Kapila, Monisha. "The Business Case for Investing in Talent." *Stanford Social Innovation
    Review* (May 7, 2014). http://www.ssireview.org/talent_matters/entry/the_
    business_case_for_investing_in_talent.

Kotter, John P. *Leading Change*. Boston: Harvard Business Press, 2012.

Landles-Cobb, Libbie, Kirk Kramer, and Katie Smith Milway. "The Nonprofit
    Leadership Development Deficit." *Stanford Social Innovation Review* (October 25,
    2015). https://ssir.org/articles/entry/the_nonprofit_leadership_development_
    deficit.

Lipman-Blumen, Jean. *Connective Leadership: Managing in a Changing World.*
    New York: Oxford University Press, 2000.

Lux, Steven, Shreeya Neupane, and Tosca Bruno-van Vijfeijken. *External Assessment of
    CARE 2020: Change Process and Progress.* 2016 (unpublished report).

Maier, Florentine, Michael Meyer, and Martin Steinbereithner. "Nonprofit
    Organizations Becoming Business-Like: A Systematic Review." *Nonprofit and
    Voluntary Sector Quarterly* 45, no. 1 (2016): 64–86.

Mayne, Ruth, Duncan Green, Irene Guijt, Martin Walsh, Richard English, and Paul
    Cairney. "Using Evidence to Influence Policy: Oxfam's Experience." *Palgrave
    Communications* 4, no. 1 (2018): 122. https://doi.org/10.1057/s41599-018-0176-7.

Mayo, Margarita. "If Humble People Make the Best Leaders,
    Why Do We Fall for Charismatic Narcissists." *Harvard
    Business Review* (April 7, 2017). https://hbr.org/2017/04/
    if-humble-people-make-the-best-leaders-why-do-we-fall-for-charismatic-narcissists.

McClelland, David C. *The Achieving Society*. New York: Free Press, 1961.

McMahon, Joe, and Alan Fowler. *Conflict Management in INGOs*. Unpublished report
    on results from survey. London/Uxbridge: InterMediation (in collaboration with
    World Vision and Amnesty International), 2015.

Miller, Jed, and Cynthia Gibson. *From Burning Platform to Building People Power*
    Mobilisation Lab (2017). https://mobilisationlab.org/burning-platform-building-
    people-power/.

Mitchell, George E. "Collaborative Propensities among Transnational NGOs Registered
    in the United States." *American Review of Public Administration* 44, no. 5 (2014): 575–
    99. https://doi.org/10.1177/0275074012474337.

Mitchell, George E., Rosemary O'Leary, and Catherine Gerard. "Collaboration and
    Performance: Perspectives from Public Managers and NGO Leaders." *Public
    Performance and Management Review* 38, no. 4 (2015): 684–716.

Mitchell, George E., and Hans Peter Schmitz. "The Nexus of Public and Nonprofit Management." *Public Performance & Management Review* 42, no. 1 (2019): 11–33. https://doi.org/10.1080/15309576.2018.1489293.

"Moving Amnesty Closer to the Ground Is Necessary, Not Simple." openDemocracy. Updated January 20, 2015. https://www.opendemocracy.net/openglobalrights/salil-shetty/moving-amnesty-closer-to-ground-is-necessary-not-simple.

O'Leary, Rosemary, Yujin Choi, and Catherine M. Gerard. "The Skill Set of the Successful Collaborator." *Public Administration Review* 72, no. supp. 1 (2012): 70–83. https://doi.org/doi:10.1111/j.1540-6210.2012.02667.x.

Pagé, Christiane. "To Challenge or Respect Constraints?: Leadership Style's Noticeable Effect on NGO Impact." *Monday Developments* (April, 2011): 23–24.

Queenan, Jeri Eckhart, Jacob Allen, and Jari Tuomala. *Stop Starving Scale: Unlocking the Potential of Global NGOs.* The Bridgespan Group (2013). https://www.bridgespan.org/bridgespan/Images/articles/stop-starving-scale-unlocking-the-potential/stopstarvingscale-unlockingthepotentialofglobalngos.pdf.

Sargeant, Adrian, and Harriet Day. *The Wake Up Call. A Study of Nonprofit Leadership in the US and Its Impending Crisis.* Plymouth, UK: Philanthropy Centre, 2018.

Sriskandarajah, Dhananjayan. "NGOs Losing the War against Poverty and Climate Change, Says Civicus Head: Charities Are No Longer Drivers of Social Change; for Many Saving the World Has Become Big Business. How Did We Lose Our Way?" The Guardian (London), August 11, 2014.

Storey, John, ed. *Leadership in Organizations: Current Issues and Key Trends.* London: Routledge, 2016.

Thomas, David A., and Robin J. Ely. "Making Differences Matter: A New Paradigm for Managing Diversity." *Harvard Business Review* 74, no. 5 (1996). 79-90.

Useem, Michael. *Leading Up: How to Lead Your Boss So You Both Win.* New York: Three Rivers Press, 2001.

CHAPTER 10
Collaboration

The TNGO sector has committed itself to expansive missions and has deployed a changing set of strategies to advance its goals (see Chapter 3). Its evolving strategies imply an increased reliance on collaboration, including a need to partner with other civil society actors, businesses, and governments.[1] Many TNGOs want to increase their membership and empower their stakeholders in the Global South while remaining relevant and competitive as they coexist with a range of new actors and institutional forms. Collaboration represents a powerful tool to accomplish these goals, but it also creates major demands on organizations to adapt to new ways of working. Collaboration is especially needed to deal with issues that "don't fit neatly within the boundaries of a single organization"[2] including so-called wicked problems.[3] Collaboration promises enhanced legitimacy and impact, but it also imposes transaction costs and generates new reputational risks, particularly when working with businesses and governments.[4] TNGOs were often founded in response to an urgent need or to offer a unique approach to problem-solving. Their founding myths and senses of self-perceived uniqueness and importance are integral to many of their identities, but can conflict with investments in capacities needed to effectively work across organizational boundaries.

Many larger TNGOs are themselves an institutional embodiment of long-term collaborations bringing together different national sections into (con)federations or networks. Internally, they seek to develop structures facilitating greater responsiveness to stakeholders, more agility, and a more networked approach to mission and goal accomplishment. Collaboration is not only key to pooling and scaling-up the impact of individual organizations, but also to effectively managing the organizational change required to make TNGOs fit for the future. Externally, TNGOs are discovering more opportunities to collaborate not only with other civil society organizations and movements, but also with governmental agencies and businesses, especially as low- and middle-income countries and their governments rise in prominence and influence and many for-profit investors and organizations embrace social missions.

Collaboration comes in many forms and may involve a range of partners, including local communities and social movements, intergovernmental organizations, governments, peer organizations, businesses, and impact investors.[5] Collaboration is frequently recommended and increasingly required by institutional donors as being essential to accomplishing goals and scaling impact. Unfolding collaborations and partnerships are shifting attention to issues outside of traditional organizational and sectoral boundaries as collective impact approaches[6] and outcome-oriented philanthropy orientations[7] are taking hold in many areas. It is clear that TNGOs with ambitious missions must collaborate to scale up their work, but they can face major disincentives to do so, largely because collaboration can be costly and does not necessarily produce short-term gains. Commitments to collaboration often clash with the realities of unique organizational cultures, differences across missions, or the lack of leadership capacities to lead without having control (see Chapter 9).

The reality of many external collaborations often differs starkly from the ideal of deliberate and strategic action in support of clearly articulated goals. The nature of working across organizational boundaries raises additional, and frequently neglected, issues related to how partners think about the collaborative process and understand the importance of constructing the meaning of a joint venture. Collaboration as an emerging process requires leaders to not just focus on formal transactions, but also to pay attention to the informal behaviors and understandings emerging in the process of working together. While formal arrangements such as contracts or memoranda of understanding are important, they frequently fail to capture the real challenges of managing expectations and sense-making across two or more sometimes very different organizations. The challenges to collaboration are frequently normative and cultural in nature, especially in the TNGO context when working across sectors in intersectoral arrangements.

VARIETIES OF COLLABORATION

As external collaborations can assume many different forms, each with unique opportunities and challenges, it is useful to distinguish between

Table 10.1 EXTERNAL COLLABORATION EXAMPLES

		Network	Cooperation	Coordination	Alliance	Merger or acquisition
Intrasectoral	TNGOs and CSOs	Human rights information distributed	Specific, one-time advocacy efforts shared	Joint planning for humanitarian responses	Long-term, joint programming to scale up interventions	Governance and authority shared (See Chapter 11)
Intersectoral	Government	Secure access to decision-makers; provide information	Training of government employees; joint advisory boards	Harmonized responsibilities for public service delivery	Creation of new educational institutions or other national-level programs	
	Business	Sharing best practices with early adopters	Employee volunteering	Joint awareness-raising campaign	Social enterprise models	

different types and levels of collaboration. Table 10.1 provides examples of different collaborative forms and their possible expressions in the context of TNGOs working with other civil society actors, government, and business.

Types of collaboration

TNGOs tend to adopt one of two main collaborative styles.[8] Most TNGOs tend to strongly favor "intrasectoral" collaborations, or collaborations involving only other TNGOs or civil society organizations or movements. Many of these TNGOs work in the human rights and conflict resolution sectors, where operational independence from government and business is especially critical for maintaining organizational legitimacy. Many have specific policies in place to prohibit certain relationships, particularly with respect to funding. For many TNGOs, this orientation is the default mode of operating and underscores the traditional identity of TNGOs as independent "third sector" actors (see Chapter 2). They are also more likely to collaborate with similar organizations (in terms of organizational age, region, North-South identity, and sources of legitimacy).[9] This preference for similarity or "homophily" may be a manifestation of the in-group bias and skepticism of "others" with different values, a condition largely driven by TNGOs' strong mission focus. Compared to TNGOs that collaborate with a wider array of actors, TNGOs that engage primarily in intrasectoral collaborations are less likely to encounter cultural obstacles, are more likely to report obstacles related to the operational competencies of their partners, and are less likely to regard funding, legitimacy, and credibility as benefits of collaboration.[10]

Other TNGOs are more willing to work across sectors in "intersectoral" collaborations. Intersectoral collaborations may be focused on specific developmental issues, for example the partnership between CBM (a TNGO), Peek Vision (a for-profit social enterprise), and the Pakistani government to address preventable blindness. Or it may involve representatives of each sector serving in intersectoral advisory or board roles. Such recent collaborations have emerged between Oxfam and Unilever as a result of the Behind the Brands campaign, and the presence of an IKEA representative on the global board of Save the Children, for instance.

Especially for TNGOs that lack local brand awareness, maintaining ties with respected businesses and government agencies can signal legitimacy. Traditionally, such entanglements may have been seen to compromise a TNGO's credibility and legitimacy by creating dependencies and interests that erode organizational independence, but in some circumstances TNGOs can benefit reputationally. Although some government agencies and businesses are culpable for abuses of power and corruption, others may have reputations for delivering services at a high level. In many situations, intersectoral collaboration is a precondition for scaling up coverage and impact. In the development sector, the proliferation of the rights-based approach requires TNGOs to no longer aim to substitute for government services, but to strengthen government capacities for improving and expanding rights enjoyment.[11]

Collaborations with businesses involve different sets of issues than do collaborations with government agencies. The TNGO sector may lack an adequate understanding of evolving business mindsets,[12] including the shift from corporate social responsibility to more integrative shared-value or collaborative value-creation mindsets, for example.[13] Although TNGO-business collaborations can risk co-optation or the compromise of TNGO autonomy[14] based on power differentials—notably funding, learning, networking, and branding[15]—TNGOs can also implement a variety of strategies for maintaining autonomy and resisting resource dependence. For example, TNGOs can employ revenue diversification, niche specialization, selectivity in partner selection, and partner education strategies to preserve their autonomy.[16]

Greater effectiveness is often a prominent interest and central to much of the rhetoric around intersectoral collaboration, although such collaborations can also invite reputational risks. For example, three large environmental organizations—WWF, the Nature Conservancy, and the Sierra Club—experimented over the past decades with corporate partnerships to enhance their mission effectiveness. All three faced significant criticisms for developing financial ties to the corporate sector, especially as the associated businesses reaped significant reputational benefits and profits without having to fundamentally change their behavior.[17]

An alternative approach was taken in Oxfam's Behind the Brands campaign. Rather than starting out with a collaborative arrangement, Oxfam targeted food companies on various labor and environmental issues by releasing critical research reports and grading their actions at regular intervals. Subsequently, some of the food companies responded to the advocacy by working with Oxfam to address their shortcomings.[18] In this model, the TNGO is more likely to be viewed as an equal partner because it relies on a "carrot-and-stick" approach, rather than accepting the rules of the game set by corporate partners.

TNGOs have much in common with public sector agencies, as both typically claim to represent broad constituencies in support of a social purpose while being similarly subjected to the nondistribution constraint (see Chapter 2), public demands for accountability, and a perpetual need to maintain legitimacy (see Chapter 5).[19] TNGOs have even been regarded as a form of "third party government" where public sector agencies play an important role in providing guidance and financial support to the sector through grants, contracts, and often tax benefits.[20] From the perspective of public managers, TNGOs are often critically important subcontractors or direct service providers.[21] Broadly speaking, the motivations for collaboration are strikingly similar between TNGO leaders and some government managers. For example, in the US context, public managers at both the local and the national levels overwhelmingly engage in collaboration for the same reasons indicated by TNGO leaders.[22] These reasons include leveraging resources, achieving better outcomes, and improving the scope and quality of services. Interestingly, it is public sector managers who are comparatively more likely to feel a moral or cultural imperative to collaborate—often stating that collaboration is simply the "right thing to do," whereas TNGO leaders tend to stress the pragmatic benefits of collaboration. Public managers and TNGO leaders also perceive similar obstacles to collaboration in terms of mission incompatibility and potential losses of power or control. Government actors are not always unlike-minded partners and may sometimes have more in common with the motives and missions of TNGOs than might be expected, although this depends heavily on the specific context. This does not reduce the importance of caution when approaching intersectoral collaborations but does reinforce the notion that governance is an inherently intersectoral process that often requires collaboration among many different types of organization.

North-South collaboration

North-South partnerships represent another often very challenging dimension to collaboration. While many traditionally "Northern TNGOs" have expressed principled commitments to increasing their Southern membership and empowering Southern stakeholders, the realties on the ground suggest that significant obstacles frequently still stand in the way. Criticisms often point to the problematic role of Northern organizations typically as funders, organizational systems and processes that distort accountability, and frequent differences in organizational size and capacity that undermine equality.[23] In terms of campaigning, by some assessments resultant losses of Southern TNGO autonomy can lead collaborative North-South campaigns to fall into one of two patterns: (1) lengthy but ineffective campaigns with high visibility or (2) campaigns that produce rapid victories followed by exit after adversities materialize.[24] Other criticisms of Northern TNGOs have noted the poaching of staff, inappropriate credit-taking, and problems due to language barriers.[25]

Part of the problem is that the architecture within which TNGOs operate is largely predicated on a principal-agent model of accountability that tends to cast Northern TNGOs and their donors in the role of principals and Southern partners and stakeholders in the role of agents, subcontractors, or passive "recipients." Common across many critiques of North-South collaboration patterns is a tendency for accountability systems to serve primarily the needs of Northern donors through mainly upward financial reporting mechanisms.[26]

Northern TNGOs' internal systems, and often their donors' policies as well, are typically designed for upward financial accountability rather than prioritizing responsiveness to Southern partners and their practices and capacities. This can undermine organizational autonomy and constrain the policies, procedures, and systems of Southern TNGOs. "Herein lies the challenge for [Northern TNGOs] wishing to address remaining barriers to creating stronger partnerships with Southern NGOs. The principles of collaboration conflict with the established principles of accountability."[27] Although resources for strengthening accountability practices are increasingly available from initiatives such as Keystone Accountability and Accountable Now,[28] addressing the fundamental problem of the broader accountability architecture would require a large-scale collective effort. Meanwhile, TNGOs are likely to continue to struggle to balance competing imperatives for, on the one hand, satisfying traditional expectations for upward financial accountability, and on the other hand, ensuring organizational relevance and legitimacy through more effective and equitable North-South collaborations.

Levels of collaboration

Collaboration also varies along a continuum ranging from more irregular exchanges of information to mergers or acquisitions involving two or more entities. Some definitions of collaboration highlight the "process in which autonomous actors interact through formal and informal negotiation, jointly creating rules and structures governing their relationships,"[29] while others emphasize the desired outcome of achieving "jointly what could not be achieved by organizations in one sector separately."[30] Research focused on intrasectoral and intersectoral collaboration is expanding, but there is no common language in classifying such arrangements. In addition to definitional differences, research linking collaboration to various outcomes rarely agrees on common standards in operationalizing and measuring effectiveness or other outcomes. The expanding research on collaboration across different disciplines has rarely translated into accumulated knowledge overall, which has led some to call for "better conceptualization and definitions of collaboration."[31]

Collaborative arrangements can include networking, cooperation, coordination, alliances, and mergers and acquisitions (see Table 10.1). What is common across all such terms is an implicit understanding that increasing levels of integration across organizations involves greater possible risks and rewards and requires more investment in maintaining the relationship. Networking is primarily about information exchange between autonomous entities. Cooperation involves working together often for short- or medium-term mutual benefit on discrete projects, whereas coordination involves harmonization and often joint long-term planning in the pursuit of common goals. An alliance emphasizes sustained joint programming and describes many TNGOs organized in (con)federated structures as well as many campaigning and public education-focused initiatives.[32] Mergers or acquisitions (M&A), discussed in Chapter 11, represent a special case of collaboration leading to the emergence of a new organizational entity.

The intensity of collaboration is not necessarily an indicator of subsequent success or effectiveness. In the TNGO context, even low levels of collaboration, such as networking, play a key role in scaling impact. This is particularly true for advocacy and the capacity of TNGOs to shape policy outcomes (see Chapter 4). Transnational advocacy networks (TANs), for instance, emphasize the significance of horizontal and sustained networking not only within the TNGO sector, but also with other societal groups or individuals in government.[33] The core idea of TANs is that TNGOs scale their impact by mobilizing others with a shared normative outlook while avoiding the trappings of hierarchy and bureaucracy. Networks allow activists to remain nimble, exchange information even in repressive environments, and collaborate horizontally across different organizational contexts.

Moving beyond the "organization"

The distinction between service delivery and advocacy sometimes maps onto the difference between "organization" and "network." Although some organizations have clear boundaries and recognizable brands, many have considered how to change public perceptions about themselves and shed traditional images. Many mid- to large-size TNGOs view their own roles as shifting from direct providers of services or advocacy to becoming conveners, brokers, facilitating platforms, networks, or even a community (see Chapter 8). At the same time, some TNGOs express aspirations to become more networked organizations internally, to enhance agility and flexibility, and to practice shared, horizontal leadership (see Chapter 9).[34]

These new labels indicate a move away from the "organization" toward an emphasis on collaboration as a means for fostering a democratic culture. This may partly counter perceptions of Northern dominance and paternalism[35] and represent an embrace of different leadership models. For example, digital platforms represent an example of new forms of mobilizing and organizing with the potential for significantly reduced brick-and-mortar operations and overhead (see Chapter 6). While many larger TNGOs have experienced growth and professionalization over time, many now aspire to unlearn some of the associated hierarchical behaviors and acquire distinct collaborative competencies.[36]

Ambitious and complex theories of change require new strategies and tactics, but also substantial changes in organizational form. This shift away from hierarchy toward more networked and collaborative forms of governance and operations is particularly pronounced among organizations seeking to develop an authentic global presence while shifting to new roles. Although the idea of replacing hierarchical structures with more collaboration may be a prudent step in addressing the pitfalls of traditional service delivery and advocacy, it also creates new challenges. Shifting toward being a platform or network may respond to long-standing criticisms, but it raises new difficulties with regard to establishing common agendas and assessing impact.[37] For example, the complexities of measuring impact and agency-level results discussed in Chapter 7 are significantly amplified when multiple organizations attempt to define and contribute to a collective outcome. Moreover, the devolution of power through internal decentralization embraced by some TNGOs may not only reduce their ability to act quickly, but may also cause leaders and staff to pay more attention to internal processes.

General approaches to collaboration

Many of the pressures faced by TNGOs have led them to increasingly talk about collaboration. There are at least two core dimensions to consider when working across organizational boundaries, as illustrated in Table 10.2.[38] The first dimension concerns the time horizon. Since TNGOs often have difficulty ascertaining their long-term impact, especially beyond the program level, it can be difficult to make reasoned decisions about the likely role that a collaborative arrangement may play in the future. The second dimension pertains to information. Information about potential partners and the external environment may be somewhat easier to obtain if an organization has established a solid strategic planning process and regularly scans its environment, including for possible competitors and partners.

Without a clear sense of impact or strategic focus, any decision about collaboration is likely to be reactive and deficiency-oriented—that is, organizations start thinking about it because it has become inevitable or is imposed

Table 10.2 COLLABORATION MATRIX

		Information available	
		Limited	Extensive
Time horizon	Long-term	Speculative	Strategic
	Short-term	Reactive	Opportunistic

from the outside. Being reactive is unlikely to lead to collaborations with the potential to bring about transformative change, but it is often the default for organizations with limited resources and planning capacities. Moving from limited to extensive information will improve the chances of success because the organization and its leaders are able to perform due diligence to at least anticipate major problems that may arise. Moving from a short-term to long-term time horizon ensures that an organization is not just making better decisions about working across its boundaries, but actually identifies the best options for collaborations in the first place. In the special case of mergers and acquisitions discussed in Chapter 11, this means being able to identify and choose among collaborative options, rather than react to the only available option and hope for the best. However, although adopting longer-term time horizons may seem advantageous in principle, in practice it can be difficult to plan ahead, particularly in unpredictable environments that require complex systems thinking.

Many TNGO collaborations are reactive, speculative, or opportunistic in nature. This does not mean that they are necessarily bad, but they may require different management approaches based on a clear understanding of these origins. A reactive approach with limited information and a short-term time horizon will require significant risk management in the collaborative process, especially to avoid mission drift and unwarranted transaction costs in return for lowest-common-denominator outcomes. A speculative approach may be the only option when trying to address a social problem with unknown and emerging solutions. An opportunistic approach may be taken when TNGOs are able to scale up a program through collaboration without necessarily risking their core activities. Although many TNGOs will refer to their collaborations and partnerships as strategic in nature, truly strategic partnerships have clearly defined long-term objectives and extensive shared knowledge.

GENERAL COLLABORATION DRIVERS AND CHALLENGES

At the sector level, changes over the past decades have contributed to a rhetorical, principled commitment to collaboration. The sector is naturally fragmented as citizens across many democratic countries can establish new associations with relatively minimal impediments. In the United States and elsewhere, fragmentation is by design and also extends to oversight of the sector.[39] But during the past decade, many institutional donors as well as some competitors such as digital platforms have claimed that the sector is too fragmented and under-scaled, as many organizations have similar missions and the sector overall likely wastes resources by sustaining too many small players. More organizations may increase overall resources as fundraising expands,[40] but this does not necessarily translate into enhanced aggregate impact. As the sector expands, fragmentation can also provide fertile ground for ethical lapses accommodated by lax oversight, while also locking organizations into patterns of increased competition.[41]

In response, many have called for more and deeper collaboration throughout the sector. For example, the "collective impact" body of practice advances a collaborative programming approach in specific localities typically involving public, private (including foundations and businesses), and nonprofit organizations.[42] It asks the partners to (1) agree on common goals, (2) develop shared measurement approaches and indicators, (3) engage in mutually reinforcing activities, (4) continuously communicate, and (5) rely on a strong "backbone" organization or structure that provides coordination and synchronization. While collective impact has been criticized for failing to focus sufficiently on local needs and community strengths, neglecting system-level change, imposing high transaction costs, and other difficulties,[43] the remarkable attention that it has received shows how collaboration has become a major focus for many throughout the sector.[44]

Geopolitical trends also have important ramifications for collaborative behavior. As Western donors reduce their aid budgets and promote their own financial and strategic self-interests,[45] many increasingly rely on larger grants. This means that only the largest TNGOs typically based in the Global North can compete with for-profit development agencies such as Chemonics, Abt Associates, or John Snow Inc., while small and medium-sized TNGOs find it more difficult to access this type of funding. This increases pressures on TNGOs to professionalize[46] and also to engage in partnerships to improve their fundraising chances and to remain relevant in areas they have dominated for decades.

While many TNGOs agree that working collaboratively is more essential than ever, they also face more competition and many traditionally reliable sources of income such as government grants or child sponsorships are leveling off or declining.[47] As a result, TNGOs are subject to conflicting external incentives. On the one hand, there is pressure to collaborate to reduce costs and increase impact. On the other hand, increased competition gives TNGOs reasons to defend their independence and niche in the sector's ecosystem. The competitive imperative to promote TNGO brand loyalty coexists uneasily with sectoral trends toward more collaborative approaches, underscoring the need for more deliberate and strategic approaches to collaboration that more explicitly address credit-sharing as well as shared monitoring and evaluation practices and systems.

Benefits of collaboration

The anticipated and perceived benefits of collaborations include better results, broader program coverage, potentially reduced costs, increased access to funding sources, enhanced knowledge and local capabilities, and access to decision-makers.[48] Additionally, many donors desire or even require grantees to collaborate, particularly with partners that have local recognition and capacities. Even if collaboration ultimately fails to reduce costs or generate efficiencies, it can nevertheless improve the scale and reach of programs by attracting more resources and leveraging complementary strengths.

Another benefit associated with collaboration is an enhanced capacity of TNGOs for innovation, nimbleness, and participation. Collaboration facilitates the regular import of new ideas. As many organizations have aging donor bases and mature growth rates, they face increased competition from new players, including digital platforms, social enterprises, and the business sector. Projecting an image of innovation, transparency, and participation can be important components of renewing the brand, connecting with new audiences, and establishing the adaptive capacity and agility increasingly central to surviving in a rapidly changing global context. Additionally, under the right conditions collaboration can enhance legitimacy and relevance, especially in intersectoral and North-South collaborations.

Obstacles to collaboration

Collaboration has become a buzzword for TNGOs because it is associated—rightly or wrongly—with all the good things that the sector values. However, evidence about the effectiveness and efficiency of collaboration is relatively scarce and not always encouraging.[49] TNGOs with a limited understanding of their own organizational effectiveness may find it difficult to establish and then assess criteria for collaborative success.

TNGO leaders identify a variety of challenges to collaboration, including mission incompatibility, muddled management, potentially reduced funding due to sharing finite resources, transaction costs in terms of time as well as money, differences in organizational cultures, perceived losses of control, and insufficient confidence in partners.[50] Leaders in the development sector mention collaboration difficulties related to fragmentation, poor coordination among donors, a dearth of appropriate partners, incompatible values, competitive impulses, and the persistence of institutional silos.[51] Differences in organizational cultures are frequently an important source of observed barriers.[52]

Part of the challenge is that TNGOs have to be sufficiently outwardly focused even to be able to recognize strategic opportunities for collaboration. Reactive and opportunistic approaches often prevail because TNGOs and their leaders do not spend enough time scanning the external environment (see Chapter 9).[53] Even when organizations share the same basic goals, their internal cultures are often very different and practitioners instinctively want to hold on to what they perceive makes their organizations unique. This uniqueness is fostered by highly deliberative and consultative cultures internally. Within some large TNGOs with a (con)federated or broadly democratic network structure,[54] organizations can expend significant energy managing and negotiating their own internal processes. Leaders regularly report complex and time-intensive processes through which internal proposals or initiatives need to pass to become accepted and approved. National sections or affiliates can easily slow down such processes by calling for more deliberation, while the more powerful sections typically can veto proposals or refuse to join or implement initiatives. As a result, organizations such as Amnesty International regularly experience situations where its leadership is "frustrated by their inability to turn often extremely perceptive analyses of what did not work into meaningful organizational change."[55] Overly cumbersome, conservatively minded, or inefficient internal decision-making procedures can therefore prevent leadership and staff from being more externally focused.[56]

The internal focus is reinforced by external incentives for pushing the brand and engaging in extensive "flag-planting" to demonstrate a comparative advantage over the perceived competition. Leaders and staff may be inherently disinterested or even suspicious of other organizations and discourses[57] because they do not emerge from their own organization and its commitment to a specific set of truths and normative commitments.[58]

BEING MORE COLLABORATIVE

The boundaries of TNGOs can become more porous in the process of engaging in major sustained collaborations. Such efforts then require becoming more welcoming of other types of actors and their diverse perspectives typically underrepresented within the TNGO sector. Organizations can become more open-minded by introducing and multiplying "membranes" that function as permanent exchanges between the inside and the outside world.[59] For example, a particular program may rest formally within a single organization, but it may also be designed to facilitate an information and learning flow with external stakeholders. TNGOs can also increase their reliance on associates who act as bridge builders[60] by being simultaneously part of the wider world and the organization. Even without dedicated translators and interlocutors, TNGOs can increase their collective awareness of complexity[61] by explicitly seeking out dissent, involving multiple stakeholders early on in strategic planning, and by looking at a problem from an opponents' perspective.[62]

Creating organizational "membranes" must be combined with the right incentive system for rewarding staff engaged in new types of collaborations and multi-stakeholder efforts. Managerially, this highlights careful attention to incentivization as well as deliberate, transparent, and inclusive institutional design among relevant stakeholders. A collaboration may make a lot of sense from the top leadership perspective, but it is likely to fail if the motives and perspectives of TNGO staff at the frontline are not taken seriously in setting up collaborative efforts. To become more externally focused also requires an awareness of how and with whom leaders and staff spend their time in terms of internal and external engagement. Team meetings can be used to scan the external environment and identify new actors with whom to engage. Collaboration and external scans more likely to be effective when they are mainstreamed throughout the organizations, rather than charged to a separate "strategy unit." Similar to mainstreaming other important practices (e.g., use of digital tools or a measurement culture), a priority for collaboration has to become the default, rather than just one option.

Such a default approach is essential because demonstrating effectiveness in collaborative arrangements is challenging. The complexity of measuring "collective impact" is substantial since it is based on a joint initiative with "long-term commitments to a common agenda by the group of cross-sector actors needed to realize system-wide change around a social problem."[63] Because defining and measuring collective impact can be difficult, an adequate managerial infrastructure or backbone mechanism that includes strong monitoring and evaluation capabilities is essential—not only for basic performance management and accountability, but also to maintain momentum and to coordinate efforts over time. To be meaningful, collective impact must be measured in terms of the quality of the collaboration and its results rather than simply funding, but this requires the existence of effective and interoperable monitoring and evaluation systems that are difficult and time consuming to develop. Moreover, many of these necessary prerequisites for successful collaboration require not only a long-term commitment and significant managerial capacity, but also unrestricted funding to support substantial indirect costs.[64]

CONCLUSION

One core challenge of collaboration derives from the tension between scaling up impact and the need of each organization to get credit for its contributions. On the one hand, TNGOs have established increasingly ambitious agendas and embraced complex theories of change that cannot be implemented without working with others. This is increasingly recognized as some TNGOs have adopted identities as movements or communities in which organizational boundaries essentially envelop external actors.[65] On the other hand, the same organizations have to also compete in an increasingly crowded marketplace pushing them to demonstrate organizational effectiveness and distinguish themselves from the competition. Many pressing social problems require collective solutions, but the existing sectoral architecture generally lacks the requisite support systems and incentive structures that would allow TNGOs to invest more in collaboration and do so more strategically. Moreover, organizational cultures that prize uniqueness and harbor skepticism of outsiders impose limits on the effective use of collaborations to increase impact.

While TNGOs attempt to be more collaborative, donors and other external stakeholders have changing expectations and no longer necessarily regard consistently supporting individual TNGOs as the best way to advance causes. The TNGO sector as a whole is not yet well prepared to organize, evaluate, and market itself on the basis of delivering shared solutions to social problems through coordinated individual contributions. Instead, the traditional architecture was designed mainly to convey financial support to specific organizations, not necessarily to mobilize multiple stakeholders around collective problem-solving. Collective impact and strategic philanthropy approaches may be part the future, but to unlock their potential will require not just organizational but sectoral and ecosystemic change as well.[66]

To successfully transform into new roles, particularly as partners, brokers, conveners, facilitators, and agents of empowerment and social transformation, TNGOs will have to collaborate more fluidly with communities, peers, government agencies, and the business sector. One critical implication is that TNGOs will need to think more strategically and act more deliberately to create change coalitions that clearly and reliably align individual interests with collective outcomes. Moreover, organizations must be willing not only to create change, but also to genuinely be changed in meaningful ways through greater open-mindedness, listening, and inclusion, and especially through the empowerment of dissenting voices.

REFERENCES

Ashman, Darcy. "Strengthening North-South Partnerships for Sustainable Development." *Nonprofit and Voluntary Sector Quarterly* 30, no. 1 (2001): 74–98.

Atouba, Yannick C., and Michelle Shumate. "International Nonprofit Collaboration: Examining the Role of Homophily." *Nonprofit and Voluntary Sector Quarterly* 44, no. 3 (2015): 587–608.

Austin, James E., and Maria May Seitanidi. "Collaborative Value Creation: A Review of Partnering between Nonprofits and Businesses. Part 1. Value Creation Spectrum and Collaboration Stages." *Nonprofit and Voluntary Sector Quarterly* 41, no. 5 (2012): 726–58.

Austin, James E., and Maria May Seitanidi. "Collaborative Value Creation: A Review of Partnering between Nonprofits and Businesses. Part 2: Partnership Processes and Outcomes." *Nonprofit and Voluntary Sector Quarterly* 41, no. 6 (2012): 929–68.

Baur, Dorothea, and Hans Peter Schmitz. "Corporations and NGOs: When Accountability Leads to Co-Optation." *Journal of Business Ethics* 106, no. 9 (2011): 9–21.

Beaton, Erynn, and Hyunseok Hwang. "Increasing the Size of the Pie: The Impact of Crowding on Nonprofit Sector Resources." *Nonprofit Policy Forum* 8, no. 3 (2017): 211–35.

Bermeo, Sarah Blodgett. "Aid Allocation and Targeted Development in an Increasingly Connected World." *International Organization* 71, no. 4 (2017): 735–66. https://doi.org/10.1017/S0020818317000315.

Bingham, Lisa Blomgren, Rosemary O'Leary, and Christine Carson. "Frameshifting: Lateral Thinking for Collaborative Public Management." In *Big Ideas in Collaborative Public Management*, edited by Lisa Blomgren Bingham and Rosemary O'Leary, 3–16. Armonk, NY: M. E. Sharpe, 2008.

Bouchard, Mathieu, and Emmanuel Raufflet. "Domesticating the Beast: A 'Resource Profile' Framework of Power Relations in Nonprofit-Business Collaboration." *Nonprofit and Voluntary Sector Quarterly* 48, no. 6 (2019): 1186–1209. https://doi.org/10.1177/0899764019853378.

Brehm, Vicky Mancuso. *Autonomy or Dependence? North-South NGO Partnerships.* Oxford: INTRAC, 2004.

Brest, Paul. "A Decade of Outcome-Oriented Philanthropy." *Stanford Social Innovation Review* (Spring 2012). http://www.ssireview.org/articles/entry/a_decade_of_outcome_oriented_philanthropy.

Brest, Paul. "Strategic Philanthropy and Its Discontents." *Stanford Social Innovation Review* (April 27, 2015). https://ssir.org/up_for_debate/article/strategic_philanthropy_and_its_discontents.

Brown, L. David. "Bridge-Building for Social Transformation." *Stanford Social Innovation Review* (Winter 2015): 34–39.

Brown, L. David, Alnoor Ebrahim, and Srilatha Batliwala. "Governing International Advocacy NGOs." *World Development* 40, no. 6 (2012): 1098–108. https://dx.doi.org/10.1016/j.worlddev.2011.11.006.

Bryson, John M., and Barbara C. Crosby. "Failing into Cross-Sector Collaboration Successfully." In *Big Ideas in Collaborative Public Management*, edited by Lisa Blomgren Bingham and Rosemary O'Leary, 55–78. Armonk, NY: M. E. Sharpe, 2008.

Coase, Ronald H. "The Nature of the Firm." *Economica* 4, no. 16 (1937): 386–405.

DiMaggio, P. J., and W. W. Powell. "The Iron Cage Revisited: Institutional Isomorphism and Collective Rationality in Organizational Fields." *American Sociological Review* 48 (1983): 147–60.

Ebrahim, Alnoor, and V. Kasturi Rangan. "Acumen Fund: Measurement in Impact Investing." Boston: Harvard Business School Publishing, 2011.

Eisenberg, Pablo. "A Crisis in the Nonprofit Sector." *National Civic Review* 86, no. 4 (1997): 331–41.

Elbers, Willem, and Lau Schulpen. "Corridors of Power: The Institutional Design of North-South NGO Partnerships." *Voluntas* 24, no. 1 (2013): 48–67. https://doi.org/10.1007/s11266-012-9332-7.

Foster, Robert J. "Corporations as Partners: 'Connected Capitalism' and the Coca-Cola Company." *PoLAR: Political and Legal Anthropology Review* 37, no. 2 (2014): 246–58. https://doi.org/doi:10.1111/plar.12073.

Gibson, David. "Awash in Green: A Critical Perspective on Environmental Advertising." *Tulane Environmental Law Journal* 22, no. 2 (2009): 423–40.

Gneiting, Uwe. "How Can Campaigners Influence the Private Sector? 4 Lessons from the Behind the Brands Campaign on Big Food." *From Poverty to Power* (June 8, 2016). http://oxfamblogs.org/fp2p/how-can-campaigners-influence-the-private-sector-4-lessons-from-the-behind-the-brands-campaign-on-big-food.

Gratton, Lynda, and Tamara J. Erickson. "8 Ways to Build Collaborative Teams." *Harvard Business Review* 85, no. 11 (2007): 100–9.

Green, Duncan. "If Annoying, Talking Down to, or 'Othering' People Is a Terrible Way to Influence Them, Why Do We Keep Doing It? (Research Edition)." *From Poverty to Power* (February 12, 2015). https://oxfamblogs.org/fp2p/if-annoying-talking-down-to-or-othering-people-is-a-terrible-way-to-influence-them-why-do-we-keep-doing-it-research-edition/.

Hargrave, Russell. "Save the Children CEO on a New Era of Competition for Aid." *Devex* (January 11, 2018). https://www.devex.com/news/save-the-children-ceo-on-a-new-era-of-competition-for-aid-91723.

Hopgood, Stephen. "Amnesty International's Growth and Development since 1961." In *50 Years of Amnesty International: Reflections and Perspectives*, edited by Wilco de Jonge, Brianne McGonigle Leyh, Anja Mihr, and Lars van Troost, 75–100. Utrecht: Universiteit Utrecht, 2011.

ICSC. *Exploring the Future.* Berlin: International Civil Society Centre, 2016.

Ingram, George, and Kristin M. Lord. *Global Development Disrupted: Findings from a Survey of 93 Leaders.* Washington, DC: Brookings Institution, 2019.

Jordan, Thomas, Pia Andersson, and Helena Ringnér. "The Spectrum of Responses to Complex Societal Issues: Reflections on Seven Years of Empirical Inquiry." *Integral Review* 9, no. 1 (2013): 34–70.

Kajenthira, Arani, and Philippe Sion. "Collective Impact without Borders: Successful, Multi-National, Collective Impact Efforts Require That Organizations Carefully Consider Two Dimensions of Their Approach." *Stanford Social Innovation Review* (August 29, 2017).

Kania, John, and Mark Kramer. "Collective Impact." *Stanford Social Innovation Review*, no. Winter (2011): 36–41. https://ssir.org/articles/entry/collective_impact_without_borders.

Keast, Robyn, Kerry Brown, and Myrna Mandell. "Getting the Right Mix: Unpacking Integration Meanings and Strategies." *International Public Management Journal* 10, no. 1 (2007): 9–33.

Keck, Margaret E., and Kathryn Sikkink. *Activists beyond Borders: Advocacy Networks in International Politics*. Ithaca, NY: Cornell University Press, 1998.

Landsman, Greg, and Erez Roimi. "Collective Impact and Systems Change: Missing Links." *Nonprofit Quarterly* (February 12, 2018). https://nonprofitquarterly.org/2018/02/12/collective-impact-systems-change-missing-links/.

Lecy, Jesse D., George E. Mitchell, and Hans Peter Schmitz. "Advocacy Organizations, Networks, and the Firm Analogy." In *Rethinking Advocacy Organizations*, edited by Aseem Prakash and Mary Kay Gugerty, 229–51. Cambridge: Cambridge University Press, 2010.

Manji, Firoze. "Collaboration with the South: Agents of Aid or Solidarity?" *Development in Practice* 7, no. 2 (1997): 175–78.

Mayer, Lloyd Hitoshi. "Fragmented Oversight of Nonprofits in the United States: Does It Work?—Can It Work?" *Chicago-Kent Law Review* 91, no. 3 (2016): 937–64.

Milward, H. Brinton, and Keith G. Provan. "The Hollow State: Private Provision of Public Services." In *Public Policy for Democracy*, edited by Helen Ingram and Steven Rathgeb Smith, 222–37. Washington, DC: Brookings Institution Press, 1993.

Milward, H. Brinton, and Keith G. Provan. *A Manager's Guide for Choosing and Using Collaborative Networks*. Washington, DC: IBM Center for the Business of Government, 2006.

Mitchell, George E. "Collaborative Propensities among Transnational NGOs Registered in the United States." *American Review of Public Administration* 44, no. 5 (2014): 575–99. https://doi.org/10.1177/0275074012474337.

Mitchell, George E. "Strategic Responses to Resource Dependence among Transnational Ngos Registered in the United States." *Voluntas* 25, no. 1 (2014): 67–91.

Mitchell, George E., Rosemary O'Leary, and Catherine Gerard. "Collaboration and Performance: Perspectives from Public Managers and NGO Leaders." *Public Performance and Management Review* 38, no. 4 (2015): 1–33. https://doi.org/10.1080/15309576.2015.1031015.

Mitchell, George E., and Hans Peter Schmitz. "The Nexus of Public and Nonprofit Management." *Public Performance & Management Review* 42, no. 1 (2019): 11–33. https://doi.org/10.1080/15309576.2018.1489293.

Mitchell, George E., and Hans Peter Schmitz. "Principled Instrumentalism: A Theory of Transnational NGO Behaviour." *Review of International Studies* 40, no. 3 (2014): 487–504. https://doi.org/10.1017/S0260210513000387.

Pallas, Christopher L., and Johannes Urpelainen. "Mission and Interests: The Strategic Formation and Function of North-South NGO Campaigns." *Global Governance* 19, no. 3 (2013): 401–23.

Pattberg, Philipp, and Oscar Widerberg. *Transnational Multi-Stakeholder Partnerships for Sustainable Development: Building Blocks for Success*. Berlin: International Civil Society Centre, 2015.

Peterson, Kyle, Adeeb Mahmud, Neeraja Bhavaraju, and Aaron Mihaly. *The Promise of Partnerships: A Dialogue between INGOs and Donors*. Washington, DC: FSG, 2014.

Pfeffer, Jeffrey, and Gerald R. Salancik. *The External Control of Organizations: A Resource Dependence Perspective*. Stanford Business Classics. Stanford, CA: Stanford University Press, 2003.

Prakash, Aseem, and Mary Kay Gugerty, eds. *Advocacy Organizations and Collective Action*. New York: Cambridge University Press, 2010.

Redvers, Louise. "NGOs: Bridging the North South Divide." *The New Humanitarian* (June 8, 2015). http://www.thenewhumanitarian.org/analysis/2015/06/08/ngos-bridging-north-south-divide.

Salamon, Lester M. "Of Market Failure, Voluntary Failure, and Third-Party Government: Toward a Theory of Government-Nonprofit Relations in the Modern Welfare State." *Journal of Voluntary Action Research* 16, nos. 1–2 (1987): 29–49.

Schmidt, Arthur "Buzz". "Divining a Vision for Markets for Good." In *Selected Readings: Making Sense of Data and Information in the Social Sector*, edited by Eric J. Henderson, 61–81. Stanford, CA: Markets for Good, 2014.

Schmitz, Hans Peter, and George E. Mitchell. "The Other Side of the Coin: NGOs, Rights-Based Approaches, and Public Administration." *Public Administration Review* 76, no. 2 (2016): 252–62. https://doi.org/10.1111/puar.12479. http://dx.doi.org/10.1111/puar.12479.

Smith, Steven Rathgeb. "Nonprofit Organizations and Government: Implications for Policy and Practice." *Journal of Policy Analysis and Management* 29, no. 3 (2010): 621–25.

Smith, Steven Rathgeb. "Nonprofits and Public Administration: Reconciling Performance Management and Citizen Engagement." *The American Review of Public Administration* 40, no. 2 (2010): 129–52.

Smith, Steven Rathgeb, and K. A. Grønbjerg. "Scope and Theory of Government-Nonprofit Relations." In *The Nonprofit Sector: A Research Handbook*, edited by W. W. Powell and R. Steinberg, 221–42. New Haven, CT: Yale University Press, 2006.

Smith, Steven Rathgeb, and Michael Lipsky. *Nonprofits for Hire: The Welfare State in the Age of Contracting.* Cambridge, MA: Harvard University Press, 2009.

Stachowiak, Sarah, and Lauren Gase. "Does Collective Impact Really Make an Impact?" *Stanford Social Innovation Review* (August 8, 2018). https://ssir.org/articles/entry/does_collective_impact_really_make_an_impact?utm_source=Enews&utm_medium=Email&utm_campaign=SSIR_Now&utm_content=Title.

Stephenson, Max, and Elisabeth Chaves. "The Nature Conservancy, the Press, and Accountability." *Nonprofit and Voluntary Sector Quarterly* 35, no. 3 (2006): 345–66. https://doi.org/10.1177/0899764006287886.

Thomson, Ann Marie, and James L. Perry. "Collaboration Processes: Inside the Black Box." *Public Administration Review* 66 (2006): 20–32. https://doi.org/10.1111/j.1540-6210.2006.00663.x.

Weber, Edward P., and Anne M. Khademian. "Wicked Problems, Knowledge Challenges, and Collaborative Capacity Builders in Network Settings." *Public Administration Review* 68, no. 2 (2008): 334–49.

Williamson, Oliver E. "The Economics of Organization: The Transaction Cost Approach." *American Journal of Sociology* 87, no. 3 (1981): 548–77.

Wolff, Tom. "Ten Places Where Collective Impact Gets It Wrong." *Global Journal of Community Psychology Practice* 7, no. 1 (2016): 1–11.

CHAPTER 11
Mergers and Acquisitions

Mergers and acquisitions (M&A) are an important yet sometimes overlooked strategic option for TNGOs as they attempt to acquire new capabilities and advance expanded missions.[1] M&As represent an endpoint on the continuum of collaborative behaviors when two or more organizations join together. In theory, combining organizations can result in the scale-up of programs, greater overall effectiveness, and more efficient processes due to greater economies of scale. Some recent high-profile M&As in the TNGO sector have included Save the Children's acquisition of Merlin (2013), ActionAid's integration of the Danish group Mellemfolkeligt Samvirke (2010), Plan International USA's acquisition of the Centre for Development and Population Activities (CEDPA, 2011), Mercy Corps' mergers with the Conflict Management Group (2004) and NetAid (2007), and the transfer of the Academy for Educational Development (AED) assets to Family Health International to form FHI 360 in 2011.[2]

Merger activities are certainly not new to the TNGO sector. The International Rescue Committee (IRC) was founded in 1942 as a result of a merger between two organizations, the International Relief Organization and the Emergency Rescue Committee, for example. TNGO "families" have been (re)organizing into federated, confederated, and networked structures for decades—Oxfam, CARE, World Vision, ActionAid, and Save the Children are just a few examples.[3] In the past, the main impetus for the emergence of these "families" as forms of "merged action" was the desire to combine local relevance and participation in the form of a national footprint with global influence and economies of scale.

Despite many examples, M&A remains strikingly rare in the TNGO sector and is seldom approached strategically as a practical tool for improving efficiency and effectiveness. In a recent survey of US TNGO leaders, for example, M&A was overwhelmingly rated as the least likely area for future organizational change.[4] Relatedly, between 2008 and 2015 in the United States, large nonprofit mergers occurred only at a rate of one tenth of that of business, despite the impact of the Great Recession that resulted in significant upheaval and a funding crunch lasting for several years.[5]

Like businesses, TNGOs have to consider the relative benefits of M&As as an option to remain relevant and competitive. But unlike in the business world, the existing TNGO architecture does not favor M&A. Without a shareholder system, there is no easy way for one organization to take over another. Funders rarely invest in explorations of M&A, and the practice is often viewed with suspicion, both because it seems like a businesslike approach and because it seems to run counter to cultural values related to autonomy, uniqueness, and an ethos of "letting a thousand flowers bloom."[6] When M&A is not a mainstream consideration and regular external scans are not a standard operating procedure in the sector, then cultural factors can become additional major barriers.

In the TNGO sector, discussion about M&A often emerges as a response to crisis or to external pressures, rather than a deliberate strategic effort. Such a reactive approach typically means that one organization finds itself in a much weaker position than the other. The resulting process and outcomes are thus often fraught with struggles over recognition and relative power. In such cases, it is less likely that M&A will yield the synergies that make M&A worthwhile. Identifying the right reasons for exploring such an option, approaching a partner, and executing the process are important and still undervalued capacities for many TNGOs and their leaders.

LIMITATIONS ON M&A ACTIVITIES AMONG TNGOS

Many of the obstacles to M&A reflect the architectural characteristics that affect the sector. These barriers negatively affect the likelihood of M&A being considered and initiated by TNGOs and can undermine the successful completion of M&A processes. Table 11.1 summarizes some of the main impediments to M&A activities among TNGOs.

Significant legal and cultural barriers prevent organizations from exploring M&A as part of their regular environmental scans. In the United States and elsewhere, the legal architecture governing the sector emphasizes autonomy and the independence of nonprofits and their boards. For

Table 11.1 BARRIERS TO M&A ACTIVITIES

Barrier	Implications for M&A
Institutional form	Privileges autonomy, independence, and asset protection No shareholders or hostile takeovers No material incentives for M&A among board members Lack of incentives for financial institutions to support M&A Contract buyouts may be interpreted as illegal private inurement
Organizational and sectoral norms	Cultures of uniqueness and perceptions of mission incompatibility deter M&A Organizational success construed as financial growth and brand survival; M&A construed as organizational demise Short-term M&A transaction costs seen as diversions from supporting the mission
Donors	Perceived potential losses in terms of influence, attachments, and other investments create resistance
Absence of M&A matchmakers and marketplaces	The lack of external resources to support M&A exploration puts pressure on scarce unrestricted funds Limited expertise to successfully explore and execute M&A Strategic M&A is rare; many beneficial M&A opportunities unlikely to be discovered and pursued

example, the assets of nonprofits typically enjoy special protections to uphold the nondistribution constraint (see Chapter 2). Unlike in the business sector, "hostile takeovers" via shareholders are not possible. TNGOs have no shareholders who stand to materially benefit from M&A and who would therefore have a corresponding interest in supporting it. As well as lacking material incentives to support M&A, some board members may also stand to lose "warm glow," prestige, and reputational benefits derived from their service. Individual donors have often little influence or stake, while institutional funders may not want to lose influential relationships with organizations that they have supported and view as implementing their specific objectives.

Even if some of these barriers were to be addressed, other major barriers would remain. There are virtually no institutionalized marketplaces or significant matchmakers within the sector's ecosystem facilitating merger discussions.[7] Without direct support from shareholders or matchmakers, the costs of M&A exploration must be typically paid out of an organization's own unrestricted funds, consuming precious resources and increasing overhead. Institutional donors may be inclined to support M&A rhetorically, but may not be accustomed to bear the costs. The absence of a more widespread M&A culture then also limits the available expertise among organizations and their leaders. Most important, internal resistance is inevitable since M&A is often viewed as a sign of failure. Mission-focused organizations with dedicated staff and prized organizational cultures face particularly powerful internal barriers, even if the actual cause would be better served by bringing two or more organizations together.

The obstacles making M&A less likely to be explored are also likely to generate challenges during the process of negotiating mergers and acquisitions. Projected fiscal benefits and improved efficiencies may not materialize for many years, and prohibitions on private inurement create a challenging environment for the contract buyouts that may be needed to smooth transitions. During negotiations, cultural and emotional barriers make it more difficult to create "alignment within the boards, defining roles for senior staff, and blending the brands."[8] While leaders may clearly understand that working together is key for achieving impact, the lack of basic tools aiding in developing common agendas and establishing processes of increasingly integrated joint action limit the widespread adoption of effective collaborative practices leading to M&A.

Rather than being focused on enhancing impact through M&A, the architecture's existing norms and structures push leaders toward insularity. There is arguably too little emphasis even in relatively well-run organizations on honestly assessing whether the organization is reaching its potential or simply maintaining the status quo and growing financially. And if or when the financial situation becomes precarious, it is often too late for a more deliberate approach to M&A.

CATALYSTS FOR M&A

Increasing awareness of the barriers to M&A has prompted a few funders to dedicate resources to support mergers and acquisitions and to track best practices and highlights.[9] M&As have received increased attention in the TNGO sector, and some have even predicted "a coming wave of nonprofit mergers, partnerships, and collaborations."[10] To bring M&A more into mainstream discussions, the practice can be legitimized by having "highest-impact organizations begin to look at M&A as a possible avenue," and having external funders invest in M&A, including creating a "marketplace" that allows nonprofits to "explore potential merger options safely."[11]

Three core conditions appear to make M&A more likely: (1) a large number of small nonprofits in a given market, (2) high competition due to comparable metrics and large dominant donors, and (3) limited opportunities for growth due to saturated markets, regulations, and high-asset requirements.[12] Looking across TNGOs, the humanitarian subsector has the closest resemblance to these characteristics, especially with regard to direct competition. However, TNGOs overall operate in much less integrated markets, across more diverse economic and cultural settings, and are nowhere close to the widespread adoption of common metrics about effectiveness and impact. As a result, larger TNGOs are not exposed to M&A pressures at levels similar to the business sector.

In the ideal case, pursuing M&A represents one of a number of strategic options that organizations can regularly explore as they focus on their overall mission, including (1) improvements in outcomes, (2) greater future efficiency, (3) increased fundraising capacity, (4) enhanced skill sets, and (5) geographic and programmatic scale-up. A wide range of collaborative arrangements, including M&A, can be instrumental to accomplishing such goals and can be evaluated in comparison to other strategic options, such as organic growth or the adoption of innovative practices. Beyond the dominance of financial considerations, in a few cases M&As may be driven by reputational issues or by institutional donors encouraging acquisitions to preserve service delivery channels or to improve overall coherence and efficiency in their focal area.[13]

M&A is particularly promising when organizations can combine complementary strengths that are difficult to produce in-house by either partner. Although TNGOs can hire specific talent, M&A stands out as a way of integrating proven and successful programs that allow the new organization to do more than the merging organizations can accomplish separately. For example, the promise of these benefits for improved impact motivated the Task Force for Child Survival and the International Trachoma Initiative to merge in 2009 to form the Task Force for Global Health with the goal of intensifying the struggle to eliminate the leading cause of preventable blindness.

A more common cause for exploring M&A is a growing mismatch between organizational capacities and program ambitions. For example, the UK-based health TNGO Merlin, founded in 1993, explored a merger with Save the Children because it increasingly struggled to raise sufficient unrestricted income from private donations and became too reliant on grants from institutional donors.[14] Before the merger in 2013, Merlin employed 4,000 staff in seventeen countries, but was unable to increase its private donations or mobilize other sources of funding with fewer or no restrictions. Merlin was not in an immediate crisis situation, but its limited ability to raise private donations made it wholly dependent on institutional donors unwilling to support investments in capacity.[15] From Save the Children's perspective, the merger was about expanding its efforts in emergency health work by adding Merlin's staff and expertise. While the merger certainly also reflects a response to increased competitive pressures, its deliberate nature highlights a focus on increasing impact rather than merely pursuing organizational survival. Save the Children and Merlin shared common goals and brought together complementary competencies at different levels to produce greater efficiencies.[16]

Another typical example of the marriage between a larger, established group and a smaller and younger organization is Mercy Corps' acquisition of NetAid. While NetAid struggled to develop sustainable funding streams beyond its annual televised rock concerts, Mercy Corps saw an opportunity to reach younger audiences and venture into online advocacy.[17]

Looking at recent M&A activity among TNGOs more broadly, the dominant pattern is often marked by relatively small organizations finding themselves unable to scale and keep up with increasing competition, external demands, and costs. A sudden loss of core funding and a lack of resources to acquire new donors on the part of a smaller organization are common drivers for M&A. Enter a larger organization looking for assets that complement its strengths and also enhance its abilities to remain competitive and deliver distinct programs. The dominant form is then not a merger of equals, but an acquisition involving either the full dissolution of one organization or its effectually becoming a subsidiary. Organizations of similar size may be more likely to face obstacles related to merging brands and organizational cultures, dealing with the reassignment of leadership roles, and other internal and external stakeholders resisting the merger.

Financial stress due to a loss of funding is a major catalyst for M&A primarily because it directly threatens survival and investment in organizational change and innovation. Examples of external shocks to the sector include the then-conservative Canadian government's decision in 2008 to shift funding priorities away from gender equality to advancing private sector partnerships.[18] In Europe, the Dutch bilateral aid agency dropped in 2014 its commitment to aid levels at 0.75 percent of gross national income, and DFID in the UK discontinued in 2016 large block grants to select TNGOs.[19] Many TNGOs in the Global North have also struggled since the Great Recession because their traditional individual donor bases are no longer expanding and recruiting donors in new markets is costly and often takes much longer than anticipated. As costs for doing business (e.g., providing security or investing in digital infrastructure) increase every year, many organizations find themselves in a bind of being unable to keep up with new demands and the need to innovate to stay vibrant and relevant.

THE M&A PROCESS IN TWO STAGES

The M&A process can be divided into two phases: the pre-merger phase and the implementation and post-merger stage.[20] Some factors, including resources to facilitate each stage, will matter throughout the entire process, while others play a more prominent role at specific points of the M&A process. For example, existing pre-merger relations and a supportive external environment matter greatly for a successful initiation, while a focus on staff retention will take on great significance during and after the merger process. There are a number of factors to consider before deciding whether to explore a merger or acquisition. These considerations include (1) the intrinsic motivation for the merger or acquisition, (2) a prior record of collaboration, (3) the degree of consensus within and across the boards and top leadership, and (4) assent or pressure from outside funders on the need for a merger or acquisition. If this exploratory process matures, attention turns to considerations of implementation. This includes the normal due diligence that any organization would undertake and a focus on (1) generating full support among the boards and their senior staff, including defining future roles of board members, chairs, and senior leaders; (2) developing detailed plans and contingencies for the merger or acquisition and for subsequent operations; (3) likely pre- and post-M&A budgets, cash flows, and reserves; (4) commitments of core funder support;[21] and (5) options for the future use of the brand equity that both organizational names bring to the new arrangement.

Pre-merger phase

TNGOs typically will start the exploration of a potential M&A by having detailed discovery conversations with another TNGO to ascertain the extent to which the two organizations have compatible values, cultures, and goals. They also explore the extent of strategic alignment with regard to synergies across stakeholders, revenue models, cost structures, geographic areas served, and program implementation. Leaders also consider the compatibility of organizations in terms of political ideologies and theories of change, closely held belief systems, and strategic visions. At the programmatic level, one organization may be more partner-led while the other may be more operational in nature, for instance. There may also be differences in the extent to which policy work and advocacy are part of the organizations' approaches. At this level, peers may leap to judgments about perceived differences in the quality of programming and evaluation approaches, which can be stumbling blocks during the pre-M&A phase. Sometimes, a TNGO that is acquiring another organization may want to "cherry-pick" some of that organization's programmatic elements and let others fade out. Such actions can lead to staff resistance and can create long-term problems for the M&A process.

Equally at the operational level there are potential hurdles to address during this initial phase, which may involve managing joint overhead costs (which often are one of the financial drivers involved in considering M&A in the first place), different time frames, and substantial sunk costs in different internal systems (e.g., information technology, finance, etc.). The attitude and response of institutional donors are best assessed early on to determine their support of a merger or acquisition, their trust in both organizations, the implications for accountability, and their willingness to invest in a joint venture by shouldering some of the transaction, project management, and due diligence costs.

Board chairs are typically directly involved in due diligence work, including the careful consideration of potential legal consequences, financial liabilities, and staffing implications. It is important at this point that the egos of leaders involved do not become an obstacle. Some organizations survey their boards, staff, and external constituents and key supporters, including high-net-worth individuals and institutional donors to solicit their opinions and any potential concerns. Strong board involvement throughout the entire process is an important positive factor in producing a "positive image, reputation, or public support" for the merged entity.[22] This must also include decisions about the future roles of board members, chairs, and senior leaders.

The most critical consideration is to determine whether the organization would be better served by relying on other forms of collaboration (see Chapter 10) or by entering a formal merger or acquisition. Alternatives may include joint ventures, structured partnerships, or the sharing of back-office services and systems.[23] Joint ventures driven by program or funding opportunities are common and such co-owned entities may become successful as independent organizations (e.g., the Start network, the Fairtrade Foundation, and the Disasters Emergency Committee). Structured partnerships are also common on specific advocacy issues or in the form of a consortium bid for large grants. At a smaller, local scale, the sharing of offices in program countries can substantially reduce administrative costs.

Once a decision has been made to move forward, leaders need to project confidence and vision while encouraging dialogue, building a shared sense of urgency, and forming a broad-based coalition to support the M&A process.[24] Organizational assets, liabilities, and business systems need to be analyzed and consequences for personnel management need to be explored, including possible redundancies. Boards and senior leadership have to set the tone and signal their willingness to work toward the creation of a new culture befitting the new entity.[25] Practical approaches to preparing for M&A include organizing regular joint team meetings, allowing plenty of opportunity for social gatherings, and peer mentoring. Such informal efforts can play an important role in limiting the emergence of perceptions of "winners" and "losers" as specific decisions are announced. The intense passion of staff for their own organization's expertise and culture requires specific efforts to address existing organizational cultural issues. Outside consultants may be helpful as facilitators who take a more dispassionate view and guide staff in the organizations through the process.

Implementation and post-M&A

Leadership and board involvement in general continue to be important throughout and after implementation. Often the new board will consist of members of the former boards of each of the legacy organizations. In addition, carryover board members will need to recruit and develop new board members who are able to look at the new organization with fresh eyes.

In terms of personnel management, high-performing people may depart early as a result of perceptions of uncertainty over the future. This is another major reason TNGOs are generally wary of M&As because they often are heavily reliant on key personnel. Leadership therefore needs to focus not only on the minutiae of the merger but also on establishing open lines of communication with key staff whom they wish to retain. The board, CEOs, and senior leaders have to be willing to see the staff in the other organization as equally competent, passionate, and with valid perspectives compared to their own people. Who gets picked for future senior roles and which teams stay will define (for staff and for external perceptions in the sector as a whole) how much it is a merger among equals. Leaders also need to articulate clearly and regularly the benefits of the merger or acquisition and explain its overall purpose and role in making the combined organization more effective. Transparency and honesty about the ambiguities and uncertainties can enhance trust and confidence in leadership.

Challenges during the implementation of M&A include factors that are resource-related, stakeholder-focused, and cultural. Resources play a key role in facilitating a successful implementation process. TNGOs may require outside grants to explore the implications of a potential merger or acquisition and to subsequently implement the merger or acquisition successfully.

In the case of Save the Children's merger with Merlin, for example, DFID was a major funder of both organizations and offered ad hoc support to cover the costs. For DFID, this seemed like a good investment as it no longer funded two separate entities, resulting in anticipated savings.[26] Resources are required to research the case for M&A, to facilitate conversations across organizations at different levels, and to offer financial incentives to senior staff who may depart.[27] Mergers rarely create cost savings and efficiencies in the short-term as is sometimes anticipated,[28] and the inherent implementation risks can present significant obstacles.

In addition to resources, M&A is about the power and control of donors and boards. The interests and influences of major stakeholders, including the board and senior staff, typically need to be realigned, and dedicated resources are only one part of facilitating such a transition. A merger of boards and the reassignment of senior staff raise delicate issues about who controls resources and decision-making. When a smaller TNGO merges with or is acquired by a larger TNGO, the core institutional donors of the acquired TNGO may sense a strong loss of control, a loss of perceived ability to see where their money goes with a clear "line of sight," and a loss of ability to hold the national board of the merging TNGO to account. In addition, when national TNGOs join a larger (con)federation they typically have to agree to a membership fee or levy. Institutional and individual donors may have difficulties accepting such costs in addition to potential losses of autonomy and identity (also see Table 11.1).

Finally, there are important cultural implications for M&A,[29] including issues that will likely surface in discussions about resources and stakeholder interests. Staff and longtime donors may feel a strong attachment to their organization and brand. Existential organizational change is always a threat to those attachments, even if mitigating strategies are undertaken to combine brands or preserve distinct brands. Stakeholders in a merger may feel a need to preserve not only brand identity but also a degree of equality between brands. For example, given that organizational cultures represent often unspoken belief systems and assumptions about appropriate social behavior (see Chapter 2), it took Save the Children and Merlin considerable time and effort to determine whether their cultures were sufficiently compatible and complementary to facilitate cultural convergence and acclimation. In this case, the challenges were surmountable, but due to the generally abstract, intangible nature of culture, and the long-term time horizon needed for cultural change, this element can be hard to assess as part of a due diligence process.[30] Table 11.2 summarizes major considerations, activities, and risks across the M&A process.

Table 11.2 THE M&A PROCESS

	Pre-merger phase	Implementation and post-M&A
Considerations	Existing relations	Generating and maintaining support
	Supportive external environment (including funders and other key external stakeholders)	Strategic and contingency planning
	Intrinsic motivation	Legal, financial, and business systems (related to due diligence)
	Board consensus	
	Extent of synergies	Securing funder support
	Overhead costs	Brand equity options
	Sunk costs	Transparency
	Timeframes for anticipated results	Control
	Potential benefits	Branding
	M&A alternatives	Staff retention
	Cultural change	Opportunity costs
Activities	Discovery conversations	Due diligence
	Securing funding for process costs	Continued leadership involvement
	Taking soundings	Board member development and recruitment
	Create change coalition and sense of urgency	Leadership communication
	Retain facilitating consultants	
Risks	Leaping to judgments	Personnel departures
	Cherry-picking	Insufficient resources
	Egos	Losses of control and autonomy
	Winner-loser mindset	

GOAL AND OXFAM: WHEN A MERGER MADE SENSE, BUT FAILED TO COMPLETE

Oxfam International emerged as a confederation in 1996. It has grown primarily through the joining of independent national organizations with similar values, visions, and high degrees of overlap in mission and mandates. However, such efforts to expand the organization sometimes fail, even when they make fundamental sense from an efficiency and effectiveness perspective. One such example is the attempted effort to merge GOAL with Oxfam Ireland.[31] Similar to a majority of cases in the TNGO sector, merger talks were initially driven by concerns about financial sustainability and reputational risks. GOAL experienced a major crisis in early 2016 over allegations of financial mismanagement relating to procurement in the Turkey-Syria program, leading to the resignation of its chief executive. Its chief operating officer also resigned. GOAL had doubled its income in the four years prior to the crisis, primarily in grants for work in Syria and Ethiopia. The organization had grown restricted income rapidly while not having significantly increased unrestricted income from individual donors.[32] As in the case of Merlin, this put pressure on liquidity and reserves.

GOAL's work in Syria on food security was very successful, reaching over 800,000 people trapped in Idlib province. Indeed, GOAL's approach meant that it had, and still has, a well-known ability to work in very difficult to reach communities. This is why institutional funders were so keen to partner with GOAL. Humanitarian staff in the sector understand just how difficult it is to operate in these environments, including the ability to manage financial processes such as procurement and disbursements.

GOAL international staff were based in Turkey for safety and security reasons and work was done through national staff and community partners. When the procurement issue came to light, the possible fraud was for a relatively small amount of money compared to the total program spending in Syria. USAID, the main funder of GOAL's Syria program, and in effect of GOAL as whole, imposed an administrative agreement with stringent requirements as conditions for continued funding. An interim general manager was put in place while the board considered next steps. Above all, the organization wanted to ensure the survival of important programs.

As the crisis was consuming significant amounts of reserves, a merger was proposed as a way forward. This was not a new idea, as GOAL had previously explored a merger with Mercy Corps. The board requested other organizations to submit proposals. Several organizations with similar mandates, reach, and thematic focus expressed their wish to explore the idea. Oxfam Ireland's proposal, titled "The Power of Two," emphasized the opportunity to leverage two different sets of competences for greater overall impact—rather than a rationale based primarily on high levels of program thematic overlap and efficiencies. It proposed that this increased impact could be achieved by combining GOAL's agile humanitarian responsiveness with Oxfam's global reach, humanitarian capacity, and public-facing advocacy work in Ireland and globally. The power of the two organizations' brand was also addressed right from the start with "Oxfam GOAL" as the proposition—a model used elsewhere in the Oxfam confederation and attractive to an organization worried about losing its sense of history and identity in a time of crisis.

Oxfam Ireland was significantly smaller than GOAL but brought with it the Oxfam confederation that was six times larger than GOAL. In addition to global reach, GOAL would have been able to access wider technical skill sets as well as some of the systems and processes that it needed to handle its growing programs and income. For the Oxfam confederation the benefit would have been extra humanitarian capacity and GOAL technical expertise and approaches. However, food security and nutrition were not strategic themes for Oxfam, and a merger would have required significant effort to manage programmatic alignment.

As an affiliate, Oxfam Ireland had the authority to conduct a merger on its own sovereign territory but wanted to balance this with ensuring that it would not create strategic, operational, and financial challenges for the Oxfam confederation in excess of the benefits. During the pre-merger phase, both parties held high-level meetings with major donors, including Irish Aid, ECHO, and USAID. At the same time, leaders in both organizations wanted to assure GOAL staff that this was not a takeover. Considerable effort was put into facilitating peer discussions across the two entities and organizing visits and presentations by individuals from each organization to the staff in the other organization. At the country level, Oxfam's and GOAL's country directors met personally to discuss possible opportunities and challenges to respective country strategies. In most cases, these discussions identified few challenges, except for GOAL's two largest programs operating in Syria and Ethiopia and Oxfam's programs in those countries.

GOAL staff had developed a distinctive and passionately held culture celebrating GOAL's agility, "can-do" attitude, and real-time problem-solving needed for successful life-saving responses. Both organizations had strong identities going into the process. For GOAL, this included the pride of being a "GOALie," while for Oxfam this involved their global impact through the scale of their humanitarian and development programming and their extensive reach in global and national advocacy. Understandably, some of GOAL's remaining senior staff were wary of being subsumed and losing the expertise and approach at which GOAL excels, especially the agility that could be threatened by the sometimes slower decision-making processes of a large confederation (see Chapter 8). While this was partly addressed by the proposed Oxfam GOAL branding and other assurances, some senior staff in GOAL felt that surviving the crisis and rebuilding were a much better option for ensuring their long-term impact.

Despite the existential financial stress experienced by GOAL, the GOAL general manager and Oxfam Ireland's CEO still had to spend significant time and resources on pitching the merger to wary and concerned GOAL staff. The Oxfam Ireland program director and colleagues across the confederation's program team focused on aligning program approaches, themes, and countries, as well as on identifying potential risks and opportunities in funding.

GOAL's external affairs director and Oxfam Ireland's public engagement director spent significant efforts on the alignment of messaging in Ireland, including how to identify opportunities to recruit supporters and address risks to donor retention. GOAL brought external expertise to match Oxfam Ireland's COO's extensive experience in commercial mergers.

The merger efforts required navigating both the convergent and divergent needs of three core participating entities (GOAL, Oxfam International, and Oxfam Ireland) as well as donors. At the same time, promoting the merger had to focus on the morale of staff and a constant emphasis on the vision of more impact. As the discussions at each of the boards moved on to more detailed and complex areas, differences in program approach, financial arrangements, and institutional donors became clearer. The merger was mutually and respectfully called off as the detailed analysis of the envisioned complementarity based on different strategic approaches was possibly outweighed by the efforts required to achieve it. Funding complexities also created challenges.

GOAL remained an independent organization with a reduced country footprint and annual budget (€109 million in 2019 compared to €163 million in 2016). GOAL's board publicly observed that the due diligence process provided invaluable insights into the organization's operating effectiveness, which has helped them to continue to provide critical humanitarian aid to the difficult to reach communities with which they work. Consequently, they continue to put extensive effort into managing operational risks including grant management, fraud, theft, and corruption. A head of ethics and compliance was appointed with direct line to the board. A wide-ranging new set of policies, known as GOAL's "integrity framework," built with high-level fraud and corruption specialists, means that GOAL has been building what could end up being a "best-in-class" capacity to prevent, identify, investigate, and resolve such issues. However, the underlying issue that threatened GOAL's existence continues to be a challenge. In 2018 GOAL's unrestricted fundraising from the public still represented only 3 percent of its income. GOAL is putting a large amount of effort into rebuilding public fundraising and diversifying its income. Whether it succeeds in this will determine the nature of its near- to medium-term existence and thus its ability to deliver its much-needed programs.

PLAN INTERNATIONAL USA AND CEDPA: THE FRIENDLY TAKEOVER

The acquisition of CEDPA by Plan International USA (Plan USA) in 2012 is an example of a "friendly takeover."[33] The primary driver for the acquisition was to preserve the capacities of an organization that was struggling to remain financially viable. Following the loss of several large US government contracts, CEDPA leadership began discussions with its board about organizational sustainability roughly two years prior to opening conversations with Plan USA. CEDPA's strong preference was to remain independent, so internal discussions initially centered on reaching out to other organizations to establish joint ventures or shared back offices. CEDPA leadership soon realized that it was difficult to find other organizations with similar interests and a shared sense of urgency. Without management expertise or support from funders or matchmakers, acting on their intent to secure their future independence turned out to be more difficult than anticipated. Over a two-year period, senior leadership and the board of CEDPA explored options with several organizations. They came close to finalizing a merger with another TNGO, but negotiations failed in the final stages due to cultural and management differences. Facing a critical shortage of unrestricted funds, CEDPA had to then explore new options more quickly.

The initial contact and conversations between Plan USA and CEDPA were the result of opportunity. A first lunchtime conversation in late 2011 occurred between Plan USA's CEO Tessie San Martin and Holly Wise, a CEDPA board member. This led to more sustained conversations between Tessie San Martin and CEDPA CEO Carol Peasley. For Plan USA, the core interest initially revolved around bringing in additional expertise and scale, but the organization had no prior experience in completing a merger or acquisition. Both organizations faced serious capacity constraints, lacking the necessary bandwidth to systematically scan the environment to identify potential partners or to proactively lead or drive discussions on available options. There was no funder support for either organization to approach this opportunity strategically, or to consider possible alternatives to the acquisition.

As Plan USA and CEDPA began to explore an acquisition, their discussions focused on mission, cultural fit, and potential synergies in geography, programs, fundraising, and staff retention. Leadership initially focused entirely on these elements rather than on operational details related to the formal components of an acquisition. In short, form followed substance, and the acquisition was driven by CEDPA's struggles to remain financially sustainable.[34] The two organizations also did identify important geographic, program, and fundraising synergies.

With only limited issues pertaining to their overall compatibility, staff retention became one of the most important challenges. Making decisions about who stays and who does not, and on what terms, became critical to a successful acquisition. This included the identification of key staff and their core competencies, personal networks, and abilities to add value to the new entity. Potential redundancies had to be identified and decisions had to be made as to whether staff from CEDPA would replace Plan USA staff or whether CEDPA staff would be reallocated or retrained. The compensation structure also had to be reevaluated. In this case, pay equalization needed to happen in a very short time frame to avoid establishing a two-tiered pay structure that could create grounds for resentment and "us versus them" attitudes. Staff retention was directly related to the capacity of Plan USA as the acquiring organization. Existing organizational systems, business processes, and people needed to have the ability to accommodate the additional throughput and personnel. The acquisition process also imposed opportunity costs. These notably included costs in the form of elements of the operating plan that would not get done as a result of redirected efforts. This was particularly important for fundraising and support functions.

Having fit CEDPA within Plan USA's multiyear strategic plan, the two signed a memorandum of understanding and non-disclosure agreements, which provided for strict confidentiality and gave Plan International USA time for due diligence and strategic planning, without immediately committing to the merger. This included exploring a range of critical financial, operational, and reputational issues. Once Plan USA established that it could overcome certain financial hurdles and capacity constraints, they made sure to quickly gain buy-in from relevant stakeholders. This was especially important for integration planning with respect to programming, fundraising, and support functions. Critical to gaining stakeholder support was understanding capacity constraints as well as the comparative opportunity costs of either going ahead with the acquisition or deciding not to pursue it any further.

The acquisition was structured as an asset acquisition. This was done to manage actual and potential liability. To preserve good title and limited liability, CEDPA negotiated settlements with each of its creditors prior to its acquisition, and Plan USA negotiated with CEDPA donors about taking over CEDPA grants and other program activities. Having almost a year to move from initial discussions in late 2011 to completion in late 2012 proved to be important. To manage material risks, Plan USA assumed project liability from the acquisition date for certain projects, and where necessary, negotiated a form of shared liability for pre-acquisition, capped at a percentage of remaining revenues. Plan USA's target was to be cash positive in the first year. This would provide the necessary lead time to develop a pipeline of incremental CEDPA revenue and avoid the pitfall of a large majority of acquisitions failing to add incremental value over time. Plan USA also took account of costs incurred throughout the acquisition process, and developed worst-case, base, and best-case scenarios for growing the portfolio. The ability to grow or leverage the CEDPA portfolio involved estimating a number of hard-to-assess and intangible factors. Name and brand awareness, program effectiveness, donor and partner networks, and ownership of copyrights all had to be included into future revenue projections. Plan USA not only acquired an organization with a strong sectoral reputation, but also took on new donor relationships that offered potential new funding opportunities for existing Plan USA program areas. Although Plan USA's assessments did not explicitly account for opportunity costs, these were nevertheless an important consideration throughout the acquisition. Given the strain placed on the acquiring organization, understanding the time and resources lost to pursue the acquisition required significant consideration. With CEDPA's solid programming and sufficient time for planning, the acquisition ultimately succeeded.[35]

CONCLUSION

Common M&A drivers in the TNGO sector include critical shortages of unrestricted funds, an inability to make long-term strategic investments, and difficulties scaling up to achieve efficiencies of scale. These challenges are indicative of the architectural constraints under which TNGOs operate that can make strategic investments in areas such as M&A difficult. Options for scalingup to seek new opportunities and long-term programmatic and financial benefits are already limited by organizational forms that forbid equity investment and cultural norms that can make substantial debt financing difficult.[36] M&A is one possible means of pursuing more rapid growth and scaled-up impact while coping with these restrictions, but M&A itself is difficult to undertake within the existing architecture. Few stakeholders have the interest and ability to support strategic M&A, which too often relegates M&A to a tool of last resort. Additionally, pride in organizational brands, cultures of uniqueness, and personal feelings of attachment can present further obstacles to M&A.

The main drivers for M&A are key to predicting their likelihood of success. Of course, these drivers are not necessarily mutually exclusive. Finances and impact both factor into an organization's value propositionand so reducing costs and increasing impact are often put forward as rationales for M&A. For instance, ActionAid's strategy to seek a merger with Mellemfolkeligt Samvirke Denmark explicitly aimed to achieve both. In the long term, M&As can help TNGOs reduce transaction costs from continued external collaboration, catalyze growth, obtain new capacities, reach greater economies of scale, and ultimately increase impact. M&A can be more than merely a means to solve short-term financial problems and sudden crises, but can be a strategic option to be explored alongside other strategies for geographic or issue-based program expansion.

Mergers and acquisitions carry their risks both during the process and after completion. The emerging larger organizations will face challenges with regard to their governance and local responsiveness, especially if the motivation was primarily focused on increasing efficiencies and competitiveness. Difficulties can multiply if the process is not embedded in a broader strategy focused on defining the purpose of the new organization and knowing how it will deliver more value to those it serves. Because M&As are costly and carry risks, they will not always be the best option nor will they always be successful when pursued. However, given the potential for M&As to help TNGOs acquire new capacities necessary for their future success, M&As appear to deserve greater strategic consideration.

REFERENCES

Alliage Morales, John. "Merlin: Anatomy of a Doomed INGO Business Model." *Devex* (July 30, 2013). https://www.devex.com/news/merlin-anatomy-of-a-doomed-ingo-business-model-81537.

Anonymous. "Secret Aid Worker: The UK NGO Sector Is Facing a Funding Crisis." *The Guardian* (August 2, 2016). https://www.theguardian.com/global-development-professionals-network/2016/aug/02/secret-aid-worker-projectitis-dfid-civil-society.

Calabrese, Thad D., and Cleopatra Grizzle. "Debt, Donors, and the Decision to Give." *Journal of Public Budgeting, Accounting, and Financial Management* 24, no. 2 (2012): 221–54.

Carrington, Oliver, Iona Joy, Katie Boswell, Sonali Patel, and Tom Collinge. *Let's Talk Mission and Merger*. London: New Philanthropy Capital, 2018.

Charles, Cleopatra. "Nonprofit Arts Organizations: Debt Ratio Does Not Influence Donations—Interest Expense Ratio Does." *American Review of Public Administration* 48, no. 7 (2018): 659–67.

Conner, Daryl, and Ed Boswell. *Cultural Implications of INGO Mergers and Acquisitions*. Atlanta: Conner Advisory, 2018. http://3vcego17hhlq3f2du63lx87v.wpengine.netdna-cdn.com/wp-content/uploads/2018/06/Cultural-Implications-of-INGO-Mergers-and-Acquisitions.pdf.

Cook, Stephen. "Analysis: Merlin and Save the Children." *Third Sector* (July 30, 2013). https://www.thirdsector.co.uk/analysis-merlin-save-children/governance/article/1193125.

Cortez, Alexander, William Foster, and Katie Milway. *Nonprofit M&A. More Than a Tool for Tough Times*. Boston: Bridgespan Group, 2009.

Department of Justice. "Washington, DC–Based Academy for Educational Development Pays More Than $5 Million to Settle False Claims Act Allegations."

Washington, DC: Office of Public Affairs, 2011. https://www.justice.gov/opa/pr/washington-dc-based-academy-educational-development-pays-more-5-million-settle-false-claims.

InterAction. *Supporting Your NGO Future: US NGO Executive Thoughts on the Future*. Washington, DC: InterAction, 2019.

Jones, Richard. "Oxfam Chief: INGO Mergers 'Not a Trend'." *Devex* (2013). https://www.devex.com/news/oxfam-chief-ingo-mergers-not-a-trend-81486.

Knight, Melanie, and Kathleen Rodgers. "'The Government Is Operationalizing Neo-Liberalism': Women's Organizations, Status of Women Canada, and the Struggle for Progressive Social Change in Canada." *NORA—Nordic Journal of Feminist and Gender Research* 20, no. 4 (2012): 266–82. https://doi.org/10.1080/08038740.2012.747786.

La Piana, David. "Merging Wisely." *Stanford Social Innovation Review* (Spring 2010): 28–33.

MAP for Nonprofits/Wilder Research. *What Do We Know about Nonprofit Mergers?* Saint Paul, MN: Wilder Research, 2011.

McLaughlin, Thomas A. *Nonprofit Mergers & Alliances*. Hoboken, NJ: John Wiley & Sons, 2010.

Mercy Corps. *Building a Smarter, Stronger, and Broader Youth Constituency in the United States to Fight Global Poverty*. New York: Rockefeller Brothers Fund, 2007.

Mitchell, George E., and Thad D. Calabrese. "Proverbs of Nonprofit Financial Management." *American Review of Public Administration* 49, no. 6 (2019): 649–61. https://doi.org/10.1177/0275074018770458.

Nahavandi, Afsaneh, and Ali R. Malekzadeh. "Acculturation in Mergers and Acquisitions." *Academy of Management Review* 13, no. 1 (1988): 79–90.

Santamaria, Carlos. "Are INGO Mergers the Wave of the Future?" *Devex* (July 24, 2013). https://www.devex.com/news/are-ingo-mergers-the-wave-of-the-future-81500.

Smith Milway, Katie, Maria Orozco, and Cristina Botero. "Why Nonprofit Mergers Continue to Lag." *Stanford Social Innovation Review* (Spring 2014): 48–54.

Worthington, Sam, and Alexander Grashow. *NGO Board Reckoning*. Washington, DC: InterAction and Good Wolf Group, 2018.

CHAPTER 12
Change

Geopolitical shifts, the emergence of new competitors, greater demands for accountability, and gaps between rhetoric and practice present profound challenges to the future of TNGOs. Yet the relative comfort of the status quo encourages complacency and incremental action, not transformative change, in the face of these challenges. If TNGOs genuinely want to be agents of fundamental change, not simply charitable conduits, then they need to take more decisive steps beyond moving their headquarters, adopting the latest digital tools, and diversifying staff and leadership. Such measures in themselves are important, but the sector's full potential can only be realized through an even more radical questioning of the sector's own architecture. Many of the current measures taken by TNGOs reflect repeated reactive adaptations to mounting external pressures without challenging the broader systems within which TNGOs operate. What is missing are more proactive and audacious steps designed to change the legacy structures that shape how TNGOs understand their purpose, make strategic decisions, and operate globally.

Many future-oriented practitioners are well aware of the challenges that the TNGO sector faces. Even as many of them acknowledge the need for change, many also remain hesitant about diverting organizational attention and resources to addressing the sector's own internal issues. To overcome these anxieties and ambivalences, it is important to first identify the root causes of the perceptions of a crisis in the sector as well as the reasons for why decisive actions are so difficult to take.

While many TNGOs have adopted expansive commitments to achieving long-term sustainable impact through fundamental transformation, they also operate in a restrictive normative and institutional context. Observers have frequently argued that individual TNGOs have become too large, financially successful, and preoccupied with organizational survival to deliver on their promises.[1] As a result, the argument goes, they have too often lost touch with their principled identities, become too focused on business models and the satisfaction of (usually Northern) donors, and have too often pursued self-serving behaviors incompatible with their espoused values.[2] However, the core problem may not be what the TNGO sector has become over time (e.g., arguably more competitive, professionalized, and detached), but how it has failed to evolve its own norms and institutions apace with its expanding aspirations and commitments to new roles. The fact that TNGOs have reached a certain size and attained a certain degree of power is not a problem in itself, but it turns into a major cause for crisis when a still-expanding sector makes expansive promises of social transformation without having the underlying capabilities or "architectural affordances" to carry them out. It is not the often-alleged abandonment of principles that threatens to undermine the legitimacy of the sector, so much as a reluctance to change organizational forms and norms to enable a more promising future. To return to the metaphor from Chapter 2, the soul of the TNGO appears to be as strong as ever, but the architecture limits its self-expression.

Although charities and transnational organizations have existed for centuries,[3] the concept of a socially transformative TNGO capable of addressing root causes with sustainable solutions is a relatively modern idea. As many TNGOs intellectually may have already made the shift from a charity to a sustainable impact mindset, they nevertheless remain embedded in an architectural context prioritizing low-cost intermediation over value-adding innovation, short-term outputs and results over long-term social change, and upward financial accountability to donors over primary stakeholder empowerment. The sector's historical legacy creates expectations, and even requirements, for TNGOs to serve as trustworthy stewards of resources provided by the wealthy, not necessarily as change agents seeking to fundamentally transform social structures. TNGOs are a constitutive part of a global system, even as they critique its inequities. If TNGOs continue to conform to this legacy architecture, rather than challenging it, they will continue to face major constraints on their impact. In effect, TNGOs will be complicit in undermining their own future potential.

This is not to say that all TNGOs are or ought to be pursuing sustainable impact and social transformation, or that short-term aid is no longer relevant or necessary—clearly it is. TNGOs will likely always have a significant role to play providing critical humanitarian and life-saving assistance in times of crisis. But for a large and growing number of organizations that have embraced the rhetoric of sustainable impact and social transformation, many of the cultural beliefs, norms, and institutional forms that evolved out of ancient traditions of almsgiving and charity no longer match their current aspirations. The legacy architecture is not necessarily problematic for all TNGOs, but for those aspiring to certain new roles it represents a significant constraint. To realize the potential of TNGOs with expanded missions and strategies, the architecture must change.

As organizations with espoused commitments to social change, TNGOs wield a kind of ideational power that leverages legitimacy to exercise authority. When TNGOs no longer limit their engagements to direct aid and short-term advocacy, but effectually participate in social and environmental governance, they incur an obligation to acquire and maintain new forms of legitimacy in their exercise of power. Many organizational changes that TNGOs are considering or are implementing are directly related to this imperative to derive—or strengthen—legitimacy. The adoption of various digital technologies, enhanced measurement systems, and governance reforms, for example, all offer pathways for enhanced legitimacy. Legitimacy matters greatly when seeking deeper transformations of societies, particularly for historically Northern TNGOs wishing to become more responsive and relevant to stakeholders in the Global South. Transformative TNGOs need mandates for such changes, and such external change mandates require a foundation.

But the legacy architecture has a certain very powerful appeal. Its demands are modest (e.g., minimize overhead, avoid scandals, etc.), its benefits are lucrative (e.g., often tax benefits, giving incentives, and an automatic baseline of trustworthiness), and the risks are minimal (i.e., fiscal survival is virtually decoupled from mission success, as considered in Chapter 2). Conformity to the architecture has allowed TNGOs to dramatically increase their numbers and resources over the course of the latter half of the twentieth century, but it has also frustrated many TNGO efforts to evolve for the future.

The power of TNGOs, as measured by their numbers and resources, has been in large part supported by a combination of adherence to pre-twenty-first-century norms of fiscal propriety, effective branding, and expanding promises to donors about what these organizations can achieve. Now, TNGOs that aspire to transform social structures and achieve sustainable impact face a crucial dilemma: to deliver on their lofty promises they must do things that conventional charities are not supposed to do. For example, many TNGOs have discovered that they need to do more "indirect" programming in the forms of facilitation, knowledge brokering, research, and empowerment, to invest more in themselves internally and as a sector, and to become more politically engaged to sustainably address root causes over longer-term time horizons. TNGOs have rhetorically and strategically evolved well beyond the legacy charity model from which they emerged, but still find themselves bound by its archaic architecture.

SUCCESSFUL IRRELEVANCE

As a sector, TNGOs will likely continue to survive and grow, perhaps even faster and with more financial success than ever before. However, not all TNGOs that survive will also be relevant and impactful. While the legacy architecture has been historically effective for resource mobilization, especially in the Global North, it is much less conducive to the production of long-term sustainable impact and societal transformation that so many TNGOs desire. This is partly because conformity to the architecture deters TNGOs from making precisely those kinds of investments necessary to secure their future relevance. The architecture's accountability model is a case in point. It demands that TNGOs prioritize donor compliance and rigorous upward financial reporting—typically to stakeholders in the Global North—concentrating power and control with those who already have it. Only more rarely (although increasingly) do a TNGO's primary stakeholders have real voice and power. Without significant change, TNGOs risk "successful irrelevance"—continuing to survive by satisfying the expectations of the architecture but without necessarily providing relevant solutions for those they claim to serve.

While TNGOs are being asked—and are trying—to enhance constituency voice and downward accountability; to improve diversity, inclusion, and equity in internal leadership and governance structures; to address fundamental (often political) underlying causes in their programming; and to produce rigorous evidence of results (that require sophisticated systems), the legacy architecture imposes constraint after constraint. For example, meaningful downward accountability and primary stakeholder empowerment is constrained by a governance model in which boards and leaders feel primarily responsible for satisfying funder demands. Enhancing equity in internal governance structures is constrained by norms that equate contributed resources with power. Addressing root causes is constrained by the need to demonstrate short-term results without offending political sensibilities or transgressing legal restrictions designed to keep charities out of politics. Building up internal systems capable of producing rigorous evidence of social change in complex environments is constrained by the imperative to minimize the "overhead" costs of research and evaluation. The list could continue.

The constraints of the architecture can explain a wide array of organizational problems: underinvestment in core systems (e.g., information technology, measurement and evaluation, accountability, learning, transparency, and responsiveness), inverted accountabilities that prioritize donors and finances above primary stakeholders and impact, underinvestment in leadership development, restricted funding models that create fragmentation and inefficiency,[4] and inadequate support and interest in strategic M&A, just to name a few examples. This is emphatically not a question of simply striking a better balance with respect to different accountabilities and resource uses but represents fundamental tensions regarding the soul of the TNGO and its institutional embodiment and ecosystem.

The design of the architecture also means that many TNGOs could, in principle, continue to exist indefinitely without ever necessarily delivering on their lofty promises.[5] Real change would require abandoning legacy ways of operating that may have worked well in the past. This is one reason why organizational cultural change can prove to be so difficult. Nevertheless, significant external changes are already underway, and in time, TNGOs that fail to adapt may find not only their own relevance dwindling but also overall trust and confidence in the sector as a whole.

Some TNGOs may decide to revert to legacy roles while ceding the "post-charity model" to social enterprises, public-private partnerships, digital organizations, impact investors, and other institutional vehicles perhaps better able to invest in long-term change and demonstrable impact. But this would betray TNGOs' principled commitments to serving their primary stakeholders. It would also rob the world of a set of distinctly positioned organizations continuously improving and reimagining their roles to address social problems that businesses and governments have neglected, or in many cases, are responsible for creating in the first place. Of course, TNGOs could also continue to push the boundaries of what is possible to achieve within the existing architecture, but those boundaries will continue to push back, circumscribing the transformative potential of the sector. A more fundamental kind of change will be needed.

The three major, complementary ingredients for the sector's own transformation include (1) organizational metamorphosis, (2) leading change within, and (3) bringing about fundamental change in the institutional and normative architecture. Many TNGOs have been or are currently considering or implementing significant organizational changes involving polycentrism, facilitation, hybridity, deeper collaborations, mergers and acquisitions, and investments in core operational platforms. Such initiatives require significant change leadership capabilities. In addition to internal changes, TNGOs can consider collective actions to transform their own environment into one more conducive to their aspirations.

METAMORPHOSIS

Many TNGOs are implementing organizational changes with the aim of securing their future relevance and credibility. In this context, these organizations are not only reconsidering their business models, but also questioning their structures, cultures, and the very roles that they play in advancing their respective missions. As a result of this deeper questioning of organizational roles, some TNGOs are considering fundamentally altering their institutional forms—in addition to changes in strategy, location, fundraising, business systems, staffing, reward systems, and so forth.[6] There are a number of more transformative changes that are already taking place in the sector that illustrate how TNGOs are attempting to cope with, modify, or transcend their existing forms.

The polycentric model

TNGOs face a shift in economic opportunities away from the Global North to other regions of the world. This shift also requires abandoning traditional unidirectional models of organizing fundraising, programming, and governance. The polycentric model seeks an optimal balance between global standardization and national customization regarding strategy formation, policies, program standards, business systems, and processes.[7] Some large (con)federated organizations such as Oxfam and CARE show strong allegiance to that model while seeking structural changes to create a stronger foundation or center within a relatively flat network of members or affiliates. Others, such as ActionAid, have adopted a fully federated model through a principled move toward "internationalization" in the early 2000s. Amnesty International (like Greenpeace International) instead sought to "move closer to the ground" by decreasing its secretariat's size and influence over research and campaigning, while increasing its regional and national presence, and especially the ability of regional offices and sections to lead research and campaigning. The aims are to better ground their activism in locally relevant normative frameworks, to conduct campaigning more effectively through hands-on, locally vetted political power analysis and influencing tools, and to use a broader set of influencing methods that goes beyond traditional models of producing high-quality research and communication products for dissemination in-country. Amnesty International's theory of change focuses on significantly increasing its Global South support base and improving its capacity to partner with strong national and regional organizations—something that TNGOs such as Amnesty and Greenpeace have sometimes struggled with in the past. In a somewhat similar vein, Greenpeace's organizational change is moving away from a staff-centric model of campaign direction to a supporter-led form of activism ("people-powered campaigning") in which Greenpeace staff primarily play a facilitative role.

A deliberate, strategic movement toward a polycentric model can help to address important problems with traditional governance models that concentrate strategy-making and decision-making power in the Global North. It can also provide a check on Northern stakeholders that often exercise influence proportional to their financial contributions.

The facilitative model

Facilitative approaches such as people-powered campaigning challenge TNGOs to cede substantial control to communities of activists, yet significant (and costly) organizational infrastructure is generally still required to convert supporter energy into tangible campaign wins. Some TNGOs may discover that embracing more facilitative roles that put activists and local communities in charge risks alienating traditional donors and upending historically reliable funding models. Some stakeholders may balk at the prospect of losing real or perceived influence over campaign messages and priorities. Moreover, in many countries supporting people-powered campaigns could jeopardize a TNGO's charitable status (see Chapter 6). Activist-led campaigns that begin with general issue advocacy could potentially evolve to include specific policy asks, calls to action, and political endorsements. In countries such as the United States, such activities require different legal forms and may run counter to cultural norms prescribing appropriate behavior for organizations regarded as "charities."

Hybridity

The institutional form of the charity that many TNGOs adopt around the world was never meant for addressing root causes by facilitating supporter-led activism in pursuit of fundamental social transformation. The historical traditions of charity and almsgiving from which modern TNGOs emerged largely took deprivation, conflict, and inequality for granted and sought mainly to help people cope. Today, many are finding that the traditional model in which organizations such as TNGOs operate as perpetual intermediaries between "haves" and "have nots" is not necessarily the best way to make a lasting difference in the world.

The steady growth in alternative philanthropic vehicles, such as social enterprises, benefit corporations, and limited liability companies (e.g., the Chan-Zuckerberg Initiative, Omidyar Network, Emerson Collective, etc.), may be instructive that the institutional form of the charity is mismatched with modern aspirations and strategies for social change. Such hybrid ventures (partially) operate outside of the restrictions of the legacy architecture. They are designed to better facilitate for-profit impact investments in new technologies and can engage in more political advocacy by supporting specific policies, ballot initiatives, and political candidates.[8] These vehicles often have fewer transparency requirements and face greater public suspicion, but their success may ultimately be measured by how well they deliver on their stated goals. This does not necessarily imply that alternative organizational forms would always deliver better results, but it does suggest that moving beyond (or perhaps reforming) the institutional form of the charity is one avenue for innovation.

For TNGOs, similar opportunities exist to grow outside of the constraints of the charity model by creating hybrid entities capable of mobilizing different kinds of resources and engaging in nontraditional activities. For example, several digital platforms discussed in Chapter 6 that focus on facilitating and scaling up supporter-led activism are not registered charities but have incorporated as various alternative forms such as for-profit businesses. These digital organizations have additional opportunities to combine online and offline activism to maximize supporter engagement and improve campaigning outcomes.

Apart from creating new platforms and governance systems, digital tools can facilitate the transformation of organizations from staff-led to more supporter-led activism. TNGOs have to make choices about how far they want to go in mobilizing digital opportunities for purposes of overcoming the constraints of the legacy architecture. They may limit online engagement to broadcasting their messages to wider audiences or to improving the segmentation of their supporter base for more targeted fundraising appeals. Or they can abandon the staff-led approach and use digital tools to grow into new roles as facilitators and brokers. This may also entail moving away from the model of staff-defined topics and letting supporters do the talking and storytelling. This will require developing skill sets for TNGO leaders and their staff that include a strong emphasis on inquiry, discovery, and empathy as conditions for understanding how to improve the traction of neglected issues in public discourse.

On the input side, the financial benefits of hybridization can include more efficient capitalization through the selling of equity and easier borrowing, which in turn can support investments in core systems and more rapid scaling. On the output side, it can enable organizations to engage more directly in nontraditional activities that may be otherwise prohibited by law or difficult to undertake for cultural reasons. Additionally, some TNGOs have experimented with incubation strategies to foster innovation, such as in the case of Mobilisation Lab within Greenpeace and later CIVICUS.[9] Hybridity is also consistent with a cultural shift to a greater emphasis on data-driven decision-making.

Collaboration and M&A

Collaborations and other forms of a networked or collective impact approach are increasingly recognized as essential for achieving fundamental social and political transformations. Collaboration of different forms aims to create synergies to deliver significantly more than each partner can deliver on its own. However, many TNGOs still struggle with important aspects of collaboration (e.g., to engage productively with unlike-minded actors, to embrace constructive conflict, to acquire and hone interest-based negotiation skills, and to develop "non-othering" perspectives). In many instances, organizations stand to gain from deeper collaborations. However, a variety of obstacles—including personal egos and various financial and cultural constraints (see Chapter 10)—limit the depth of collaboration as a strategic instrument.

Beyond collaboration, M&A can be pursued strategically to acquire new capabilities and achieve greater scale, reduced transaction costs, and enhanced impact. Although sustained collaboration will likely remain a core strategy for many TNGOs, M&A can potentially provide additional benefits, especially for small- to mid-sized TNGOs wishing to acquire new capabilities and achieve greater economies of scale. However, M&A activity is hampered by attributes of the legacy architecture (see Chapter 11). For example, the lack of an ownership structure eliminates material incentives for board members and financial institutions to take a strong interest in M&A; contract buyouts that may be necessary to secure buy-in and smooth transitions may be normatively improper or illegal; M&A may be construed culturally as organizational failure or demise; and TNGOs may lack sufficient unrestricted funds to bear the upfront costs of exploration.

Organizational leadership plays a key role in collaborations and M&As. Top leadership typically takes the first steps of exploring joint actions, gathering intelligence for strategic decision-making, and communicating the case to staff and other stakeholders. Defining how different organizations will be better off as a result of collaborating or merging is a central condition for a successful process. In particular, positive collaborative attitudes require shifting away from mindsets that view one's own organization as superior and unique and accepting an emphasis on how to build a new and more promising venture to advance shared missions.

Operational platforms

Although the legacy architecture creates significant barriers, TNGOs can also become more global and streamlined by improving internal operational platforms to increase efficiencies, reduce costs, and enhance program quality and effectiveness. Some TNGO families are already in the process of more tightly coordinating program implementation worldwide. This was, for instance, one of the important outcomes of the organizational transformation in Save the Children documented in 2012.[10] CARE International also had as part of its change platform an aspiration to unify its line management in "CARE Global," envisioning a stronger role for the CARE International Secretariat. In the meantime, bringing operational platforms to scale through the sharing of services among different members or affiliates of mid- to large-sized TNGOs, and the building of integrated organizational systems for human resources, procurement, legal services, information technology, measurement and evaluation, etc., to create more efficiencies, is now underway in many large TNGOs (e.g., WWF, CARE, and Oxfam).[11]

Larger TNGOs such as Save the Children, CARE, Oxfam, and World Vision are among the many that are moving in this direction, despite the fact that these are complex systems changes with uncertain financial benefits and substantial risks attached. Multiple ongoing reform processes may also overlap and create unforeseen interactions, making it difficult to implement changes sequentially and adding to the complexity of change management. CARE USA, for example, experienced significant internal upheaval when it tried unsuccessfully to implement a new financial management system (PAMODZI). As a result, its staff became weary of subsequent change efforts and less supportive of the broader CARE 2020 agenda.

Many TNGOs tend to underinvest significantly in information technology, procurement, evaluation systems, and staff capacity-building and leadership development, among other areas, compared to the public and private sectors. They have been deterred from doing so thus far in large part because of the architecture's legacy imperative to demonstrate fiscal leanness more or less regardless of the effects on processes and outcomes. However, significant gains are available for TNGO (con)federations that are able to invest in systems that take advantage of scale. In this way, TNGOs can strengthen their backbone role by maintaining and providing core systems that facilitate the work of offices, members, affiliates, and partners around the world. At the same time, small and mid-sized TNGOs can economize by sharing services through co-op models in which vendors offer discounted externally sourced services for co-op members, such as what Humentum and InterAction have tried, for example.

TNGOs can also use operational platforms to enhance legitimacy and attract resources by improving systems for measuring program outcomes and agency-level results. As described across several chapters of this book, organizational legitimacy is essential to a TNGO's power and relevance, but the foundations of this legitimacy have shifted over time. In particular, TNGOs' commitments to missions of social transformation have ratcheted up expectations and drawn greater attention to the gap between their rhetoric about, and their evidence of, impact. In theory, TNGOs could establish trustworthiness not by practicing fiscal austerity but by demonstrating their cost-effective solutions to social problems. While the latter is much more difficult and costly, it could help to establish an environment considerably more aligned with what TNGOs aspire to do.

LEADING ORGANIZATIONAL CHANGE

TNGOs engaged in changing their organizational forms need expertise and leadership in how to manage large-scale organizational change processes, including cultural change.[12] Many TNGOs have significant gaps between their officially espoused values and their real in-use values, behaviors, and actions. The gaps are visible across a range of key areas, including with regard to accountability (at the individual or organizational level), how power is used within organizations, and how organizations respond to violations of codes of conduct by staff, for example.

The first challenge that TNGOs and their leaders typically face is establishing a sense of urgency for change.[13] This may be surprising for organizations whose mission it is to bring about change. Organizational inertia in the TNGO sector is not simply a problem of growth in size, but of widely distributed operations and multiple internal stakeholder groups with sometimes limited opportunities to regularly interact. Additionally, some TNGO staff may not be entirely honest is disclosing their self-interests in organizational change processes. Such processes may impact staff through their units and budgets, as well as through individual identity, social standing and prestige, and personal desires to "do good" or feel "warm glow" (see Chapter 2). Aspects of organizational culture can also convince internal stakeholders that their organization is unique, contributing to organizational narcissism[14] and resistance as a force working against the case for change.

When a sense of urgency is established, leaders of major change efforts still have to forge coalitions for specific proposals and facilitate compromises across institutional members of different sizes, cultural backgrounds, and interests. Internal transformation has to be framed as going beyond formal relations to emphasize that "change needs to be about people and behaviors, trust, and not primarily about structures or systems."[15] Leading such people-focused change typically requires first establishing a greater sense of community across the entire organization by fostering greater interdependence through a "network of peers" or "global glue" (as it has been called in CARE). Despite the rhetoric of common values, TNGO leaders cannot take for granted deeply shared understandings of common purpose across the organization. Change also requires devolving change management capacities to managers, rather than creating a separate, high-level change management unit that can develop a "bunker mentality" and may be too detached from everyday operations.[16]

Creating common purpose can serve as an important complement to a more hard-nosed internal power analysis at the outset of a desired change process. TNGOs apply such a tool regularly in their advocacy work, but much less so internally. Such an analysis plays an important role in distinguishing between different forms of resistance, and can be decisive in engaging with skeptics more productively. A power analysis enables leaders to identify specific change champions and distinguish strategies of direct and indirect influencing.[17]

External consultants may be helpful in very limited ways, but they are not always effective in the context of TNGO organizational change. They may come in with outside business sector perspectives that are insufficiently attuned to the TNGO setting, may not really be able to help with issues of creating urgency and consent, and often face immediate skepticism from staff accustomed to different symbols and language. Since the major challenges of bringing everyone onboard evolve differently across different TNGOs, commonly offered toolkits and blueprints can be of limited value.[18] Leaders have to be involved personally in change management, communicate often and in meaningful and multifold ways, and show regular presence.

Leaders are typically well ahead of the rest of the organization with regard to change processes, and may need to make sufficient space for staff grieving processes and for acknowledging past contributions that may no longer be needed or may become less important over time. Communicating urgency and resolve for change can be accompanied by celebrating both past accomplishments and by lighting the path from the old to the new organization. Staff will be more tied to the old organization because it valued their skills and capacities, and this may not be the case moving forward. There has to be room to discuss long-internalized expectations about the organization that never had to be discussed previously, but are challenged by change processes. As a result, leaders have to understand the "bottom-up" perspective on change and be able to switch between different lenses, such as the political, structural, human resource, and symbolic lenses, when being in charge of major organizational transformations.[19]

Transformative change has progressed at very different speeds across TNGOs.[20] ActionAid's decision to give all member affiliates the same power was made quickly and implemented immediately, with relatively little planning for possible practical or negative ramifications.[21] Yet, without having moved quickly they might not have made the leap. Amnesty International, in contrast, debated for more than a decade its Global Transition Programme to establish regional offices, but then took only four years to implement it (2012–2016). Quick implementation can prevent sources of resistance from overpowering momentum, but it can be devastating for the organization if it lacks adequate change management capacities. In the case of Amnesty, the broader goals of being closer to the ground were accomplished, but at high internal costs for staff morale and well-being.[22]

Significant change processes can also compete with other important issues for attention and resources, and staff may develop resentment if change processes are seen to divert too much attention from core activities related to programing or campaigning.[23] Strategies to address such concerns include clearly communicating the expected long-term benefits of change as well as tracking critical milestones and regularly sharing evaluations and lessons-learned throughout the change process.[24]

Polycentricism, facilitation, hybridity, collaborations, M&A, and enhanced operational platforms can help to transform individual organizations, especially when accompanied by effective change leadership. Such initiatives can be more than simply passive reactions to external pressures, but can be proactive transmutations designed to create a new fit between form and desired function. Over the past decades, many TNGOs have made major decisions about the direction of their organizational transformations. Although significant progress has been made in many areas, the possibilities for fundamental changes throughout the sector to enhance accountability, legitimacy, effectiveness, and relevance are circumscribed by the architecture itself.

The sector overall is challenged to stop reproducing its own problematic architecture and historical modes of operating. This is a difficult step to take because it destabilizes a status quo to which TNGOs are relatively well adapted. It requires not just transformations of individual organizations, but also changes in how the sector is governed, held accountable, and how it maintains its legitimacy. TNGOs seeking new roles cannot become the organizations they want to be until they let go of being what they were. This means addressing the root causes of their own problems by transforming the architecture.

The sector's future may need to involve changing how TNGOs are fundamentally constituted in law and understood as cultural objects. Such changes will certainly face the greatest resistance, with stakeholders struggling to conceive of what an alternative vision of TNGOs may even look like. Moreover, TNGOs lack short-term incentives to collectively organize to advocate for changes that would ultimately impose greater demands upon them, particularly when the status quo is relatively comfortable and appealing, at least in the short term.

Macrostructural efforts would likely entail exploring changes to regulatory frameworks as well as challenging the normative expectations imposed on the sector. Institutionally, TNGOs are constrained by the absence of formal legal recognition at the global level. An explicit international legal personality could provide TNGOs with a source of legitimacy supporting their operations across countries, while also establishing clearer and more relevant expectations with regard to their conduct and capacity to deliver on promises.[25] Although national nonprofit or charitable legal status confers important benefits for TNGOs in many contexts, the attendant regulatory frameworks often limit the capacities of TNGOs to wholeheartedly embrace new roles.

At national levels, major changes can be made in how TNGOs and nonprofits more generally are established and regulated. This does not necessarily mean making it harder to establish such organizations but rather implies a need for designing more appropriate regulatory frameworks and legal forms that are better aligned with TNGOs' missions. For example, because so many TNGOs exist to carry out activities that produce social or environmental benefits, an appropriate accounting regime would focus on TNGOs' activities and outcomes, and perhaps even cost-effectiveness, rather than just emphasizing finances, as is the case in the United States. The point is not to loosen financial oversight or make the sector more businesslike,[26] but to exchange outdated structures and practices with ones more aligned with TNGOs' current and future aspirations.[27] Conventional regulatory frameworks and accounting regimes focused purely on finances at best do nothing to account for what TNGOs exist to accomplish, and at worst create perverse incentives that can distract TNGOs from their missions and prevent them from adequately investing in the capacities they need to be effective. The so-called nonprofit starvation cycle derived from this surveillance regime seems to have outlived any usefulness it may have once had, yet the sector still perpetuates it.[28] Although some institutional donors are starting to pledge to support the full costs of delivering programs,[29] such commitments fall well short of changing the fundamental architecture within which such pledges become necessary in the first place.

In some national contexts TNGOs have attempted to use voluntary self-regulation initiatives to regain public trust and forestall legal changes perceived to be adverse, but such initiatives are rarely effective.[30] Despite the challenges, the sector would be better off developing a collective capacity to control its own destiny, rather than allow complacency to erode the sector's status and relevance. A major architectural transformation, whether at the international or national level, would invite controversy and expose organizations to new risks. The sector's existing incentive structures militate against such collective action, and its norms do not necessarily favor aggressive and honest confrontation. However, to be relevant, effective, and legitimate actors in the world, TNGOs cannot exempt themselves and their sector from the disruptive processes of fundamental transformation that they so often prescribe for others.

FROM ANXIETY TO STRATEGY

There is an urgent need for a vibrant and healthy TNGO sector capable of addressing challenging social and environmental problems throughout the world. History has shown that markets and governments have not only failed to address, but in many cases have caused or exacerbated, global problems such as climate change and inequality. TNGOs are committed to addressing such issues holistically, but TNGOs risk being increasingly outpaced by a combination of mounting global problems and their own lagging capacities to legitimately bring about change.

Around the world, such concerns have given rise to distrust of TNGOs[31] and various critiques of the third sector and philanthropy, including arguments that TNGOs' efforts are structurally incapable of transforming societies, are undemocratic, and sustain the power of the wealthy by pacifying dissent.[32] However, the diversity among TNGOs precludes such broad generalizations condemning the sector. More promising is to understand the sector's evolution and power as shaped by its institutional and normative context, and to explore how to evolve by transforming the conditions under which the sector operates. Some TNGOs may be able to thrive by staying the course, but survival alone will not make them more accountable, effective, or relevant. The sector needs to become collectively more proactive and better at demonstrating its distinctive value to the world. By confronting the legacy architecture, TNGOs can reassert who they are and what they want to accomplish. The solution to ensuring their relevance and impact is not to accept the seductive comfort of the status quo, but to embrace a more promising future in which the forms and norms of the architecture have been brought into harmony with the soul of the TNGO.

REFERENCES

Balboa, Cristina M. *The Paradox of Scale: How NGOs Build, Maintain, and Lose Authority in Environmental Governance.* Cambridge: MIT Press, 2018.

Bolman, Lee G., and Terrence E. Deal. *Reframing Organizations: Artistry, Choice, and Leadership.* 6th ed. San Francisco: Jossey-Bass, 2017.

Boswell, Ed, and Daryl Conner. *Leading Successful Change Amidst a Disruptive INGO Environment.* Atlanta: Conner Advisory, 2017. http://3vcego17hhlq3f2du63lx87v. wpengine.netdna-cdn.com/wp-content/uploads/2018/06/Leading-Successful-Change-Amidst-a-Disruptive-INGO-Environment.pdf.

Breen, Oonagh B., Alison Dunn, and Mark Sidel, eds. *Regulatory Waves: Comparative Perspectives on State Regulation and Self-Regulation Policies in the Nonprofit Sector.* New York: Cambridge University Press, 2017.

Bruno-van Vijfeijken, Tosca, Steven J. Lux, Shreeya Neupane, and Ramesh Singh. *Final Assessment: Amnesty's Global Transition Program.* Syracuse, NY: Moynihan Institute of Global Affairs, 2017.

Conner, Daryl, and Ed Boswell. *Organizational Culture and Its Impact on Change in the Civil Society Sector.* Atlanta: Conner Advisory, 2018. http://3vcego17hhlq3f2du63lx87v. wpengine.netdna-cdn.com/wp-content/uploads/2018/06/Organizational-Culture-and-Its-Impact-on-Change-in-the-Civil-Society-Sector.pdf.

Cooley, Alexander, and James Ron. "The NGO Scramble: Organizational Insecurity and the Political Economy of Transnational Action." *International Security* 27, no. 1 (2002): 5–39.

Crowley, James, and Morgana Ryan. *Building a Better International NGO: Greater Than the Sum of Its Parts?* Boulder, CO: Kumarian Press, 2013.

Crowley, James, and Morgana Ryan. *Navigating Change for International NGOs: A Practical Handbook.* Boulder, CO: Kumarian Press, 2017.

Davies, Rhodri. "Philanthropy Is at a Turning Point. Here Are 6 Ways It Could Go." *World Economic Forum Global Agenda* (April 29, 2018). https://www.weforum.org/agenda/2019/04/philanthropy-turning-point-6-ways-it-could-go/.

Davies, Thomas. *NGOs: A New History of Transnational Civil Society.* New York: Oxford University Press, 2014.

Duchon, Dennis, and Michael Burns. "Organizational Narcissism." *Organizational Dynamics* 37, no. 4 (2008): 354–64.

Edelman. *2019 Edelman Trust Barometer: Global Report.* New York, NY: Daniel J. Edelman Holdings, 2019.

Galbraith Jay R. Designing Organizations: An Executive Briefing on Strategy, Structure, and Process. San Francisco, CA: Jossey-Bass, 1995.

Garvin, David A. "The Processes of Organization and Management." *MIT Sloan Management Review* 39, no. 4 (1998): 33–51.

Giridharadas, Anand. *Winners Take All: The Elite Charade of Changing the World.* New York: Penguin Random House, 2018.

Gregory, Ann Goggins and Don Howard, "The Nonprofit Starvation Cycle." *Stanford Social Innovation Review* 7, no. 4 (2009): 49–53.

Gugerty, Mary Kay. "The Effectiveness of NGO Self-Regulation: Theory and Evidence from Africa." *Public Administration and Development* 28, no. 2 (2008): 105–18.

Gugerty, Mary Kay, and Dean Karlan. *The Goldilocks Problem: Right-Sized Monitoring and Evaluation for Development NGOs.* New York, NY: Oxford University Press, 2018.

Kotter, John P. *Leading Change.* Boston: Harvard Business Press, 2012.

Lecy, Jesse D., and Elizabeth A. M. Searing. "Anatomy of the Nonprofit Starvation Cycle: An Analysis of Falling Overhead Ratios in the Nonprofit Sector." *Nonprofit and Voluntary Sector Quarterly* 44, no. 3 (2015): 539–63. https://doi.org/10.1177/0899764014527175.

Martens, Kerstin. "Examining the (Non-)Status of NGOs in International Law." *Indiana Journal of Global Legal Studies* 10, no. 2 (2003): 1–24.

Mitchell, George E. "Creating a Philanthropic Marketplace through Accounting, Disclosure, and Intermediation." *Public Performance and Management Review* 38, no. 1 (2014): 23–47.

Moore, Mark H. "Managing for Value: Organizational Strategy in for-Profit, Nonprofit, and Governmental Organizations." *Nonprofit and Voluntary Sector Quarterly* 29, no. 1 (2000): 183–204.

Oxfam International. "SMS Learning Loop Tool Kit." Oxford, UK: Oxfam International, 2012.

Pallotta, Dan. *Uncharitable: How Restraints on Nonprofits Undermine Their Potential.* Boston: Tufts University Press, 2008.

Piper, Kelsey. "Why This Billion-Dollar Foundation Is Becoming a Corporation." *Future Perfect* (February 7, 2019). https://www.vox.com/future-perfect/2019/2/7/18207247/arnold-foundation-corporation-nonprofit-charity.

Queenan, Jeri Eckhart, Jacob Allen, and Jari Tuomala. *Stop Starving Scale: Unlocking the Potential of Global NGOs.* The Bridgespan Group (April 2013). https://www.

bridgespan.org/bridgespan/Images/articles/stop-starving-scale-unlocking-the-potential/stopstarvingscale-unlockingthepotentialofglobalngos.pdf.

Sidel, Mark.. "Regulation of Nonprofit and Philanthropic Organizations: An International Perspective." *Nonprofit Quarterly* (Summer 2016). https://nonprofitquarterly.org/2016/07/25/regulation-philanthropic-organizations/.

Sriskandarajah, Dhananjayan. "NGOs Losing the War against Poverty and Climate Change, Says Civicus Head: Charities Are No Longer Drivers of Social Change; for Many Saving the World Has Become Big Business. How Did We Lose Our Way?" *The Guardian* (London), August 11, 2014.

Stroup, Sarah S., and Wendy Wong. *The Authority Trap: Strategic Choices of International NGOs*. Ithaca, NY: Cornell University Press, 2017.

Tremblay-Boire, Joannie, Aseem Prakash, and Mary Kay Gugerty. "Regulation by Reputation: Monitoring and Sanctioning in Nonprofit Accountability Clubs." *Public Administration Review* 76, no. 5 (2016): 1–11. https://doi.org/10.1111/puar.12539.

Vijfeijken, Tosca Bruno-van, and Steven Lux. "From Alliance to International: The Global Transformation of Save the Children." *E-PARCC Collaborative Governance Initiative* (2012). https://www.maxwell.syr.edu/uploadedFiles/moynihan/tngo/2013-1A-Case-LuxBrunovanVijfeijken.pdf.

Younis, Mohamed, and Andrew Rzepa. *One in Three Worldwide Lack Confidence in NGOs*. Gallup and Wellcome (2019). https://news.gallup.com/opinion/gallup/258230/one-three-worldwide-lack-confidence-ngos.aspx.

AFTERWORD

BY BARNEY TALLACK

The decades of work by the TNGOs that originated in the Global North mostly in the twentieth century have made profound differences to the lives of many people and the causes of social and environmental justice. There are tens of millions of people who have benefited from TNGOs' direct life-saving work at times of rapid-onset, emerging, and politically created humanitarian crises. Northern TNGOs acting in solidarity with communities and civil society organizations in the Global South have supported hundreds of millions of citizens who are now better able to claim and exercise their human rights locally to globally.

It could be argued that the success of TNGOs, in concert with other actors, in keeping social justice, international development, and environmental issues on the local, national, and global agendas of citizens and those in power has been a worthwhile end in itself. The unwelcome recent rise in nativism demonstrates both that global social values and the spirit of solidarity cannot be taken for granted and continue to need defending.

The majority of the organizations referenced in this book came into existence in the early twentieth century or following World War II. Their original founders might be pleased with the successes and wins for the causes but also surprised at how these TNGOs have developed their organizational form, size, and role in the world. They might be even more surprised that what were initially unrelated small groups of passionately driven volunteers working on different specific missions have become "the sector."

PROFESSIONALIZATION, RUNNING THE MACHINE, AND EMERGENT EXISTENTIAL CRISIS

However, it can be argued that the sector as a whole has, for many of the reasons outlined in this book, become increasingly constrained or driven by its own existential needs. The unifying idea running through this book is that the achievement of the missions of TNGOs in recent, and even more so in future decades, is constrained by "forms and norms."

The authors describe well the rise of professionalization and the need to manage growth. Front-line staff delivering programs might express frustrations about internal organizational arrangements and ways of working. Alongside this there is a completely legitimate demand from TNGOs' stakeholders for demonstration of impact and, increasingly, accountability and transparency. What was easier to demonstrate when the organization was a handful of volunteers cannot be substituted with a "we do good, therefore, trust us in how we do it" assumption.

However, opponents of social justice have increasingly and disingenuously used the "TNGOs as self-perpetuating businesses with highly paid CEOs, big HQs and management costs" card as a weapon to undermine TNGOs demands for the powerful to address social, environmental justice and inequality. Trust in TNGOs and NGOs in general has declined since the beginning of the twenty-first century.

It is fair to say that some TNGO leaders (boards and executive leaders) do run the risk of thinking about their organizations as institutions that need to be self-perpetuating and sustained at all costs and that this does trickle down into culture and ways of working. This might be appropriate in some contexts where they are, and will continue to be, providers of essential services in the absence of state actors. It is far less so where their mission is to achieve transformational and lasting change for communities or global citizens. There is an irony that these organizations that are predominantly focused on change are unable to change themselves. The Gandhian advice that you must "be the change you wish to see in the world" is as relevant as ever. TNGOs increasingly struggle to align their present practices that have evolved over the last decades with the expanding missions and profound social change they want to achieve.

As the authors of this book have made clear, Northern TNGOs (or at least the majority of them) must transform themselves if they are to continue to play a useful role in the achievement of progressive change on a local, national, or global level. How current supporters, volunteers, and staff see many TNGOs in the 2030s will need to be as surprising to them as the current organizational forms would be surprising to their founders.

WHY "SOUL" AND ORIGIN STORIES ARE IMPORTANT IN THINKING ABOUT ORGANIZATIONAL FORM

Whether brought into being by solidarity and love (which is what charity means, after all) or righteous outrage at social and environmental injustice, it is clear that issues caused small groups of individuals to self-organize. It is unlikely that any of the individuals involved at the first meeting at someone's house, a church, or a university was doing so with the aim of founding a TNGO with thousands of staff and a century-plus lifespan. These origin stories are worth revisiting when leaders fret about "threats" from disintermediation and digitally savvy youth movements.

One of the more interesting responses to the closing of civil society space is for some TNGO leaders to respond to the risk by playing down the values and drivers that brought their TNGO into existence in the first place. An example of this is the quite radical toning down in some countries of the Christian identity of TNGOs originally founded as very much Christian organizations. Local populations do have a right not to be on the receiving end of proselytizing aid programs. However, this is not the same as being mildly embarrassed about publically acknowledging the organization's founding values. TNGOs with Islamic origins (who are achieving some of the greatest and highly sophisticated transformations in normative thinking) face similar contextual challenges in an increasingly Islamophobic Global North.

HOW PASSION CAN LEAD EITHER TO PRODUCTIVE SELF-CRITIQUE OR TO ORGANIZATIONAL HUBRIS

What moves much more slowly—and sometimes not at all—is the self-critical analysis of the mission and role of each TNGO. Reading the strategic plans and internal reports for many TNGOs, one will find the very similar descriptions of that organization's "unique" role. In reality this often means working with broadly the same mandates, in the same countries, and with the same partner organizations on very similar thematic programs. The inherent unwillingness and lack of external drivers for organizations to merge leaves both institutional donors and program partners somewhat frustrated. Consortia are helpful but partial responses, as multiple reporting requirements, contradictory policy positions, and so on do not make life easier for program partners.

TNGO boards, members, and leaders can all too easily convince themselves that their TNGO's added value, role, thematic niche, or program approach is unique even though the same "uniqueness" is evident in other

TNGOs. Even where a TNGO recognizes that other organizations also claim uniqueness, the response at the leadership level is often to assert that their TNGO is far better than other TNGOs, and thus still unique. Current examples to be heard at board and leadership meetings are a TNGO's excellence and uniqueness in "real participatory approaches," "convening," "innovating," and "advocacy that is grounded in real programs." These are almost articles of faith that are often unsupported by benchmarking against peers.

Trustees (or equivalent) mostly feel honored to be on the board and simultaneously proud of the organization's achievements. This is good. However, they also have limited exposure to the reality of the success and failures in the achievement of the mission and generally spend less time actively questioning the impact of the organization than perhaps they should. Measures such as fundraising growth, number of countries of operation, and UN meetings attended give trustees comfort but are not sufficient to be proxies for impact.

Individual passion and pride—including in the breadth of the organization's work—can lead to collective organizational hubris. Hubris does not sit well with hearing evidence of whether the organization's role, focus, or performance is really optimized for achievement of the mission. Purposefully stopping, phasing out, or handing over parts of the organization's work to others is not something that TNGOs are that good at.

GOVERNANCE

The 5S model of governance—Strategy, Stretch, Stewardship, Scrutiny, and Support—is a useful framework for understanding why the norms of TNGO boards are constraining TNGOs' ability to transform.

Stretch versus Support

Performance management is a commonly observed challenge for boards. There can be an unintended level of collusion or ignoring of performance issues. The deep values and people-centric mindsets of board members are combined with a passion and determination that the mission must be achieved. When organizational or personal performance is not up to the standards needed, rather than addressing the need for focus or hold executive leadership to account for that, boards often opt for more comfortable approaches of suggesting, deferring, or giving a bit more time for the issue to resolve itself or to suggest coaching or mentoring. As one governance staff member in a faith-based TNGO put it, "our sixth organizational value is being too nice." For these all too understandable reasons, some TNGOs exhibit a "low performance, high persistence" approach (see Chapter 2) in the hope that the latter, in and of itself, will solve the former.

Scrutiny

Often when trustees do question how well the organization is achieving the mission it is based on a narrow understanding of programmatic complexity, leaving program directors and executive teams frustrated by requests for somewhat simplistic answers in terms of the short-term quantifiable impact of programs versus dollars spent. Program leadership unconsciously (or consciously?) is sometimes very happy if discussions about impact, program quality, and complexity are left off the board agenda.

Strategy versus stewardship

In addition to the challenges around the ability to operate in program countries, there are many technical challenges arising from the relatively recent and blunt tools of Western governments in relation to legislation on terrorism financing, bank roles in international corruption, and so forth. For these reasons—and the very real existential challenges in fundraising—the risk appetite of boards has changed dramatically. Questions of strategy and breaking out of the existing but constraining organizational form are uncomfortable.

Most TNGOs have four-to-five-year strategy periods, if not longer. Significant effort is put in by boards, leadership teams, and others to create a strategy for sign-off. A common frustration expressed in informal groupings of TNGO directors of strategy is that performance is rarely assessed against the strategy and the need for midterm review or adjustments is rarely discussed after sign-off. Some TNGOs have been very successful at operationalizing the strategy and using it to guide decision-making and organizational change. Save the Children and Plan are good examples of a bold new unifying strategy idea leading to consequential organization-wide transformations. For many other TNGOs the strategy is often overly aspirational in either breadth of themes, scale, or funding ambition, has failed to make tough choices for focus, and is rarely supported by clear resourcing plans.

As identified by the authors, even when the need to transform has been acknowledged and bold decisions made, change management and work on culture are disciplines that most TNGOs have very limited expertise in. One of the underlying themes of this book is that organizational culture is hugely overlooked. Experience tells us that some TNGO leaders either do not see work on culture and change management as a significant and necessary component of their roles or see it as an operational strand of work to be initiated after board and executive leadership decisions have been made. Multiple functional cultures can manifest in very problematic ways in multi-mandate TNGOs. For example, humanitarian "first phase response" operating culture and decision-making may come up against consensus-building approaches or the risks to delivery from the (rightly challenging) external positions of advocacy work. Tensions produced by these operating culture frictions from multiple mandates can significantly hinder TNGOs from transforming themselves.

NOT ALL TNGOS NECESSARILY DISTINGUISH BETWEEN BEING INTERNATIONAL AND BEING GLOBAL

As cited by the authors, the external megatrends affecting TNGOs are profound. Externally, the changing location and structure of poverty and inequality is on its own a reason to revisit organizational roles. Projections for the 2030s strongly suggest a rump of fragile and conflicted states still focused on internal issues and the rest of the world's population living in middle- or high-income countries trying to deal with globally common challenges of resource scarcity, inequality, and environmental degradation. Governments and populations in the Global South rightly challenge perceived neocolonial behaviors by Northern governments and populations. Southern civil society has for some decades challenged "charitable" Northern TNGOs to question whether the role they currently play is well-meaning but also (unintentionally) neocolonial. The need for social justice and solidarity between communities across the globe will persist, although some Southern civil society organizations (CSOs) strongly question whether many of the older Northern TNGOs are needed at all. Converting a country office to an independent national member with a local board doesn't wash with local CSOs when the power to set global strategic direction is still a function of the financial contribution of the Northern members of the family. It is also worth noting that TNGO boards and executive teams are often largely made up of a generation of people who grew up in national movements and in a pre–digitally connected global context.

LEGITIMACY AND ACCOUNTABILITY

As the book identifies, the sector has an accountability challenge. Despite the best efforts of InterAction, Accountable Now, Sphere, and the Core Humanitarian Standard, it can be argued that TNGO leaders have taken public trust for granted. The book shows clearly that TNGO leaders are playing catch-up on the need to demonstrate impact beyond that of immediate humanitarian lifesaving service delivery.

Additionally, the challenging fundraising context for unrestricted funding throws up another dissonance. An average individual donor getting an email or direct mail update on the results of his or her child sponsorship is probably less aware of the funding for that TNGO's New York or Brussels advocacy office. Indeed, there has been an alarming backtracking by some TNGO members on the sector-wide agreements from the 1990s not to use "victim" and "flies in their eyes" imagery for individual supporter fundraising. It is still a brave CEO or VP who consistently and systematically promotes fundraising asks that are completely aligned with the TNGO's program approach and theory of change.

IT IS HARD NOT TO LET MONEY AND THUS POWER DICTATE ORGANIZATIONAL FORM

The inconvenient truth is that the money, and the power to determine the organization's future that goes with it, drives more decision-making than leaders would like it to or will acknowledge. The governance of many TNGOs insist that they genuinely operate with a participatory, consensus-based, or "one member, one vote" approach. However, global structures, cultures, and ways of working are very heavily influenced by underlying disparities in power. In a TNGO family with a dominant member it can create an environment in which an unspoken veto exists and where the capacity (not always the same as capability) of individual larger members dominates strategic and thought leadership.

There is the often unmentioned but very real dependency on the negotiated indirect cost rate agreement that comes with institutional funding to cover head office and management costs. For many TNGOs with declining financial supporter bases this is a real issue. The growth in legacy income from aging supporters recruited in the 1960s to 1990s masks but does not solve the long-term challenge of aging supporter bases and dramatically reduced returns on investment in individual fundraising.

Many TNGOs have turned to institutional funding not just because it can support programs at scale but also because the contribution to management costs enables the organization to keep going (in the short term). Boards and leadership teams across the sector frequently express a yearning for the unrestricted funding ratios of previous decades but can be less open to considering decreasing their dependency and opportunistic grant-seeking in institutional funding. This and the assertions about uniqueness of contribution and the importance of a multi-mandate approach does not lend itself to focus on fewer areas of deeper, evidenced strategic competence.

Are we reaching the end of the Golden Age of TNGOs?[1] Much like the G7 states in global politics, the speed of growth and dominance of "traditional" Northern TNGOs in global civil society has probably reached its high tide mark. In addition to geopolitical changes, Northern governments have cut or repurposed development cooperation budgets available to TNGOs.

FUTURE ROLE AND POTENTIAL EXISTENTIAL OUTCOMES

Is there a future role for TNGOs? Yes, because progressive change is not linear (as the current rise of nativism and attacks on human rights shows us), and although the nature of issues might change, there will, unfortunately, continue to be a need for advances in social and environmental justice. What is less clear is whether TNGOs founded in the Global North will be the ones playing this role equally alongside newer, Southern, or digital organizations, or will have been replaced by them.

Rather than look from this end of the telescope, Northern TNGOs could instead look backward from 2050 and at the legacy that they would ideally bequeath to global civil society. This could include having finally "locked in" normative thinking about rights, decades of monitoring, evaluation, and learning and technical knowledge being truly bequeathed as creative commons, having genuinely become part of networked communities aligned around global or local issues, as well as very specific knowledge and technical transfers.

Do especially Northern TNGOs need to change? As the authors assert: Yes, absolutely! Not changing is the only course of action more guaranteed to end the existence of a TNGO. To put it bluntly, TNGOs can either transform radically, decide that their existence should "end well," or, because they are not in strategic control of their destiny, "end badly."

Transform radically

There are a number of ways in which TNGOs need to transform radically to remain relevant in the future. In some cases transforming radically may mean purposefully getting smaller or not growing in size. For example, some TNGOs may need to consider moving from generalist, multi-mandate organizations to being more focused and thus valued by the rest of the movement of which they are a part. Boards and leaders need to be honest with themselves about their real competence and niche in order to recognize the most effective role that the organization can play within the wider movement for change. Likewise, the multi-mandate mantra in some organizations that "we have to do humanitarian crisis response and long-term development and advocacy" needs to be strongly questioned. Not every organization needs, or can, be the leading expert in all areas. Ceasing or transferring work in some areas to other parts of the movement, doing only what they are good at, and working collaboratively with them should be considered major signs of success.

Even those Northern TNGOs primarily focused on a life-saving assistance mandate need to change radically. Many have already taken the step to refocus from 60, 70, or even 100-plus countries down to 20 to 30 countries (often the fragile and conflict-affected states) and become more expert and focused on their niche (e.g., WASH, hunger and food security, etc.) and capacity-building partners. For example, Concern Worldwide made the decision some time ago to focus only on the "poorest" countries and has since followed through. Within the need to focus, there is also the need to respond meaningfully to the localization agenda (handing over power to Southern actors) and to the difficulties of saturated Northern fundraising markets, aging supporter profiles, and so forth.

TNGOs can decide to take a smaller but deeper role in the wider civil society environment. The more self-critical TNGOs are currently, or have already, looked at where their niche lies in relation to the rest of their movement. The organizational hubris that says, "we are the only expert in every aspect of what we currently do" is unhelpful to movements as a whole. It creates unnecessary competition and poor cross-organizational relationships that undermine collective efforts. Genuinely honest TNGOs need to be asking the other stakeholders in their movements to act as critical friends telling them what they think the TNGO is actually strong at, where it is useful and valuable, and what contribution they think it could best make alongside some truths about where it is not succeeding or adding value. This requires a level of humility and a servant leadership type of mindset alongside lived values around a "nothing for us without us" mentality, solidarity, collaboration not competition, and genuine partnership based on solidarity and respect.

Global issues require global organizations with local roots and legitimacy. As identified by the authors, transformation, by programmatic necessity, needs to be even more profound in those organizations working on global issues that require global solutions (e.g., climate change, inequality, nativism, etc.). The challenges to their underlying economic models are just as intense. Greater than these are the challenges of legitimacy, relevance, and accountability in middle-income countries. The promotion of rights-based approaches alongside Western aid is less attractive to many governments than Chinese foreign direct investment.

While many TNGOs are "globalizing" by converting program countries into full and equal national members, affiliates, or partners, the time scales are very long and require significant investments of unrestricted funds. How much local civil society and governments see these national members as being legitimate is dependent on how much power is actually transferred from the Northern founding members. Doing this properly requires embracing radical transformation.

Returning to or becoming a grassroots popular mobilization type of organization might appear elusive but is probably essential for some campaigning organizations. Since the late 1990s many TNGOs have added or are adding more advocacy and policy work to their existing programs. This is a logical extension that does achieve scale, addresses root causes, and brings about sustainable change. While being grounded in program reality is essential, that does not necessarily mean all the program work needs to be delivered by the TNGO. A number of successful policy, think tank, research, or convening organizations did not start with their own "on-the-ground" programs. TNGOs regularly capacity-build and fund the work of such organizations. It is certainly an option for some TNGOs to become radically smaller and transform into such research or policy organizations, especially as platforms "owned" or funded by the partner organizations that use them.

Governance is an area where change is especially needed. Reading the "who we are" and "how we are governed" pages of Northern TNGO websites goes a long way to explaining some of the self-generated "forms and norms" constraining change. Individually, every trustee or board member is to be celebrated and gratitude should be expressed for their contribution and passion. But several changes do need to happen. These include actually addressing the diversity and inclusion question rather than just promising to do so, ensuring that people with lived experience of the TNGO's issues are involved, and living the "nothing for us without us" principle regarding legitimacy, relevance, and accountability.

Although perhaps not the most popular course of action, it will also be necessary for many TNGOs to reduce dependencies on institutional funding. It is not just the dependency on one donor for a large percentage of a TNGO's funding or for matched funding. There is also the carefully constructed but complex matrix of funding, which can mean that the failure to secure a relatively small proportion of funding from one donor jeopardizes the whole.

Some TNGOs have become more opportunistic and less competency-driven in the proposals they put forward to funders. This creates a vicious cycle as the TNGO becomes less focused and its competency is spread thinner. Some of the more established, progressive, and long-standing donors (e.g., EU, SIDA, DFID, Irish Aid, etc.) have politely pointed this out and are more interested in strategic partnerships with TNGOs that have well-articulated theories of change, program approaches, or thematic competence aligned with the donor's focus.

Reducing the dependency also increases the ability of the organization and governance to act strategically. This author has operated on a charity board in which the management had, opportunistically, created such a dependency on a certain type of institutional funding that management wanted to change the charitable objects to maintain it. The board, however, chose to exit that work, halving the size of the organization but keeping true to the mission.

The notion of "soul" is also essential. A national NGO that has become a small TNGO and then a large TNGO can slowly and almost imperceptibly lose its soul. The authors describe this well in Chapter 2. A TNGO's soul can be a somewhat nebulous concept and occasionally one used as an excuse for failing to change or disguising low performance. It would, however, serve TNGOs well to reexamine their origin stories, recognizing that they came from movements and not a desire to build a large TNGO with a predetermined organizational form. In both a pre-digital and digital world, movements are self-organizing. The technology is just a modality, just as church halls and local community spaces were, and still are.

Recapturing passion and soul is not straightforward but there are some ways that boards and leaders can do this. They can examine whether the organization lives its founding values in all its activities by paying attention to whether the strategic and operational decisions meet the tests of legitimacy, relevance, and accountability. Leaders help to determine culture and soul. They can put dedicated, continuous effort into understanding the reality of their organizational cultures and addressing the known but ignored negative aspects of them.

More TNGOs will reshape their work to include more domestic programming. This goes beyond raising public awareness around humanitarian and development issues in the Global South and addresses, for example, individual consumption, holding duty-bearers to account, mobilizing, and even in some cases delivering services. With the move to more middle-income countries it is not inconceivable that the role and activity of Northern members of TNGO families become exactly the same as Southern members. That is, they raise funds, do awareness-raising, and maintain programs in their own country as part of a shared global strategy. Already the European members of many TNGOs have started doing work on migration as a result not of East Asia, Southern Africa, or Latin American migration (all of which are pre-existing and bigger), but as a consequence of the post–Arab Spring migration from Syria, Libya, etc., into Europe.

As an example, one TNGO once struggled to reconcile its roots in international development in "poor" countries with whether or not to do have programs "at home." The decision to do so was the result of an intervention by the country directors. Their collective letter pointed out that the denial that the causes of poverty did not exist in the "home" country was a fundamentally neocolonial attitude.

It is worth asking whether it is worth merging more of the humanitarian response arms of TNGOs. As far back as the 2004 tsunami response it was clear that Northern TNGOs were falling over each other in delivering lifesaving and reconstruction work. The UNHCR cluster approach has helped, but how many TNGOs are needed to deliver the most effective WASH, child rights, and livelihoods responses? Can every TNGO be unique in its focus and in having the best-quality response in all of the areas it works on? As cash and voucher responses have increasingly become part of effective responses, this has had some effect. This and work on true localization must force changes, even though it is often unpopular with fundraisers who find it easier to "sell" more traditional and tangible ideas of what humanitarian response means.

Another question worth asking is whether a given national member is a member of the right TNGO family. Most of the TNGOs with multiple national members struggle to create shared theories of change and programmatic and fundraising approaches. The identity of a national member in one country can be very different from that of members in other countries. For example, this can be observed in the different desire or ability of national members to be political or do public campaigning. It can also be observed in the wish or perceived need to do more fundraising or more work on one thematic area and none of another area. Whether a three-member or forty-member family, the ability to focus and bring the best of every member together is an ongoing headache for boards, CEOs, and directors of strategy (and governance support) staff.

It takes only a cursory comparison of the publicly available mission statements, strategy, and annual report documents or web pages across TNGOs to see the outward expression of this challenge. Some TNGOs will describe five, six, seven, or eight goals and then within each of those many more sub-thematic areas. These are not necessarily a reflection of competence and added value in all of those areas but more often a result of different national members wanting to see "their thing" in the strategy.

In addition to the challenge of focus, TNGOs are not necessarily good at discussing and owning a shared understanding of theories of change and thematic and program approaches. This then surfaces at the CEO or governance level in arguments about lower-level areas of operations and lower-level structures. The frustration of country directors and other program staff who are trying to deliver programs that align to the country context while national CEOs argue is substantial. Often a national member is so much in dispute with the majority of the rest of the family that it would actually be more effective (and happier) in one of the other TNGO families with which it is better aligned. Perhaps it is not entirely fanciful to consider a "dating agency" that helps match national members to the right family and facilitates the exchanging of national members.

End well

Some traditional charities established prior to the twentieth century came into existence for very similar reasons as modern TNGOs, but usually with a national focus (e.g., enabling children from poorer families to access free schooling; the provision of health services; welfare provision for ex-sailors, tailors, and drapers; the anti-slavery movement; universal suffrage; etc.). Many of these incredibly useful and successful charities no longer exist. This can be because the issue no longer exists in the same way, the state or duty-bearer has taken on responsibility, or the funding environment changed. In some cases it is simply because the funding ran out or the cause ceased to be as popular.

Likewise, turning an existing "supertanker" into an emerging youth-led, grassroots, digitally enabled organization is a massive, probably impossible exercise in which huge costs would be expended. The transformations in Save the Children, Oxfam, and ActionAid are all journeys of ten years and counting. In all three cases these have been multi-phase journeys where the second phase had to be triggered because the organizational form developed in the first phase (i.e., Save's "Unified Presence," Oxfam's "Single Management Structure") had not gotten far enough, fast enough. For those TNGOs coming to that first decision point to transform, it could well be too late. There are also TNGOs that have made tentative decisions but are putting in place new organizational forms that look remarkably like the mid- to late-2000s first redesigns that Save the Children, ActionAid, and Oxfam subsequently moved on from.

In other sectors, large and once successful parts of the organization are purposefully closed or allowed to fade out as "cash cows" and new investments are put into building new organizations unencumbered by the structures, systems, processes, operating cultures, and "baggage" that are no longer fit for purpose. Is it more effective to try and nudge the supertanker or to build new speedboats instead? Does it make sense to slowly adjust the supertanker to compete with the newer dynamic and agile movements? If you cannot build the speedboats yourself, then fund the building of those organizations and hand over your useful capabilities if they want them.

Ending well can be a positive outcome for a TNGO. Searching for new work for the continued existence of an organization is not the best way if there is already another organization better equipped or better located to do it. Some TNGOs have done this in very small and localized ways (e.g., handing programs over to a partner or spinning out new organizations owned locally). Others have capacity-built local Southern NGOs to access funding directly rather than its going through the TNGO's books. BRAC is a good example of a local TNGO supported in this way in its early years and that is now bigger than most of the largest TNGOs.

As the authors have highlighted, very few organizations have let themselves be subsumed or merged into another TNGO. Where mergers have happened, it is often because of external funding crises. The operational and practical obstacles to this have been articulated well. They do not undermine the argument that the achievement of a particular mission could be better effected through merging expertise, name, and resources into a larger TNGO that can leverage these to deliver impact at scale (and with more efficiency).

Instead of globalizing through building more national members, a more meaningful response to localization, the need for legitimacy, and disintermediation could be to hand over Northern TNGOs' assets, power, and decision-making authority to Southern civil society. Some very small organizations have done this fully, where expertise or donor funding is the main asset; among the larger TNGOs, ActionAid has embraced this approach.

Some TNGOs—often unitary ones—are very keen to open fund-raising offices in emerging middle-income countries while retaining decision-making power in the North. The conversion of Northern members into fundraising offices for a Southern-owned unitary organization could be one outcome worth considering.

Another form of ending well would be to merge or transfer the assets to a digital organization platform owned by others or even (heresy though it might be for some TNGOs) to a state or private sector actor.

There are many assets that are already welcomed by partners as part of capacity-building and could be transferred to a degree or in their entirety at a national or supranational level. These include thematic knowledge, program learning, and connections to other actors (ministries, global corporations, Northern governments, etc.). These assets can be truly handed over rather than mediated by the TNGO or the TNGO playing a nebulous broker or convener role that is actually more like a "middle man."

Another variation of ending well is to transfer assets to Southern partners or national members of the same family to a point where the Northern organization operates as the smaller member. Taking this point further, ending well could also involve merging into or facilitating being taken over by a Southern TNGO. However, this would take even more bold leadership at the board and CEO level than a merger between Northern organizations.

End badly

Some Northern TNGOs have grasped, albeit tentatively, the need to transform themselves and have recognized that by 2025–2030 the world is going to be very different from the past golden age. Whether all those transformations succeed and those TNGOs are still significant actors in 2030 is yet to be seen. Some may not make it, even despite recognizing the need, for all the reasons described in this book.

All the causes and drivers that make ending well an outcome worth considering are also relevant for those organizations that are still in denial, less willing to critique their roles and evaluate their real added value, or are suffering from organizational hubris. If they do not successfully transform, or do not purposefully phase out, then they will crash and burn. The horizon that is used to guide the longer-term strategic direction and organizational form for many of these TNGOs even today is still only three to five years out. This is about the same length of time as the program contracts that they sign today. Or, perhaps as one TNGO leader admitted, the hand-to-mouth nature of their funding means that more than eighteen months out is a long way off.

Partnerships with corporations and new more private sector–type business models have been touted for many years but are not (yet) of significant size. Many TNGOs need to get over themselves and their simplistic "private sector bad, states OK, third sector good" mentality. This mentality has also created a sometimes rigid approach in which advocacy is only focused on pushing states to constrain the worst of the private sector through regulation. The addition of working in alliance to enable more Unilevers and Patagonias so that they are the norm and not the exception is possible (in some sectors).

The biggest challenge is that of the financial dependency on large grants and funding from institutional donors. Even the positives of the disintermediation of Northern TNGOs and localization threaten the ability of TNGOs to secure funding for the overhead that comes with being a large professional organization.

This author has worked with many TNGOs that needed to close or realign fundraising business units achieving lower and lower yields but were unwilling or unable to do so because they feared it would crystallize very significant costs of change. The soaking up of costs in unproductive areas constrains their ability to invest in or grow new "products" and channels. This inability to innovate, invest in the future, and realign can become a death spiral.

If financial crises have already triggered some failures and will trigger more, then reputational crises are not far behind. TNGOs aspire to hold the strongest of values and the public expects them to live those. Yes, delivering 100 percent on these expectations is highly unrealistic in some of the contexts in which TNGOs work, but TNGOs have set themselves up for a fall as well. A combination of lack of transparency in reporting, an assumption that all staff live the same values, and a reluctance to communicate the messiness of international development, program complexity, and difficulties in attributing impact means that the gap between what the public expects versus the reality is very large. Fundraising pitches that give the simplistic impression that the organization is doing easy concrete work like building schools, when it is actually achieving program impact on education in very different ways, does not help. Being an outspoken organization challenging vested interests' destruction of the environment or inequality and injustice—shouting loudly in the streets and in the media—is very necessary if some TNGOs are to achieve their missions. It is core, for example, to Greenpeace or Amnesty's ability to create impact. Being outspoken and having had some degree of success means that TNGOs need to take their accountability and living their values seriously. It also brings opponents. TNGOs that are still organized, registered, and perceived as traditional charities by the public are vulnerable.

The frenzied and escalating attack by parts of the media hostile to international aid spending and political activity by charities in the UK has damaged the ability of the sector to carry out its main aims for many years to come. It has certainly given a catalyzing shock to the entire sector. Safeguarding became the priority topic on TNGO board agendas throughout 2018, all the inter-agency conferences majored on it, and TNGOs rapidly upgraded or put in place new policies and processes and communicated that to their supporters. Fortunately for the sector, the vast majority of TNGO supporters could see the difference between what was a genuine failing that needed to be addressed and an over-the-top media and political response that ignored the complexity of operating in challenging contexts. However, their near miss does not guarantee surviving a second time if they cannot rebuild public trust and also do better at explaining how what they actually do is different from the twentieth-century charity paradigm understood by the public.

In the longer term, the insular nativist, divisive, anti-migrant shift in Northern government policy and sections of the public's normative thinking, combined with the rise of middle-income countries, fans the "if they can fund a space program, why do they need our help" mantra. The diminishing relative geopolitical power of Northern countries in the global economy makes Northern governments even more unwilling to jeopardize trade relations and inward investment from countries with some of the worst human rights abuses. Even funding and campaigning activity for some of the most severe humanitarian crises is harder than it was (see Yemen as an example, and that is one of the more high-profile crises).

The route for Northern TNGOs through this is ultimately about relevance and legitimacy. Those that have kept their "soul," critically assess their role, and are less monolithic and superstructure-heavy might survive. Those that have not or are not may face ending badly or experiencing a long and painful decline to nonexistence.[2]

CONCLUSION

There is a future role for TNGOs. The imperative to respond to humanitarian crises in fragile and conflict-affected states will exist for decades to come. There must be a flourishing civil society to achieve local and global social justice—global issues such as climate change necessitate it—but Northern TNGOs' role and function, and thus their organizational forms and norms, must change. Their role must be better situated within a global movement in which Southern civil society is an equal partner or leads. TNGO impact is only as good, deep, and sustainable as that of the movement as a whole.

The rapidly changing external context not only dramatically changes how the mission is achieved, but brings dramatic existential and funding challenges for TNGOs as well. This means that they need to change their role, function, and organizational form. However, the creation and institutionalization of forms and norms over the decades since their founding makes it much harder for large Northern TNGOs to make the tough decisions and implement the consequent changes.

TNGOs will live, prosper, and achieve impact, especially new and Southern organizations. Northern TNGOs can continue to exist, although collectively are unlikely to grow. That continued existence will be helped dramatically where they can reduce their dependency on institutional funding and cease equating size with impact. Becoming smaller, more focused thematically, more rooted in a coherent theory of change, more strategic, and less opportunistic are all ways forward. Some may be able to leapfrog through youth mobilization, technology, innovation, and far more collaboration. All should do better at demonstrating their added value and cogently explaining the complexity of achieving impact. They will also need to move from being a "jack of all trades" to having a smaller set of core competencies and working with other actors who have more competence in other areas. These transformations need to be accompanied by leaders revitalizing the soul that recognizes values, legitimacy, relevance, accountability, and solidarity to be the foundation of everything that they do.

REFERENCE

Roche, Chris, and Andrew Hewett. "The End of the Golden Age of International NGOs?" ACFID/University Linkage Conference, Australia, November 21–22, 2013.

NOTE ON SOURCES

This book reflects our accumulated experience based on more than fifteen years of academic and professional engagement with the TNGO community. Our collaboration began in 2004 as cofounders of the Transnational NGO Initiative at the Moynihan Institute of Global Affairs at the Maxwell School of Citizenship and Public Affairs at Syracuse University. The Initiative was designed to create virtuous feedback loops between research, education, and practice. We obtained our first major research grant from the National Science Foundation (NSF) in 2005 to complete an interview study focused on TNGO leadership perspectives about effectiveness, governance, collaboration, and other key challenges faced by the sector.[1] In parallel, we turned to practitioner experts for advice and feedback. In 2006, we consulted senior TNGO leaders to help us generate insights about how the Initiative may benefit the practitioner community. This group included, among others, Harriet Stanley, then a senior leader at PATH; Phil Robertson, who currently has a leadership position in Human Rights Watch; and Sarah Newhall, who then was CEO of Pact. As a result of their and others' input, the Initiative began to complement academic research with other activities, including consultancies, annual Leadership Institutes, Senior Leadership Development Programs, and visitor programs.

We each have also gained from our regular interactions with practitioners in graduate-level courses on TNGO and nonprofit management, civil society, evaluation, human rights, and other topics. This includes students at the Maxwell School of Syracuse University, the Colin Powell School for Civic and Global Leadership at the City College of New York, the Austin W. Marxe School of Public and International Affairs at Baruch College, and the School of Leadership and Education Sciences at the University of San Diego.

Our approach synthesizes decades of academic research with the experiential learnings of hundreds of contemporary TNGO practitioners. Our reliance on a variety of data sources through research, practitioner engagement, and teaching has allowed us to develop the core themes and insights presented in the book. Although specific data sources are indicated in notes and references throughout each chapter, we provide below a synopsis of our original academic research and professional engagements that have informed the arguments of this book.

TRANSNATIONAL NGO INTERVIEW STUDY

The academic centerpiece of the collaboration at Syracuse University was the Transnational NGO Interview Study, which was an in-depth, mixed-method study of 152 US-based transnational NGO leaders. The core interview study covered topics such as organizational goals, strategies, activities, transnationalism, effectiveness, accountability, communications, networks and partnerships, and leadership development. The semi-structured interviews averaged an hour and 23 minutes each, generating a combined 209 hours of recordings. The interviews were transcribed, coded, and processed using computer-aided qualitative data analysis software and statistical software to produce qualitative and quantitative datasets. After the completion of the NSF study, these datasets have been made available to other researchers. Table N.1 provides an overview of the interview study sample. A portion of the academic research cited throughout the book is derived from this study.[2]

ACADEMIC RESEARCH

In addition to numerous white papers and applied "pracademic" publications cited throughout this book, we have written many academic articles about TNGOs and nonprofits that have appeared in peer-reviewed journals of TNGO and nonprofit studies, public administration, international relations, and related fields. In addition to the original NSF study, much of this research is based on subsequent interviews with TNGO leaders, survey data, government records, and conceptual and theoretical analysis. George Mitchell's research has examined topics including organizational effectiveness,[3] evaluation and reporting,[4] financial management,[5] strategic management,[6] collaboration,[7] operational strategy,[8] organizational theory,[9] and sectoral context.[10] Hans Peter Schmitz's work has explored the composition and power of policy networks,[11] risks and opportunities associated with intersectoral collaborations,[12] scholarly debates about organizational effectiveness,[13] the role of digital tools in transforming transnational advocacy,[14] TNGO leadership perspectives on intrasectoral collaboration,[15] and the evolution of transnational activism, especially in the area of human rights and international development.[16] Tosca Bruno-van Vijfeijken's academic research has addressed TNGO accountability,[17] future challenges faced by the sector,[18] planned organizational closure,[19] and organizational culture.[20] Our academic research is regularly presented at conferences organized by the Association for Research on Nonprofit Organizations and Voluntary Action, the International Society for Third-Sector Research, the International Studies Association, and other venues.

RESEARCH CONDUCTED IN PREPARATION FOR THIS BOOK

To further develop the major themes of this book, we interviewed fifteen "thought leaders" to explore their views on the sector's challenges and future. These interviewees included (among others) John Clark, former head of civil society at the World Bank; Ramesh Singh, CEO of ActionAid; Ingrid Srinath, secretary-general of CIVICUS; and Alan Fowler, honorary professor chair in African philanthropy, Wits Business School, Johannesburg, and emeritus professor, Institute of Social Studies, Erasmus University. Over the years, we have conducted about 450 interviews and conversations as part of our research, conference attendance,[21] and hosting of visitors to the Transnational NGO Initiative. Professional titles used throughout this book to identify individuals reflect those current at the time of engagement unless otherwise noted.

Additionally, between August 2014 and May 2016, we conducted eighteen interviews with TNGO leaders and senior managers responsible for digital communications. The study focused on the use of digital tools by a variety of organizations, including traditional and "digitally native" organizations. The interviews focused on how these organizations use social media and other digital tools, what opportunities and challenges they saw, and what primary goals they pursued in establishing an online presence. Since digital strategies are particularly relevant in recruiting new supporters outside of the Global North, the sample reflected a strong representation of experts from middle-income countries.[22]

In April 2015, we hosted a forum titled "Breaking Digital" at the Center for Strategic and International Studies (CSIS) in Washington, DC. Panelists included Jason Cone (communications director, MSF USA), Blair Glencorse (founder and executive director, Accountability Lab), David Karpf (assistant professor, George Washington University), Steven Livingston (professor, George Washington University), Andrea Koppel (vice president of global engagement and policy, Mercy Corps), Robtel Neajai Pailey (academic, activist, and author, SOAS, University of London), Michael Silberman (global director of the Digital Mobilization Lab, Greenpeace), Mark Smith (senior director for humanitarian emergencies, World Vision USA), and Ben Wikler (Washington director of MoveOn.org).

LEADERSHIP INSTITUTE

In 2009, the Transnational NGO Initiative embarked on developing a new training program designed for senior TNGO personnel. We began by hosting a forum of TNGO leaders to discuss the outlines of a week-long senior leadership training program. Fifteen leaders, including Sam Worthington (CEO of InterAction) and Nyaradzayi Gumbonzvanda (secretary-general of World

Table N.1 SAMPLE DESCRIPTION

	Count	Percent
Sector		
Environment	22	14
Human rights	21	14
Humanitarian relief	32	21
Sustainable development	64	42
Conflict resolution	13	9
Total	152	100
Size[a]		
Small	56	37
Medium	64	42
Large	32	21
Total	152	100
Function		
Advocacy	34	22
Service	70	46
Both	48	32
Total	152	100

[a] The three categories of budget size are small (less than $1 million), medium ($1 million to $10 million), and large (greater than $10 million).

YWCA), among others, helped to shape the initial focus and agenda of what became the Leadership Institute (LI). We then formed a LI Steering Group of eminent TNGO leaders that operated from 2010 to 2014. Steering Group members included, among others, Lindsay Coates (president of InterAction and later managing director of the Ultra Poor Graduation Initiative for BRAC), Susan Hayes (CEO, ReSurge International), Sherine Jayawickrama (head of the Development and Relief NGO Domain at the Hauser Center for Nonprofit Organizations, Harvard University), Mark Sidel (professor of law, University of Wisconsin, and president, International Society for Third-Sector Research, ISTR), Ramesh Singh (CEO, ActionAid International from 2004 to 2010 and later international organization director of Greenpeace), Ingrid Srinath (secretary-general, CIVICUS), Inge Wallage (director of communications, Greenpeace), Adriano Campolina (CEO of ActionAid International from 2014 to 2019), and Adam Weinberg (president and CEO, World Learning).

The LI was first offered in 2011 and its purpose was defined as helping next-generation TNGO leaders from across the world to develop leadership skills required to promote internal and external change. Our conversations on this topic repeatedly focused on the struggles that even larger TNGOs have with respect to investing in and proactively developing leadership capacities among their own staff. The LI's curriculum was explicitly focused on how to make the "leadership leap" from the senior level to the top C-suite level. Members of the Steering Group were explicitly selected based on their personal experience in making the "leadership leap" in recent years and being able to share their firsthand experiences.

The program attracted a global, cross-sectoral pool of rising leaders from small, mid- and large-sized TNGOs across the Global South, East, and North. Each cohort consisted of sixteen to eighteen participants. Representatives from several institutional donors (such as the Ford Foundation) contributed funds over multiple years to financially support the attendance of participants from TNGOs founded in the Global South. Overall, 57 percent of participants identified as female and 43 percent were based in the Global South. About half of the participants worked for organizations with global coverage, while the other half came from TNGOs with a specific regional focus. Thirty-six percent of participants represented the development sector, followed by human rights (13%), public health (9%), humanitarian aid (7%), governance and democracy (6%), advocacy and campaigning (6%), civil society promotion (5%), environmental protection (4%), and other areas (12%).[23] Some of the graduates of the program have subsequently moved into top leadership positions, including Adriano Campolina (CEO of ActionAid International), Jason Cone (executive director of Médecins Sans Frontières, USA), and Joel Charny (director of Norwegian Refugee

Council USA). Both our conversations with these top leaders since 2011 in co-creating the program and our in-program discussions with participants over the years have allowed us to understand better the diversity and key challenges faced by the sector.

SENIOR LEADERSHIP DEVELOPMENT PROGRAM

The reputation of the Leadership Institute led to a request by ActionAid International in 2012 to design and host an annual, customized Senior Leadership Development Program (SLDP). Similar to the Leadership Institute, the program lasted for about one week and was offered in-residence. The majority of the programs took place in Arusha, Tanzania, with one in Bangkok, Thailand. During the first two years, the program was offered exclusively to ActionAid's country directors, heads of unit, and heads of function. In 2015, ActionAid invited senior leaders from Amnesty International, Greenpeace International, and Oxfam International to join the program to facilitate an exchange of perspectives across primarily campaign-focused TNGOs. In 2018, CIVICUS leaders joined the program as well. The US-based TNGO Population Council also tapped the Transnational NGO Initiative to offer three iterations of a customized SLDP for its leaders in 2014 and 2015. About twenty-five senior leaders participated in each of the three programs, which were held in Long Island, New York.

In preparation for each iteration of the SLDP, we read (often confidential) internal organizational documents on strategy, organizational change, leadership-level performance management systems, and competency systems. We also interviewed top leadership of each of these TNGOs to develop an understanding of what current strategic issues should be highlighted in the curriculum design. Again, this learning across program design and delivery allowed us to acquire important insights about the challenges faced by these large transnational campaigning organizations. The adaptation of the SLDP to the needs of Population Council offered opportunities to better understand the specific organizational and leadership development challenges faced by a mid-sized, more research and service delivery–focused organization.

NGO CHANGE MANAGEMENT LEARNING GROUP

In addition to a strong focus on senior leadership development, we also developed a broad knowledge base on organizational change management and change leadership. Such issues are a prominent component of the senior leadership training programs. Based on this expertise, Tosca was invited to co-facilitate an informal NGO Learning Group of change managers who met virtually and face-to-face several times annually from 2012 to 2016. Leaders represented organizations such as Oxfam, World Wildlife Fund, Islamic Relief, CARE, Water Aid, Catholic International Development Charity (CAFOD), Trócaire, World Vision, and Save the Children, among others. We documented lessons-learned by TNGO change managers and presented aggregated observations at academic and practitioner conferences. Through attending many practitioner-oriented conferences since 2005, we obtained firsthand insights into the concerns on the minds of senior TNGO leaders and their stakeholders (such as institutional donors and corporate actors). Such venues included meetings organized by INTRAC, CIVICUS, InterAction, and the International Civil Society Centre in Berlin.

VISITING FELLOWS

The original interview study not only produced research publications and educational materials, but also facilitated more than a decade of sustained interactions with TNGO practitioners. These interactions ranged from short visits to the Maxwell School to long-term relationships we fostered to solicit regular feedback on the research needs of the TNGO community. Since 2005, we annually hosted three to six TNGO practitioners—often senior leaders—for short visits, during which time we conducted research interviews and informal conversations.

Since 2007, we hosted one or two senior TNGO leaders annually as Visiting Moynihan NGO Fellows for periods of two to three weeks. These visits involved the identification of a specific research topic focused on organizational or leadership challenges, with an emphasis on stepping outside of the day-to-day management of an organization. For example, one visiting fellow focused on the legacy that Northern TNGOs should leave to effectively empower a global civil society movement in the 2030s. Another fellow explored the ways in which Millennials will be motivated to donate time, talent, and their networks and money. A third focused on the profile of the CEO of the future (see Chapter 9).

In each case, the process commenced with the recruitment of volunteer students who worked with faculty in completing a thorough literature review prior to the visit. After the arrival of the fellow, he or she would have to time to read and write, give presentations, serve as a resource to the Maxwell community, and provide feedback to the current and future agenda of the Transnational NGO Initiative.[24] Conversational interviews were recorded with virtually all visitors to build an online library of TNGO leadership perspectives for classroom instruction and research. The video archives are freely available online.[25]

COLLABORATION WITH THE CENTER FOR CREATIVE LEADERSHIP

In collaboration with the Center for Creative Leadership (CCL) in the United States, the Transnational NGO Initiative undertook an interview study between 2013 and 2016 on "next and best practices" in in-house leadership development. The interviews involved leaders from organizations including World Vision, Plan International, ActionAid, Oxfam, Médecins Sans Frontières, Amnesty International, and Transparency International. We interviewed a total of three individuals from each organization, including a CEO or other top leader, the heads of Organizational Development or Human Resources, and one person who had in the past been the beneficiary of leadership development and was viewed as a "rising leader."

CONSULTANCIES

Consultancies played a crucial role in our learnings about the TNGO sector. Our knowledge on organizational change processes in TNGOs was greatly enhanced when we had the opportunity to observe significant transformational change processes in several large TNGOs in real time. From 2011 to 2017, Save the Children International, Heifer International, Oxfam International, CARE International, and Amnesty International invited us to help them document, learn from, and critically review organizational change management processes and capacities. We also performed meta-analyses of program evaluations and an analysis of program implementation for Plan Guatemala and Plan USA. Working with stakeholders such as InterAction and the DMA Nonprofit Federation, we were also involved in analyzing various financial and accountability standards developed for the TNGO and broader nonprofit sectors. TNGOs typically gave us complete access to internal documents and allowed us to conduct participant observation of important events and meetings, to facilitate focus group discussions, and to interview and survey staff. This resulted in the documentation of lessons-learned in the form of case studies, internal reports, evaluations, and presentations.

Plan Guatemala and Plan USA

In 2009–2010, Tosca, Hans, Uwe Gneiting, and local staff completed an evaluation of Plan Guatemala's transition to Child Centered Community Development (CCCD). In this effort, Plan Guatemala, a member of the federated, child-focused Plan International family, was primarily interested in understanding which parts of their new rights-based agenda were particularly successful and which lagged behind.[26] In 2011, Plan USA requested a meta-analysis of program evaluations to ascertain the extent to which CCCD was applied in field operations.[27] As part of our ongoing engagement with ActionAid (starting in 2005), we also gained comparative insights into how different TNGOs define and implement rights-based approaches (RBA). The RBA-focused consultancies also generated knowledge about the nature of strategic change processes in TNGOs, especially how these actors mainstream new program activities. It also offered opportunities to compare the academic literature on RBA with practitioner experiences on the ground.[28]

DMA Nonprofit Federation

In 2010 George consulted for the DMA Nonprofit Federation to analyze the organizational ratings systems of the major US nonprofit information intermediaries or so-called watchdogs. This produced a report about the measurement and mismeasurement of organizational effectiveness, which was presented during their annual conference in New York and subsequently covered in the media.[29]

Save the Children International

In 2010, Tosca and Steve Lux (head of executive education at the Maxwell School) wrote a case study about Save the Children International's transformational change process toward internationalization of its program implementation and the formation of a more tightly coordinated and integrated network. The focus of the case study was on change management and leadership. Sources included internal document reviews, approximately twenty in-depth, semi-structured interviews with leaders of the change process, and repeated conversations with the main change manager over the duration of the assignment. The case study became an award-winning (and publicly available) teaching case.[30]

Oxfam International

In 2013–2014, Tosca and Karla Dominga Gonzalez (Humphrey Fellow at the Maxwell School) undertook an external assessment of the organizational learning that emanated from Oxfam International's Single Management Systems (SMS) change process. SMS was the first step toward Oxfam's attempt to reduce its operating costs, streamline operations, strengthen the measurement of program outcomes, and give Southern member sections a greater voice. The specific goals included having only one Oxfam section operate in a given country as well as establishing a globally balanced and well-governed confederation. The analysis relied on internal document reviews, repeated conversations with Oxfam's main change managers over the duration of the assignment, and twenty-two in-depth, semi-structured interviews with leaders of the change process.

Heifer International

In 2014 and 2015, Tosca completed two consultancies for Heifer International through strategic planning session facilitation. To prepare for each facilitation, she had access to internal documents and undertook ten interviews with key internal informants and peer organizations. This engagement provided high-level insights into how a well-known US-based TNGO embraced a new theory of change, including new business models, evaluation indicators, and underlying culture to remain relevant and scale organizational impact.

CARE International

Between 2013 and 2016, Steven Lux, Shreeya Neupane (program director, Transnational NGO Initiative from 2014 to 2016), and Tosca were "semi-embedded" in the Transformational Change Task Force of CARE International to help that unit learn from its change management experiences under the CARE 2020 change process. We had full access to in-house confidential documentation and undertook twenty-two interviews with key change champions as well as staff and leaders impacted by the change process. The research team regularly debriefed the Task Force, especially after major decision moments. Tosca also facilitated several virtual and face-to-face learning sessions between CARE and Oxfam change managers after the two organizations had concluded that they shared many commonalities. This resulted in an internal report to the secretary-general of CARE International and the Transformational Change Task Force.

Amnesty International

From 2013 to 2017, the Transnational NGO Initiative was asked to provide external interim and final assessments of Amnesty International's Global Transition Program (GTP; also known as "Moving Closer to the Ground"). GTP's goals included the establishment of eleven distributed Regional Offices, the redistribution of power between the London-based International Secretariat and the Regional Offices, greater integration of function across the entire organization, and a significant increase of individual membership in the Global South. Steve Lux, Hans, Shreeya Neupane, and Tosca undertook approximately seventy-five interviews, two surveys with global Amnesty staff, twelve to fifteen focus group discussions, recurring debriefing sessions with Amnesty's GTP Task Force, participant observation at several global leadership meetings, and eight interviews with external peers and partner organizations. The team had full access to the internal documents associated with the GTP process. The Final External Assessment of the GTP is publicly available.[31]

InterAction

In 2015–2016, Tosca coauthored a white paper and executive brief on agency-level measurement (ALM), commissioned by a number of InterAction NGO members.[32] This opportunity highlighted the growing emphasis on evaluation and performance measurement. ALM is now an aspiration for many mid- to large-sized NGOs, and this work allowed us to learn about the pros and cons of assessing whole-of-organization programmatic performance. This learning was supplemented with additional interviews that George conducted with practitioners from Pact, Mercy Corps, and the International Rescue Committee.

In 2017–2018, Tosca and George were involved in an effort to revise InterAction's Code of Conduct, which is the basis of a biannual self-evaluation required of all InterAction member organizations. Initiated by InterAction and many of its member CEOs, one important goal for revising the Code of Conduct was the strengthening of its standards pertaining to outcome measurement. Tosca, as a board member of InterAction and co-chair of the Task Force on Standards Revision within its Board Committee on

Membership and Standards, was involved in research on how to strengthen sector-wide standards for outcome measurement. George and Mary Kay Gugerty (professor, University of Washington) consulted with InterAction to complete a review of the landscape for outcome measurement among peers and competitors, and developed recommendations for concrete new standards language adopted by InterAction's board in 2018.[33] As part of the consultancy, George and Mary Kay conducted twenty-one interviews with CEOs and other practitioners from InterAction member organizations, as well as from stakeholders from GuideStar, Charity Navigator, and the International Civil Society Centre (which houses the Global Standard for CSO Accountability). George and Mary Kay also conducted an on-site workshop at InterAction's annual CEO retreat with thirty-three CEOs.

BOARD MEMBERSHIPS

The Transnational NGO Initiative was one of the first associate members of InterAction, and Tosca has been the first associate member representative on InterAction's board (2016–2019). She also served on the boards of ProLiteracy, an organization focused on adult literacy promotion (2009–2015), and Public Interest Registry (PIR), the nonprofit operator of the .org, .ngo, and .ong Internet domain names (2016–2019). From 2012 to 2015, she also served on the Advisory Panel of Charity Navigator as it was testing its ratings system to include measures of transparency and effectiveness (the rating systems were called "Charity Navigator 2.0 and 3.0"). As part of this effort, Maxwell School students performed beta testing of Charity Navigator's proposed 3.0 dimensions, which offered important insights into the complexities of an intermediary trying to obtain information at scale about programmatic activities across a wide range of US nonprofits. Since 2009, Tosca has served as board director for Cadasta Foundation, a US-based international land rights documentation focused start-up organization. This sustained board-level engagement has offered a number of benefits, including establishing a bird's-eye perspective on the TNGO sector overall (InterAction), an in-depth understanding of the nexus between the Internet and civil society, and a broad perspective on how TNGO boards actually function.

ADDITIONAL DATA SOURCES

This book has also benefited from the experiential learnings of Barney Tallack. Barney has over twenty-five years of experience in the TNGO, social justice, and UK nonprofit sectors, and has held senior leadership and board member roles in a variety of international and UK-based organizations.

As director of strategy for Oxfam International, Barney ran the global strategy process, and for five years he led the global transformation program and change process affecting all of Oxfam's 10,000 staff and €1 billion annual budget in over ninety countries. He was also responsible for running Oxfam International's governance and various support functions, for supporting the relocation of Oxfam's global headquarters to Nairobi, and for the development of smaller member organizations in the Oxfam family. Additionally, in his role as director of strategy he provided coaching and accompaniment support to a number of change leaders in other TNGOs.

He has also held trustee and non–executive director roles for a range of nonprofits and social enterprises. He is currently a board member of the Fairtrade Foundation and the Forest People's Programme (FPP). Previous board roles have included the Conservation Volunteers, International Health Exchange (now part of RedR), the Charity Retail Association, Oxfam's commercial arm, and fundraising entities in South Korea and Sweden.

He has been active in the TNGO community in a variety of other roles as well. In 2009, he established the INGO Transformation Directors' Group, bringing together leaders of transformation programs from twenty of the largest TNGOs. He has been involved with the International Civil Society Centre based in Berlin, including through membership of its horizon scanning group and involvement in Accountable Now (formerly the INGO Accountability Charter), a global accountability platform for TNGOs. He has also held senior leadership roles in a number of fundraising, finance, and operational areas, and as a consultant, he has worked with CBM International, Islamic Relief Worldwide, Forest Peoples Programme (FPP), and the International Institute for Environment and Development. He also provides pro bono coaching to individuals in other TNGOs and UK nonprofits. Barney has lectured extensively on TNGO transformations and futures, and in 2017 he was a visiting fellow at the Transnational NGO Initiative at Syracuse University. Insights from Barney's extensive experiences are featured prominently in Chapters 8 and 11. He also provided feedback across the entire book and contributed the Afterword.

REFERENCES

Baur, Dorothea, and Hans Peter Schmitz. "Corporations and NGOs: When Accountability Leads to Co-Optation." *Journal of Business Ethics* 106, no. 1 (2012): 9–21. https://doi.org/10.1007/s10551-011-1057-9.

Berlan, David, and Tosca Bruno-van Vijfeijken. "The Planned Close of an NGO: Evidence for a New Organizational Form?" *Voluntas* 24, no. 1 (2013): 262–75. https://doi.org/10.1007/s11266-012-9300-2.

Boyer, E. J., A. Kolpakov, and Hans Peter Schmitz. "Do Executives Approach Leadership Differently When They Are Involved in Collaborative Partnerships?: A Perspective from International Nongovernmental Organizations (INGOs)." *Public Performance & Management Review* 42, no. 1 (2018): 213–40.

Bruno-van Vijfeijken, Tosca. "Culture Is What You See When Compliance Is Not in the Room." *Nonprofit Policy Forum* 10, no. 4 (2019), https://doi.org/10.1515/npf-2019-0031.

Bruno-van Vijfeijken, Tosca, Uwe Gneiting, and Hans Peter Schmitz. *How Does CCCD Affect Program Effectiveness and Sustainability?: A Meta Review of Plan's Evaluations.* Syracuse, NY: Moynihan Institute of Global Affairs, 2011.

Bruno-van Vijfeijken, Tosca, Steven J. Lux, Shreeya Neupane, and Ramesh Singh. *Final Assessment: Amnesty's Global Transition Program.* Syracuse, NY: Moynihan Institute of Global Affairs, 2017.

Bruno-van Vijfeijken, Tosca, and Hans Peter Schmitz. "Commentary: A Gap between Ambition and Effectiveness." *Journal of Civil Society* 7, no. 3 (2011): 287–92. https://doi.org/10.1080/17448689.2011.604998.

Gneiting, Uwe, and Hans Peter Schmitz. "Comparing Global Alcohol and Tobacco Control Efforts: Network Formation and Evolution in International Health Governance." *Health Policy and Planning* 31, no. suppl. 1 (2016): i98–i109. https://doi.org/10.1093/heapol/czv125.

Gneiting, Uwe, and Hans Peter Schmitz. *From Assistance to Agency to Rights: The Experience of Transnational Development NGOs in Guatemala.* Syracuse, NY: Moynihan Institute of Global Affairs, 2008.

Gugerty, Mary Kay, and George E. Mitchell. *Summary and Recommendations for Impact Measurement Standards: Report for the Interaction Standards Task Force.* Washington, DC: InterAction, 2018.

Hall, Nina, Hans Peter Schmitz, and J. Michael Dedmon. "Transnational Advocacy and NGOs in the Digital Era: New Forms of Networked Power." *International Studies Quarterly* (August 7, 2019). https://doi.org/10.1093/isq/sqz052.

Hermann, Margaret G., Jesse D. Lecy, George E. Mitchell, Christiane Pagé, Paloma Raggo, Hans Peter Schmitz, and Lorena Viñuela. *Transnational NGOs: A Cross-Sectoral Analysis of Leadership Perspectives.* Syracuse, NY: Moynihan Institute of Global Affairs, 2010.

Lecy, Jesse D., Ines Mergel, and Hans Peter Schmitz. "Networks in Public Administration: Current Scholarship in Review." *Public Management Review* 16, no. 5 (2014): 643–55.

Lecy, Jesse D., Hans Peter Schmitz, and Haley Swedlund. "Non-Governmental and Not-for-Profit Organizational Effectiveness: A Modern Synthesis." *Voluntas* 23, no. 2 (2012): 434–57. https://doi.org/10.1007/s11266-011-9204-6.

Levine, Carlisle J., Tosca Bruno-van Vijfeijken, and Sherine Jayawickrama. *Measuring International NGO Agency-Level Results.* Washington, DC: InterAction, 2016.

Lux, Steven J., and Tosca Bruno-van Vijfeijken. *From Alliance to International: The Global Transformation of Save the Children.* Syracuse, NY: Maxwell School of Citizenship and Public Affairs, 2012.

Mitchell, George E. "The Attributes of Effective NGOs and the Leadership Values Associated with a Reputation for Organizational Effectiveness." *Nonprofit*

Management and Leadership 26, no. 1 (2015): 39–57. https://doi.org/doi:10.1002/nml.21143.

Mitchell, George E. "Collaborative Propensities among Transnational NGOs Registered in the United States." *The American Review of Public Administration* 44, no. 5 (2014): 575–99.

Mitchell, George E. "The Construct of Organizational Effectiveness: Perspectives from Leaders of International Nonprofits in the United States." *Nonprofit and Voluntary Sector Quarterly* 42, no. 2 (2013): 324–45. https://doi.org/10.1177/0899764011434589.

Mitchell, George E. "Creating a Philanthropic Marketplace through Accounting, Disclosure, and Intermediation." *Public Performance & Management Review* 38, no. 1 (2014): 23–47. https://doi.org/10.2753/PMR1530-9576380102.

Mitchell, George E. "Fiscal Leanness and Fiscal Responsiveness: Exploring the Normative Limits of Strategic Nonprofit Financial Management." *Administration & Society* 49, no. 9 (2017): 1272–96.

Mitchell, George E. "Modalities of Managerialism: The 'Double Bind' of Normative and Instrumental Nonprofit Management Imperatives." *Administration & Society* (2016): 1037–68. https://doi.org/10.1177/0095399716664832.

Mitchell, George E. "NGOs in the United States." In *Routledge Handbook of NGOs and International Relations*, edited by Thomas Davies, 415–32. New York: Routledge, 2019.

Mitchell, George E. "Reframing the Discussion about Nonprofit Effectiveness." Washington, DC: DMA Nonprofit Federation, 2010.

Mitchell, George E. "The Strategic Orientations of US-Based NGOs." *Voluntas* 26, no. 5 (2015): 1874–93. https://doi.org/10.1007/s11266-014-9507-5.

Mitchell, George E. "Strategic Responses to Resource Dependence among Transnational NGOs Registered in the United States." *Voluntas* 25, no. 1 (2014): 67–91.

Mitchell, George E. "Why Will We Ever Learn? Measurement and Evaluation in International Development NGOs." *Public Performance & Management Review* 37, no. 4 (2014): 605–31. https://doi.org/10.2753/PMR1530-9576370404.

Mitchell, George E., and David Berlan. "Evaluation and Evaluative Rigor in the Nonprofit Sector." *Nonprofit Management and Leadership* 27, no. 2 (2016): 237–50. https://doi.org/doi:10.1002/nml.21236.

Mitchell, George E., and David Berlan. "Evaluation in Nonprofit Organizations: An Empirical Analysis." *Public Performance & Management Review* 41, no. 2 (2018): 415–37. https://doi.org/10.1080/15309576.2017.1400985.

Mitchell, George E., and Thad D. Calabrese. "Proverbs of Nonprofit Financial Management." *The American Review of Public Administration* 49, no. 6 (2018): 649–61. https://doi.org/10.1177/0275074018770458.

Mitchell, George E., Rosemary O'Leary, and Catherine Gerard. "Collaboration and Performance: Perspectives from Public Managers and NGO Leaders." *Public Performance & Management Review* 38, no. 4 (2015): 684–716. https://doi.org/10.1080/15309576.2015.1031015.

Mitchell, George E., and Hans Peter Schmitz. "The Nexus of Public and Nonprofit Management." *Public Performance & Management Review* 42, no. 1 (2019): 11–33. https://doi.org/10.1080/15309576.2018.1489293.

Mitchell, George E., and Hans Peter Schmitz. "Principled Instrumentalism: A Theory of Transnational NGO Behaviour." *Review of International Studies* 40, no. 3 (2014): 487–504. https://doi.org/doi:10.1017/S0260210513000387.

Mitchell, George E., and Sarah S. Stroup. "The Reputations of NGOs: Peer Evaluations of Effectiveness." *The Review of International Organizations* 12, no. 3 (2016): 397–419.

Mwangi, Wagaki, Lothar Rieth, and Hans Peter Schmitz. "Encouraging Greater Compliance: Local Networks and the United Nations Global Compact (UNGC)." In *The Persistent Power of Human Rights: From Commitment to Compliance*, edited by Thomas Risse, Stephen Ropp, and Kathryn Sikkink, 203–21. Cambridge: Cambridge University Press, 2013.

Rodio, Emily B., and Hans Peter Schmitz. "Beyond Norms and Interests: Understanding the Evolution of Transnational Human Rights Activism." *International Journal of Human Rights* 14, no. 3 (2010): 442–59.

Schmitz, Hans Peter, J. Michael Dedmon, Tosca Bruno-van Vijfeijken, and Jaclyn Mahoney. "Democratizing Advocacy?: How Digital Tools Shape International Non-Governmental Activism." *Journal of Information Technology & Politics* (2020). https://doi.org/10.1080/19331681.2019.1710643.

Schmitz, Hans Peter. "The Global Health Network on Alcohol Control: Successes and Limits of Evidence-Based Advocacy." *Health Policy and Planning* 31, no. 1 (2016): i87–i97.

Schmitz, Hans Peter. "A Human Rights–Based Approach (HRBA) in Practice: Evaluating NGO Development Efforts." *Polity* 44, no. 4 (2012): 523–41. https://doi.org/10.1057/pol.2012.18.

Schmitz, Hans Peter. "International Criminal Accountability and Transnational Advocacy Networks (TANs)." In *Oxford Handbook of International Security*, edited by Alexandra Gheciu and William C. Wohlforth, 697–710. New York: Oxford University Press, 2018.

Schmitz, Hans Peter, and George E. Mitchell. "The Other Side of the Coin: NGOs, Rights-Based Approaches, and Public Administration." *Public Administration Review* 76, no. 2 (2016): 252–62. https://doi.org/10.1111/puar.12479.

Schmitz, Hans Peter, Paloma Raggo, and Tosca Bruno-van Vijfeijken. "Accountability of Transnational NGOs: Aspirations vs. Practice." *Nonprofit and Voluntary Sector Quarterly* 41, no. 6 (2012): 1175–94. https://doi.org/10.1177/0899764011431165.

Shiffman, Jeremy, Kathryn Quissell, Hans Peter Schmitz, David L. Pelletier, Stephanie L. Smith, David Berlan, Uwe Gneiting, et al. "A Framework on the Emergence and Effectiveness of Global Health Networks." *Health Policy and Planning* 31, no. suppl. 1 (2016): i3–i16. https://doi.org/10.1093/heapol/czu046.

NOTES

PREFACE

1. National Science Foundation Grant No. SES-0527679 (Agents of Change: Transnational NGOs as Agents of Change: Toward Understanding Their Governance, Leadership, and Effectiveness). The research was also supported by funds from the Moynihan Institute of Global Affairs at Syracuse University.
2. For example, a case study on Save the Children is publicly available: Steven J. Lux and Tosca Bruno-van Vijfeijken, *From Alliance to International: The Global Transformation of Save the Children* (Syracuse, NY: Maxwell School of Citizenship and Public Affairs, 2012). See: https://www.maxwell.syr.edu/moynihan/tngo/Publications/.
3. On the topic of mergers and acquisitions, Barney provided direct input into the GOAL-Oxfam case. His experience includes his being part of the merger exploration team between GOAL and Oxfam and the successful merger of International Health Exchange and RedR. He has had direct experience with organizations becoming part of larger TNGOs (e.g., Oxfam International merging with IBIS, UCODEP, Agir Ici, and Vamos), as well as with the long-term implications of organizations leaving a federation (such as Fairtrade USA and others). Additionally, John McGeehan, former executive vice president and COO of Plan International USA, provided invaluable insights into the Plan-CEDPA case. Annie Msosa, alumna of the Maxwell Executive Masters of Public Administration Program; Rudy von Bernuth, retired director of international programs at Save the Children International; and James Crowley, independent consultant and associate at Accenture Development Partnership, also contributed greatly to our understanding of mergers and acquisitions.

CHAPTER 1

1. Gani Aldashev and Cecilia Navarra, "Development NGOs: Basic Facts," *Annals of Public and Cooperative Economics* 89, no. 1 (2018), https://doi.org/10.1111/apce.12188; Sarah S. Stroup and Wendy Wong, *The Authority Trap. Strategic Choices of International NGOs* (Ithaca, NY: Cornell University Press, 2017).
2. Fidelity Charitable, *The Future of Philanthropy: Where Individual Giving Is Going*, (Boston: Fidelity Charitable, 2016). In the United States, giving to international causes as a percentage of overall charitable contributions has increased from around 2 percent in the 1990s to over 5 percent today. In 2018, overall charitable giving dropped by 1.7 percent, while international giving increased by 7 percent.

Emily Haynes and Michael Theis, "Gifts to Charity Dropped 1.7 Percent Last Year, Says 'Giving USA'," *The Chronicle of Philanthropy* 31, no. 9 (2019)..

3. See, for example: Cristina M. Balboa, *The Paradox of Scale: How NGOs Build, Maintain, and Lose Authority in Environmental Governance* (Cambridge, MA: MIT Press, 2018). Also see interviews with Sophie Delauny, executive director, MSF USA, published on April 9, 2015 (https://www.youtube.com/watch?v=4sOgZR8pku0&list=PL384pgKdeHvDtxM6TCA5CR3LfST1hDhgo&index=23) and James Crowley, associate, Accenture Development Partnerships, published on March 31, 2014 (https://www.youtube.com/watch?v=K7AIMKFQkFA&index=18&list=PL384pgKdeHvDtxM6TCA5CR3LfST1hDhgo).

4. David Ransom, "The Big Charity Bonanza," *New Internationalist* (October 2, 2005), https://newint.org/features/2005/10/01/keynote; Mark Curtis, "Charity or Justice," *New Internationalist* (October 1, 2005), https://newint.org/features/2005/10/01/politics; Dhananjayan Sriskandarajah, "NGOs Losing the War against Poverty and Climate Change, Says Civicus Head: Charities Are No Longer Drivers of Social Change; for Many Saving the World Has Become Big Business. How Did We Lose Our Way?," *The Guardian* (London) (August 11, 2014).

5. Civicus, *State of Civil Society Report 2011* (Johannesburg: Civicus, 2012), 47–88; Balboa, *The Paradox of Scale: How NGOs Build, Maintain, and Lose Authority in Environmental Governance.*

6. Richard Youngs, *Civic Activism Unleashed: New Hope or False Dawn for Democracy?* (Oxford: Oxford University Press, 2019).

7. Jeffrey S. Hornsby et al., "Entrepreneurship Everywhere: Across Campus, across Communities, and across Borders," *Journal of Small Business Management* 56, no. 1 (2018), https://doi.org/10.1111/jsbm.12386. For a critique of such approaches to social change, see Marshall Ganz, Tamara Kay, and Jason Spicer, "Social Enterprise Is Not Social Change," *Stanford Social Innovation Review* 16, no. 2 (2018).

8. Thomas R. Davies, *NGOs: A New History of Transnational Civil Society* (Oxford: Oxford University Press, 2014).

9. InterAction, *Supporting Your NGO Future: US NGO Executive Thoughts on the Future,* (Washington, DC: InterAction, 2019).

10. George Ingram and Kristin M. Lord, *Global Development Disrupted: Findings from a Survey of 93 Leaders* (Washington, DC: Brookings Institution, 2019); IARAN, *The Future of Aid INGOs in 2030* (Inter-Agency Regional Analysts Network, 2017), http://iaran.org/futureofaid/The_Future_Of_Aid_INGOs_In_2030-33.pdf.

11. See: https://bcorporation.net/.

12. Cheng Cheng, *The Logic behind China's Foreign Aid Agency* (New York: Carnegie-Tshinghua Center for Global Policy, 2019).

13. Steve Davis, "China's Emerging Role in Social Innovation for Global Good," *Stanford Social Innovation Review* (May 9, 2017), https://ssir.org/articles/entry/chinas_emerging_role_in_social_innovation_for_global_good.

14. International Center for Not-for-Profit Law, "Closing Civic Space: Impact on Development and Humanitarian CSOs," *Global Trends in NGO Law* 7, no. 3 (2016); Alexandra V. Orlova, ""Foreign Agents," Sovereignty, and Political Pluralism: How the Russian Foreign Agents Law is Shaping Civil Society," *Penn State Journal of Law & International Affairs* 7, no. 2 (2019); Kendra Dupuy, James Ron, and Aseem Prakash, "Hands Off My Regime! Governments' Restrictions on Foreign Aid to Non-Governmental Organizations in Poor and Middle-Income Countries," *World Development* 84 (2016).

15. Civicus, *State of Civil Society Report 2011*; Dupuy, Ron, and Prakash, "Hands Off My Regime!"

16. Thomas Carothers, "Closing Space for International Democracy and Human Rights Support," *Journal of Human Rights Practice* 8, no. 3 (2016), https://doi.org/10.1093/jhuman/huw012.

17. Douglas Rutzen, "Civil Society under Assault," *Journal of Democracy* 26, no. 4 (2015); Mark Sidel, *Regulation of the Voluntary Sector: Freedom and Security in an Era of Uncertainty* (London: Routledge, 2009).

18. Sakia Brechenmacher and Thomas Carothers, *Examining Civil Society Legitimacy* (Washington, DC: Carnegie Endowment for International Peace, 2018).

19. Matthew D. Stephen and Michael Zürn, eds., *Contested World Orders: Rising Powers, Non-Governmental Organizations, and the Politics of Authority Beyond the Nation-State* (Oxford: Oxford University Press, 2019).

20. The International Budget Partnership, *"Thats How the Light Gets In." Making Change in Closing Political Environments* (Washington, DC: The International Budget Partnership, 2016).

21. Charles Kenny, *Getting Better: Why Global Development Is Succeeding—And How We Can Improve the World Even More* (New York: Basic Books, 2012); Kathryn Sikkink, *Evidence of Hope. Making Human Rights Work in the 21st Century* (Princeton, NJ: Princeton University Press, 2017).

22. Edelman, *2019 Edelman Trust Barometer: Global Report* (New York, NY: Daniel J. Edelman Holdings, 2019).

23. Mohamed Younis and Andrew Rzepa, *One in Three Worldwide Lack Confidence in NGOs* (Gallup and Wellcome, 2019), https://news.gallup.com/opinion/gallup/258230/one-three-worldwide-lack-confidence-ngos.aspx.

24. Mary Kay Gugerty and Dean Karlan, *The Goldilocks Challenge: Right-Fit Evidence for the Social Sector* (New York: Oxford University Press, 2018).

25. Kellie C. Liket and Karen Maas, "Nonprofit Organizational Effectiveness: Analysis of Best Practices," *Nonprofit and Voluntary Sector Quarterly* 44, no. 2 (2015), https://doi.org/10.1177/0899764013510064.

26. John Clark, "Civil Society in the Age of Crisis," *Journal of Civil Society* 7, no. 3 (2011).

27. Fay Twersky, Phil Buchanan, and Valerie Threlfall, "Listening to Those Who Matter Most, the Beneficiaries," *Stanford Social Innovation Review* 11 (2013); Didier Fassin, "The Predicament of Humanitarianism," *Qui Parle* 22, no. 1 (2013), 45, https://doi.org/10.5250/quiparle.22.1.0033.

28. Edelman, *2019 Edelman Trust Barometer*; Younis and Rzepa, *One in Three Worldwide Lack Confidence in NGOs*.

29. Daniel Emmrich, *NGOs in the 21st Century: The Opportunities Presented by Digitalization and Globalization* (Munich: Dr. Wieselhuber & Partner GmbH, 2017), 25

30. Susan M. Roberts, "Development Capital: USAID and the Rise of Development Contractors," *Annals of the Association of American Geographers* 104, no. 5 (2014), https://doi.org/10.1080/00045608.2014.924749.

31. Michael E. Porter and Mark R. Kramer, "The Big Idea: Creating Shared Value," *Harvard Business Review* (January–February 2011); Ans Kolk, Miguel Rivera-Santos, and Carlos Rufín, "Reviewing a Decade of Research on the "Base/Bottom of the Pyramid" (BOP) concept," *Business & Society* 53, no. 3 (2014).

32. Elena Lucchi, *Introducing 'For Profit' Initiatives and Actors in Humanitarian Response* (Barcelona: Médecins Sans Frontières, 2018).

33. Christopher Marquis and Andrew Park, "Inside the Buy-One Give-One Model," *Stanford Social Innovation Review* (Winter 2014).

34. Christopher Marquis, Andrew Klaber, and Bobbi Thomson, *B Lab: Building a New Sector of the Economy* (Cambridge, MA: Harvard Business School, 2011); Ramesh Mangaleswaran and Ramya Venkataraman, *Designing Philantropy for Impact* (Chennai: McKinsey & Company, 2013).

35. Alnoor Ebrahim and V. Kasturi Rangan, "Acumen Fund: Measurement in Impact Investing," (Boston: Harvard Business School Publishing, 2011).

36. Clay Shirky, *Here Comes Everybody: The Power of Organizing without Organizations* (New York: Penguin, 2008).

37. Steven J. Lux and Tosca Bruno-van Vijfeijken, *From Alliance to International: The Global Transformation of Save the Children* (Syracuse, NY: Maxwell School of Citizenship and Public Affairs, 2012).

38. Michael Edwards, "What's to Be Done with Oxfam?, Part 2," *openDemocracy* (February 15, 2018), https://www.opendemocracy.net/en/transformation/what-s-to-be-done-with-oxfam-part-2/; Duncan Green, *Fit for the Future?: Development Trends and the Role of International NGOs* (Oxford: Oxfam GB, 2015).

39. Stephen Hopgood, *Keepers of the Flame: Understanding Amnesty International* (Ithaca, NY: Cornell University Press, 2006).

40. Additionally, organizational culture has long been identified as a major factor in shaping innovation. James R. Detert, Roger G. Schroeder, and John J. Mauriel, "A Framework for Linking Culture and Improvement Initiatives in Organizations," *The Academy of Management Review* 25, no. 4 (2000), https://doi.org/10.2307/259210, including claims that "a strongly shared culture might not be appropriate for fostering innovation." Kristina Jaskyte and Audrone Kisieliene, "Organizational Innovation: A Comparison of Nonprofit Human-Service Organizations in Lithuania and the United States," *International Social Work* 49, no. 2 (2006): 171.

41. Kavita Avula, Lisa McKay, and Sébastien Galland, *Amnesty International: Staff Well-being Review* (Washington, DC: The Konterra Group, 2019).

42. Cristina M. Balboa, "How Successful Transnational Non-Governmental Organizations Set Themselves Up for Failure on the Ground," *World Development* 54 (February 2014), http://dx.doi.org/10.1016/j.worlddev.2013.09.001.

43. For example, critics have faulted TNGOs for sometimes being "too close for comfort" in their relations with powerful states, too large to be responsive to local needs, and overly concerned self-interest focused on organizational survival. See: Aseem Prakash and Mary Kay Gugerty, eds., *Advocacy Organizations and Collective Action* (Cambridge: Cambridge University Press, 2010); Clifford Bob, *The Marketing of Rebellion: Insurgents, Media, and International Activism* (New York: Cambridge University Press, 2005); Stroup and Wong, *The Authority Trap*; Nicola Banks, David Hulme, and Michael Edwards, "NGOs, States, and Donors Revisited: Still Too Close for Comfort?," *World Development* 66 (2015), https://doi.org/10.1016/j.worlddev.2014.09.028.

44. Thomas Davies, *NGOs: A New History of Transnational Civil Society* (New York: Oxford University Press, 2014).

45. Peter Willetts, *Non-Governmental Organizations in World Politics: The Construction of Global Governance* (New York: Routledge, 2011), 7; Norbert Götz, "Reframing NGOs: The Identity of an International Relations Non-Starter," *European Journal of International Relations* 14, no. 2 (2008), https://doi.org/10.1177/1354066108089242.

46. Kerstin Martens, "Mission Impossible. Defining Nongovernmental Organizations," *Voluntas* 13, no. 3 (2002).

47. Criteria are adapted from the eligibility requirements for the .ngo and .ong domains established by Public Interest Registry. See: https://pir.org/policies/ngo-ong-policies/registration-policies-for-ngo-ong/.

48. Stephen Rainey, Kutoma Wakunuma, and Bernd Stahl, "Civil Society Organisations in Research: A Literature-Based Typology," *Voluntas* (December 2016), https://doi.org/10.1007/s11266-016-9816-y.

49. The table is based on Barney Tallack, *INGO Typologies and Organizational Forms* (2018), and L. David Brown, Alnoor Ebrahim, and Srilatha Batliwala, "Governing International Advocacy NGOs," *World Development* 40, no. 6 (2012), http://dx.doi.org/10.1016/j.worlddev.2011.11.006.. The organizational structure only provides a rough picture of internal power relations and decision-making. Leadership, resource distribution, and other factors also shape in what ways each organization ultimately behaves.

50. Stroup and Wong, *The Authority Trap*.

51. However, we occasionally adopt the terminology of underlying sources as necessary to avoid mischaracterizations.

52. "Do you still use the word 'beneficiary'?," Feedback Labs, updated September 6, 2015, accessed August 26, 2019, https://feedbacklabs.org/blog/do-you-still-use-the-word-beneficiary/. "In international aid, people should be seen as consumers not 'beneficiaries'," *The Guardian*, updated May 13, 2015, accessed August 26, 2019, https://www.theguardian.com/global-development-professionals-network/2015/may/13/international-aid-consumers-beneficiaries.

53. Elizabeth Bloodgood and Hans Peter Schmitz, "The INGO Research Agenda: A Community Approach to Challenges in Method and Theory," in *Routledge Handbook of International Organization*, ed. Bob Reinalda (New York: Routledge, 2013).

54. Willetts, *Non-Governmental Organizations in World Politics*.

55. Organization ecology is one approach to a better understanding of the dynamics of the TNGO population. Scholars have previously argued that variation in density can explain rates of founding and failure. See: Paul J. DiMaggio and Helmut K. Anheier, "The Sociology of Nonprofit Organizations and Sectors," *Annual Review of Sociology* 16, no. 1 (1990). Levels of low density attract more organizations to emerge and facilitate mutually reinforcing peer support. As levels of density rise, competition creates incentives to develop niche differentiation and rates of organizational death increase. See: Michael T. Hannan and John Freeman, "The Population Ecology of Organizations," *American Journal of Sociology* 82, no. 5 (1977); Sarah Bush and Jennifer Hadden, "Density and Decline in the Founding of International NGOs in the United States," *International Studies Quarterly* (August 2019).

56. Susan Cotts Watkins, Ann Swidler, and Thomas Hannan, "Outsourcing Social Transformation: Development NGOs as Organizations," *Annual Review of Sociology* 38 (2012). A sector-wide perspective on the evolution of the sector would add considerable value not only to the scholarly literature Erica Johnson and Aseem Prakash, "NGO Research Program: A Collective Action Perspective," *Policy Sciences* 40 (2007), but also to the capacity of the sector for self-reflection and learning.

57. William F. Fisher, "Doing Good?: The Politics and Anti-Politics of NGO Practices," *Annual Review of Anthropology*, no. 26 (1997).

58. Colette Chabbott, "Development INGOs," in *Constructing World Culture*, ed. John Boli and George M. Thomas (Stanford: Stanford University Press, 1999); Jennifer N. Brass et al., "NGOs and International Development: A Review of Thirty-five Years of Scholarship," *World Development* 112 (2018), https://doi.org/10.1016/j.worlddev.2018.07.016.

59. Michael Edwards, *Civil Society*, 3rd ed. (Cambridge: Polity Press, 2014).

60. Union of International Associations, *Yearbook of International Organizations*, 5 vols. (Leiden: Brill, 2016).

61. Thomas M. Weiss, D. Conor Seyle, and Kelsey Coolidge, *The Rise of Non-State Actors in Global Governance: Opportunities and Limitations* (Broomfield, CO: One Earth Future Foundation, 2013). Lester M. Salamon, "Putting the Civil Society Sector on the Economic Map of the World," *Annals of Public and Cooperative Economics* 81, no. 2 (2010), found that among the forty-two countries for which data were available that civil society organizations represented a $2.2 trillion industry (accounting for about 5.6 percent of the economically active populations).

62. We follow the UN's use of the term NGO when describing their statistics. For a list of current NGOs with UN consultative status, see http://csonet.org/.

63. Eric Werker and Faisal Z. Ahmed, "What Do Nongovernmental Organizations Do?," *Journal of Economic Perspectives* 22, no. 2 (2008).

64. Organisation for Economic Co-operation and Development, *Aid for CSOs* (Paris: OECD, 2015).

65. Aldashev and Navarra, "Development NGOs."

66. Jesse D. Lecy and David M. Van Slyke, "Nonprofit Sector Growth and Density: Testing Theories of Government Support," *Journal of Public Administration Research and Theory* 23, no. 1 (2013), https://doi.org/10.1093/jopart/mus010.

67. George E. Mitchell, "NGOs in the United States," in *Routledge Handbook of NGOs and International Relations*, ed Thomas Davies (New York: Routledge, 2019).

68. Ken Caldwell, *ICSO Global Financial Trends* (London: Baobab, 2015), 4

69. Nicola Banks and Dan Brockington, *Mapping the UK's Development NGOs: Income, Geography, and Contributions to International Development* (Manchester: Global Development Institute/The University of Manchester, 2019).

70. CARE, Médecins Sans Frontières (MSF), Oxfam International, Plan International, Save the Children, World Vision, and the World Wide Fund for Nature (WWF).

71. Brice S. McKeever, *The Nonprofit Sector in Brief 2015: Public Charities, Giving, and Volunteering* (Washington, DC: Urban Institute, 2015), 9

72. Caldwell, *ICSO Global Financial Trends*.

73. Michael Edwards and David Hulme, "Too Close for Comfort?: The Impact of Official Aid on Nongovernmental Organizations," *World Development* 24, no. 6 (1996).

CHAPTER 2

1. Or more precisely, its form consists of a variety of legal entities, some or most of which are registered charities (or their legal equivalents) or other entities substantially related to one or more such organizations.

2. For information about specific charitable sectors throughout the world, see: The International Center for Not-for-Profit Law (www.icnl.org), the Johns Hopkins Center for Civil Society Studies Comparative Nonprofit Sector Project (http://ccss.jhu.edu/research-projects/comparative-nonprofit-sector-project/), CIVICUS

(www.civicus.org), and the Council on Foundations (https://www.cof.org/country-notes). Also see: Oonagh B. Breen, Alison Dunn, and Mark Sidel, eds., *Regulatory Waves: Comparative Perspectives on State Regulation and Self-Regulation Policies in the Nonprofit Sector* (New York: Cambridge University Press, 2017).

3. William F. Meehan III and Kim Starkey Jonker, *Engine of Impact: Essentials of Strategic Leadership in the Nonprofit Sector* (Stanford: Stanford Business Books, 2017).

4. Robert A. Gross, "Giving in America: From Charity to Philanthropy," in *Charity, Philanthropy, and Civility in American History*, ed Lawrence J. Friedman and Mark D. McGarview (New York: Cambridge University Press, 2003). Also see: William MacAskill, "Effective Altruism: An Introduction," *Essays in Philosophy* 18, no. 1 (2017).

5. In the past, TNGOs have sometimes successfully challenged the restrictions of their institutional form. For example, when Oxfam UK faced pressures in the 1990s to stop its newly expanded advocacy efforts, it successfully resisted. As a result, limits on political activities imposed by the UK's Charity Commissioners Guidelines eased over time David Bryer and John Magrath, "New Dimensions of Global Advocacy," *Nonprofit and Voluntary Sector Quarterly* 28, no. 1 suppl. (1999), https://doi.org/10.1177/089976499773746500.

6. Richard Steinberg, "Economic Theories of Nonprofit Organizations," in *The Nonprofit Sector: A Research Handbook*, ed Walter W. Powell and Richard Steinberg (Thousand Oaks, CA: Sage, 2006); Burton A. Weisbrod, "Toward a Theory of the Voluntary Non-Profit Sector in a Three-Sector Economy," in *Altruism, Morality, and Economic Theory*, ed. Edmund S. Phelps (New York: Russell Sage Foundation, 1975).

7. Technically, public goods are said to be "nonexcludable" (no one can be prevented from enjoying them) and "nonrivalrous" (one person's enjoyment does not impede the ability of others to enjoy them).

8. Mancur Olson, *The Logic of Collective Action: Public Goods and the Theory of Groups* (Cambridge, MA: Harvard University Press, 1965).

9. Such government failure is especially problematic in diverse societies with high demand heterogeneity.

10. Lester M. Salamon, "Of Market Failure, Voluntary Failure, and Third-Party Government: Toward a Theory of Government-Nonprofit Relations in the Modern Welfare State," *Journal of Voluntary Action Research* 16, nos. 1–2 (1987), https://doi.org/10.1177/089976408701600104.

11. Research has suggested that the government and nonprofit sectors are complementary. See, for instance: Jesse D. Lecy and David M. Van Slyke, "Nonprofit Sector Growth and Density: Testing Theories of Government Support," *Journal of Public Administration Research and Theory* 23, no. 1 (2013), https://doi.org/10.1093/jopart/mus010.

12. George E. Mitchell and Hans Peter Schmitz, "The Nexus of Public and Nonprofit Management," *Public Performance & Management Review* 42, no. 1 (2018), https://doi.org/10.1080/15309576.2018.1489293.

13. Henry B. Hansmann, "The Role of Nonprofit Enterprise," *The Yale Law Journal* 89, no. 5 (1980), https://doi.org/10.2307/796089; Burton A. Weisbrod, *The Nonprofit Economy* (Cambridge, MA: Harvard University Press, 1989).

14. Hansmann, "The Role of Nonprofit Enterprise."

15. Hansmann, "The Role of Nonprofit Enterprise."

16. Roger A. Lohmann, "And Lettuce Is Nonanimal: Toward a Positive Economics of Voluntary Action," *Nonprofit and Voluntary Sector Quarterly* 18, no. 4 (1989).

17. Steinberg, "Economic Theories of Nonprofit Organizations."
18. Estelle James, "Why Do Different Countries Choose a Different Public-Private Mix of Educational Services?," *Journal of Human Resources* 28, no. 3 (1993).
19. Martha Finnemore and Kathryn Sikkink, "International Norm Dynamics and Political Change," *International Organization* 52, no. 4 (1998): 897.
20. Sanjay K. Pandey et al., "Public Service Motivation Research Program: Key Challenges and Future Prospects," in *Foundations of Public Administration*, ed Jos Raadshelders and Richard Stillman (Irvine, CA: Melvin and Leigh, 2017), 324; Leonard Bright, "Is Public Service Motivation a Better Explanation of Nonprofit Career Preferences Than Government Career Preferences?," *Public Personnel Management* 45, no. 4 (2016), https://doi.org/10.1177/0091026016676093; George E. Mitchell and Hans Peter Schmitz, "The Nexus of Public and Nonprofit Management," *Public Performance & Management Review* 42, no. 1 (2019), https://doi.org/10.1080/15309576.2018.1489293.
21. David Knoke, *Organizing for Collective Action: The Political Economies of Associations* (New York: Routledge, 1990).
22. Dennis R. Young, *If Not for Profit, for What?: A Behavioral Theory of the Nonprofit Sector Based on Entrepreneurship* (Heath, MA: Lexington Books, 1983).
23. René Bekkers and Pamala Wiepking, "A Literature Review of Empirical Studies of Philanthropy: Eight Mechanisms That Drive Charitable Giving," *Nonprofit and Voluntary Sector Quarterly* 40, no. 5 (2011).
24. Heidi Crumpler and Philip J. Grossman, "An Experimental Test of Warm Glow Giving," *Journal of Public Economics* 92 (2008).
25. James Andreoni and A. Abigail Payne, "Charitable Giving," in *Handbook of Public Economics*, ed Alan A. Auerbach et al. (Amsterdam: North Holland, 2013); C. Null, "Warm Glow, Information, and Inefficient Charitable Giving," *Journal of Public Economics* 95 (2011).
26. For example, see: https://www.radiaid.com/social-media-guide.
27. James Andreoni, "Impure Altruism and Donations to Public Goods: A Theory of Warm-Glow Giving," *The Economic Journal* 100, no. 401 (1990).
28. Wolfgang Seibel, "Successful Failure," *American Behavioral Scientist* 39, no. 8 (1996), https://doi.org/10.1177/0002764296039008006. Wolfgang Seibel, "Organizational Behavior and Organizational Function: Towards a Micro-Macro Theory of the Third Sector," in *The Third Sector: Comparative Studies of Nonprofit Organizations*, ed. Helmut K. Anheier and Wolfgang Seibel (Berlin: de Gruyter, 1990).
29. George E. Mitchell and Thad D. Calabrese, "Instrumental Philanthropy, Nonprofit Theory, and Information Costs," *Nonprofit Policy Forum* (2020).
30. Lant Pritchett, "It Pays to Be Ignorant: A Simple Political Economy of Rigorous Program Evaluation," *The Journal of Policy Reform* 5, no. 4 (2002).
31. Curtis Child and Eva M. Witesman, "Optimism and Bias When Evaluating a Prosocial Initiative," *Social Science Quarterly* (2019), https://doi.org/10.1111/ssqu.12585.
32. Seibel, "Successful Failure": 1023.
33. C. Wayne Gordon and Nicholas Babchuk, "A Typology of Voluntary Associations," *American Sociological Review* 24, no. 1 (1959); Peter Frumkin, *On Being Nonprofit: A Conceptual and Policy Primer* (Cambridge, MA: Harvard University Press, 2002).
34. Paul Brest, "Strategic Philanthropy and Its Discontents," *Stanford Social Innovation Review* (April 27, 2015), https://ssir.org/up_for_debate/article/strategic_philanthropy_and_its_discontents; Paul Brest, "A Decade of Outcome-Oriented

Philanthropy," *Stanford Social Innovation Review* (2012), http://www.ssireview. org/articles/entry/a_decade_of_outcome_oriented_philanthropy. This takes many forms, including so-called value for money approaches. See: Bond and Itad, *Value for Money: What It Means for UK NGOs* (London: Bond, 2012).

35. For a description of the historical origins of TNGOs as principally religious organizations, see: Thomas Davies, *NGOs: A New History of Transnational Civil Society* (New York: Oxford University Press, 2014). Regarding the US context, see: Peter Dobkin Hall, "Historical Perspectives on Nonprofit Organizations in the United States," in *The Jossey-Bass Handbook of Nonprofit Leadership and Management*, ed David O. Renz (San Francisco: Jossey-Bass, 2010).

36. George E. Mitchell, "NGOs in the United States," in *Routledge Handbook of NGOs and International Relations*, ed Thomas Davies (New York: Routledge, 2019); Barber, Putnam, and Megan M. Farwell. "The Relationships between State and Nonstate Interventions in Charitable Solicitation Law in the United States." In *Regulatory Waves: Comparative Perspectives on State Regulation and Self-Regulation Policies in the Nonprofit Sector*, ed. Oonagh B. Breen, Alison Dunn and Mark Sidel (New York, NY: Cambridge University Press, 2017), 199–220.

37. Mitchell, George E., and Thad D. Calabrese, "Proverbs of Nonprofit Financial Management," *American Review of Public Administration* 49, no. 6 (2019), https:// doi.org/10.1177/0275074018770458.

38. Mark H. Moore, "Managing for Value: Organizational Strategy in For-Profit, Nonprofit, and Governmental Organizations," *Nonprofit and Voluntary Sector Quarterly* 29, no. 1 (2000).

39. Jesse D. Lecy and Elizabeth A. M. Searing, "Anatomy of the Nonprofit Starvation Cycle: An Analysis of Falling Overhead Ratios in the Nonprofit Sector," *Nonprofit and Voluntary Sector Quarterly* 44, no. 3 (2015), https://doi.org/10.1177/ 0899764014527175; George E. Mitchell and Thad D. Calabrese, "Proverbs of Nonprofit Financial Management," *The American Review of Public Administration* 49, no. 6 (2018), https://doi.org/10.1177/0275074018770458, http://journals. sagepub.com/doi/abs/10.1177/0275074018770458; Kennard Wing and Mark A. Hager, *Getting What We Pay For: Low Overhead Limits Nonprofit Effectiveness* (Washington, DC: Nonprofit Overhead Cost Project/Urban Institute, 2004); Jason Coupet and Jessica L. Haynie, "Toward a Valid Approach to Nonprofit Efficiency Measurement," *Nonprofit Management & Leadership* 29, no. 2 (2019), https://doi.org/10.1002/nml.21336; "The Overhead Myth," GuideStar, 2013, accessed June 24, 2013, http://overheadmyth.com/wp-content/uploads/2013/ 06/GS_OverheadMyth_Ltr_ONLINE.pdf.

40. Mitchell and Calabrese, "Proverbs of Nonprofit Financial Management"; George E. Mitchell, "Modalities of Managerialism: The 'Double Bind' of Normative and Instrumental Nonprofit Managerial Imperatives," *Administration & Society* 50, no. 7 (2018), https://doi.org/10.1177/0095399716664832.

41. Indeed, the rationale for the charity model essentially requires that demonstrable impact is either (1) logically precluded, because if impact was demonstrable then informational problems would not arise and donors would contract with businesses, (2) unworthwhile, because the costs exceed the benefits, or (3) counterproductive, because the purpose of the charitable sector is to generate warm glow and a feeling that something is being done, admitting of the possibility that nothing really ever has or can be done. As an institutional form, the charity model lacks design features conducive to an impact focus, making it a questionable choice for impact-oriented TNGOs.

42. InterAction, *Supporting Your NGO Future: US NGO Executive Thoughts on the Future* (Washington, DC: InterAction, 2019).

43. Mats Alvesson and Stefan Sveningsson, *Changing Organizational Culture: Cultural Change Work in Progress* (New York: Routledge, 2015).

44. Edgar H. Schein, *Organizational Culture and Leadership* (San Francisco: Jossey-Bass, 2010). We are grateful to Catherine Gerard at the Maxwell School for informing many of the insights discussed in this section.

45. M. Slaughter and H. Grant, "How Culture Change Really Happens," NeuroLeadership Institute, 2016.

46. Schein, *Organizational Culture and Leadership*; Stephen R. Block and Steven Rosenberg, "Toward an Understanding of Founder's Syndrome: An Assessment of Power and Privilege among Founders of Nonprofit Organizations," *Nonprofit Management and Leadership* 12, no. 4 (2002), https://doi.org/10.1002/nml.12403.

47. Ronald A. Heifetz, Marty Linsky, and Alexander Grashow, *The Practice of Adaptive Leadership: Tools and Tactics for Changing Your Organization and the World* (Boston: Harvard Business School Publishing, 2009).

48. Sarah S. Stroup, *Borders among Activists: International NGOs in the United States, Britain, and France* (Ithaca, NY: Cornell University Press, 2012).

49. Mike Hudson, *Managing without Profit: The Art of Managing Non-Profit Organizations* (Harmondsworth: Penguin, 1999); Dorothea Hilhorst and Nadja Schmiemann, "Humanitarian Principles and Organisational Culture: Everyday Practice in Médecins Sans Frontiéres–Holland," *Development in Practice* 12, nos. 3–4 (2002), https://doi.org/10.1080/0961450220149834.

50. David Lewis, "NGOs, Organizational Culture, and Institutional Sustainability," *The Annals of the American Academy of Political and Social Science* 590, no. 1 (2003): 220

51. Dennis Duchon and Brian Drake, "Organizational Narcissism and Virtuous Behavior," *Joural of Business Ethics* 85, no. 3 (2009). Dennis Duchon and Michael Burns, "Organizational Narcissism," *Organizational Dynamics* 37, no. 4 (2008).

52. Kavita Avula, Lisa McKay, and Sébastien Galland, *Amnesty International: Staff Well-Being Review* (Washington, DC: The Konterra Group, 2019), 27 "Othering" is often particularly focused on non-NGO interlocutors, especially in the government and private sector. In the case of campaigning organizations, it can also be seen inside the organization.

53. ICSC Online Forum as part of Culture Change Task Force proceedings, 2015 (unpublished).

54. ICSC Online Forum as part of Culture Change Task Force proceedings, 2015 (unpublished).

55. Leaders have frequently self-reported this in TNGO Initiative Leadership Institute trainings.

56. Denise Rousseau, *Psychological Contracts in Organizations: Understanding Written and Unwritten Agreements* (Thousand Oaks, CA: Sage, 1995).

57. Personal communication between Tosca Bruno-van Vijfeijken and a member of the International Civil Society Centre Culture Change Task Force, 2015.

58. Leaders have frequently self-reported this in TNGO Initiative Leadership Institute trainings.

59. M. O'Hara and A. Omer, "Virtue and the Organizational Shadow: Exploring False Innocence and the Paradoxes of Power," in *Humanity's Dark Side: Evil, Destructive Experience, and Psychotherapy*, ed A. C. Bohart et al. (Washington, DC: American Psychological Association, 2013).

60. Michael Edwards, "What's to Be Done with Oxfam?, Part 2," *openDemocracy* (February 15, 2018), https://www.opendemocracy.net/en/transformation/what-s-to-be-done-with-oxfam-part-2/.

61. Paul DiMaggio and Walter Powell, "The Iron Cage Revisited: Institutional Isomorphism and Collective Rationality in Organizational Fields," *American Sociological Review* 48 (1983).

62. Joseph Galaskiewicz and Wolfgang Bielefeld, *Nonprofit Organizations in an Age of Uncertainty* (New York: Aldine de Gruyter, 1998).

63. Dennis R. Young and Richard Steinberg, *Economics for Nonprofit Managers* (New York: The Foundation Center Press, 1995).

64. Mitchell and Calabrese, "Proverbs of Nonprofit Financial Management"; Mitchell, "Modalities of Managerialism"; George E. Mitchell, "Fiscal Leanness and Fiscal Responsiveness: Exploring the Normative Limits of Strategic Nonprofit Financial Management," *Administration & Society* 49, no. 9 (2017), https://doi.org/10.1177/0095399715581035.

65. Examples of such norms include an overhead rate below 35 percent, an average cost to raise one dollar of less than $0.10, holding about six months' worth of net available assets, and maintaining a liabilities-to-assets ratio under 5 percent. For additional context and examples, see: Mitchell and Calabrese, "Proverbs of Nonprofit Financial Management"; Mitchell, "Modalities of Managerialism."

66. See, for example, Nicholas P. Marudas, TeWhan Hahn, and Fred A. Jacobs, "An Improved Model of Effects of Accounting Measures of Inefficiency on Donations," *Journal of Finance and Accountancy* 15 (2014); Daniel Tinkelman and Kamini Mankaney, "When Is Administrative Efficiency Associated with Charitable Donations?," *Nonprofit and Voluntary Sector Quarterly* 36, no. 1 (2007); Fred A. Jacobs and Nicholas P. Marudas, "The Combined Effect of Donation Price and Administrative Inefficiency on Donations to US Nonprofit Organizations," *Financial Accountability & Management* 25, no. 1 (2009), https://doi.org/doi:10.1111/j.1468-0408.2008.00464.x; Karen Kitching, "Audit Value and Charitable Organizations," *Journal of Accounting and Public Policy* 28, no. 6 (2009).

67. DiMaggio and Powell, "The Iron Cage Revisited."

68. Ann Goggins Gregory and Don Howard, "The Nonprofit Starvation Cycle," *Stanford Social Innovation Review* (Fall 2009); Lecy and Searing, "Anatomy of the Nonprofit Starvation Cycle."

69. Coupet and Haynie, "Toward a Valid Approach to Nonprofit Efficiency Measurement"; Kennard Wing and Mark A. Hager, *Getting What We Pay For: Low Overhead Limits Nonprofit Effectiveness*, Urban Institute Center on Nonprofits and Philanthropy and Indiana University Center on Philanthropy (2004).

70. DiMaggio and Powell, "The Iron Cage Revisited."

71. Mayer N. Zald and Michael Lounsbury, "The Wizards of Oz: Towards an Institutional Approach to Elites, Expertise, and Command Posts," *Organization Studies* 31, no. 7 (2010).

72. Danielle Beswick et al., "International Development NGOs, Representations in Fundraising Appeals, and Public Attitudes in UK-Africa Relations," in *Britain and Africa in the Twenty-First Century*, ed Danielle Beswick, Jonathan Fisher, and Stephen R. Hiurt (Manchester: Manchester University Press, 2019).

73. Susan Cotts Watkins, Ann Swidler, and Thomas Hannan, "Outsourcing Social Transformation: Development NGOs as Organizations," *Annual Review of Sociology* 38 (2012): 286

74. Arthur "Buzz" Schmidt, "Divining a Vision for Markets for Good," in *Selected Readings: Making Sense of Data and Information in the Social Sector*, ed. Eric J. Henderson (N.p.: Markets for Good, 2014).

75. For a discussion of past waves of regulatory reforms across several countries, see: Breen, Dunn, and Sidel, *Regulatory Waves*.

CHAPTER 3

1. Peter Singer, *The Life You Can Save: How to Do Your Part to End World Poverty* (New York: Random House, 2010).

2. Linda Rabben, *Fierce Legion of Friends: A History of Human Rights Campaigns and Campaigners* (Hyattsville: Quixote Center, 2002), 186

3. A 1981 study of the US section of Amnesty International concluded about its members and their motives that "AIUSA [Amnesty International USA] offers an alternative to, or even retreat from, more confrontative political action." Jan Eckel, "The International League for the Rights of Man, Amnesty International, and the Changing Fate of Human Rights Activism from the 1940s through the 1970s," *Humanity* 4, no. 2 (2013): 200.

4. Renée C. Fox, *Doctors without Borders: Humanitarian Quests, Impossible Dreams of Médecins Sans Frontières* (Baltimore: Johns Hopkins University Press, 2014).

5. Hans Peter Schmitz, "Menschenrechtswächter: Partielle Midlife-crisis. INGOs, Vereinte Nationen, und Weltöffentlichkeit," *Vereinte Nationen* 49, no. 1 (2001).

6. Also see: Robert A. Gross, "Giving in America: From Charity to Philanthropy," in *Charity, Philanthropy, and Civility in American History*, ed. Lawrence J. Friedman and Mark D. McGarview (New York: Cambridge University Press, 2003).

7. Emma Saunders-Hastings, "Charity, Philanthropy, and Trusteeship," *HistPhil* (November 18, 2015), https://histphil.org/2015/11/18/charity-philanthropy-and-trusteeship/.

8. Cash transfers represent a strategic shift in a different direction and, whether conditional or unconditional, pose a fundamental challenge to traditional service delivery models. Aided by the rise of digital technologies, organizations such as GiveDirectly and Kiva claim that cutting out intermediaries increases the total amount of aid while also reducing the paternalism of the traditional aid model. Cash assistance is also becoming increasingly popular as an alternative to in-kind humanitarian assistance. See: Aniek Woodward et al., "Research Agenda-Setting on Cash Programming for Health and Nutrition in Humanitarian Settings," *Journal of International Humanitarian Action* 3, no. 1 (2018), https://doi.org/10.1186/s41018-018-0035-6. Research on cash transfers has become popular, especially in economics, where scholars have begun to explore the effects of such interventions on a wide variety of outcomes, including household spending, psychological well-being, environmental behaviors by the poor, and communal conflict. See: Johannes Haushofer and Jeremy Shapiro, "The Short-Term Impact of Unconditional Cash Transfers to the Poor: Experimental Evidence from Kenya," *The Quarterly Journal of Economics* 131, no. 4 (2016), https://doi.org/10.1093/qje/qjw025; Benjamin Crost, Joseph H. Felter, and Patrick B. Johnston, "Conditional Cash Transfers, Civil Conflict, and Insurgent Influence: Experimental Evidence from the Philippines," *Journal of Development Economics* 118 (2016), https://doi.org/10.1016/j.jdeveco.2015.08.005. As cash transfers have only recently become a more widespread practice, much of the evidence remains preliminary and critics have challenged the assumption that cash transfers are effective in the absence of a context of services, including

high-quality education and information. See: Kevin Starr and Laura Hattendorff, "GiveDirectly?: Not So Fast," *Stanford Social Innovation Review* (March 11, 2014). Cash transfers also lack strategies designed to explicitly address the root causes of poverty, including persistent discrimination, power structures, entrenched elites, and political repression that may prevent cash recipients from improving their lives in more fundamental ways. Nevertheless, the popularity of cash transfers enabled by digital technology underscores the threat of disintermediation throughout the TNGO sector, particularly for organizations committed to the legacy public charity model with its emphasis on resource pass-through.

9. Adrien Bouguen et al., "Using Randomized Controlled Trials to Estimate Long-Run Impacts in Development Economics," *Annual Review of Economics* 11, no. 1 (2019), https://doi.org/10.1146/annurev-economics-080218-030333.

10. Andrew Carnegie, *The Gospel of Wealth* (New York: Carnegie Corporation of New York, 1889/2017).

11. Benjamin Soskis, "The Indeterminate Politics of the Charity vs. Philanthropy Divide," *HistPhil* (November 30, 2015), https://histphil.org/2015/11/30/the-indeterminate-politics-of-the-charity-vs-philanthropy-divide/.

12. InterAction, *Supporting Your NGO Future: US NGO Executive Thoughts on the Future* (Washington, DC: InterAction, 2019).

13. Thomas Davies, *NGOs: A New History of Transnational Civil Society* (New York: Oxford University Press, 2014); Steve Charnovitz, "Two Centuries of Participation: NGOs and International Governance," *Michigan Journal of International Law* 18, no. 2 (1997).

14. Paul J. Nelson and Ellen Dorsey, "At the Nexus of Human Rights and Development: New Methods and Strategies of Global NGOs," *World Development* 31, no. 12 (2003); Paul J. Nelson and Ellen Dorsey, "Who Practices Rights-Based Development?: A Progress Report on Work at the Nexus of Human Rights and Development," *World Development* 104 (2018).

15. Peter Uvin, *Human Rights and Development* (Bloomfield, CT: Kumarian Press, 2004).

16. For example, Amnesty International started out with a singular focus on the release of individual prisoners of conscience, but adopted in the 1990s a more campaign-style advocacy aimed to address root causes of repeated human rights violations. Ellen Dorsey, "Managing Change. Amnesty International and Human Rights NGOs," in *50 Years of Amnesty International: Reflections and Perspectives*, ed. Wilco de Jonge et al. (Utrecht: Universiteit Utrecht, 2011).

17. Marc Lindenberg and Coralie Bryant, *Going Global: Transforming Relief and Development NGOs* (Bloomfield, CT: Kumarian Press, 2001), ch. 7.

18. Paul O'Brien, "Politicized Humanitarianism: A Response to Nicolas de Torrente," *Harvard Human Rights Journal* 17 (2004).

19. Didier Fassin, *Humanitarian Reason: A Moral History of the Present* (Berkeley: University of California Press, 2011), 7

20. Andrei Florin Marin and Lars Otto Naess, "Climate Change Adaptation through Humanitarian Aid?: Promises, Perils, and Potentials of the New Humanitarianism?," *IDS Bulletin* 48, no. 4 (2017).

21. David Bryer and John Magrath, "New Dimensions of Global Advocacy," *Nonprofit and Voluntary Sector Quarterly* 28, no. 1 suppl. (1999), https://doi.org/10.1177/089976499773746500.

22. Lindenberg and Bryant, *Going Global*; Steven J. Lux and Tosca Bruno-van Vijfeijken, *From Alliance to International: The Global Transformation of Save the Children* (Syracuse, NY: Maxwell School of Citizenship and Public Affairs, 2012).

23. Plan International, *Promoting Child Rights to End Child Poverty* (UK: Plan Limited, 2010), https://plan-international.org/publications/promoting-child-rights-end-child-poverty#download-options.

24. Nelson and Dorsey, "At the Nexus of Human Rights and Development"; Peter Uvin, "From the Right to Development to the Rights-Based Approach: How 'Human Rights' Entered Development," *Development in Practice* 17, nos. 4/5 (2007).

25. Peter Uvin, "From the Right to Development to the Rights-Based Approach"; Paul Gready, "Rights-Based Approaches to Development: What Is the Value-Added?," *Development in Practice* 18, no. 6 (2008), http://www.informaworld.com/10.1080/09614520802386454.

26. Dambisa Moyo, *Dead Aid: Why Aid Is Not Working and How There Is a Better Way for Africa* (New York: Farrar, Straus and Giroux, 2009); Hans Holmén, *Snakes in Paradise: NGOs and the Aid Industry in Africa* (Bloomfield, CT: Kumarian Press, 2010).

27. George E. Mitchell and Sarah S. Stroup, "The Reputations of NGOs: Peer Evaluations of Effectiveness," *The Review of International Organizations* 12, no. 3 (2016), https://doi.org/10.1007/s11558-016-9259-7; George E. Mitchell, "The Attributes of Effective NGOs and the Leadership Values Associated with a Reputation for Organizational Effectiveness," *Nonprofit Management & Leadership* 28, no. 1 (2015).

28. Susan H. Holcombe, "Structuring a Global NGO for a Rights-Based Change Agenda," in *Change Not Charity. Essays on Oxfam's First 40 Years*, ed. Laura Roper (Boston: Oxfam America, 2010).

29. Laure-Hélène Piron, *Learning from the UK Department for International Development's Rights-Based Approach to Development Assistance* (London: Overseas Development Institute, 2003).

30. Sofia Gruskin, Dina Bogecho, and Laura Ferguson, "'Rights-Based Approaches' to Health Policies and Programs: Articulations, Ambiguities, and Assessment," *Journal of Public Health Policy* 31, no. 2 (2010); Srirak Plipat, *Developmentizing Human Rights: How Development NGOs Interpret and Implement and Human Rights–Based Approach to Development Policy* (PhD thesis, University of Pittsburgh, 2005); Hans Peter Schmitz and George E. Mitchell, "The Other Side of the Coin: NGOs, Rights-Based Approaches, and Public Administration," *Public Administration Review* 76, no. 2 (2016), https://doi.org/10.1111/puar.12479.

31. Hans Peter Schmitz, "A Human Rights–Based Approach (HRBA) in Practice: Evaluating NGO Development Efforts," *Polity* 44, no. 4 (2012), https://doi.org/10.1057/pol.2012.18.

32. Pierre Ly and Geri Mason, "Individual Preferences over Development Projects: Evidence from Microlending on Kiva," *Voluntas* 23, no. 4 (2012), https://doi.org/10.1007/s11266-011-9255-8.

33. Philip Mader, "Rise and Fall of Microfinance in India: The Andhra Pradesh Crisis in Perspective," *Strategic Change* 22, nos. 1–2 (2013), https://doi.org/10.1002/jsc.1921.

34. Raj Kumar, *The Business of Changing the World: How Billionaires, Tech Disrupters, and Social Entrepreneurs Are Transforming the Global Aid Industry* (Boston: Beacon Press, 2019).

35. Helen Yanacopulos, "The Strategies That Bind: NGO Coalitions and Their Influence," *Global Networks* 5, no. 1 (2005), https://doi.org/10.1111/j.1471-0374.2005.00109.x

36. Thomas P. Lyon, *Good Cop/Bad Cop: Environmental NGOs and Their Strategies toward Business* (Washington, DC: Resources for the Future, 2010).

37. Hans Peter Schmitz, "Non-State Actors in Human Rights Promotion," in *The Sage Handbook of Human Rights*, ed. Anja Mihr and Mark Gibney (London: Sage, 2014).

38. Christie Miedema, "Impartial in the Cold War?: The Challenges of Détente, Dissidence, and Eastern European Membership to Amnesty International's Policy of Impartiality," *Humanity* 10, no. 2 (2019).

39. Tom Buchanan, "'The Truth Will Set You Free': The Making of Amnesty International," *Journal of Contemporary History* 37, no. 4 (2002).

40. In the case of Amnesty International, a letter of resignation by an early member of the policy committee stated: "I have never really believed that direct action by small, and ill-informed, groups scattered around the world could ever be effective. [. . .] So I must leave [. . .] such amateur 'do-gooder' movements to those who can have faith in them. And good luck to them." Rabben, *Fierce Legion of Friends*, 188.

41. Brendan Cox, *Campaigning for International Justice* (London: Bond, 2011).

42. Robert O'Brien et al., *Contesting Global Governance: Multilateral Economic Institutions and Global Social Movements* (Cambridge: Cambridge University Press, 2000).

43. Nigel S. Rodley, "Amnesty International's Work on Personal Integrity—A Personal Reflection," in *50 Years of Amnesty International: Reflections and Perspectives*, ed. Wilco de Jonge et al. (Utrecht: Universiteit Utrecht, 2011).: 52

44. Margaret E. Keck and Kathryn Sikkink, *Activists beyond Borders: Advocacy Networks in International Politics* (Ithaca, NY: Cornell University Press, 1998).

45. Schmitz, "Non-State Actors in Human Rights Promotion."

46. CIVICUS, *State of Civil Society Report 2018* (Johannesburg: CIVICUS, 2018), https://www.civicus.org/documents/reports-and-publications/SOCS/2018/socs-2018-overview_top-ten-trends.pdf; Sarah Albrecht, "Shrinking, Closing, Shifting: A Changing Space for Civil Society," *Alliance Magazine* (2017), https://www.alliancemagazine.org/blog/shrinking-closing-shifting-changing-space-civil-society/; ICNL; "Survey of Trends Affecting Civic Space: 2015–2016," *Global Trends in NGO Law* 7, no. 4 (2016).

47. David Kennedy, *The Dark Sides of Virtue: Reassessing International Humanitarianism* (Princeton, NJ: Princeton University Press, 2004).

48. Ana Fernández-Aballí, "Advocacy for Whom? Influence for What? Abuse of Discursive Power in International NGO Online Campaigns: The Case of Amnesty International," *American Behavioral Scientist* 60, no. 3 (2016), https://doi.org/10.1177/0002764215613407; Makau Mutua, "Savages, Victims, and Saviors: The Metaphor of Human Rights," *Harvard International Law Journal* 42, no. 1 (2001).

49. Charles Duhigg, "Why Don't You Donate for Syrian Refugees?: Blame Bad Marketing," *New York Times* (June 14, 2017), https://www.nytimes.com/2017/06/14/business/media/marketing-charity-water-syria.html.

50. OECD, *The Challenge of Capacity Development: Working towards Good Practice* (Paris: OECD, 2006), 11

51. George E. Mitchell, "The Strategic Orientations of US-Based NGOs," *Voluntas* 25, no. 5 (2014), https://doi.org/10.1007/s11266-014-9507-5.

52. Lisa Denney, "$15bn Is Spent Every Year on Training, with Disappointing Results: Why the Aid Industry Needs to Rethink 'Capacity Building'," in Duncan Green, ed., *From Poverty to Power* (blog), January 5, 2018.

53. OECD, *The Challenge of Capacity Development*, 7.

54. Haley Swedlund, *The Development Dance: How Donors and Recipients Negotiate the Delivery of Foreign Aid* (Ithaca, NY: Cornell University Press, 2017).

55. Lisa Denney, Richard Mallett, and Matthew S. Benson, *Service Delivery and State Capacity: Findings from the Secure Livelihoods Research Consortium* (London: Secure Livelihoods Research Consortium, 2017).

56. Naila Kabeer, Simeen Mahmud, and Jairo Guillermo Isaza Castro, *NGOs' Strategies and the Challenge of Development and Democracy in Bangladesh*, IDS Working Paper 343 (Brighton: IDS, 2010).

57. Derick W. Brinkerhoff and Peter J. Morgan, "Capacity and Capacity Development: Coping with Complexity," *Public Administration and Development* 30, no. 1 (2010), https://doi.org/10.1002/pad.559.

58. Duncan Green, *How Change Happens* (New York: Oxford University Press, 2017).

59. INASP, *Approaches for Developing Capacity for the Use of Evidence in Policy Making* (Oxford: INASP, 2016).

60. Duncan Green, "If Top Down Control Is Unavoidable, Can We Still Make Aid More Compatible with Systems Thinking?," *From Poverty to Power* (July 17, 2019), https://oxfamblogs.org/fp2p/if-top-down-control-is-unavoidable-can-we-still-make-aid-more-compatible-with-systems-thinking/.

61. For an excellent critique of linear change models, see: Green, *How Change Happens*.

62. Adriana Matta, Fábio da Gonçalves, and Lisiane Leyser Bizarro, "Delay Discounting: Concepts and Measures," *Psychology & Neuroscience* 5, no. 2 (2012); George E. Mitchell and Thad D. Calabrese, "Instrumental Philanthropy and the Problem of Institutional Design" (Philanthropy and Social Impact: A Research Symposium, The Center on Philanthropy & Public Policy, Sol Price School of Public Policy, University of Southern California, 2019).

CHAPTER 4

1. Since the 1970s, the following TNGOs and campaigns received the Nobel Peace Prize: Amnesty International (1977), International Physicians for the Prevention of Nuclear War (1985), Pugwash Conferences on Science and World Affairs (1995), International Campaign to Ban Landmines (ICBL, 1997), Médecins Sans Frontières (1999), and the International Campaign to Abolish Nuclear Weapons (ICAN, 2017).

2. Margaret E. Keck and Kathryn Sikkink, *Activists beyond Borders. Advocacy Networks in International Politics* (Ithaca, NY: Cornell University Press, 1998), provide the classical statement on these transnational advocacy networks (TANs) bringing together like-minded individuals across a broad range of governmental and private organizations.

3. For example, see: CIVICUS, *State of Civil Society Report 2018* (Johannesburg: CIVICUS, 2018), https://www.civicus.org/documents/reports-and-publications/SOCS/2018/socs-2018-overview_top-ten-trends.pdf.

4. Steve Charnovitz, "Nongovernmental Organizations and International Law," *The American Journal of International Law* 100, no. 2 (2006), http://www.jstor.org/stable/3651151.

5. Sarah S. Stroup and Wendy Wong, *The Authority Trap: Strategic Choices of International NGOs* (Ithaca, NY: Cornell University Press, 2017); George E. Mitchell and Sarah S. Stroup, "The Reputations of NGOs: Peer Evaluations of Effectiveness," *The Review of International Organizations* 12, no. 3 (2016).

6. L. David Brown and Vanessa Timmer, "Civil Society Actors as Catalysts for Transnational Social Learning," *Voluntas* 17, no. 1 (2006), https://doi.org/10.1007/s11266-005-9002-0.

7. Mark C. Suchman, "Managing Legitimacy: Strategic and Institutional Approaches," *The Academy of Management Review* 20, no. 3 (1995): 574

8. Anna Holzscheiter, "Discourse as Capability: Non-State Actors' Capital in Global Governance," *Millennium* 33, no. 3 (2005), https://doi.org/doi:10.1177/03058298050330030301.

9. Thomas Olesen, *Global Injustice Symbols and Social Movements* (Basingstoke: Palgrave Macmillan, 2015).

10. Mette Eilstrup-Sangiovanni and Teale N. Phelps Bondaroff, "From Advocacy to Confrontation: Direct Enforcement by Environmental NGOs," *International Studies Quarterly* 58, no. 2 (2014).

11. Paul Wapner, "Horizontal Politics: Transnational Environmental Activism and Global Cultural Change," *Global Environmental Politics* 2, no. 2 (2002).

12. Political restrictions are relatively common. See: Oonagh B. Breen, Alison Dunn, and Mark Sidel, eds., *Regulatory Waves: Comparative Perspectives on State Regulation and Self-Regulation Policies in the Nonprofit Sector* (New York: Cambridge University Press, 2017). In the United States the charitable sector recently opposed efforts to remove restrictions on political activity by charities by repealing the so-called Johnson Amendment, largely out of concerns about undermining public trust in the sector. See: Ruth McCambridge, "National Council of Nonprofits Launches Coalition Campaign to Oppose Repeal of Johnson Amendment," *Nonprofit Quarterly* (March 2, 2017), https://nonprofitquarterly.org/2017/03/02/national-coalition-nonprofits-launches-campaign-oppose-repeal-johnson-amendment/; Editors, "Losing the Johnson Amendment Would Destroy the Unique Political Role of Nonprofits," *Nonprofit Quarterly* (February 6, 2017), https://nonprofitquarterly.org/2017/02/06/losing-johnson-amendment-destroy-unique-political-role-nonprofits/. For more overt political activities, including supporting political candidates for office, nonprofits have may create separate entities (such as a 501(c)(4) in the US context).

13. Hadii M. Mamudu, MariaElena Gonzalez, and Stanton Glantz, "The Nature, Scope, and Development of the Global Tobacco Control Epistemic Community," *American Journal of Public Health* 101, no. 11 (2011), https://doi.org/10.2105/ajph.2011.300303.

14. Bronwyn Leebaw, "The Politics of Impartial Activism: Humanitarianism and Human Rights," *Perspectives on Politics* 5, no. 2 (2007).

15. Sally Engle Merry, *Human Rights and Gender Violence: Translating International Law into Local Justice* (Chicago: University of Chicago Press, 2006).

16. John Ackerman, "Co-Governance for Accountability: Beyond 'Exit' and 'Voice,'" *World Development* 32, no. 3 (2004), http://www.sciencedirect.com/science/article/pii/S0305750X03002341; Jale Tosun, Sebastian Koos, and Jennifer Shore, "Co-governing Common Goods: Interaction Patterns of Private and Public Actors," *Policy and Society* 35, no. 1 (2016), https://doi.org/10.1016/j.polsoc.2016.01.002.

17. Mai'a K. Davis Cross, "The Limits of Epistemic Communities: EU Security Agencies," *Politics and Governance* 3, no. 1 (2015), 91, https://doi.org/doi:10.1017/S0260210512000034

18. Heidi Nichols Haddad, *The Hidden Hands of Justice: NGOs, Human Rights, and International Courts* (New York: Cambridge University Press, 2018).

19. Milli Lake, "Strong NGOs and Weak States: Pursuing Gender Justice in the Democratic Republic of Congo and South Africa" (Cambridge: Cambridge University Press, 2018).

20. Steven Lukes, *Power. A Radical View*, 2nd ed. (Basingstoke: Palgrave Macmillan, 2005).

21. John Gaventa, *Power after Lukes: A Review of the Literature* (Brighton: Institute of Development Studies, 2003).

22. Audie Klotz, *Norms in International Relations: The Struggle against Apartheid* (Ithaca, NY: Cornell University Press, 1995).

23. Jennifer M. Dixon, "Rhetorical Adaptation and Resistance to International Norms," *Perspectives on Politics* 15, no. 1 (2017); Thomas Olesen, "Power and Transnationalist Activist Framing," in *Power and Transnational Activism*, ed. Thomas Olesen (Abingdon: Routledge, 2011), 5–8.

24. Jeremy Shiffman et al., "A Framework on the Emergence and Effectiveness of Global Health Networks," *Health Policy and Planning* 31, no. suppl. 1 (2016), https://doi.org/10.1093/heapol/czu046: i9–10); Keck and Sikkink, *Activists beyond Borders*.

25. Shiffman et al., "A Framework on the Emergence and Effectiveness of Global Health Networks," i9–10.

26. Sarah B. Pralle, *Branching Out, Digging In: Environmental Advocacy and Agenda Setting* (Washington, DC: Georgetown University Press, 2006).

27. Paul A. Sabatier, "An Advocacy Coalition Framework of Policy Change and the Role of Policy-Oriented Learning Therein," *Policy Sciences* 21 (1988).

28. Amy Pollard and Julius Court, *How Civil Society Organisations Use Evidence to Influence Policy Processes: A Literature Review* (London: ODI, 2005), 15–17

29. Uwe Gneiting, "From Global Agenda-Setting to Domestic Implementation: Successes and Challenges of the Global Health Network on Tobacco Control," *Health Policy and Planning* 31, no. suppl. 1 (2016), https://doi.org/10.1093/heapol/czv001.

30. Shiffman et al., "A Framework on the Emergence and Effectiveness of Global Health Networks."

31. Keck and Sikkink, *Activists beyond Borders*.

32. The Global Burden of Disease Study represents such a global effort to assess harm comparatively; see, for example, Haidong Wang et al., "Global, Regional, and National Life Expectancy, All-Cause Mortality, and Cause-Specific Mortality for 249 Causes of Death, 1980–2015: A Systematic Analysis for the Global Burden of Disease Study 2015," *The Lancet* 388, no. 10053 (2016), https://doi.org/10.1016/S0140-6736(16)31012-1.

33. Jen Iris Allan and Jennifer Hadden, "Exploring the Framing Power of NGOs in Global Climate Politics," *Environmental Politics* 26, no. 4 (2017), https://doi.org/10.1080/09644016.2017.1319017.

34. Deborah A. Stone, "Causal Stories and the Formation of Policy Agendas," *Political Science Quarterly* 104, no. 2 (1989).

35. Amartya Sen, *Development as Freedom* (Oxford: Oxford University Press, 1999).

36. David G. Chandler, "The Road to Military Humanitarianism: How the Human Rights NGOs Shaped a New Humanitarian Agenda," *Human Rights Quarterly* 23, no. 3 (2001); Hans Peter Schmitz, "International Criminal Accountability and Transnational Advocacy Networks (TANs)," in *Oxford Handbook of International Security*, ed. Alexandra Gheciu and William C. Wohlforth (New York: Oxford University Press, 2018).

37. Meena Ahmed, *The Principles and Practice of Crisis Management: The Case of Brent Spar* (Basingstoke: Palgrave, 2006).

38. Anne Schneider and Helen Ingram, "Social Construction of Target Populations: Implications for Politics and Policy," *American Political Science Review* 87, no. 2 (1993).

39. Kathryn Quissell, "The Impact of Stigma and Policy Target Group Characteristics on Policy Aggressiveness for HIV/AIDS and Tuberculosis" (PhD, American University, 2017); R. Charli Carpenter, *Forgetting Children Born of War: Setting the Human Rights Agenda in Bosnia and Beyond* (New York: Columbia University Press, 2010).

40. R. Charli Carpenter, *"Lost" Causes: Agenda-Setting and Agenda-Vetting in Global Issue Networks* (Ithaca, NY: Cornell University Press, 2014).

41. Tim Bartley and Curtis Child, "Shaming the Corporation: The Social Production of Targets and the Anti-Sweatshop Movement," *American Sociological Review* 79, no. 4 (2014), https://doi.org/doi:10.1177/0003122414540653

42. David S. Meyer and Debra C. Minkoff, "Conceptualizing Political Opportunity," *Social Forces* 82, no. 4 (2004), https://doi.org/10.1353/sof.2004.0082, http://dx.doi.org/10.1353/sof.2004.0082.

43. Drew B. Margolin et al., "Normative Influences on Network Structure in the Evolution of the Children's Rights NGO Network, 1977–2004," *Communication Research* 42, no. 1 (2015), https://doi.org/10.1177/0093650212463731.

44. Sidney Tarrow, *The New Transnational Activism* (Cambridge: Cambridge University Press, 2005), 26–27; Robert O'Brien et al., *Contesting Global Governance. Multilateral Economic Institutions and Global Social Movements* (Cambridge: Cambridge University Press, 2000).

45. Thomas Risse-Kappen, ed., *Bringing Transnational Relations Back In: Non-State Actors, Domestic Structures, and International Institutions* (Cambridge: Cambridge University Press, 1995).

46. Christoph Aluttis, Thomas Krafft, and Helmut Brand, "Global Health in the European Union—A Review from an Agenda-Setting Perspective," *Global Health Action* 7, no. 1 (2014), https://doi.org/10.3402/gha.v7.23610.

47. Keith G. Provan and Patrick Kenis, "Modes of Network Governance: Structure, Management, and Effectiveness," *Journal of Public Administration Research and Theory* 18, no. 2 (2008), https://doi.org/10.1093/jopart/mum015.

48. Martha Finnemore and Kathryn Sikkink, "International Norm Dynamics and Political Change," *International Organization* 52, no. 4 (1998).

49. John W. Kingdon, *Agendas, Alternatives, and Public Policies* (New York: Longman, 1995), 165–66

50. Nina Reiners, "Transnational Lawmaking Coalitions for Human Rights" (PhD, Universität Potsdam, 2017).

51. Tana Johnson, *Organizational Progeny: Why Governments Are Losing Control over the Proliferating Structures of Global Governance* (New York: Oxford University Press, 2014).

52. Naghmeh Nasiritousi, Mattias Hjerpe, and Björn-Ola Linnér, "The Roles of Non-State Actors in Climate Change Governance: Understanding Agency through Governance Profiles," *International Environmental Agreements: Politics, Law and Economics* 16, no. 1 (2016), https://doi.org/10.1007/s10784-014-9243-8.

53. Thomas Nash and Richard Moyers, *Global Coalitions: An Introduction to Working in Civil Society Partnerships* (London: Action on Armed Violence, 2011).

54. Richard Price, "Reversing the Gun Sights: Transnational Civil Society Targets Land Mines," *International Organization* 52, no. 3 (1998).

55. Brendan Cox, *Campaigning for International Justice* (London: Bond, 2011), 20

56. Cox, *Campaigning for International Justice*, 4.

57. Wendy H. Wong, *Internal Affairs: How the Structure of NGOs Transforms Human Rights* (Ithaca, NY: Cornell University Press, 2012).

58. Stephen Hopgood, *Keepers of the Flame. Understanding Amnesty International* (Ithaca, NY: Cornell University Press, 2006).

59. Keck and Sikkink, *Activists beyond Borders*.

60. Keck and Sikkink, *Activists beyond Borders*, 205.

61. https://www.behindthebrands.org.

62. Emily McAteer and Simone Pulver, "The Corporate Boomerang: Shareholder Transnational Advocacy Networks Targeting Oil Companies in the Ecuadorian Amazon," *Global Environmental Politics* 9, no. 1 (2009), https://doi.org/10.1162/glep.2009.9.1.1.

63. Tim Bartley and Curtis Child, "Shaming the Corporation: The Social Production of Targets and the Anti-Sweatshop Movement," *American Sociological Review* 79, no. 4 (2014), https://doi.org/10.1177/0003122414540653.

64. Nash and Moyers, *Global Coalitions*.

65. Chris Rose, *How to Win Campaigns: Communications for Change* (London: Earthscan, 2010), 46

66. R. Charli Carpenter, "Studying Issue (Non)-Adoption in Transnational Advocacy Networks," *International Organization* 61 (2007).

67. William A. Schabas, *The Abolition of the Death Penalty in International Law* (New York: Cambridge University Press, 2002): 282

68. Salil Shetty, "The Value of International Standards in the Campaign for Abolition of the Death Penalty," *Brown Journal of World Affairs* 21, no. 1 (2014).

69. Price, "Reversing the Gun Sights."

70. Jody Williams, Stephen D. Goose, and Mary Wareham, *Banning Landmines: Disarmament, Citizen Diplomacy, and Human Security* (Lanham: Rowman & Littlefield, 2008).

71. Ann Christiano and Annie Neimand, "Stop Raising Awareness Already," *Stanford Social Innovation Review* (Spring 2017).

72. Sean Bex and Stef Craps, "Humanitarianism, Testimony, and the White Savior Industrial Complex: *What Is the What* versus *Kony 2012*," *Cultural Critique* 92, no. 1 (2016): 33

73. Joshua W. Busby, "Bono Made Jesse Helms Cry: Jubilee 2000, Debt Relief, and Moral Action in International Politics," *International Studies Quarterly* 51, no. 2 (2007).

74. Abhay T. Bang et al., "Effect of Home-Based Neonatal Care and Management of Sepsis on Neonatal Mortality: Field Trial in Rural India," *The Lancet* 354, no. 9194 (1999); Jeremy Shiffman, "Network Advocacy and the Emergence of Global Attention to Newborn Survival," *Health Policy and Planning* 31, no. suppl. 1 (2016), https://doi.org/10.1093/heapol/czv092.

75. Roger W. Cobb and Charles D. Elder, *Participation in American Politics: The Dynamics of Agenda-Building* (Baltimore: Johns Hopkins University Press, 1972); Kingdon, *Agendas, Alternatives, and Public Policies*, 3. Agendas are fluid and issues are not simply "on" or "off," but the "political struggle around agenda-setting is concerned with moving issues higher up the agenda or pushing them down." Sebastiaan Princen, "Agenda-Setting in the European Union: A Theoretical

Exploration and Agenda for Research," *Journal of European Public Policy* 14, no. 1 (2007): 28, https://doi.org/10.1080/13501760601071539.

76. Ian Smilie, *The Kimberley Process Certification Scheme for Rough Diamonds: Comparative Case Study 1* (London: Verifor/ODI, 2005), 2

77. Marlies Glasius, *The International Criminal Court: A Global Civil Society Achievement* (London and New York: Routledge, 2006), 10–11

78. Kathryn Sikkink, *The Justice Cascade: How Human Rights Prosecutions Are Changing World Politics* (New York: W. W. Norton, 2011).

79. Cox, *Campaigning for International Justice*; Duncan Green, *How Change Happens* (New York: Oxford University Press, 2017), ch. 2.

80. Michele M. Betsill and Elisabeth Corell, *NGO Diplomacy: The Influence of Nongovernmental Organizations in International Environmental Organizations* (Cambridge, MA: MIT Press, 2008), 34/5

81. Jonas Tallberg et al., "NGO Influence in International Organizations: Information, Access, and Exchange," *British Journal of Political Science* (2015), https://doi.org/10.1017/S000712341500037X; Reiners, "Transnational Lawmaking Coalitions for Human Rights."

82. Glasius, *The International Criminal Court*, 47–60.

83. Cox, *Campaigning for International Justice*, 50.

84. Nick Paumgarten, "Magic Mountain: What Happens at Davos?," *New Yorker* (February 28, 2012). In 2009, Naidoo was appointed international executive director of Greenpeace, and in 2018 he became secretary-general of Amnesty International.

85. Charlotte Dany, "Ambivalenzen der Partizipation: Grenzen des NGO-Einflusses auf dem Weltgipfel zur Informationsgesellschaft," *Zeitschrift für Internationale Beziehungen* 19, no. 2 (2012).

86. Charlotte Dany, *Global Governance and NGO Participation: Shaping the Information Society in the United Nations* (London: Routledge, 2013).

87. TNGOs were unable (1) to attain clear statements privileging the free exchange of knowledge over the protection of property rights, (2) to strengthen indigenous control over traditional knowledge, and (3) to convince wealthy states to adopt financing mechanisms for infrastructure investments in the developing world.

88. Dany, "Ambivalenzen der Partizipation."

89. John Burroughs and Jacqueline Cabasso, "Confronting the Nuclear-Armed States in International Negotiating Forums: Lessons for NGOs," *International Negotiation* 4, no. 3 (1999): 474

90. Dixon, "Rhetorical Adaptation and Resistance to International Norms"; Jonathan Symons and Dennis Altman, "International Norm Polarization: Sexuality as a Subject of Human Rights Protection," *International Theory* 7, no. 1 (2015), https://doi.org/10.1017/S1752971914000384.

91. Thomas Risse-Kappen, "Bringing Transnational Relations Back In: Introduction," in *Bringing Transnational Relations Back In: Non-State Actors, Domestic Structures, and International Institutions*, ed. Thomas Risse-Kappen (Cambridge: Cambridge University Press, 1995).

92. Thomas Risse, ed., *Governance without a State: Policies and Politics in Areas of Limited Statehood* (New York: Columbia University Press, 2013).

93. For example, these issues may include supply chains affecting violent conflict, Michael John Bloomfield, *Dirty Gold: How Activism Transformed the Jewelry Industry* (Boston: MIT Press, 2017); contemporary slavery, Austin Choi-Fitzpatrick, *What Slaveholders Think: How Contemporary Perpetrators Rationalize*

What They Do (New York: Columbia University Press, 2017); or consumption patterns affecting public health, Karen Farquharson, "Influencing Policy Transnationally: Pro- and Anti-Tobacco Global Advocacy Networks," *Australian Journal of Public Administration* 62, no. 4 (2003).

94. Gneiting, "From Global Agenda-Setting to Domestic Implementation."

95. Olesen, "Power and Transnationalist Activist Framing."

96. Anja Jetschke, *Human Rights and State Security: Indonesia and the Philippines* (Philadelphia: University of Pennsylvania Press, 2011).

97. Sarah Sunn Bush, *The Taming of Democracy Assistance: Why Democracy Promotion Does Not Confront Dictators* (Cambridge: Cambridge University Press, 2015).

98. Amanda M. Murdie and David R. Davis, "Shaming and Blaming: Using Events Data to Assess the Impact of Human Rights INGOs," *International Studies Quarterly* 56 (2012).

99. Lisbeth Zimmermann, "Same Same or Different?: Norm Diffusion between Resistance, Compliance, and Localization in Post-Conflict States," *International Studies Perspectives* 17, no. 1 (2016), https://doi.org/10.1111/insp.12080.

100. Richard Price, "Transnational Civil Society and Advocacy in World Politics," *World Politics* 55, no. 4 (2003): 596; Nina Hall, "What Is Adaptation to Climate Change?: Epistemic Ambiguity in the Climate Finance System," *International Environmental Agreements: Politics, Law, and Economics* 17, no. 1 (2017), https://doi.org/10.1007/s10784-016-9345-6.

101. Margolin et al., "Normative Influences on Network Structure in the Evolution of the Children's Rights NGO Network, 1977–2004."

102. Karisa Cloward, *When Norms Collide: Local Responses to Activism against Female Genital Mutilation and Early Marriage* (New York: Oxford University Press, 2016).

103. Cloward, *When Norms Collide*, 230.

104. World Health Organization, *Eliminating Female Genital Mutilation: An Interagency Statement* (Geneva: World Health Organization, 2008).

105. Merry, *Human Rights and Gender Violence*.

106. Zimmermann, "Same Same or Different?"

107. Bodille Arensman, Margit van Wessel, and Dorothea Hilhorst, "Does Local Ownership Bring About Effectiveness?: The Case of a Transnational Advocacy Network," *Third World Quarterly* 38, no. 6 (2017), https://doi.org/10.1080/01436597.2016.1257908.: 1322

108. Phillip M. Ayoub, "Contested Norms in New-Adopter States: International Determinants of LGBT Rights Legislation," *European Journal of International Relations* 21, no. 2 (2015): 296

109. Shareen Hertel, *Unexpected Power: Conflict and Change among Transnational Activists* (Ithaca, NY: Cornell University Press, 2006).

110. Teju Cole, "The White-Savior Industrial Complex," *The Atlantic* (March 21, 2012).

111. Cloward, *When Norms Collide*.

112. Rebecca Koenig, "Some International Groups Saying Hiring More Locals Boosts Results," *Chronicle of Philanthropy* (May 21, 2018), https://www.philanthropy.com/article/International-Groups-Shift/243469.

113. Duncan Green, *Fit for the Future?: Development Trends and the Role of International NGOs* (Oxford: Oxfam GB, 2015); Michael Edwards, *Civil Society*, 3rd ed. (Cambridge: Polity Press, 2014), 127; Barbara Klugman et al., *Towards a New Ecology of the Human Rights Movement* (Johannesburg: Barbara Klugman Concepts, 2017).

CHAPTER 5

1. Sarah Kenyon Lischer, *Dangerous Sanctuaries: Refugee Camps, Civil War, and the Dilemmas of Humanitarian Aid* (Ithaca, NY: Cornell University Press, 2015).

2. Michael Edwards, "What's to Be Done with Oxfam?," *openDemocracy* (August 1, 2016), https://www.opendemocracy.net/transformation/michael-edwards/what-s-to-be-done-with-oxfam.

3. Cristina M. Balboa, *The Paradox of Scale: How NGOs Build, Maintain, and Lose Authority in Environmental Governance* (Cambridge, MA: MIT Press, 2018).

4. George E. Mitchell, "Collaborative Propensies among Transnational NGOs Registered in the United States," *American Review of Public Administration* 44, no. 5 (2014), https://doi.org/10.1177/0275074012474337.

5. Michael Meyer, Renate Buber, and Anahid Aghamanoukjan, "In Search of Legitimacy: Managerialism and Legitimation in Civil Society Organizations," *Voluntas* 24 (2013): 169.

6. Ellen Gutterman, "The Legitimacy of Transnational NGOs: Lessons from the Experience of Transparency International in Germany and France," *Review of International Studies* 40 (2014): 394.

7. Gutterman, "The Legitimacy of Transnational NGOs," 418.

8. Balboa, *The Paradox of Scale*; Jonathan G. S. Koppell, "Pathologies of Accountability: ICANN and the Challenge of 'Multiple Accountabilities Disorder'," *Public Administration Review* 65, no. 1 (2005), https://doi.org/10.1111/j.1540-6210.2005.00434.x.

9. David Beetham, *The Legitimation of Power* (Basingstoke: Palgrave Macmillan, 2013).: 38

10. Helen Yanacopulos, *International NGO Engagement, Advocacy, Activism: The Faces and Spaces of Change* (Basingstoke: Palgrave Macmillan, 2015), 50; Erla Thrandardottir, *NGO Audiences: A Beethamite Analysis* (London: City University of London, 2017).

11. Jennifer C. Rubenstein, "The Misuse of Power, Not Bad Representation: Why It Is Beside the Point That No One Elected Oxfam," *Journal of Political Philosophy* 22, no. 2 (2014), https://doi.org/10.1111/jopp.12020, http://dx.doi.org/10.1111/jopp.12020.

12. Iain Atack, "Four Criteria for Development NGO Legitimacy," *World Development* 27, no. 5 (1999).

13. Christopher L. Pallas, David Gethings, and Max Harris, "Do the Right Thing: The Impact of INGO Legitimacy Standards on Stakeholder Input," *Voluntas* 26, no. 4 (2015), https://doi.org/10.1007/s11266-014-9475-9.

14. Maryam Zarnegar Deloffre and Hans Peter Schmitz, "INGO Legitimacy: Challenges and Responses," in *Routledge Handbook of NGOs and International Relations*, ed. Thomas Davies (New York: Routledge, 2019).

15. Pallas, Gethings, and Harris, "Do the Right Thing."

16. HERE Geneva, *Humanitarian Priorities for People in Crises—The Foundations for a More Effective Response* (Geneva: Humanitarian Exchange and Research Centre Geneva, 2016).

17. Peter Ellis, "The Ethics of Taking Sides," in *Ethical Questions and International NGOs*, ed. Keith Horton and Chris Roche (New York: Springer, 2010).

18. Paul J. Nelson, "Social Movements and the Expansion of Economic and Social Human Rights Advocacy among International NGOs," in *Closing the Rights Gap: From Human Rights to Social Transformation*, ed. LaDawn Haglund and Robin Stryker (Berkeley: University of California Press, 2015).

19. Rinku Bhattacharya and Daniel Tinkelman, "How Tough Are Better Business Bureau/Wise Giving Alliance Financial Standards?," *Nonprofit and Voluntary Sector Quarterly* 38, no. 3 (2009); George E. Mitchell, "Creating a Philanthropic Marketplace through Accounting, Disclosure, and Intermediation," *Public Performance and Management Review* 38, no. 1 (2014); "The Overhead Myth," GuideStar, 2013, accessed June 24, 2013, http://overheadmyth.com/wp-content/ uploads/2013/06/GS_OverheadMyth_Ltr_ONLINE.pdf; George E. Mitchell and Thad D. Calabrese, "Proverbs of Nonprofit Financial Management," *American Review of Public Administration* 49, no. 6 (2019), https://doi.org/10.1177/ 0275074018770458; George E. Mitchell, "Modalities of Managerialism: The 'Double Bind' of Normative and Instrumental Nonprofit Managerial Imperatives," *Administration & Society* 50, no. 7 (2018), https://doi.org/10.1177/ 0095399716664832, 2016.

20. Paul Ronalds, *The Change Imperative: Creating the Next Generation NGO* (Sterling, VA: Kumarian Press, 2010).

21. Meyer, Buber, and Aghamanoukjan, "In Search of Legitimacy."

22. For an elaboration on this notion, see: Maureen O'Hara and Aftab Omer, "Virtue and the Organizational Shadow: Exploring False Innocence and the Paradoxes of Power," in *Humanity's Dark Side: Evil, Destructive Experience, and Psychotherapy* (Washington, DC: American Psychological Association, 2013).

23. In the United States, proponents of this emerging view have included Ken Berger, CEO of Charity Navigator, who spearheaded an initiative to shift attention away from cost ratios in favor of measures of results reporting and transparency. The William and Flora Hewlett Foundation was a major supporter of efforts to change metrics at Charity Navigator. The foundation's former president, Paul Brest, traces the outcome movement to a growing number of influential thought leaders, as well as to organizations such as the Center for Effective Philanthropy, Grantmakers for Effective Organizations, the Abdul Latif Jameel Poverty Action Lab (J-PAL), and information intermediaries such as GiveWell, Root Cause, and Philanthropedia, among others. Paul Brest, "A Decade of Outcome-Oriented Philanthropy," *Stanford Social Innovation Review* (2012), http://www.ssireview.org/articles/entry/a_decade_of_outcome_ oriented_philanthropy; K. Lynch and Kate Cooney, "Moving from Outputs to Outcomes: A Review of the Evolution of Performance Measurement in the Human Service Nonprofit Sector," *Administration in Social Work* 35, no. 4 (2011); Joanne G. Carman, "The Accountability Movement: What's Wrong with This Theory of Change?," *Nonprofit and Voluntary Sector Quarterly* 39, no. 2 (2010); George E. Mitchell, "The Construct of Organizational Effectiveness: Perspectives from Leaders of International Nonprofits in the United States," *Nonprofit and Voluntary Sector Quarterly* 42, no. 2 (2013), https://doi.org/10.1177/ 0899764011434589; Mitchell, "Creating a Philanthropic Marketplace through Accounting, Disclosure, and Intermediation." Other important advocates driving the cultural shift include GuideStar veterans Bob Ottenhoff and Arthur Schmidt, who have long sounded warnings about the perils of using financial data gleaned from Internal Revenue Service (IRS) Forms 990 to evaluate organizational performance.

24. Although some research finds that only a minority of households in the United States are "impact-oriented," a more recent survey of American millennials (born after 1979) found "demonstrating how gifts lead to results" to be the second largest issue identified for charitable giving. Hope Consulting, *Money for Good: The*

US Market for Impact Investments and Charitable Gifts from Individual Donors and Investors (May 2010); Derrick Feldmann et al., *The 2013 Millennial Impact Report*, The Millennial Impact Research (2013), http://www.themillennialimpact.com/past-research.

25. Personal communication from Jacob Harold, CEO, GuideStar, January 26, 2018.
26. Mitchell, George E. "Fiscal Leanness and Fiscal Responsiveness: Exploring the Normative Limits of Strategic Nonprofit Financial Management," *Administration & Society* 49, no. 9 (2017), https://doi.org/10.1177/0095399715581035.
27. Joanne G. Carman, "Nonprofits, Funders, and Evaluation: Accountability in Action," *The American Review of Public Administration* 39, no. 4 (2009).
28. Joanne G. Carman, "Understanding Evaluation in Nonprofit Organizations," *Public Performance and Management Review* 34, no. 3 (2011); Juan L. Gandia, "Internet Disclosure by Nonprofit Organizations: Empirical Evidence of Nongovernmental Organizations for Development in Spain," *Nonprofit and Voluntary Sector Quarterly* 40, no. 1 (2011).
29. Susan Houchin and Heather Johnston Nicholson, "Holding Ourselves Accountable: Managing by Outcomes in Girls Incorporated," *Nonprofit and Voluntary Sector Quarterly* 31, no. 2 (2002).
30. Mitchell and Calabrese, "Proverbs of Nonprofit Financial Management."
31. National Council of Nonprofits, *Investing for Impact: Indirect Costs Are Essential for Success* (Washington, DC: National Council of Nonprofits, 2013).
32. Deloffre and Schmitz, "INGO Legitimacy."
33. Mary Kay Gugerty, "Signaling Virtue: Voluntary Accountability Programs among Nonprofit Organizations," *Policy Sciences* 42, no. 3 (2009); Joannie Tremblay-Boire, Aseem Prakash, and Mary Kay Gugerty, "Regulation by Reputation: Monitoring and Sanctioning in Nonprofit Accountability Clubs," *Public Administration Review* 76, no. 5 (2016), https://doi.org/10.1111/puar.12539; Mary Kay Gugerty, Mark Sidel, and Angela L. Bies, "Introduction to the Minisymposium: Nonprofit Self-Regulation in Comparative Perspective—Themes and Debates," *Nonprofit and Voluntary Sector Quarterly* 39, no. 6 (2010).
34. See: http://www.csostandard.org.
35. See: https://corehumanitarianstandard.org and http://www.sphereproject.org.
36. For example, this is the case with InterAction, the TNGO alliance organization in the United States. See: https://www.interaction.org.
37. For more information about these initiatives, see: Mary Kay Gugerty and Aseem Prakash, eds., *Voluntary Regulation of NGOs and Nonprofits: An Accountability Club Framework* (New York: Cambridge University Press, 2010); Aseem Prakash and Mary Kay Gugerty, "Trust but Verify?: Voluntary Regulation Programs in the Nonprofit Sector," *Regulation & Governance* 4, no. 1 (2010); Tremblay-Boire, Prakash, and Gugerty, "Regulation by Reputation"; Maryam Zarnegar Deloffre, "NGO Accountability Clubs in the Humanitarian Sector: Social Dimensions of Club Emergence and Design," in *Voluntary Regulation of NGOs and Nonprofits: An Accountability Club Framework*, ed. Mary Kay Gugerty and Aseem Prakash (Cambridge: Cambridge University Press, 2010); Mary Kay Gugerty, "The Effectiveness of NGO Self-Regulation: Theory and Evidence from Africa," *Public Administration and Development* 28, no. 2 (2008).
38. Oonagh B. Breen, Alison Dunn, and Mark Sidel, eds., *Regulatory Waves: Comparative Perspectives on State Regulation and Self-Regulation Policies in the Nonprofit Sector* (New York: Cambridge University Press, 2017).

39. In the United States, GuideStar offers a "Platinum" data transparency platform, Charity Navigator remains in a state of transition, GiveWell emphasizes impact and cost-effectiveness, and ImpactMatters has adopted an explicit impact auditing role. See: www.guidestar.org, https://www.charitynavigator.org, https://www.givewell.org, and https://www.impactm.org.

40. Ken Berger, Robert Penna, and Jeremy Kohomban, "Mergers and Collaborations for Charity Navigator?," *Stanford Social Innovation Review* (August 10, 2012).

41. These include Malaria Consortium, Evidence Action's Deworm the World Initiative, Helen Keller International, Against Malaria Foundation, Schistosomiasis Control Initiative, Sightsavers, END Fund, and GiveDirectly. All of the recommended organizations have a narrow focus on a specific problem and with relatively easy ways of assessing impact.

42. Interview with Sean Conley, research analyst, and Catherine Hollander, outreach associate, GiveWell, by George Mitchell, September 23, 2015.

43. Interview with Jacob Harold, CEO, GuideStar, by George Mitchell, January 26, 2018.

44. For example, organizations may misreport financial information. See: George E. Mitchell, "Fiscal Leanness and Fiscal Responsiveness: Exploring the Normative Limits of Strategic Nonprofit Financial Management," *Administration & Society* 49, no. 9 (2017), https://doi.org/10.1177/0095399715581035; Ranjani Krishnan, Michelle H. Yetman, and Robert J. Yetman, "Expense Misreporting in Nonprofit Organizations," *The Accounting Review* 81, no. 2 (2006).

45. Interview with Maliha Khan, director for learning, evaluation, and accountability at OXFAM America, by Tosca Bruno-van Vijfeijken, March 25, 2014.

46. René Bekkers, "Trust, Accreditation, and Philanthropy in the Netherlands," *Nonprofit and Voluntary Sector Quarterly* 32, no. 4 (2003).

47. Gandia, "Internet Disclosure by Nonprofit Organizations."

48. Gregory D. Saxton, Daniel G. Neely, and Chao Guo, "Web Disclosure and the Market for Charitable Contributions," *Journal of Accounting and Public Policy* 33, no. 2 (2014).

49. Linda M. Parsons, "The Impact of Financial Information and Voluntary Disclosures on Contributions to Not-For-Profit Organizations," *Behavioral Research in Accounting* 19 (2007); Saxton, Neely, and Guo, *Web Disclosure and the Market for Charitable Contributions.*

50. Alnoor Ebrahim and V. Kasturi Rangan, *Acumen Fund: Measurement in Venture Philanthropy (A),* N9-310-011 (Cambridge, MA: Harvard Business School, 2009).

51. An L3C is a legal entity created in the United States that establishes a for-profit venture with an explicitly stated social mission instead of maximizing profits. It combines the legal and tax flexibility of a traditional limited liability company (LLC) with the social benefits of a nonprofit.

52. Christopher Marquis, Andrew Klaber, and Bobbi Thomson, *B Lab: Building a New Sector of the Economy* (Cambridge, MA: Harvard Business School, 2011).

53. Beth Richardson, "Sparking Impact Investing through GIIRS," *Stanford Social Innovation Review* (2012), http://ssir.org/articles/entry/sparking_impact_investing_through_giirs; Ronald A. Heifetz, Marty Linsky, and Alexander Grashow, *The Practice of Adaptive Leadership: Tools and Tactics for Changing Your Organization and the World* (Boston: Harvard Business School Publishing, 2009).

54. Interview with Ken Berger, CEO of Charity Navigator, by Tosca Bruno-van Vijfeijken, May 29, 2013.

55. Abhilash Mudaliar and Hannah Dithrich, *Sizing the Impact Investing Market* (New York: Global Impact Investing Network, 2019), https://thegiin.org/assets/Sizing%20the%20Impact%20Investing%20Market_webfile.pdf.

56. "Safeguarding Guidance and Resources," 2018, https://www.bond.org.uk/ngo-support/safeguarding.

57. Michael Edwards, "What's to Be Done with Oxfam?, Part 2," *openDemocracy* (February 15, 2018), https://www.opendemocracy.net/en/transformation/what-s-to-be-done-with-oxfam-part-2/.

58. Lore Wellens and Marc Jegers, "Beneficiary Participation as an Instrument of Downward Accountability: A Multiple Case Study," *European Management Journal* 32, no. 6 (2014); Elena McCollim, "A Tale of Two Influences: An Exploration of Downward Accountability in World Vision International" (University of San Diego, 2019).

59. Hugo Slim, "By What Authority?: The Legitimacy and Accountability of Non-Governmental Organisations," International Meeting on *Global Trends and Human Rights—Before and after September 11* (Geneva, January 10–12, 2002), http://www.gdrc.org/ngo/accountability/by-what-authority.html.

60. BFM, *Using Beneficiary Feedback to Improve Development Programmes: Findings from a Multi-Country Pilot*, World Vision, INTRAC, Social Impac Lab, CDA (2016), http://feedbackmechanisms.org/public/files/BFM-key-findings-summary.pdf; INTRAC, *DFID Beneficiary Feedback Mechanisms (BFM) Pilot: End-Point Review: Synthesis Report*, Social Impact Lab, INTRAC, World Vision (2016), http://feedbackmechanisms.org/public/files/BFM%20End-point%20Synthesis%20-%20full%20report.pdf.

61. Disaster Accountability Project, "The Republic of NGOs," in *Tectonic Shifts: Haiti Since the Earthquake*, ed. Mark Schuller and Pablo Morales (Sterling, VA: Kumarian Press, 2012).

62. National Contact Point of Switzerland, *Final Statement: Specific Instance Regarding the World Wide Fund for Nature International (WWF) Submitted by the Survival International Charitable Trust* (Berne: Swiss NCP, 2017).

CHAPTER 6

1. Nina Hall and Phil Ireland, "Transforming Activism: Digital Era Advocacy Organizations," *Stanford Social Innovation Review* (July 6, 2016), https://ssir.org/articles/entry/transforming_activism_digital_era_advocacy_organizations.

2. Piotr Czerski, "We, the Web Kids (Trans. M. Szreder)," *The Atlantic* (February 21, 2012).

3. Kari Dunn Saratovsky and Derrick Feldmann, *Cause for Change: The Why and How of Nonprofit Millennial Engagement* (San Francisco: Jossey-Bass, 2013); Derrick Feldmann, *A Generation for Causes: A Four-Year Summary of the Millennial Impact Report* (Indianapolis: Achieve/Case Foundation, 2014).

4. David Karpf, *Analytic Activism: Digital Listening and the New Political Strategy* (New York: Oxford University Press, 2016).

5. Cost increases for traditional NGOs are driven by a range of factors, including the development of more sophisticated MEAL systems, the need to hire and properly remunerate competent staff with subject matter expertise and thought leader capacity, and the rising costs of maintaining physical offices and paying for security in complex operating environments.

6. Sasha Dichter, Tom Adams, and Alnoor Ebrahim, "The Power of Lean Data," *Stanford Social Innovation Review* (Winter 2016).

7. Specifically, 97 percent of leaders overall said digital transformation would impact their organizations, some (38%), significantly (41%), or fundamentally (18%). InterAction, *Supporting Your NGO Future: US NGO Executive Thoughts on the Future* (Washington, DC: InterAction, 2019).

8. Frank Jacob, "The Role of M-Pesa in Kenya's Economic and Political Development," in *Kenya after 50: Reconfiguring Education, Gender, and Policy*, ed. Mickie Mwanzia Koster, Michael Mwenda Kithinji, and Jerono P. Rotich (New York: Palgrave Macmillan, 2016), 89–100. For an overview of major technological innovations for social change, see the Engineroom (https://www.theengineroom.org/).

9. Steven Livingston and Gregor Walter-Drop, eds., *Bits and Atoms: Information and Communication Technology in Areas of Limited Statehood* (New York: Oxford University Press, 2014); Patrick Meier, *Digital Humanitarians: How Big Data Is Changing the Face of Humanitarian Response* (London: Routledge, 2015).

10. In an effort to understand better its own effectiveness, Amnesty International also relied on digital volunteers to code more than 25,000 Urgent Action appeals issued since 1973. The subsequent analysis documented that 67 percent of all appeals had been successful. Milena Marin, "Amnesty International on Small Tasks, Big Data, and Massive Engagement," *Exposing the Invisible* (January 23, 2017), https://exposingtheinvisible.org/resources/micro-tasking-amnesty-international. It also showed that appeals focused on individual women were most successful (76%), followed by those focused on individual men (69%) and those defending groups (65%).

11. "GIS for SDGs: 'See Things That Were Impossible to See,' Esri Founder Says," DevEx, updated July 12, 2019, https://www.devex.com/news/facebook-s-digital-currency-libra-why-nonprofits-are-joining-95142.

12. Nina Hall, Hans Peter Schmitz, and J. Michael Dedmon, "Transnational Advocacy and NGOs in the Digital Era: New Forms of Networked Power," *International Studies Quarterly* (2019), https://doi.org/10.1093/isq/sqz052 .

13. Luis E. Hestres, "Climate Change Advocacy Online: Theories of Change, Target Audiences, and Online Strategy," *Environmental Politics* 24, no. 2 (2015): 207

14. Andrew Chadwick and James Dennis, "Social Media, Professional Media, and Mobilisation in Contemporary Britain: Explaining the Strengths and Weaknesses of the Citizens' Movement 38 Degrees," *Political Studies* 65, no. 1 (2017), https://doi.org/10.1177/0032321716631350.

15. Ron Kohavi and Stefan Thomke, "The Surprising Power of Online Experiments," *Harvard Business Review* 95, no. 5 (2017). For details on the role of "analytic activism," see Karpf, *Analytic Activism*.

16. Michael Silberman, "What Advocacy Organizations Need to Win Today," *MobLab* (March 28, 2019), https://mobilisationlab.org/stories/what-advocacy-organisations-need-to-win-today.

17. Ben Brandzel, *The 8-fold Path of New Organizing: DNA-Level Operating Principles for Building a Progressive People's Movement in the 21st Century* (unpublished manuscript on hand with authors, n.d.).

18. Bert Fraussen and Darren Halpin, "How Do Interest Groups Legitimate Their Policy Advocacy?: Reconsidering Linkage and Internal Democracy in Times of Digital Disruption," *Public Administration* 96, no. 1 (2018), https://onlinelibrary.wiley.com/doi/abs/10.1111/padm.12364.

19. Silberman, "What Advocacy Organizations Need to Win Today."

20. Achieve, *The 2016 Millennial Impact Report: Cause Engagement Following an Election Year* (Washington, DC: Case Foundation, 2016).

21. Saratovsky and Feldmann, *Cause for Change*.

22. Robert H. Wicks et al., "Correlates of Political and Civic Engagement among Youth during the 2012 Presidential Campaign," *American Behavioral Scientist* 58, no. 5 (2014), https://doi.org/10.1177/0002764213515226.

23. W. Lance Bennett and Alexandra Segerberg, *The Logic of Connective Action: Digital Media and the Personalization of Contentious Politics* (New York: Cambridge University Press, 2013).

24. Doug McAdam, *Political Process and the Development of Black Insurgency, 1930–1970*, 2nd ed. (Chicago: University of Chicago Press, 1999).

25. Jason Mogus and Austen Levihn-Coon, "What Makes Nonprofit Digital Teams Successful Today?," *Stanford Social Innovation Review* (February 6, 2018), https://ssir.org/articles/entry/what_makes_nonprofit_digital_teams_successful_today.

26. Jessica Word and Heather Carpenter, "The New Public Service?: Applying the Public Service Motivation Model to Nonprofit Employees," *Public Personnel Management* 42, no. 3 (2013), https://doi.org/10.1177/0091026013495773; Xavier Ballart and Guillem Rico, "Public or Nonprofit? Career Preferences and Dimensions of Public Service Motivation," *Public Administration* 96, no. 2 (2018), https://doi.org/doi:10.1111/padm.12403.

27. This is sometimes self-reported by staff and leaders, and is also evident in our own participant observation in the sector.

28. Teju Cole, "The White-Savior Industrial Complex," *The Atlantic* (March 21, 2012).

29. As one observer explained: "I don't think that the large NGOs know how to work informal spaces and I think social movements are much better because they're subversive, they're cheeky and the big NGOs can't be subversive and cheeky" (anonymous interview cited in: Helen Yanacopulos, *International NGO Engagement, Advocacy, Activism: The Faces and Spaces of Change* (Basingstoke: Palgrave Macmillan, 2015), 139.

30. Evgeny Morozov, "Why Social Movements Should Ignore Social Media," *New Republic* (February 5, 2013).

31. Lucy Bernholz and Lyndon Ormond-Parker, "The Ethics of Designing Digital Infrastructure," *Stanford Social Innovation Review* 16, no. 3 (2018).

32. "Facebook's Digital Currency Libra: Why Nonprofits Are Joining," *DevEx*, updated June 24, 2019, https://www.devex.com/news/facebook-s-digital-currency-libra-why-nonprofits-are-joining-95142.

33. Dragana Kaurin, "Why Libra Needs a Humanitarian Fig Leaf," *Medium* (July 8, 2019), https://medium.com/berkman-klein-center/why-libra-needs-a-humanitarian-fig-leaf-79ae6a463c8.

34. This section summarizes research previously published in Hall, Schmitz, and Dedmon, "Transnational Advocacy and NGOs in the Digital Era."

35. Mogus and Levihn-Coon, "What Makes Nonprofit Digital Teams Successful Today?."

36. The framework and table presented in this section have been adapted from: Hall, Schmitz, and Dedmon, "Transnational Advocacy and NGOs in the Digital Era."

37. Andrew Chadwick, *The Hybrid Media System: Politics and Power* (New York: Oxford University Press, 2013), 190; Fraussen and Halpin, "How Do Interest Groups Legitimate their Policy Advocacy?," 27.

38. Sally Heaven, "How World Wildlife Fund Used Segmentation to Activate Social Influencers for Their Cause," *npEngage* (March 10, 2017), https://npengage.com/advocacy/how-world-wildlife-fund-used-segmentation-to-activate-social-influencers-for-their-cause.

39. Brandzel, *The 8-fold Path of New Organizing*.

40. Chadwick and Dennis, "Social Media, Professional Media and Mobilisation in Contemporary Britain," 56.

41. Karpf, *Analytic Activism*.

42. Becky Bond and Zach Exely, *Rules for Revolutionaries: How Big Organizing Can Change Everything* (White River Junction, VT: Chelsea Green Publishing, 2016).

43. Lisen Selander and Sirkka Jarvenpaa, "Digital Action Repertories and Transforming a Social Movement Organization," *Management Information Systems Quarterly* 40, no. 2 (2016): 346

44. Karpf, *Analytic Activism*; "Want to Fund the Resistance? Test Everything. How Greenpeace UK Went on a Mission to Test Everything and What They Learned about Process, Culture (and Engagement) along the Way," MobLab, updated May 22, 2017, https://mobilisationlab.org/stories/want-to-fund-the-resistance-test-everything-fast/.

45. See: https://www.change.org/about/business-model.

46. "Donations to GetUp are not tax-deductible. This is an important measure to ensure that GetUp's campaign and advocacy work remains independent from government," https://www.getup.org.au/about/faqs#.

47. Avaaz is registered in the United States as a 501(c)(4) social welfare organization. "Most charities offer tax deductibility for donations. But this means that they are, in a way, partially taxpayer funded, and governments use that to place a very thick set of rules on what they can and can't do. Chief among them is restricting what they can say to criticise, support, or oppose a politician. Avaaz is very rare in that our donations are not tax deductible, leaving us 100% free to say and do whatever we need to do get leaders to listen to people. Since so many important issues are won and lost in the political realm, this makes us much more effective than advocacy groups that shy away from speaking out politically." See: https://secure.avaaz.org/campaign/en/why_donate_to_avaaz.

48. Jascha Galaski, "Germany: Outdated Law Risks Strangling Civic Activism," *Liberties* (October 27, 2019) https://www.liberties.eu/en/news/germany-outdated-law-risks-strangling-civic-activism/18284.

49. Ruth McCambridge, "National Council of Nonprofits Launches Coalition Campaign to Oppose Repeal of Johnson Amendment," *Nonprofit Quarterly* (March 2, 2017) https://nonprofitquarterly.org/2017/03/02/national-coalition-nonprofits-launches-campaign-oppose-repeal-johnson-amendment/; Editors, "Losing the Johnson Amendment Would Destroy the Unique Political Role of Nonprofits," *Nonprofit Quarterly* (February 6, 2017), https://nonprofitquarterly.org/2017/02/06/losing-johnson-amendment-destroy-unique-political-role-nonprofits/.

50. Margaret E. Keck and Kathryn Sikkink, *Activists beyond Borders: Advocacy Networks in International Politics* (Ithaca, NY: Cornell University Press, 1998).

51. The framework and table presented in this section have been adapted from: Hall, Schmitz, and Dedmon, "Transnational Advocacy and NGOs in the Digital Era."

52. James Sloam, "'The Outraged Young': Toung Europeans, Civic Engagement, and the New Media in a Time of Crisis," *Information, Communication & Society* 17, no. 2 (2014); Josep-Lluis Micó and Andreu Casero-Ripollés, "Political Activism Online: Organization and Media Relations in the Case of 15M in Spain," *Information, Communication & Society* 17, no. 7 (2014); Livingston and Walter-Drop, *Bits and Atoms*.

53. Andrew Chadwick and Jennifer Stromer-Galley, "Digital Media, Power, and Democracy in Parties and Election Campaigns: Party Decline or Party Renewal?," *The International Journal of Press/Politics* 21, no. 3 (2016), https://doi.org/10.1177/1940161216646731.

54. Maria Bakardjieva, "Subactivism: Lifeworld and Politics in the Age of the Internet," *The Information Society* 25, no. 2 (2009): 103.

55. Giovanna Mascheroni, "Performing Citizenship Online: Identity, Subactivism, and Participation," *Observatorio* 7, no. 3 (2013).

56. Ralph Schroeder, *Social Theory after the Internet: Media, Technology, and Globalization* (London: UCL Press, 2018), ch. 3.

57. Jennifer Oser, Marc Hooghe, and Sofie Marien, "Is Online Participation Distinct from Offline Participation?: A Latent Class Analysis of Participation Types and Their Stratification," *Political Research Quarterly* 66, no. 1 (2013), https://doi.org/10.1177/1065912912436695.

58. Kay Lehman Schlozman, Sidney Verba, and Henry E. Brady, "Weapon of the Strong?: Participatory Inequality and the Internet," *Perspectives on Politics* 8, no. 2 (2010); Sara Vissers and Dietlind Stolle, "The Internet and New Modes of Political Participation: Online versus Offline Participation," *Information, Communication & Society* 17, no. 8 (2014).

59. Kevin Hernandez and Tony Roberts, *Leaving No One Behind in a Digital World*, K4D Emerging Issues Report (Brighton: Institute of Development Studies, 2018).

60. MobLab, *The Anatomy of People-Powered Campaigns* (Mobilisation Lab, n.d.), https://mobilisationlab.org/resources/the-anatomy-of-people-powered-campaigns.

61. See: https://greenwire.greenpeace.org/usa/en.

62. Jennifer S. Light, "Putting Our Conversation in Context: Youth, Old Media, and Political Participation 1800–1971," in *From Voice to Influence: Understanding Citizenship in a Digital Age*, ed. Jennifer S. Light and Danielle Allen (Chicago: University of Chicago Press, 2015).

63. Joel Penney, "Social Media and Symbolic Action: Exploring Participation in the Facebook Red Equal Sign Profile Picture Campaign," *Journal of Computer-Mediated Communication* 20, no. 1 (2015).

64. Jeremy Heimans and Henry Timms, *New Power: How Power Works in Our Hyperconnected World* (New York: Doubleday, 2018).

65. Shelley Boulianne, "Social Media Use and Participation: A Meta-Analysis of Current Research," *Information, Communication & Society* 18, no. 5 (2015).

66. Sebastián Valenzuela, "Unpacking the Use of Social Media for Protest Behavior: The Roles of Information, Opinion Expression, and Activism," *American Behavioral Scientist* 57, no. 7 (2013).

67. Francis Lee and Joseph Man Chan, "Digital Media Activities and Mode of Participation in a Protest Campaign: A Study of the Umbrella Movement," *Information, Communication & Society* 19, no. 1 (2016).

68. Oser, Hooghe, and Marien, "Is Online Participation Distinct from Offline Participation?"

69. Divya Titus, "Social Media as a Gateway for Young Feminists: Lessons from the #IWillGoOut Campaign in India," *Gender & Development* 26, no. 2 (2018), https://doi.org/10.1080/13552074.2018.1473224.

70. "What evidence we do have about social media platforms suggests that the most active political users are social movement activists, politicians, party workers and those who are already fully committed to political causes." Brian D. Loader and Dan Mercea, "Networking Democracy?: Social Media Innovations and Participatory Politics," *Information, Communication & Society* 14, no. 6 (2011): 761.

71. See: https://guide.change.org. Digital organizations are not the only groups providing such information. Advocacy toolkits have been made available by TNGOs for a few decades, typically on their websites.

72. G. Albert Ruesga and Barry Knight, "The View from the Heights of Arnstein's Ladder: Resident Engagement by Community Foundations," *National Civic Review* 102, no. 3 (2013).

73. Mogus and Levihn-Coon, "What Makes Nonprofit Digital Teams Successful Today?"

74. Michael Silberman, cited in: Hestres, "Climate Change Advocacy Online," 206.

75. Karpf, *Analytic Activism.*

76. Karpf, *Analytic Activism.*

77. Sadie Hale and Erin Niimi Longhurst, *Make It Social: Tips & Tricks for #SocialMedia Success* (London: Social Misfits Media, 2019).

78. Michael Silberman and Jackie Mahendra, "Moving beyond Vanity Metrics," *Stanford Social Innovation Review* (2015).

79. Kohavi and Thomke, "The Surprising Power of Online Experiments."

80. For a resource about combating disinformation generally, see: Sarah Oh and Travis L. Adkins, *Disinformation Toolki,* (Washington, DC: InterAction, 2018).

81. Personal communications with board members of the Public Interest Registry (PIR), which administers the .org and .ngo domains under a contract with ICANN, the global governance body for the Internet.

CHAPTER 7

1. Center for Global Development, *When Will We Ever Learn?: Improving Lives through Impact Evaluation* (Washington, DC: Center for Global Development, 2006).

2. See: https://www.3ieimpact.org.

3. World Bank, *World Development Report* (Washington, DC: The World Bank, 2016); Organisation for Economic Co-operation and Development, *Measuring and Managing Results in Development Cooperation: A Review of Challenges and Practices among DAC Members and Observers* (Paris: OECD, 2014).

4. For a discussion of what an impact-oriented architecture might look like, see: George E. Mitchell, "Creating a Philanthropic Marketplace through Accounting, Disclosure, and Intermediation," *Public Performance and Management Review* 38, no. 1 (2014).

5. For example, the International Rescue Committee adopts such an approach; International Rescue Committee, *Research at the International Rescue Committee: Top Insights from 2018, What to Watch for in 2019* (New York: International Rescue Committee, 2019), https://www.rescue.org/report/ircs-top-research-findings-2018-and-2019.

6. Interviews with CEOs and measurement and evaluation staff in InterAction member organizations, December 2017–March 2018, as part of a consultancy jointly undertaken by Mary Kay Gugerty of the University of Washington and George Mitchell to inform InterAction impact measurement standards.

7. Also see: Curtis Child and Eva M. Witesman, "Optimism and Bias When Evaluating a Prosocial Initiative," *Social Science Quarterly* (2019), https://doi.org/10.1111/ssqu.12585.

8. George E. Mitchell and David Berlan, "Evaluation in Nonprofit Organizations: An Empirical Analysis," *Public Performance and Management Review* 41, no. 2 (2018), https://doi.org/10.1080/15309576.2017.1400985; George E. Mitchell and David Berlan, "Evaluation and Evaluative Rigor in the Nonprofit Sector," *Nonprofit Management & Leadership* 27, no. 2 (2016), https://doi.org/10.1002/nml.21236; George E. Mitchell, "*Why* Will We Ever Learn?: Measurement and Evaluation in

International Development NGOs," *Public Performance and Management Review* 37, no. 4 (2014).

9. Extended time series evaluations that aim to assess the long-term sustainability of program effects are also relatively uncommon.

10. Impact measurement requires a comparison between a factual condition, which describes what actually happened in the presence of the program, and a counterfactual condition, which speculates about what would have happened in the absence of the program; George E. Mitchell, "Accounting for Outcomes: Monitoring and Evaluation in the Transnational NGO Sector," in *In Leading and Managing in the Social Sector: Strategies for Advancing Human Dignity and Social Justice*, ed. Aqeel Tirmizi and John Vogelsang (New York: Springer, 2017).

11. Naeve, Katie, Julia Fischer-Mackey, Jyotsna Puri, Raag Bhatia, and Rosaine N. Yegbemey. *Evaluating Advocacy: An Exploration of Evidence and Tools to Understand What Works and Why*. 3ie Working Paper 29. (New Delhi: International Initiative for Impact Evaluation, 2017). https:// www.3ieimpact.org/evidence-hub/publications/working-papers/ evaluating-advocacy-exploration-evidence-and-tools.

12. Neil MacDonald and Nigel Simister, *Outcome Mapping* (Oxford: INTRAC, 2015); Sarah Earl, Fred Carden, and Terry Smutylo, *Outcome Mapping: Building Learning and Reflection into Development Programs* (Ottawa: International Development Research Centre, 2001).

13. Nigel Simister and Allison Napier, *Outcome Harvesting* (Oxford: INTRAC, 2017); Ricardo Wilson-Grau and Heather Britt, *Outcome Harvesting* (Cairo: Ford Foundation, 2012).

14. Jim Coe and Rhonda Schlangen, *No Royal Road: Finding and Following the Natural Pathways in Advocacy Evaluation* Center for Evaluation Innovation (2019), https://www.evaluationinnovation.org/wp-content/uploads/2019/03/ No-Royal-Road.pdf.

15. For example, one approach claims that in "more transformative advocacy" efforts "concepts of measurable outcomes (beyond the short term) and definable contribution break down." See: Coe and Schlangen, *No Royal Road*, 48.

16. For example, see: Naeve, Katie, Julia Fischer-Mackey, Jyotsna Puri, Raag Bhatia, and Rosaine N. Yegbemey. *Evaluating Advocacy: An Exploration of Evidence and Tools to Understand What Works and Why*. 3ie Working Paper 29. (New Delhi: International Initiative for Impact Evaluation, 2017). https://www.3ieimpact.org/evidence-hub/publications/working-papers/ evaluating-advocacy-exploration-evidence-and-tools; Annette L. Gardner and Claire D. Brindis, *Advocacy and Policy Change Evaluation: Theory and Practice* (Stanford: Stanford Business Books, 2017).

17. Mitchell and Berlan, "Evaluation and Evaluative Rigor in the Nonprofit Sector."

18. Laura Quinn, "In Search of Better Data about Nonprofits' Programs," in *Markets for Good* (Bill & Melinda Gates Foundation, 2013); Johanna Morariu, Katherine Athanasiades, and Ann Emery, *State of Evaluation 2012: Evaluation Practice and Capacity in the Nonprofit Sector* (Washington, DC: Innovation Network, 2012).

19. Mitchell and Berlan, "Evaluation and Evaluative Rigor in the Nonprofit Sector."

20. Richard Hoefer, "Accountability in Action?: Program Evaluation in Nonprofit Human Service Agencies," *Nonprofit Management and Leadership* 11, no. 2 (2000).

21. Quinn, "In Search of Better Data about Nonprofits' Programs."

22. Doug Easterling, "Using Outcome Evaluation to Guide Grantmaking: Theory, Reality, and Possibilities," *Nonprofit and Voluntary Sector Quarterly* 29, no. 3 (2000).

23. Joanne G. Carman and Kimberly A. Fredericks, "Evaluation Capacity and Nonprofit Organizations: Is the Glass Half-Empty or Half-Full?," *American Journal of Evaluation* 31, no. 1 (2010).

24. Sarah Carnochan et al., "Performance Measurement Challenges in Nonprofit Human Service Organizations," *Nonprofit and Voluntary Sector Quarterly* 43, no. 6 (2013), https://doi.org/10.1177/0899764013508009; Morariu, Athanasiades, and Emery, *State of Evaluation 2012*; Hoefer, "Accountability in Action?"

25. Carman and Fredericks, "Evaluation Capacity and Nonprofit Organizations"; Easterling, "Using Outcome Evaluation to Guide Grantmaking"; Mitchell and Berlan, "Evaluation and Evaluative Rigor in the Nonprofit Sector."

26. Cathy Shutt and Rosie McGee, *Improving the Evaluability of INGO Empowerment and Accountability Programmes* (Brighton, UK: Centre for Development Impact, 2013).

27. Joanne G. Carman, "Nonprofits, Funders, and Evaluation: Accountability in Action," *The American Review of Public Administration* 39, no. 4 (2009).

28. Kyle Andrei et al., *The State of Nonprofit Data* (Portland, OR: NTEN, November 2012).

29. Phil Buchanan, "Which Data? And Who Will Pay for It?," in *Markets for Good: Selected Readings: Making Sense of Data and Information in the Social Sector* (2014), https://digitalimpact.io/wordpress/wp-content/uploads/2014/01/Markets-for-Good-Selected-Readings-eBook.pdf.

30. Carnochan et al., "Performance Measurement Challenges in Nonprofit Human Service Organizations."

31. World Bank, *World Development Report*; OECD, *Measuring and Managing Results in Development Cooperation*.

32. Gustavo Gordillo and Krister Andersson, "From Policy Lessons to Policy Actions: Motivation to Take Evaluation Seriously," *Public Administration and Development* 24 (2004); Ken S. Cavalluzzo and Christopher D. Ittner, "Implementing Performance Measurement Innovations: Evidence from Government," *Accounting, Organizations, and Society* 29, no. ¾ (2004); Juan L. Gandia, "Internet Disclosure by Nonprofit Organizations: Empirical Evidence of Nongovernmental Organizations for Development in Spain," *Nonprofit and Voluntary Sector Quarterly* 40, no. 1 (2011); Malin Arvidson and Fergus Lyon, "Social Impact Measurement and Non-profit Organisations: Compliance, Resistance, and Promotion," *Voluntas* (2013), https://doi.org/10.1007/s11266-013-9373-6.

33. Martin Sjöstedt, "Aid Effectiveness and the Paris Declaration: A Mismatch between Ownership and Results-Based Management?," *Public Administration and Development* 33 (2013).

34. Alnoor Ebrahim, *NGOs and Organizational Change: Discourse, Reporting, and Learning* (New York: Cambridge University Press, 2005); Hans-Martin Jaeger, "'Global Civil Society' and the Political Depoliticization of Global Governance," *International Political Sociology* 1 (2007); Susan M. Roberts, John Paul Jones III, and Oliver Frohling, "NGOs and the Globalization of Managerialism: A Research Framework," *World Development* 33, no. 11 (2005).

35. Vic Murray and Bill Tassie, "Evaluating the Effectiveness of Nonprofit Organizations," in *The Jossey-Bass Handbook of Nonprofit Leadership and*

Management, ed. Robert D. Herman and Associates (San Francisco: Jossey-Bass, 1994); Rosalind Eyben, *Uncovering the Politics of 'Evidence' and 'Results': A Framing Paper for Development Practitioners*, The Big Push Forward (2013), http://bigpushforward.net/wp-content/uploads/2011/01/The-politics-of-evidence-11-April-20133.pdf.

36. Mitchell and Berlan, "Evaluation in Nonprofit Organizations."

37. Mitchell and Berlan, "Evaluation and Evaluative Rigor in the Nonprofit Sector"; Mitchell and Berlan, "Evaluation in Nonprofit Organizations."

38. e.g. Howard White, "Theory-Based Impact Evaluation: Principles and Practice," (New Delhi: International Initiative for Impact Evaluation, 2009); Harry P. Hatry, *Performance Measurement: Getting Results*, 2nd ed. (Washington, DC: Urban Institute Press, 2007); Grantmakers for Effective Organizations, *Four Essentials for Evaluation* (Washington, DC: GEO, 2012); Peter J. York, *Learning as We Go: Making Evaluation Work for Everyone* Group (New York: TCC, 2003); Robert M. Penna, *The Nonprofit Outcomes Toolbox* (Hoboken, NJ: John Wiley & Sons, 2011); InterAction, *Introduction to Impact Evaluation* (2011); Mario Morino, *Leap of Reason: Managing to Outcomes in an Era of Scarcity* (Washington, DC: Venture Philanthropy Partners, 2011); Burt Perrin, *Linking Monitoring and Evaluation to Impact Evaluation* (Washington, DC: InterAction/Rockefeller Foundation, 2012); Elliot Stern et al., *Broadening the Range of Designs and Methods for Impact Evaluation* (London: Department for International Development, 2012); Chris Roche and Linda Kelly, *The Evaluation of Politics and the Politics of Evaluation*, (Birmingham, UK: Developmental Leadership Program, 2012).

39. Mitchell, "Accounting for Outcomes."

40. This section is based on a white paper summarizing experiences about adopting agency-level measurements across several TNGOs. Participating organizations were American Jewish Joint Distribution Committee, CARE, Catholic Relief Services, Childfund International, International Rescue Committee, JPIEGO, Lutheran World Services, Management Sciences for Health, Mercy Corps, PATH, Save the Children, and World Vision International. See: Carlisle J. Levine, Tosca Bruno van-Vijfeijken, and Sherine Jayawickrama, *Measuring International NGO Agency-Level Results*, InterAction (May 2016), https://www.interaction.org/sites/default/files/ALR_WhitePaper_FINAL_0.pdf.

41. Tosca Bruno-van Vijfeijken et al., *Rights-Based Approach to Development: Learning from Guatemala* (Syracuse, NY: Moynihan Institute of Global Affairs, 2010).

42. Neil Dillon and Amelie Sundberg, *Back to the Drawing Board: How to Improve Monitoring of Outcomes* (London: ODI/ALNAP, 2019).

43. Robert D. Behn, "The Psychological Barriers to Performance Management: Or Why Isn't Everyone Jumping on the Performance-Management Bandwagon?," *Public Performance & Management Review* 26, no. 1 (2002).

44. Ben Ramalingam, Leni Wild, and Anne L. Buffardi, *Making Adaptive Rigour Work: Principles and Practices for Strengthening Monitoring, Evaluation and Learning for Adaptive Management* (London: ALNAP, 2019).

45. For more information, see: Carlisle J. Levine, Tosca Bruno van-Vijfeijken, and Sherine Jayawickrama, *Measuring International NGO Agency-Level Results*, InterAction (May 2016), https://www.interaction.org/sites/default/files/ALR_WhitePaper_FINAL_0.pdf.

46. Information for this case was drawn from an interview with Kerry Bruce, senior director for Global Health and Measurement at Pact, by George Mitchell, on July 24, 2014, and related materials she provided to the authors.

47. Senior evaluators in peer TNGOs have voiced serious reservations about the meaningfulness of global reach indicators such as beneficiary counts. Over and beyond significant methodological concerns (double counting, level of aggregation, etc.), reach measures generally do not account for service quality, the magnitude of change, and sustainability.

48. Pact, *Measuring Pact's Mission 2018*, Pact (2018), https://www.pactworld.org/sites/default/files/Pact%20MPM%202018_WEB.pdf. Also see: https://www.pactworld.org/our-results.

49. This case is principally based on an interview with Barbara Willett, director of monitoring, evaluation, and learning at Mercy Corps by George Mitchell, on August 6, 2014, and related materials provided to the authors.

50. Mercy Corps, *Mission Metrics 2013 Report* (Portland, OR: Mercy Corps, 2013), http://www.mercycorps.org/sites/default/files/Mission%20Metrics%202013%20Report.pdf.

51. The system was developed on the impetus of board member Alan Grossman from Harvard's Kennedy School, based on the scorecard method. However, it never was able to inform strategic decision making at that level the way it was meant to do.

52. This case is principally based on an interview with Jeannie Annan, director of research and evaluation at the International Rescue Committee by George Mitchell, on October 27, 2014, and related materials provided to the authors.

53. For example, see: IRC, *Research at the International Rescue Committee: List of Projects by Outcome* (New York: International Rescue Committee, 2018), https://www.rescue.org/sites/default/files/document/2655/researchprojectlist5172018.pdf.

54. Interview with Jeannie Annan, director of research and evaluation at the International Rescue Committee by George Mitchell, on October 27, 2014.

55. Interview with Jeannie Annan.

56. James Crowley and Morgana Ryan, *Building a Better International NGO: Greater Than the Sum of the Parts* (Boulder, CO: Kumarian Press, 2013); James Crowley and Morgana Ryan, *Navigating Change for International NGOs: A Practical Handbook* (Boulder, CO: Kumarian Press, 2017).

57. Peter Singer, *The Most Good You Can Do: How Effective Altruism Is Changing Ideas about Living Ethically* (New Haven, CT: Yale University Press, 2017); William MacAskill, "Effective Altruism: An Introduction," *Essays in Philosophy* 18, no. 1 (2017); William MacAskill, *Doing Good Better: How Effective Altruism Can Help You Help Others, Do Work That Matters, and Make Smarter Choices about Giving Back* (New York: Avery, 2016).

58. Paul Brest, "Strategic Philanthropy and Its Discontents," *Stanford Social Innovation Review* (April 27, 2015), https://ssir.org/up_for_debate/article/strategic_philanthropy_and_its_discontents.

59. Paul Brest, "A Decade of Outcome-Oriented Philanthropy," *Stanford Social Innovation Review* (2012), http://www.ssireview.org/articles/entry/a_decade_of_outcome_oriented_philanthropy; Fay Twersky and Lori Grange, *A Practical Guide to Outcome-Focused Philanthropy* (Menlo Park, CA: Hewlett Foundation, 2016), https://hewlett.org/wp-content/uploads/2017/05/OFP-Guidebook-updated.pdf.

60. Arthur "Buzz" Schmidt, "Divining a Vision for Markets for Good," in *Selected Readings: Making Sense of Data and Information in the Social Sector*, ed. Eric J. Henderson (Stanford, CA: Markets for Good, 2014), https://digitalimpact.io/wordpress/wp-content/uploads/2014/01/Markets-for-Good-Selected-Readings-eBook.pdf.

61. Michael M. Weinstein and Ralph M. Bradburd, *The Robin Hood Rules for Smart Giving* (New York: Columbia University Press, 2013).

62. Valerie Bartlett et al., eds., *What Matters: Investing in Results to Build Strong, Vibrant Communities* (New York: Federal Reserve Bank of San Francisco and Nonprofit Finance Fund, 2017).

63. Bond and Itad, *Value for Money: What It Means for UK NGOs*, (London: Bond, 2012).

64. "International Rescue Committee," 2019, accessed July 10, 2019, https://www.rescue.org/. "Mercy Corps," 2019, accessed July 10, 2019, https://www.mercycorps.org/.

65. 2019, accessed July 10, 2019, https://www.pactworld.org/.

66. For examples and further discussion, see: George E. Mitchell and Thad D. Calabrese, "Proverbs of Nonprofit Financial Management," *American Review of Public Administration* 49, no. 6 (2019), https://doi.org/10.1177/0275074018770458; George E. Mitchell, "Modalities of Managerialism: The 'Double Bind' of Normative and Instrumental Nonprofit Managerial Imperatives," *Administration & Society* 50, no. 7 (2018), https://doi.org/10.1177/0095399716664832; George E. Mitchell, "Fiscal Leanness and Fiscal Responsiveness: Exploring the Normative Limits of Strategic Nonprofit Financial Management," *Administration & Society* 49, no. 9 (2017), https://doi.org/10.1177/0095399715581035.

67. Mitchell, "Modalities of Managerialism."

68. Mary Kay Gugerty and Dean Karlan, "Ten Reasons Not to Measure Impact—And What to Do Instead," *Stanford Social Innovation Review* (Summer 2018). Also see: Mary Kay Gugerty and Dean Karlan, *The Goldilocks Challenge: Right-Fit Evidence for the Social Sector* (New York: Oxford University Press, 2018).

69. Alnoor Ebrahim and V. Kasturi Rangan, "What Impact?: A Framework for Measuring the Scale and Scope of Social Performance," *California Management Review* 56, no. 3 (2014).

70. Gugerty and Karlan, "Ten Reasons Not to Measure Impact-and What to Do Instead." Also see: Gugerty and Karlan, *The Goldilocks Challenge*.

CHAPTER 8

1. Colette Chabbott, "Development INGOs," in *Constructing World Culture*, ed. John Boli and George M. Thomas (Stanford: Stanford University Press, 1999).

2. Nicola Banks, David Hulme, and Michael Edwards, "NGOs, States, and Donors Revisited: Still Too Close for Comfort?," *World Development* 66 (2014); M. Robinson, "Privatising the Voluntary Sector: NGOs as Public Service Contractors," in *NGOs, States, and Donors: Too Close for Comfort?*, ed. D. Hulme and M. Edwards (London: Macmillan, 1997); Michael Edwards and David Hulme, "Too Close for Comfort?: The Impact of Official Aid on Nongovernmental Organizations," *World Development* 24, no. 6 (1996).

3. Andy Sumner, *The New Bottom Billion: What If Most of the World's Poor Live in Middle-Income Countries?* (London: Center for Global Development, 2011).

4. Duncan Green, *Fit for the Future?: Development Trends and the Role of International NGOs* (Oxford: Oxfam GB, 2015).

5. Paul J. Nelson and Ellen Dorsey, "At the Nexus of Human Rights and Development: New Methods and Strategies of Global NGOs," *World Development* 31, no. 12 (2003).

6. Siri Eriksen et al., "Courting Catastrophe?: Humanitarian Policy and Practice in a Changing Climate," *IDS Bulletin* 48, no. 4 (2017).

7. Sam Worthington and Alexander Grashow, *NGO Board Reckoning* (Washington, DC: InterAction and Good Wolf Group, 2018).

8. Interview with Nisha Agrawal, CEO, Oxfam India, by Tosca Bruno-van Vijfeijken, November 20, 2013.

9. This section is substantially based on personal correspondence between Barney Tallack (former director of strategy, Oxfam International) and the authors.

10. INTRAC is a global capacity-building nonprofit serving as a convener and providing research on best practices.

11. See: Oxfam, *Oxfam Purpose and Beliefs* (Brussels: Oxfam International, March 24, 2011), https://www.oxfam.org/sites/www.oxfam.org/files/oxfam-purpose-and-beliefs-mar-2011.pdf.

12. Emma Crewe, "Flagships and Tumbleweed: A History of the Politics of Gender Justice Work in Oxfam GB 1986–2015," *Progress in Development Studies* 18, no. 2 (2018), https://doi.org/10.1177/1464993417750286.

13. ICSC, "Power Shift and Governance Reform: Towards More Legitimate and Effective Global Governance," news release, 2018, https://icscentre.org/wp-content/uploads/2018/05/CONCEPT-Power-Shift-and-Governance-Reform_footer-updated.pdf.

14. Steven J. Lux and Tosca Bruno-van Vijfeijken, *From Alliance to International: The Global Transformation of Save the Children* (Syracuse, NY: Maxwell School of Citizenship and Public Affairs, 2012); Burkhard Gnärig and Charles F. Maccormack, "The Challenges of Globalization: Save the Children," *Nonprofit and Voluntary Sector Quarterly* 28, no. 1 suppl. (1999), https://doi.org/10.1177/089976499773746483.

15. Stephen Cook, "Analysis: Merlin and Save the Children," *Third Sector* (July 30, 2013), https://www.thirdsector.co.uk/analysis-merlin-save-children/governance/article/1193125.

16. Barney Tallack, "How We Developed the Last Oxfam Strategic Plan" (Paper Presented at the Maxwell School of Citizenship and Public Affairs, Syracuse, NY, 2017).

17. L. David Brown, Alnoor Ebrahim, and Srilatha Batliwala, "Governing International Advocacy NGOs," *World Development* 40, no. 6 (2012): 1101

18. Wendy H. Wong, *Internal Affairs: How the Structure of NGOs Transforms Human Rights* (Ithaca, NY: Cornell University Press, 2012).

19. Sherine S. Jayawickrama, *Oxfam International: Moving Toward "One Oxfam,"* (Cambridge, MA: Center for Public Leadership/Harvard Kennedy School, 2012).

20. Interview with Colm O'Cuanachain, senior director, Office of the Secretary-General, Amnesty International, by Tosca Bruno-van Vijfeijken, April 26, 2014.

21. James Crowley and Morgana Ryan, *Building a Better International NGO: Greater Than the Sum of the Parts* (Boulder, CO: Kumarian Press, 2013).

22. Presentation provided by Barney Tallack, Transnational NGO Initiative, Syracuse University, February–March 2017.

23. On the other hand, in those TNGOs that consist of loose networks, members may seek to protect their decision rights and autonomy zealously by making sure their boards and assemblies consist of member representatives only (i.e., not allowing for independent board members from outside membership).

24. Jayawickrama, *Oxfam International*.

25. Interview with Nisha Agrawal, CEO, Oxfam India, by Tosca Bruno-van Vijfeijken, November 20, 2013. See: https://www.youtube.com/watch?v=15z2-MPDzPg.

26. Most large NGO families use the terms "member" and "affiliate" with interchangeable meaning. For example, some NGOs such as Oxfam and ActionAid prefer the term affiliate, while others such as Save the Children and CARE prefer the term member. As part of their change processes and ambitions to gain more Global South members, some have installed two-tier membership models, with a lower level of membership for incoming affiliates or members that are still developing their capacity and a higher level of membership for full affiliates or members that have a voice in governance. In some cases, such as in ActionAid, for example, the lower level of membership is called "associate" while the full member is called "affiliate."

27. Internal communications within Amnesty International observed by Tosca Bruno-van Vijfeijken, February 2017.

28. Brown, Ebrahim, and Batliwala, "Governing International Advocacy NGOs"; Jonathan G. S. Koppell, "Pathologies of Accountability: ICANN and the Challenge of 'Multiple Accountabilities Disorder'," *Public Administration Review* 65, no. 1 (2005), https://doi.org/10.1111/j.1540-6210.2005.00434.x; Alnoor Ebrahim, "The Many Faces of Nonprofit Accountability," in *The Jossey-Bass Handbook of Nonprofit Leadership and Management*, ed. David O. Renz (San Francisco: Jossey-Bass, 2010); Cristina M. Balboa, *The Paradox of Scale: How NGOs Build, Maintain, and Lose Authority in Environmental Governance* (Cambridge, MA: MIT Press, 2018).

29. Brown, Ebrahim, and Batliwala, "Governing International Advocacy NGOs."

30. Interview with Emeritus Professor Alan Fowler, Erasmus University Rotterdam, by Tosca Bruno-van Vijfeijken, December 19, 2013.

31. Wolfgang Jamann, "Digital Leadership in the International Civil Society Sector," *Disrupt & Innovate* (April 24, 2018), https://icscentre.org/2018/04/24/digital-leadership-in-the-international-civil-society-sector/.

32. See: https://consultations.worldbank.org/?map=1.

33. ActionAid International, *ActionAid International Annual Report to INGO Accountability Charter 2015* (Johannesburg: ActionAid International, 2017).

34. These voices include Burkhard Gnärig, the co-founder of the International Civil Society Centre based in Berlin. See: Daniela Costa et al., *Taking a Strategic Approach to Governance Reform in International Civil Society Organisations* (Berlin: International Civil Society Center, 2012).

35. ActionAid International, *Good Practices for ActionAid International Governance* (Johannesburg: ActionAid International, 2014).

36. Interview with Ingrid Srinath, CEO of Hivos India Advisory Services and former secretary-general of CIVICUS, by Tosca Bruno-van Vijfeijken, April 14, 2014.

37. Michael Theis and Jimena Faz Garza, "White Men Still Dominate CEO Offices at Big Charities," *The Chronicle of Philanthropy* (September 4, 2019), https://www.philanthropy.com/article/White-Men-Still-Dominate-CEO/247039?cid=pt&source=ams&sourceId=4723264.

38. Fairouz El Tom, "Diversity and Inclusion on NGO Boards: What the Stats Say," *The Guardian* (May 7, 2013), https://www.theguardian.com/global-development-professionals-network/2013/apr/29/diversity-inclusion-ngo-board.

39. In the business sector, diversity has arguably been recognized longer as a key asset and condition for success. See: Vivian Hunt et al., *Delivering through Diversity* (New York: McKinsey & Company, 2018).

40. Crowley and Ryan, *Building a Better International NGO*.

41. As reported by participants of the INGO Learning Group on Organizational Change: Marcy Vigoda, CARE; Simon Miller, World Vision International; Anil

Pant, Amnesty International; Pauline Martin, ActionAid; Barney Tallack and Franc Cortada, Oxfam International; facilitated by Philip Horgan, Oxfam International, Tosca Bruno-van Vijfeijken, Syracuse University, June 11, 2012.

42. Interview with Marcy Vigoda, deputy secretary general, CARE International, by Tosca Bruno-van Vijfeijken. April 25, 2013.

43. Richard P. Chait, William P. Ryan, and Barbar E. Taylor, *Governance as Leadership: Reframing the Work of Nonprofit Boards* (Hoboken, NJ: Wiley, 2005).

44. Personal communications between Stanley Arumugam, head of governance, leadership, and accountability at ActionAid (until 2017) and Tosca Bruno-van Vijfeijken.

45. Worthington and Grashow, *NGO Board Reckoning*.

46. Advocates for "community engagement governance" call for boards to more directly share governance decision-making with other constituents. Judy Freiwirth, "Community-Engagement Governance: Systems-Wide Governance in Action," *Nonprofit Quarterly* (May 9, 2011), https://nonprofitquarterly.org/community-engagement-governance-systems-wide-governance-in-action.

47. Long Tran, "International NGO Centralization and Leader-Perceived Effectiveness," *Nonprofit and Voluntary Sector Quarterly* (2019), https://doi.org/10.1177/0899764019861741.

48. Lee G. Bolman and Terrence E. Deal, *Reframing Organizations: Artistry, Choice, and Leadership*, 6th ed. (San Francisco: Jossey-Bass, 2017).

49. Jeri Eckhart Queenan, Jacob Allen, and Jari Tuomala, *Stop Starving Scale: Unlocking the Potential of Global NGOs*, The Bridgespan Group (April 2013), https://www.bridgespan.org/bridgespan/Images/articles/stop-starving-scale-unlocking-the-potential/stopstarvingscale-unlockingthepotentialofglobalngos.pdf.

50. This "tax" may range from 2.5 percent to 8 percent of annual income and covers shared spending on global coordination, branding, and other expenses.

51. Barney Tallack, *INGO Typologies and Organizational Forms* (2018).

52. For an assessment of TNGO accountability practices, see: Hans Peter Schmitz, Paloma Raggo, and Tosca Bruno-van Vijfeijken, "Accountability of Transnational NGOs: Aspirations vs. Practice," *Nonprofit and Voluntary Sector Quarterly* 41, no. 6 (2012), https://doi.org/10.1177/0899764011431165.

CHAPTER 9

1. Personal communication between Burkhard Gnärig, executive director of International Civil Society Centre, and Tosca Bruno-van Vijfeijken.

2. Adrian Sargeant and Harriet Day, *The Wake Up Call. A Study of Nonprofit Leadership in the US and Its Impending Crisis* (Plymouth, UK: Philanthropy Centre, 2018).

3. Florentine Maier, Michael Meyer, and Martin Steinbereithner, "Nonprofit Organizations Becoming Business-Like: A Systematic Review," *Nonprofit and Voluntary Sector Quarterly* 45, no. 1 (2016).

4. Dhananjayan Sriskandarajah, "NGOs Losing the War against Poverty and Climate Change, Says Civicus Head: Charities Are No Longer Drivers of Social Change; for Many Saving the World Has Become Big Business. How Did We Lose Our Way?," *The Guardian* (London) (August 11, 2014); James Crowley and Morgana Ryan, *Building a Better International NGO: Greater Than the Sum of the Parts* (Boulder, CO: Kumarian Press, 2013).

5. Interview with Ramesh Singh, COO, Greenpeace, by Tosca Bruno-van Vijfeijken, November 4, 2014. In the TNGO Initiative's senior leadership training programs offered since 2011, participants have indicated that successful leadership

development in the sector needs to bring in corporate sector experiences, but adapt them explicitly for the values in the government and TNGO sectors.

6. George E. Mitchell and Hans Peter Schmitz, "The Nexus of Public and Nonprofit Management," *Public Performance & Management Review* 42, no. 1 (2019), https://doi.org/10.1080/15309576.2018.1489293.

7. Benjamin E. Hermalin, "At the Helm, Kirk or Spock?: The Pros and Cons of Charismatic Leadership" (Berkeley: University of California, Berkeley, 2014).

8. These observations are based on practitioner engagement through the Transnational NGO Initiative, especially through the Leadership Institute over the course of the past several years and customized leadership trainings with several prominent TNGOs. See the Note on Sources for more detail.

9. Ruth Mayne et al., "Using Evidence to Influence Policy: Oxfam's Experience," *Palgrave Communications* 4, no. 1 (2018), https://doi.org/10.1057/s41599-018-0176-7.

10. In the TNGO Initiative's senior leadership training programs offered since 2011, negotiation exercises regularly revealed that TNGO leaders tend to remain in persuasion mode, focused on pushing positions, with insufficient attention to unearthing interests—and all of this despite their espoused collaborative approaches. This focus on persuasion is ineffective in situations where power is shared, such as within a coalition or alliance. Furthermore, it prevents the TNGO collective from moving quickly to any agreement to accomplish the task at hand. Position-based compromise is more difficult to alter and TNGOs lose the capacity to quickly adapt to changing circumstances.

11. Excerpt from a blogpost by James Whitehead, global innovation advisor, Oxfam GB, as part of an invitation-only discussion forum led by the International Civil Society Centre, February 15, 2015.

12. For a review of the broader literature, see: George B. Graen and Mary Uhl-Bien, "Relationship-Based Approach to Leadership: Development of Leader-Member Exchange (LMX) Theory of Leadership over 25 Years: Applying a Multi-Level Multi-Domain Perspective," *The Leadership Quarterly* 6, no. 2 (1995).

13. Private proceedings of the task force of the 2017 International Civil Society Centre (ICSC) Task Force on Culture Change.

14. Internal documents related to the Global Transition Program, Amnesty International; also, see: "Moving Amnesty Closer to the Ground Is Necessary, Not Simple," openDemocracy, updated January 20, 2015, https://www.opendemocracy.net/openglobalrights/salil-shetty/moving-amnesty-closer-to-ground-is-necessary-not-simple.

15. For a broader discussion, see: David A. Thomas and Robin J. Ely, "Making Differences Matter: A New Paradigm for Managing Diversity," *Harvard Business Review* 74, no. 5 (1996).

16. Jeri Eckhart Queenan, Jacob Allen, and Jari Tuomala, *Stop Starving Scale: Unlocking the Potential of Global NGOs*, The Bridgespan Group (April 2013), https://www.bridgespan.org/bridgespan/Images/articles/stop-starving-scale-unlocking-the-potential/stopstarvingscale-unlockingthepotentialofglobalngos.pdf.

17. John P. Kotter, *Leading Change* (Boston: Harvard Business Press, 2012).

18. Steven Lux, Shreeya Neupane, and Tosca Bruno-van Vijfeijken, *External Assessment of CARE 2020: Change Process and Progress* (Syracuse: Moynihan Institute of Global Affairs, 2016).

19. INGO Learning Network on Leading and Managing Organizational Change, 2012–2016. Members of this learning group were TNGO practitioners from

organizations including Oxfam, Amnesty International, HelpAge, CARE International, ActionAid International, Save the Children International, Islamic Relief, WaterAid, World Vision, and World Wildlife Fund, among others.

20. James Crowley and Morgana Ryan, *Navigating Change for International NGOs: A Practical Handbook* (Boulder, CO: Kumarian Press, 2017).

21. Tricia S. Cabrey, Amy Haughey, and Terry Cooke-Davies, *Enabling Organizational Change through Strategic Initiatives* (Newtown Square, PA: Project Management Institute, 2014). The Center for Creative Leadership's research on change in the private sector also points to similar findings, as does Daryl Conner in his work as part of the Conner Academy on Leading Change.

22. Interview with Emeritus Professor Alan Fowler, Erasmus University Rotterdam, by Tosca Bruno-van Vijfeijken, January 16, 2014.

23. Libbie Landles-Cobb, Kirk Kramer, and Katie Smith Milway, "The Nonprofit Leadership Development Deficit," *Stanford Social Innovation Review* (October 25, 2015), https://ssir.org/articles/entry/the_nonprofit_leadership_development_deficit.

24. Ira Hirshfield, "Investing in Leadership to Accelerate Philanthropic Impact," *Stanford Social Innovation Review* (2014), https://ssir.org/articles/entry/investing_in_leadership_to_accelerate_philanthropic_impact; Monisha Kapila, "The Business Case for Investing in Talent," *Stanford Social Innovation Review* (May 7, 2014), http://www.ssireview.org/talent_matters/entry/the_business_case_for_investing_in_talent.

25. Interview with Burkhard Gnärig, founder, International Civil Society Centre, by Tosca Bruno-van Vijfeijken, August 1, 2013.

26. For an overview on how political psychology has developed scientific methods for assessing leadership traits "at a distance"; Margaret G. Hermann, "Assessing Leadership Style: Trait Analysis," in *The Psychological Assessment of Political Leaders*, ed. Jerrold Post (Ann Arbor: University of Michigan Press, 2003).

27. Fred E. Fiedler, "The Contingency Model and the Dynamics of the Leadership Process," in *Advances in Experimental Social Psychology*, ed. Leonard Berkowitz (London: Academic Press, 1978); John Storey, ed., *Leadership in Organizations: Current Issues and Key Trends* (London: Routledge, 2016).

28. Christiane Pagé, "To Challenge or Respect Constraints?: Leadership Style's Noticeable Effect on NGO Impact," *Monday Developments* (2011), 23.

29. Pagé, "To Challenge or Respect Constraints?," 24.

30. Hermann,"Assessing Leadership Style."

31. Hermann, "Assessing Leadership Style."

32. Pagé, "To Challenge or Respect Constraints?" For more information about the study, see: Margaret Hermann et al., "Transnational NGOs: A Cross-Sectoral Analysis of Leadership Perspectives" (2010); Margaret G. Hermann et al., "The Transnational NGO Study: Rationale, Sampling and Research Process" (2010), http://ssrn.com/abstract=2191090. In addition to the individual leadership profiling, the analysis also focused on the range of leadership traits, styles, and preferences based on additional sets of individual psychometric surveys that participants in our various senior leadership programs have completed. In total, this cohort includes approximately 250 TNGO leaders. These tools include Meyers Briggs, the Four Frames test (*Reframing Organizations*, 2013), the Least Preferred Co-Worker test, the *Friendly* survey on communication in the workplace, an Emotional Intelligence assessment Daniel Goleman, *Emotional Intelligence* (New York: Bantam Books, 2005), a conflict management style survey,

a "Machiavellian" assessment on need for power, and a work needs assessment David C. McClelland, *The Achieving Society* (New York: Free Press, 1961) that measures individual motivation in the workplace, among others.

33. This analysis was performed on a sample of 152 US-based TNGO leaders. Subsequent analyses have focused on the leadership traits of five cohorts of about twenty TNGO leaders, each participating in the Transnational NGO Leadership Institute, and seven cohorts of about twenty-five leaders, each participating in customized senior leadership trainings for ActionAid, Greenpeace, Oxfam, and Amnesty International.

34. The term "leading self" was coined by the Center for Creative Leadership (CCL).

35. McClelland, *The Achieving Society*.

36. See: Lee G. Bolman and Terrence E. Deal, *Reframing Organizations: Artistry, Choice, and Leadership*, 6th ed. (San Francisco: Jossey-Bass, 2017).

37. As self-reported by participants in the TNGO Initiative's Leadership Institute. See the Note on Sources for more information.

38. Interview with Joel Charny, vice president for humanitarian policy and practice, InterAction, by Tosca Bruno-van Vijfeijken, October 13, 2013.

39. Interview with Ingrid Srinath, director of the Center for Social Impact and Philanthropy at Ashoka University, India, and senior leader in the Dutch NGO Hivos and former secretary-general of CIVICUS, by Tosca Bruno-van Vijfeijken, April 14, 2014.

40. Jed Miller and Cynthia Gibson, *From Burning Platform to Building People Power*, Mobilisation Lab (2017), https://mobilisationlab.org/burning-platform-building-people-power/.

41. Kirk Emerson, Tina Nabatchi, and Stephen Balogh, "An Integrative Framework for Collaborative Governance," *Journal of Public Administration Research and Theory* 22, no. 1 (2012); George E. Mitchell, "Collaborative Propensities among Transnational NGOs Registered in the United States," *American Review of Public Administration* 44, no. 5 (2014), https://doi.org/10.1177/0275074012474337; Arani Kajenthira and Philippe Sion, "Collective Impact without Borders: Successful, Multi-National, Collective Impact Efforts Require That Organizations Carefully Consider Two Dimensions of Their Approach," *Stanford Social Innovation Review* (2017); John Kania and Mark Kramer, "Collective Impact," *Stanford Social Innovation Review* (Winter 2011); George E. Mitchell, Rosemary O'Leary, and Catherine Gerard, "Collaboration and Performance: Perspectives from Public Managers and NGO Leaders," *Public Performance and Management Review* 38, no. 4 (2015).

42. Bolman and Deal, *Reframing Organizations*.

43. Rosemary O'Leary, Yujin Choi, and Catherine M. Gerard, "The Skill Set of the Successful Collaborator," *Public Administration Review* 72, no. s1 (2012), https://doi.org/doi:10.1111/j.1540-6210.2012.02667.x.

44. Joe McMahon and Alan Fowler, *Conflict Management in INGOs* (unpublished report on results from survey) (London/Uxbridge: InterMediation (in collaboration with World Vision and Amnesty International), 2015); Alan Fowler, Elizabeth Field, and Joseph McMahon, "The Upside of Conflict," *Stanford Social Innovation Review* (Winter 2019), https://ssir.org/articles/entry/the_upside_of_conflict#.

45. Interview with Emeritus Professor Alan Fowler, Erasmus University Rotterdam, by Tosca Bruno-van Vijfeijken, January 16, 2014.

46. Joyce K. Fletcher, "The Paradox of Post Heroic Leadership: An Essay on Gender, Power, and Transformational Change," *The Leadership Quarterly* 15 (2004).

47. Hande Eslen-Ziya and Itır Erhart, "Toward Postheroic Leadership: A Case Study of Gezi's Collaborating Multiple Leaders," *Leadership* 11, no. 4 (2015), https://doi.org/10.1177/1742715015591068.
48. Fletcher, "The Paradox of Post Heroic Leadership."
49. Michael Useem, *Leading Up: How to Lead Your Boss So You Both Win* (New York: Three Rivers Press, 2001).
50. Jean Lipman-Blumen, *Connective Leadership: Managing in a Changing World* (New York: Oxford University Press, 2000).
51. CARE has started several social enterprise operations inside its own organization and Habitat for Humanity has established social investment funds as an integral piece of its operations.
52. Hybrid organizations include Techsoup, PATH, and Public Interest Registry. The Public Interest Registry is the nonprofit wholesale registry for the Internet domain names .org and .ngo. Such hybrid organizations appear to be more likely to emerge in technology-related fields, where leaders and staff have backgrounds in business and innovation and also pursue a social mission.
53. Derrick Feldmann et al., *The 2013 Millennial Impact Report*, The Millennial Impact Research (2013), http://www.themillennialimpact.com/past-research; Achieve, *The 2016 Millennial Impact Report. Cause Engagement Following an Election Year* (Washington, DC: The Case Foundation, 2016).
54. Interview with Isaac Bekalo, president, International Institute of Rural Reconstruction, by Tosca Bruno-van Vijfeijken, June 6, 2013.
55. Andrew Chadwick and James Dennis, "Social Media, Professional Media, and Mobilisation in Contemporary Britain: Explaining the Strengths and Weaknesses of the Citizens' Movement 38 Degrees," *Political Studies* 65, no. 1 (2017), https://doi.org/10.1177/0032321716631350.
56. Roger Bohn, "Stop Fighting Fires," *Harvard Business Review*, 2000.
57. Ronald A. Heifetz, Marty Linsky, and Alexander Grashow, *The Practice of Adaptive Leadership: Tools and Tactics for Changing Your Organization and the World* (Boston: Harvard Business School Publishing, 2009).
58. Interview with Burkhard Gnärig, co-founder of the International Civil Society Centre, by Tosca Bruno-van Vijfeijken, August 1, 2013.
59. Excerpt from an unpublished online forum contribution by James Whitehead, global innovation advisor, Oxfam, in online forum of the Task Force on Organizational Culture Change of the International Centre for Civil Society, March 2015.
60. The idea of rhizomatic learning highlights a more networked, distributed, and evolving process of knowledge transmission and generation. Dave Cormier, "Rhizomatic Education: Community as Curriculum," *Innovate: Journal of Online Education* 4, no. 5 (2008), https://www.learntechlib.org/p/104239. Knowledge is constructed non-hierarchically by the entire community, rather than passed down by experts.
61. Adapted from a white paper contributed by Richard Marshall, World Vision, as an outcome of his fellowship at the Transnational NGO Initiative, February 2015.
62. Margarita Mayo, "If Humble People Make the Best Leaders, Why Do We Fall for Charismatic Narcissists," *Harvard Business Review* (April 7, 2017), https://hbr.org/2017/04/if-humble-people-make-the-best-leaders-why-do-we-fall-for-charismatic-narcissists.
63. Daniel M. Cable, "How Humble Leadership Really Works," *Harvard Business Review* (April 23, 2018), https://hbr.org/2018/04/how-humble-leadership-really-works.

CHAPTER 10

1. ICSC, *Exploring the Future* (Berlin: International Civil Society Centre, 2016).
2. H. Brinton Milward and Keith G. Provan, *A Manager's Guide for Choosing and Using Collaborative Networks* (Washington, DC: IBM Center for the Business of Government, 2006), 8
3. Edward P. Weber and Anne M. Khademian, "Wicked Problems, Knowledge Challenges, and Collaborative Capacity Builders in Network Settings," *Public Administration Review* 68, no. 2 (2008).
4. For more explanation about transaction costs, see: Aseem Prakash and Mary Kay Gugerty, eds., *Advocacy Organizations and Collective Action* (New York: Cambridge University Press, 2010); Ronald H. Coase, "The Nature of the Firm," *Economica* 4, no. 16 (1937); Oliver E. Williamson, "The Economics of Organization: The Transaction Cost Approach," *American Journal of Sociology* 87, no. 3 (1981).
5. This chapter refers to collaboration as the overarching term describing a broad range of activities across organizational boundaries. Scholars have also defined collaboration as a particular form of horizontal integration distinct from cooperation or coordination. See: Robyn Keast, Kerry Brown, and Myrna Mandell, "Getting the Right Mix: Unpacking Integration Meanings and Strategies," *International Public Management Journal* 10, no. 1 (2007).
6. Arani Kajenthira and Philippe Sion, "Collective Impact without Borders: Successful, Multi-National, Collective Impact Efforts Require That Organizations Carefully Consider Two Dimensions of Their Approach," *Stanford Social Innovation Review* (2017); John Kania and Mark Kramer, "Collective Impact," *Stanford Social Innovation Review* (Winter 2011).
7. Paul Brest, "A Decade of Outcome-Oriented Philanthropy," *Stanford Social Innovation Review* (2012), http://www.ssireview.org/articles/entry/a_decade_of_outcome_oriented_philanthropy. Also see: Alnoor Ebrahim and V. Kasturi Rangan, "Acumen Fund: Measurement in Impact Investing," (Boston: Harvard Business School Publishing, 2011).
8. George E. Mitchell, "Collaborative Propensities among Transnational NGOs Registered in the United States," *American Review of Public Administration* 44, no. 5 (2014), https://doi.org/10.1177/0275074012474337.
9. Yannick C. Atouba and Michelle Shumate, "International Nonprofit Collaboration: Examining the Role of Homophily," *Nonprofit and Voluntary Sector Quarterly* 44, no. 3 (2015).
10. Mitchell, "Collaborative Propensities among Transnational NGOs Registered in the United States."
11. Hans Peter Schmitz and George E. Mitchell, "The Other Side of the Coin: NGOs, Rights-Based Approaches, and Public Administration," *Public Administration Review* 76, no. 2 (2016), https://doi.org/10.1111/puar.12479.
12. ICSC, *Exploring the Future*.
13. James E. Austin and M. May Seitanidi, "Collaborative Value Creation: A Review of Partnering between Nonprofits and Businesses. Part 1. Value Creation Spectrum and Collaboration Stages," *Nonprofit and Voluntary Sector Quarterly* 41, no. 5 (2012); James E. Austin and Maria May Seitanidi, "Collaborative Value Creation: A Review of Partnering Between Nonprofits and Businesses. Part 2: Partnership Processes and Outcomes," *Nonprofit and Voluntary Sector Quarterly* 41, no. 6 (2012).
14. Dorothea Baur and Hans Peter Schmitz, "Corporations and NGOs: When Accountability Leads to Co-optation," *Journal of Business Ethics* 106, no. 9 (2011).

15. Mathieu Bouchard and Emmanuel Raufflet, "Domesticating the Beast: A 'Resource Profile' Framework of Power Relations in Nonprofit-Business Collaboration," *Nonprofit and Voluntary Sector Quarterly* (2019), https://doi.org/10.1177/0899764019853378.

16. George E. Mitchell, "Strategic Responses to Resource Dependence among Transnational NGOs Registered in the United States," *Voluntas* 25, no. 1 (2014).

17. Max Stephenson and Elisabeth Chaves, "The Nature Conservancy, the Press, and Accountability," *Nonprofit and Voluntary Sector Quarterly* 35, no. 3 (2006), https://doi.org/10.1177/0899764006287886; Robert J. Foster, "Corporations as Partners: 'Connected Capitalism' and the Coca-Cola Company," *PoLAR: Political and Legal Anthropology Review* 37, no. 2 (2014), https://doi.org/doi:10.1111/plar.12073; David Gibson, "Awash in Green: A Critical Perspective on Environmental Advertising," *Tulane Environmental Law Journal* 22, no. 2 (2009).

18. Uwe Gneiting, "How Can Campaigners Influence the Private Sector? 4 Lessons from the Behind the Brands Campaign on Big Food," *From Poverty to Power* (June 8, 2016), http://oxfamblogs.org/fp2p/how-can-campaigners-influence-the-private-sector-4-lessons-from-the-behind-the-brands-campaign-on-big-food.

19. George E. Mitchell and Hans Peter Schmitz, "The Nexus of Public and Nonprofit Management," *Public Performance & Management Review* 42, no. 1 (2019), https://doi.org/10.1080/15309576.2018.1489293.

20. Lester M. Salamon, "Of Market Failure, Voluntary Failure, and Third-Party Government: Toward a Theory of Government-Nonporfit Relations in the Modern Welfare State," *Journal of Voluntary Action Research* 16, nos. 1–2 (1987).

21. An extensive literature exists about government-nonprofit contracting and collaboration. For example, see: Steven Rathgeb Smith, "Nonprofit Organizations and Government: Implications for Policy and Practice," *Journal of Policy Analysis and Management* 29, no. 3 (2010); Steven Rathgeb Smith, "Nonprofits and Public Administration: Reconciling Performance Management and Citizen Engagement," *The American Review of Public Administration* 40, no. 2 (2010); Steven Rathgeb Smith and Michael Lipsky, *Nonprofits for Hire: The Welfare State in the Age of Contracting* (Cambridge, MA: Harvard University Press, 2009); Steven Rathgeb Smith and K. A. Grønbjerg, "Scope and Theory of Government-Nonprofit Relations," in *The Nonprofit Sector: A Research Handbook*, ed. W. W. Powell and R. Steinberg (New Haven, CT: Yale University Press, 2006); H. Brinton Milward and Keith G. Provan, "The Hollow State: Private Provision of Public Services," in *Public Policy for Democracy*, ed. Helen Ingram and Steven Rathgeb Smith (Washington, DC: Brookings Institution Press, 1993).

22. George E. Mitchell, Rosemary O'Leary, and Catherine Gerard, "Collaboration and Performance: Perspectives from Public Managers and NGO Leaders," *Public Performance and Management Review* 38, no. 4 (2015), https://doi.org/10.1080/15309576.2015.1031015.

23. Vicky Mancuso Brehm, *Autonomy or Dependence?: North-South NGO Partnerships* (Oxford: INTRAC, 2004).

24. Christopher L. Pallas and Johannes Urpelainen, "Mission and Interests: The Strategic Formation and Function of North-South NGO Campaigns," *Global Governance* 19, no. 3 (2013).

25. Louise Redvers, "NGOs: Bridging the North South Divide," *The New Humanitarian* (June 8, 2015), http://www.thenewhumanitarian.org/analysis/2015/06/08/ngos-bridging-north-south-divide.

26. Firoze Manji, "Collaboration with the South: Agents of Aid or Solidarity?," *Development in Practice* 7, no. 2 (1997).

27. Darcy Ashman, "Strengthening North-South Partnerships for Sustainable Development," *Nonprofit and Voluntary Sector Quarterly* 30, no. 1 (2001): 87.

28. See: https://keystoneaccountability.org and https://accountablenow.org.

29. Ann Marie Thomson and James L. Perry, "Collaboration Processes: Inside the Black Box," *Public Administration Review* 66 (2006): 23, https://doi.org/10.1111/j.1540-6210.2006.00663.x.

30. John M. Bryson and Barbara C. Crosby, "Failing into Cross-Sector Collaboration Successfully," in *Big Ideas in Collaborative Public Management*, ed. Lisa Blomgren Bingham and Rosemary O'Leary (Armonk, NY: M. E. Sharpe, 2008), 56

31. Lisa Blomgren Bingham, Rosemary O'Leary, and Christine Carson, "Frameshifting: Lateral Thinking for Collaborative Public Management," in *Big Ideas in Collaborative Public Management*, ed. Lisa Blomgren Bingham and Rosemary O'Leary (Armonk, NY: M. E. Sharpe, 2008), 6

32. L. David Brown, Alnoor Ebrahim, and Srilatha Batliwala, "Governing International Advocacy NGOs," *World Development* 40, no. 6 (2012), http://dx.doi.org/10.1016/j.worlddev.2011.11.006.

33. Margaret E. Keck and Kathryn Sikkink, *Activists beyond Borders: Advocacy Networks in International Politics* (Ithaca, NY: Cornell University Press, 1998).

34. Personal communications between Maret Laev, organizational development manager, Oxfam Great Britain, and Tosca Bruno-van Vijfeijken.

35. Willem Elbers and Lau Schulpen, "Corridors of Power: The Institutional Design of North-South NGO Partnerships," *Voluntas* 24, no. 1 (2013), https://doi.org/10.1007/s11266-012-9332-7

36. Also see: Lynda Gratton and Tamara J. Erickson, "8 Ways to Build Collaborative Teams," *Harvard Business Review* 85, no. 11 (2007).

37. It may also necessitate new skill sets for effective collaboration among managers and leaders (see Chapter 9).

38. This matrix was developed by Kenneth Grimes, executive director of the City Heights Community Development Corporation, San Diego, CA.

39. Lloyd Hitoshi Mayer, "Fragmented Oversight of Nonprofits in the United States: Does It Work?—Can It Work?," *Chicago-Kent Law Review* 91, no. 3 (2016).

40. Erynn Beaton and Hyunseok Hwang, "Increasing the Size of the Pie: The Impact of Crowding on Nonprofit Sector Resources," *Nonprofit Policy Forum* 8, no. 3 (2017).

41. Pablo Eisenberg, "A Crisis in the Nonprofit Sector," *National Civic Review* 86, no. 4 (1997).

42. Kania and Kramer, "Collective Impact."

43. Tom Wolff, "Ten Places Where Collective Impact Gets It Wrong," *Global Journal of Community Psychology Practice* 7, no. 1 (2016); Sarah Stachowiak and Lauren Gase, "Does Collective Impact Really Make an Impact?," *Stanford Social Innovation Review* (August 8, 2018), https://ssir.org/articles/entry/does_collective_impact_really_make_an_impact?utm_source=Enews&utm_medium=Email&utm_campaign=SSIR_Now&utm_content=Title.

44. Kajenthira and Sion, "Collective Impact without Borders."

45. Sarah Blodgett Bermeo, "Aid Allocation and Targeted Development in an Increasingly Connected World," *International Organization* 71, no. 4 (2017), https://doi.org/10.1017/S0020818317000315.

46. Russell Hargrave, "Save the Children CEO on a New Era of Competition for Aid," *Devex* (January 11, 2018), https://www.devex.com/news/save-the-children-ceo-on-a-new-era-of-competition-for-aid-91723.

47. A recent survey of leaders in the global development sector identified changes related to funding models and the emergence of new actors as the top two themes. See: George Ingram and Kristin M. Lord, *Global Development Disrupted: Findings from a Survey of 93 leaders* (Washington, DC: Brookings Institution, 2019).

48. George E. Mitchell and Hans Peter Schmitz, "Principled Instrumentalism: A Theory of Transnational NGO Behaviour," *Review of International Studies* 40, no. 3 (2014), https://doi.org/10.1017/S0260210513000387.

49. For example, in a study of 330 partnerships, only 36 percent met or partially met their goals. See: Philipp Pattberg and Oscar Widerberg, *Transnational Multi-Stakeholder Partnerships for Sustainable Development: Building Blocks for Success* (Berlin: International Civil Society Centre, 2015).

50. Mitchell and Schmitz, "Principled Instrumentalism."

51. Ingram and Lord, *Global Development Disrupted*.

52. Mitchell, "Collaborative Propensities among Transnational NGOs Registered in the United States."

53. When we have asked senior leaders of mid- to large-sized TNGOs in the TNGO Initiative's senior leadership training programs how much of their time is externally focused, a range of 10–20 percent is typically mentioned.

54. Brown, Ebrahim, and Batliwala, "Governing International Advocacy NGOs."

55. Stephen Hopgood, "Amnesty International's Growth and Development since 1961," in *50 Years of Amnesty International: Reflections and Perspectives*, ed. Wilco de Jonge et al. (Utrecht: Universiteit Utrecht, 2011).

56. This has been a common theme from more than six years of senior leadership training programs through the TNGO Initiative and in additional applied work with TNGOs on their organizational change processes.

57. These views surfaced frequently in Transnational NGO Initiative interviews, meetings of the Task Force on Culture Change of the International Civil Society Center (ICCS), and during other interactions with practitioners.

58. Some TNGOs have sought to challenge this tendency and foster innovation by hiring "external" staff and leaders with very different outlooks and frames of reference. For example, bringing in a business leader with a distinguished career typically means that a TNGO board wants to shake up the organization, reduce costs, and generally improve its financials. People with different sectoral backgrounds (private sector, technology industries, academia, etc.) are hired to challenge long-standing practices. However, approaching this kind of cultural change purely through a hiring strategy is typically a reactive move with limited chances of success. Newly hired "rebels" often face a deeply ingrained organizational culture ready to activate its "antibodies" and push out or isolate such persons relatively swiftly. This expression was used in the discussion as part of the ICCS Task Force on Culture Change in 2015 by one of its participants.

59. Statement of James Whitehead of Oxfam Great Britain during the Task Force of the International Civil Society Center on Culture Change, in which Tosca Bruno-van Vijfeijken participated.

60. L. David Brown, "Bridge-Building for Social Transformation," *Stanford Social Innovation Review* (2005).

61. Thomas Jordan, Pia Andersson, and Helena Ringnér, "The Spectrum of Responses to Complex Societal Issues: Reflections on Seven Years of Empirical Inquiry," *Integral Review* 9, no. 1 (2013).

62. Duncan Green, "If Annoying, Talking Down to or 'Othering' People Is a Terrible Way to Influence Them, Why Do We Keep Doing It? (research edition)," *From Poverty to Power* (February 12, 2015), https://oxfamblogs.org/fp2p/if-annoying-talking-down-to-or-othering-people-is-a-terrible-way-to-influence-them-why-do-we-keep-doing-it-research-edition.

63. Kyle Peterson et al., *The Promise of Partnerships: A Dialogue between INGOs and Donors* (Washington, DC: FSG, 2014), 2.

64. Peterson et al., *The Promise of Partnerships*.

65. The concept of organizational boundaries also has implications for transaction costs. See: Jesse D. Lecy, George E. Mitchell, and Hans Peter Schmitz, "Advocacy Organizations, Networks, and the Firm Analogy," in *Rethinking Advocacy Organizations*, ed. Aseem Prakash and Mary Kay Gugerty (Cambridge: Cambridge University Press, 2010).

66. See: Greg Landsman and Erez Roimi, "Collective Impact and Systems Change: Missing Links," *Nonprofit Quarterly* (February 12, 2018), https://nonprofitquarterly.org/2018/02/12/collective-impact-systems-change-missing-links/; Stachowiak and Gase, "Does Collective Impact Really Make an Impact?"; Wolff, "Ten Places Where Collective Impact Gets It Wrong"; Paul Brest, "Strategic Philanthropy and Its Discontents," *Stanford Social Innovation Review* (April 27, 2015), https://ssir.org/up_for_debate/article/strategic_philanthropy_and_its_discontents; Arthur "Buzz" Schmidt, "Divining a Vision for Markets for Good," in *Selected Readings: Making Sense of Data and Information in the Social Sector*, ed. Eric J. Henderson (. Stanford, CA: Markets for Good, 2014).

CHAPTER 11

1. Sections of this chapter are substantially based personal correspondence between Barney Tallack (former director of strategy, Oxfam International) and the authors.

2. The dissolution of AED followed an investigation by the US Justice Department into financial misconduct in managing programs for USAID in Pakistan and Afghanistan See: Department of Justice, "Washington, DC–Based Academy for Educational Development Pays More Than $5 Million to Settle False Claims Act Allegations" (Washington, DC: Office of Public Affairs, 2011), https://www.justice.gov/opa/pr/washington-dc-based-academy-educational-development-pays-more-5-million-settle-false-claims.

3. Personal correspondence between Tosca Bruno-van Vijfeijken and Winnie Byanyima, executive director of Oxfam International. Also see: Richard Jones, "Oxfam Chief: INGO Mergers 'Not a Trend'," *Devex* (2013), https://www.devex.com/news/oxfam-chief-ingo-mergers-not-a-trend-81486.

4. InterAction, *Supporting Your NGO Future: US NGO Executive Thoughts on the Future* (Washington, DC: InterAction, 2019).

5. Bridgespan webinar, March 11, 2014, with Katie Smith Milway, partner/head of knowledge, Bridgespan; Lois Savage, president, Lodestar Foundation; Elisabeth Babcock, president/CEO, Crittenton Women's Union; and Decker Ngongang, senior associate, Echoing Green, as speakers.

6. Oliver Carrington et al., *Let's Talk Mission and Merger* (London: New Philanthropy Capital, 2018).

7. See: Katie Smith Milway, Maria Orozco, and Cristina Botero, "Why Nonprofit Mergers Continue to Lag," *Stanford Social Innovation Review* (Spring 2014). More recently, some foundations have developed an interest in M&A as a part of capacity-building strategies. The Collaboration Prize supported by the Lodestar Foundation is one example, while other institutional funders with such an emphasis include the Hewlett, the Packard, and the Dyson Foundations.

8. Smith Milway, Orozco, and Botero, "Why Nonprofit Mergers Continue to Lag."

9. Smith Milway, Orozco, and Botero, "Why Nonprofit Mergers Continue to Lag."

10. Sam Worthington and Alexander Grashow, *NGO Board Reckoning* (Washington, DC: InterAction and Good Wolf Group, 2018).

11. Looking at 3,300 mergers from 1996 to 2006 in four US states, the study found that M&A activities among smaller nonprofits were similar in frequency compared to those in the business sector, but for nonprofits with budgets of USD $50 million or higher the rate dropped to one tenth of the corporate sector. See: Alexander Cortez, William Foster, and Katie Milway, *Nonprofit M&A. More Than a Tool for Tough Times* (Boston: Bridgespan Group, 2009).

12. Cortez, Foster, and Milway, *Nonprofit M&A.*

13. Personal correspondence between Tosca Bruno-van Vijfeijken and Rudy von Bernuth, retired director of international programs, Save the Children International, January 11, 2016.

14. Stephen Cook, "Analysis: Merlin and Save the Children," *Third Sector* (July 30, 2013), https://www.thirdsector.co.uk/analysis-merlin-save-children/governance/article/1193125.

15. John Alliage Morales, "Merlin: Anatomy of a Doomed INGO Business Model," *Devex* (July 30, 2013), https://www.devex.com/news/merlin-anatomy-of-a-doomed-ingo-business-model-81537.

16. Carlos Santamaria, "Are INGO Mergers the Wave of the Future?," *Devex* (July 24, 2013), https://www.devex.com/news/are-ingo-mergers-the-wave-of-the-future-81500.

17. Mercy Corps, *Building a Smarter, Stronger, and Broader Youth Constituency in the United States to Fight Global Poverty* (New York: Rockefeller Brothers Fund, 2007).

18. Melanie Knight and Kathleen Rodgers, "'The Government Is Operationalizing Neo-Liberalism': Women's Organizations, Status of Women Canada, and the Struggle for Progressive Social Change in Canada," *NORA—Nordic Journal of Feminist and Gender Research* 20, no. 4 (2012), https://doi.org/10.1080/08038740.2012.747786.

19. Anonymous, "Secret Aid Worker: The UK NGO Sector Is Facing a Funding Crisis," *The Guardian* (August 2, 2016), https://www.theguardian.com/global-development-professionals-network/2016/aug/02/secret-aid-worker-projectitis-dfid-civil-society.

20. MAP for Nonprofits/Wilder Research, *What Do We Know about Nonprofit Mergers?* (Saint Paul, MN: Wilder Research, 2011), 2

21. Bridgespan webinar, March 11, 2014, with Katie Smith Milway, partner/head of knowledge, Bridgespan; Lois Savage, president, Lodestar Foundation; Elisabeth Babcock, president/CEO, Crittenton Women's Union; and Decker Ngongang, senior associate, Echoing Green, as speakers.

22. MAP for Nonprofits/Wilder Research, *What Do We Know about Nonprofit Mergers?*

23. David La Piana, "Merging Wisely," *Stanford Social Innovation Review* (Spring 2010). An example is Hospice UK (formerly Help the Hospices), which provides "white

label" fundraising products and training services to several hundred member organizations.

24. John P. Kotter, *Leading Change* (Boston: Harvard Business Press, 2012).

25. Afsaneh Nahavandi and Ali R. Malekzadeh, "Acculturation in Mergers and Acquisitions," *Academy of Management Review* 13, no. 1 (1988).

26. Personal correspondence between Tosca Bruno-van Vijfeijken and Rudy von Bernuth, director of international programs, Save the Children International, November 19, 2013.

27. Personal correspondence between Tosca Bruno-van Vijfeijken and Rudy von Bernuth.

28. Thomas A. McLaughlin, *Nonprofit Mergers & Alliances* (Hoboken, NJ: John Wiley & Sons, 2010).

29. For a lengthier discussion of the cultural implications of M&A, see: Daryl Conner and Ed Boswell, *Cultural Implications of INGO Mergers and Acquisitions* (Atlanta: Conner Advisory, 2018), http://3vcego17hhlq3f2du63lx87v.wpengine.netdna-cdn.com/wp-content/uploads/2018/06/Cultural-Implications-of-INGO-Mergers-and-Acquisitions.pdf.

30. .Edgar H. Schein, *Organizational Culture and Leadership* (San Francisco: Jossey-Bass, 2010).

31. This case is primarily based on correspondence between Barney Tallack, former director of strategy, Oxfam International, and the authors, throughout 2019.

32. For a general discussion of related growth problems see: Queenan, Jeri Eckhart, Jacob Allen, and Jari Tuomala. April 2013. Stop Starving Scale: Unlocking the Potential of Global NGOs. The Bridgespan Group. https://www.bridgespan.org/bridgespan/Images/articles/stop-starving-scale-unlocking-the-potential/stopstarvingscale-unlockingthepotentialofglobalngos.pdf.

33. For insights on this case and extensive documentation, we thank John McGeehan, former executive vice president and COO of Plan International USA. The acquisition excluded the CEDPA India Society.

34. According to their Forms 990 ending in 2011, CEDPA's annual budget was about $7.4 million, while Plan International USA's budget was about $64 million.

35. According to John McGeehan, former executive vice president and COO of Plan International USA, "a critical benefit to Plan was learning—not just about M&A, but about itself. We understood and acknowledged to each other that we would not get everything right. This had important implications for buy-in and commitment to see this through." Personal correspondence with McGeehan, January 11, 2016.

36. See, for example: George E. Mitchell and Thad D. Calabrese, "Proverbs of Nonprofit Financial Management," *American Review of Public Administration* 49, no. 6 (2019), https://doi.org/10.1177/0275074018770458; Thad D. Calabrese and Cleopatra Grizzle, "Debt, Donors, and the Decision to Give," *Journal of Public Budgeting, Accounting, and Financial Management* 24, no. 2 (2012); Cleopatra Charles, "Nonprofit Arts Organizations: Debt Ratio Does Not Influence Donations—Interest Expense Ratio Does," *American Review of Public Administration* 48, no. 7 (2018).

CHAPTER 12

1. Sarah S. Stroup and Wendy Wong, *The Authority Trap: Strategic Choices of International NGOs* (Ithaca, NY: Cornell University Press, 2017); Cristina M. Balboa, *The Paradox of Scale: How NGOs Build, Maintain, and Lose Authority in Environmental Governance* (Cambridge, MA: MIT Press, 2018).

2. Alexander Cooley and James Ron, "The NGO Scramble: Organizational Insecurity and the Political Economy of Transnational Action," *International Security* 27, no. 1 (2002). Dhananjayan Sriskandarajah, "NGOs Losing the War against Poverty and Climate Change, Says Civicus Head: Charities Are No Longer Drivers of Social Change; for Many Saving the World Has Become Big Business. How Did We Lose Our Way?," *The Guardian* (London) (August 11, 2014).

3. Thomas Davies, *NGOs: A New History of Transnational Civil Society* (New York: Oxford University Press, 2014).

4. Jeri Eckhart Queenan, Jacob Allen, and Jari Tuomala, *Stop Starving Scale: Unlocking the Potential of Global NGOs*, The Bridgespan Group (April 2013), https://www.bridgespan.org/bridgespan/Images/articles/stop-starving-scale-unlocking-the-potential/stopstarvingscale-unlockingthepotentialofglobalngos.pdf.

5. For an articulation of the general argument, see: Mark H. Moore, "Managing for Value: Organizational Strategy in For-Profit, Nonprofit, and Governmental Organizations," *Nonprofit and Voluntary Sector Quarterly* 29, no. 1 (2000).

6. Galbraith Jay R, *Designing Organizations: An Executive Briefing on Strategy, Structure, and Process*. (San Francisco, CA: Jossey-Bass, 1995).

7. Charlie McCormack, former CEO of Save the Children, has used this term. Also see: ICSC Global Perspectives Conference, Berlin, 2012.

8. Kelsey Piper, "Why This Billion-Dollar Foundation Is Becoming a Corporation," *Future Perfect* (February 7, 2019), https://www.vox.com/future-perfect/2019/2/7/18207247/arnold-foundation-corporation-nonprofit-charity.

9. Personal correspondence between George Mitchell and Michael Silberman, global director, Mobilisation Lab, July 2019.

10. See: Tosca Bruno-van Vijfeijken and Steven Lux, "From Alliance to International: The Global Transformation of Save the Children," *E-PARCC Collaborative Governance Initiative* (2012), https://www.maxwell.syr.edu/uploadedFiles/moynihan/tngo/2013-1A-Case-LuxBrunovanVijfeijken.pdf.

11. This shift has been called for by many observers, for example, Queenan, Allen, and Tuomala, *Stop Starving Scale*; James Crowley and Morgana Ryan, *Building a Better International NGO: Greater Than the Sum of Its Parts?* (Boulder, CO: Kumarian Press, 2013); James Crowley and Morgana Ryan, *Navigating Change for International NGOs: A Practical Handbook* (Boulder, CO: Kumarian Press, 2017).

12. For a discussion of organizational cultural change, see: Daryl Conner and Ed Boswell, *Organizational Culture and Its Impact on Change in the Civil Society Sector* (Atlanta: Conner Advisory, 2018), http://3vcego17hhlq3f2du63lx87v.wpengine.netdna-cdn.com/wp-content/uploads/2018/06/Organizational-Culture-and-Its-Impact-on-Change-in-the-Civil-Society-Sector.pdf.

13. John P. Kotter, *Leading Change* (Boston: Harvard Business Press, 2012).

14. Dennis Duchon and Michael Burns, "Organizational Narcissism," *Organizational Dynamics* 37, no. 4 (2008).

15. Oxfam International, "SMS Learning Loop Tool Kit" (2012).

16. Interviews with Richard Marshall, senior director for people and culture at World Vision, and Adrian Brown, global practice leader for organisation development & change at World Vision, by Tosca Bruno-van Vijfeijken, July 16, 2014.

17. Interview with Pam Innes, change manager at Save the Children International, by Tosca Bruno-van Vijfeijken, January 26, 2012.

18. Interviews with Richard Marshall and Adrian Brown, by Tosca Bruno-van Vijfeijken, July 16, 2014.

19. Lee G. Bolman and Terrence E. Deal, *Reframing Organizations: Artistry, Choice, and Leadership*, 6th ed. (San Francisco: Jossey-Bass, 2017).

20. For a general discussion about leading organizational change, see: Ed Boswell and Daryl Conner, *Leading Successful Change amidst a Disruptive INGO Environment* (Atlanta: Conner Advisory, 2017), http://3vcego17hhlq3f2du63lx87v.wpengine. netdna-cdn.com/wp-content/uploads/2018/06/Leading-Successful-Change-Amidst-a-Disruptive-INGO-Environment.pdf.

21. Comments from Pauline Martin, international director of organisational effectiveness, ActionAid International, at the first meeting of the INGO Learning Group on Organizational Change, February 2014, Oxfam International, UK.

22. Tosca Bruno-van Vijfeijken et al., *Final Assessment: Amnesty's Global Transition Program* (Syracuse, NY: Moynihan Institute of Global Affairs, 2017).

23. Observations shared by Oxfam change managers in a series of informal learning sessions between Oxfam and CARE change managers (2013–2015).

24. David A. Garvin, "The Processes of Organization and Management," *MIT Sloan Management Review* 39, no. 4 (1998).

25. National governments could recognize an international legal status or the national law of the country where a TNGO is headquartered. For example, Belgium accords special status to international NGOs by recognizing foreign national laws as the basis for their operations. See: Kerstin Martens, "Examining the (Non-)Status of NGOs in International Law," *Indiana Journal of Global Legal Studies* 10, no. 2 (2003).

26. In the US context, some observers have called for removing financial restrictions on the sector to increase its impact, but such proposals typically ignore the need for more accountability for results and impact. See: Dan Pallotta, *Uncharitable: How Restraints on Nonprofits Undermine Their Potential* (Boston: Tufts University Press, 2008).

27. See, for example: George E. Mitchell, "Creating a Philanthropic Marketplace through Accounting, Disclosure, and Intermediation," *Public Performance and Management Review* 38, no. 1 (2014).

28. Gregory, Ann Goggins and Don Howard, "The Nonprofit Starvation Cycle." *Stanford Social Innovation Review* 7, no. 4 (2009); Lecy, Jesse D., and Elizabeth A. M. Searing. "Anatomy of the Nonprofit Starvation Cycle: An Analysis of Falling Overhead Ratios in the Nonprofit Sector." *Nonprofit and Voluntary Sector Quarterly* 44, no. 3 (2015), https://doi.org/10.1177/0899764014527175.

29. See, for example: https://philanthropynewyork.org/news/leaders-ford-open-society-macarthur-hewlett-and-packard-foundations-pledge-do-more-help.

30. Oonagh B. Breen, Alison Dunn, and Mark Sidel, eds., *Regulatory Waves: Comparative Perspectives on State Regulation and Self-Regulation Policies in the Nonprofit Sector* (New York: Cambridge University Press, 2017); Mark Sidel, "Regulation of Nonprofit and Philanthropic Organizations: An International Perspective," *Nonprofit Quarterly* (July 25, 2016), https://nonprofitquarterly. org/2016/07/25/regulation-philanthropic-organizations/; Mary Kay Gugerty and Dean Karlan, *The Goldilocks Problem: Right-Sized Monitoring and Evaluation for Development NGOs* (New York, NY: Oxford University Press, 2018); Joannie Tremblay-Boire, Aseem Prakash, and Mary Kay Gugerty, "Regulation by Reputation: Monitoring and Sanctioning in Nonprofit Accountability Clubs," *Public Administration Review* 76, no. 5 (2016), https://doi.org/10.1111/puar.12539; Mary Kay Gugerty, "The Effectiveness of NGO Self-Regulation: Theory and Evidence from Africa," *Public Administration and Development* 28, no. 2 (2008).

31. Edelman, *2019 Edelman Trust Barometer: Global Report* (New York, NY: Daniel J. Edelman Holdings, 2019); Mohamed Younis and Andrew Rzepa, *One in Three Worldwide Lack Confidence in NGOs* (Gallup and Wellcome, 2019), https://news.gallup.com/opinion/gallup/258230/one-three-worldwide-lack-confidence-ngos.aspx.
32. Rhodri Davies, "Philanthropy Is at a Turning Point: Here Are 6 Ways It Could Go," *World Economic Forum Global Agenda* (April 29, 2018), https://www.weforum.org/agenda/2019/04/philanthropy-turning-point-6-ways-it-could-go/ ; Anand Giridharadas, *Winners Take All: The Elite Charade of Changing the World* (New York: Penguin Random House, 2018).

AFTERWORD

1. Chris Roche and Andrew Hewett, "The End of the Golden Age of International NGOs?" (ACFID/University Linkage Conference, Australia, November 21–22, 2013).
2. One subsector of TNGOs that might have a potentially different trajectory is that of faith movements. Many TNGOs came out of faith movements or the faith of some of their founders. Many of the TNGOs that are visibly faith-based are able to mobilize individual supporters and volunteers through well-articulated shared values and legitimacy in the eyes of those supporters. Consequently, they also have much higher percentages of unrestricted funding. Their chances of existing for longer are, therefore, higher.

NOTE ON SOURCES

1. National Science Foundation Grant No. SES-0527679 (Agents of Change: Transnational NGOs as Agents of Change: Toward Understanding Their Governance, Leadership, and Effectiveness). Additional funding was provided by the Moynihan Institute of Global Affairs at Syracuse University.
2. For detailed technical information about the study, see Margaret G. Hermann et al., *Transnational NGOs: A Cross-Sectoral Analysis of Leadership Perspectives* (Syracuse, NY: Moynihan Institute of Global Affairs, 2010).
3. George E. Mitchell, "The Attributes of Effective NGOs and the Leadership Values Associated with a Reputation for Organizational Effectiveness," *Nonprofit Management and Leadership* 26, no. 1 (2015), https://doi.org/doi:10.1002/nml.21143; George E. Mitchell and Sarah S. Stroup, "The Reputations of NGOs: Peer Evaluations of Effectiveness," *The Review of International Organizations* (2016); George E. Mitchell, "The Construct of Organizational Effectiveness: Perspectives from Leaders of International Nonprofits in the United States," *Nonprofit and Voluntary Sector Quarterly* 42, no. 2 (April 1, 2013), https://doi.org/10.1177/0899764011434589.
4. George E. Mitchell and David Berlan, "Evaluation and Evaluative Rigor in the Nonprofit Sector," *Nonprofit Management and Leadership* 27, no. 2 (2016), https://doi.org/doi:10.1002/nml.21236; George E. Mitchell and David Berlan, "Evaluation in Nonprofit Organizations: An Empirical Analysis," *Public Performance & Management Review* 41, no. 2 (2018), https://doi.org/10.1080/15309576.2017.1400985; George E. Mitchell, "Creating a Philanthropic Marketplace through Accounting, Disclosure, and Intermediation," *Public Performance & Management Review* 38, no. 1 (2014), https://doi.org/10.2753/PMR1530-9576380102; George E. Mitchell, "Why Will We Ever Learn?: Measurement and Evaluation in International Development NGOs,"

Public Performance & Management Review 37, no. 4 (2014), https://doi.org/10.2753/PMR1530-9576370404.

5. George E. Mitchell and Thad D. Calabrese, "Proverbs of Nonprofit Financial Management," *The American Review of Public Administration* 49, no. 6 (2018), https://doi.org/10.1177/0275074018770458; George E. Mitchell, "Fiscal Leanness and Fiscal Responsiveness: Exploring the Normative Limits of Strategic Nonprofit Financial Management," *Administration & Society* 49, no. 9 (2017); George E. Mitchell, "Strategic Responses to Resource Dependence among Transnational NGOs Registered in the United States," *Voluntas* 25, no. 1 (2014).

6. George E. Mitchell, "Modalities of Managerialism: The 'Double Bind' of Normative and Instrumental Nonprofit Management Imperatives," *Administration & Society* (2016).

7. George E. Mitchell, "Collaborative Propensities among Transnational NGOs Registered in the United States," *The American Review of Public Administration* 44, no. 5 (2014); George E. Mitchell, Rosemary O'Leary, and Catherine Gerard, "Collaboration and Performance: Perspectives from Public Managers and NGO Leaders," *Public Performance & Management Review* 38, no. 4 (2015), https://doi.org/10.1080/15309576.2015.1031015.

8. George E. Mitchell, "The Strategic Orientations of US-Based NGOs," *Voluntas* 26, no. 5 (2015), https://doi.org/10.1007/s11266-014-9507-5; Hans Peter Schmitz and George E. Mitchell, "The Other Side of the Coin: NGOs, Rights-Based Approaches, and Public Administration," *Public Administration Review* 76, no. 2 (2016), https://doi.org/10.1111/puar.12479.

9. George E. Mitchell and Hans Peter Schmitz, "Principled Instrumentalism: A Theory of Transnational NGO Behaviour," *Review of International Studies* 40, no. 3 (2014), https://doi.org/doi:10.1017/S0260210513000387; George E. Mitchell and Hans Peter Schmitz, "The Nexus of Public and Nonprofit Management," *Public Performance & Management Review* 42, no. 1 (2019), https://doi.org/10.1080/15309576.2018.1489293.

10. George E. Mitchell, "NGOs in the United States," in *Routledge Handbook of NGOs and International Relations*, ed. Thomas Davies (New York: Routledge, 2019).

11. Jesse D. Lecy, Ines Mergel, and Hans Peter Schmitz, "Networks in Public Administration: Current Scholarship in Review," *Public Management Review* 16, no. 5 (2014); Jeremy Shiffman et al., "A Framework on the Emergence and Effectiveness of Global Health Networks," *Health Policy and Planning* 31, no. suppl. 1 (2016), https://doi.org/10.1093/heapol/czu046; Uwe Gneiting and Hans Peter Schmitz, "Comparing Global Alcohol and Tobacco Control Efforts: Network Formation and Evolution in International Health Governance," *Health Policy and Planning* 31, no. suppl. 1 (2016), https://doi.org/10.1093/heapol/czv125; Hans Peter Schmitz, "The Global Health Network on Alcohol Control: Successes and Limites of Evidence-Based Advocacy," *Health Policy and Planning* 31, no. 1 (2016).

12. Dorothea Baur and Hans Peter Schmitz, "Corporations and NGOs: When Accountability Leads to Co-optation," *Journal of Business Ethics* 106, no. 1 (2012), https://doi.org/10.1007/s10551-011-1057-9; Wagaki Mwangi, Lothar Rieth, and Hans Peter Schmitz, "Encouraging Greater Compliance: Local Networks and the United Nations Global Compact (UNGC)," in *The Persistent Power of Human Rights: From Commitment to Compliance*, ed. Thomas Risse, Stephen Ropp, and Kathryn Sikkink (Cambridge: Cambridge University Press, 2013).

13. Jesse D. Lecy, Hans Peter Schmitz, and Haley Swedlund, "Non-Governmental and Not-for-Profit Organizational Effectiveness: A Modern Synthesis," *Voluntas* 23, no. 2 (2012), https://doi.org/10.1007/s11266-011-9204-6.

14. Nina Hall, Hans Peter Schmitz, and J. Michael Dedmon, "Transnational Advocacy and NGOs in the Digital Era: New Forms of Networked Power," *International Studies Quarterly* (2019).

15. E. J. Boyer, A. Kolpakov, and Hans Peter Schmitz, "Do Executives Approach Leadership Differently When They Are Involved in Collaborative Partnerships?: A Perspective from International Nongovernmental Organizations (INGOs)," *Public Performance & Management Review* 42, no. 1 (2018).

16. Emily B. Rodio and Hans Peter Schmitz, "Beyond Norms and Interests: Understanding the Evolution of Transnational Human Rights Activism," *International Journal of Human Rights* 14, no. 3 (2010); Hans Peter Schmitz, "A Human Rights–Based Approach (HRBA) in Practice: Evaluating NGO Development Efforts," *Polity* 44, no. 4 (2012), https://doi.org/10.1057/pol.2012.18; Hans Peter Schmitz, "International Criminal Accountability and Transnational Advocacy Networks (TANs)," in *Oxford Handbook of International Security*, ed. Alexandra Gheciu and William C. Wohlforth (New York: Oxford University Press, 2018).

17. Hans Peter Schmitz, Paloma Raggo, and Tosca Bruno-van Vijfeijken, "Accountability of Transnational NGOs: Aspirations vs. Practice," *Nonprofit and Voluntary Sector Quarterly* 41, no. 6 (2012), https://doi.org/10.1177/0899764011431165.

18. Tosca Bruno-van Vijfeijken and Hans Peter Schmitz, "Commentary: A Gap between Ambition and Effectiveness," *Journal of Civil Society* 7, no. 3 (2011), https://doi.org/10.1080/17448689.2011.604998.

19. David Berlan and Tosca Bruno-van Vijfeijken, "The Planned Close of an NGO: Evidence for a New Organizational Form?," *Voluntas* 24, no. 1 (2013), https://doi.org/10.1007/s11266-012-9300-2.

20. Tosca Bruno-van Vijfeijken, "Culture Is What You See When Compliance Is Not in the Room," *Nonprofit Policy Forum* 10, no. 4 (2019), https://doi.org/10.1515/npf-2019-0031.

21. We regularly attend conferences organized by the American Evaluation Association, the Association for Research on Nonprofit Organizations and Voluntary Action (ARNOVA), the InterAction Forum, the International Studies Association, the International Society for Third-Sector Research (ISTR), and the Public Management Research Association, among others.

22. For details, see: Hans Peter Schmitz, J. Michael Dedmon, Tosca Bruno-van Vijfeijken, and Jaclyn Mahoney "Democratizing Advocacy?: How Digital Tools Shape International Non-Governmental Activism," *Journal of Information Technology & Politics* (2020), https://doi.org/10.1080/19331681.2019.1710643.

23. Errors due to rounding.

24. A list of past TNGO Moynihan Fellows can be found here: https://www.maxwell.syr.edu/moynihan/tngo/Past_Fellows.

25. Links to the YouTube channels for the interviews can be found here: https://www.maxwell.syr.edu/moynihan/tngo/interview_series/TNGO_Interview_Showcase.

26. See: Uwe Gneiting and Hans Peter Schmitz, *From Assistance to Agency to Rights: The Experience of Transnational Development NGOs in Guatemala* (Syracuse, NY: Moynihan Institute of Global Affairs, 2008).

27. See: Tosca Bruno-van Vijfeijken, Uwe Gneiting, and Hans Peter Schmitz, *How Does CCCD Affect Program Effectiveness and Sustainability?: A Meta Review of Plan's Evaluations* (Syracuse, NY: Moynihan Institute of Global Affairs, 2011).
28. See: Schmitz, "A Human Rights–Based Approach (HRBA) in Practice."
29. See: George E. Mitchell, *Reframing the Discussion about Nonprofit Effectiveness* (Washington, DC: DMA Nonprofit Federation, 2010).
30. See: Steven J. Lux and Tosca Bruno-van Vijfeijken, *From Alliance to International: The Global Transformation of Save the Children* (Syracuse, NY: Maxwell School of Citizenship and Public Affairs, 2012).
31. See: Tosca Bruno-van Vijfeijken et al., *Final Assessment: Amnesty's Global Transition Program* (Syracuse, NY: Moynihan Institute of Global Affairs, 2017).
32. Carlisle J. Levine, Tosca Bruno-van Vijfeijken, and Sherine Jayawickrama, *Measuring International NGO Agency-Level Results* (Washington, DC: InterAction, 2016).
33. Mary Kay Gugerty and George E. Mitchell, *Summary and Recommendations for Impact Measurement Standards: Report for the InterAction Standards Task Force* (Washington, DC: InterAction, 2018), https://www.interaction.org/documents/interaction-ngo-standards.

INDEX

Note: Tables are indicated by *t* following the page number

For the benefit of digital users, indexed terms that span two pages (e.g., 52–53) may, on occasion, appear on only one of those pages.

transnational non-governmental
organizations (TNGOs)
adaptability of, 38–39, 50, 65,
68–69, 100–1, 182–83 (see also
agility, organizational)
authority of, 63–64, 87, 101–2, 232
(see also legitimacy)
brand identity of, 11, 12t, 15, 52, 62,
195, 222, 226–27
definition of, 9–10, 10t, 11
independence of, 9–10, 88, 90, 114–15,
194–95, 197–98, 202, 212–13,
213t, 221t (see also autonomy;
three-sector economy)
organizational metamorphosis of,
19, 234–40
structure of, 9–10, 10t, 11, 12t
transnational advocacy networks
(TANs), 198–99
transparency, 91, 95–96, 100t, 155, 164,
203, 219, 221t, 2 50
data and, 92, 93, 95
lack of, 99, 264
trust, 5, 28, 39, 56, 79, 94, 250
See also trustworthiness
trustworthiness, 7–8, 26, 28, 29–31,
36, 39, 55, 64, 79, 88, 146, 231
Twitter, 111–14

Unilever, 195, 263–64
Union of International Associations
(UIA), 14

United Kingdom (UK), 4, 14–15, 25–26,
114–15, 164, 166, 216, 265
United Nations (UN), 9, 14, 49–50, 74,
76, 252
United States (US), 14–15, 25–26,
46–47, 49–50, 75–76, 91,
95–96, 114–15, 164, 166–67,
178, 180–81, 212
unlike-minded actors, 35, 68, 175–76,
178, 195
collaboration with, 77, 88, 183t, 184,
185, 192–93 (see collaboration:
types of)
skepticism towards, 35, 178, 192
US Agency for International
Development (USAID), 14,
222, 223

Viso, Mark, 141

Warshauer, Will, 141
WASH (water, sanitation and
hygiene), 260
WhatsApp, 110, 111–12
Wise, Holly, 225
World Summit on the Information
Society (WSIS), 76
World Vision, 8, 44, 49–50, 98–99,
166–67, 175, 178, 211,
239–40
World Wildlife Fund (WWF), 99, 112–13,
160, 195–96, 239